Get the eBook FREE!
(PDF, ePub, Kindle, and liveBook all included)

We believe that once you buy a book from us, you should be able to read it in any format we have available. To get electronic versions of this book at no additional cost to you, purchase and then register this book at the Manning website.

Go to https://www.manning.com/freebook and follow the instructions to complete your pBook registration.

That's it!
Thanks from Manning!

Statistics Every Programmer Needs

Statistics Every Programmer Needs

Gary Sutton

MANNING
SHELTER ISLAND

For online information and ordering of this and other Manning books, please visit www.manning.com. The publisher offers discounts on this book when ordered in quantity. For more information, please contact

>   Special Sales Department
>   Manning Publications Co.
>   20 Baldwin Road
>   PO Box 761
>   Shelter Island, NY 11964
>   Email: orders@manning.com

©2025 by Manning Publications Co. All rights reserved.

No part of this publication may be reproduced, stored in a retrieval system, or transmitted, in any form or by means electronic, mechanical, photocopying, or otherwise, without prior written permission of the publisher.

Many of the designations used by manufacturers and sellers to distinguish their products are claimed as trademarks. Where those designations appear in the book, and Manning Publications was aware of a trademark claim, the designations have been printed in initial caps or all caps.

♾ Recognizing the importance of preserving what has been written, it is Manning's policy to have the books we publish printed on acid-free paper, and we exert our best efforts to that end. Recognizing also our responsibility to conserve the resources of our planet, Manning books are printed on paper that is at least 15 percent recycled and processed without the use of elemental chlorine.

The author and publisher have made every effort to ensure that the information in this book was correct at press time. The author and publisher do not assume and hereby disclaim any liability to any party for any loss, damage, or disruption caused by errors or omissions, whether such errors or omissions result from negligence, accident, or any other cause, or from any usage of the information herein.

Manning Publications Co. 20 Baldwin Road PO Box 761 Shelter Island, NY 11964	Development editor: Ian Hough Technical editor: Rohit Goswami Review editor: Angelina Lazukić Production editor: Keri Hales Copy editor: Tiffany Taylor Proofreader: Jason Everett Typesetter and cover designer: Marija Tudor

ISBN 9781633436053
Printed in the United States of America

In memory of my Mom

brief contents

1 ■ Laying the groundwork   1
2 ■ Exploring probability and counting   16
3 ■ Exploring probability distributions and conditional probabilities   41
4 ■ Fitting a linear regression   79
5 ■ Fitting a logistic regression   111
6 ■ Fitting a decision tree and a random forest   140
7 ■ Fitting time series models   184
8 ■ Transforming data into decisions with linear programming   222
9 ■ Running Monte Carlo simulations   242
10 ■ Building and plotting a decision tree   271
11 ■ Predicting future states with Markov analysis   294
12 ■ Examining and testing naturally occurring number sequences   319
13 ■ Managing projects   349
14 ■ Visualizing quality control   378

contents

preface xiii
acknowledgments xv
about this book xvii
about the author xxiv
about the cover illustration xxv

1 Laying the groundwork 1

1.1 Stats and quant 2

Understanding the basics 2 • Why they matter 2 • The broader effect 3 • Diving deeper: Core concepts 3

1.2 Why Python? 4

Rich ecosystem 4 • Ease of learning 5 • Online support and community 5 • Industry adoption 5 • Versatility 6

1.3 Python IDEs 6

IDLE: A starting point 6 • PyCharm: A professional tool 7 Other popular IDEs 7

1.4 Benefits and learning approach 8

From statistical measures to real-world application 9 Expanding beyond traditional techniques 9 • A balanced approach to theory and practice 10

CONTENTS

1.5 How this book works 11

*Foundational learning with exploration and practice 12
Using Python for precision and efficiency 13 ▪ Adaptable learning for diverse skill levels 14*

1.6 What this book does not cover 14

2 Exploring probability and counting 16

2.1 Basic probabilities 17

Probability types 19 ▪ Converting and measuring probabilities 19

2.2 Counting rules 22

Multiplication rule 22 ▪ Addition rule 22 ▪ Combinations and permutations 23

2.3 Continuous random variables 30

Examples 31 ▪ Probability density function 31 ▪ Cumulative distribution function 33

2.4 Discrete random variables 34

Examples 35 ▪ Probability mass function 36 ▪ Cumulative distribution function 37

3 Exploring probability distributions and conditional probabilities 41

3.1 Probability distributions 42

*Normal distribution 42 ▪ Binomial distribution 50
Discrete uniform distribution 56 ▪ Poisson distribution 60*

3.2 Probability problems 63

Complement rule for probability 65 ▪ Quick reference guide 66 ▪ Applied probability: Examples and solutions 68

3.3 Conditional probabilities 72

*Examples 72 ▪ Conditional probabilities and independence 73
Intuitive approach to conditional probability 74 ▪ Formulaic approach to conditional probability 76*

4 Fitting a linear regression 79

4.1 Primer on linear regression 81

Linear equation 81 ▪ Goodness of fit 85 ▪ Conditions for best fit 85

4.2 Simple linear regression 87

*Importing and exploring the data 88 • Fitting the model 93
Interpreting and evaluating the results 95 • Testing model
assumptions 105*

5 Fitting a logistic regression 111

5.1 Logistic regression vs. linear regression 113

5.2 Multiple logistic regression 114

*Importing and exploring the data 115 • Fitting the model 125
Interpreting and evaluating the results 128 • Calculating and
evaluating classification metrics 131*

6 Fitting a decision tree and a random forest 140

6.1 Understanding decision trees and random forests 141

6.2 Importing, wrangling, and exploring the data 142

*Understanding the data 143 • Wrangling the data 144
Exploring the data 148*

6.3 Fitting a decision tree 157

*Splitting the data 158 • Fitting the model 160 • Predicting
responses 161 • Evaluating the model 161 • Plotting the
decision tree 163 • Interpreting and understanding decision
trees 164 • Advantages and disadvantages of decision
trees 173*

6.4 Fitting a random forest 174

*Fitting the model 175 • Predicting responses 177 • Evaluating
the model 177 • Feature importance 179 • Extracting random
trees 181*

7 Fitting time series models 184

7.1 Distinguishing forecasts from predictions 185

7.2 Importing and plotting the data 186

*Fetching financial data 186 • Understanding the data 189
Plotting the data 190*

7.3 Fitting an ARIMA model 191

*Autoregression (AR) component 192 • Integration (I)
component 192 • Moving average (MA) component 192
Combining ARIMA components 192 • Stationarity 193
Differencing 195 • Stationarity and differencing applied 197
AR and MA components 205 • Fitting the model 207
Evaluating model fit 209 • Forecasting 213*

CONTENTS

7.4 Fitting exponential smoothing models 215

Model structure 216 ▪ Applicability 216 ▪ Mathematical properties 216 ▪ Types of exponential smoothing models 216 Choosing between ARIMA and exponential smoothing 217 SES and DES models 217 ▪ Holt–Winters model 218

8 Transforming data into decisions with linear programming 222

8.1 Problem formulation 223

The scenario 224 ▪ The challenge 224 ▪ The approach 225 Feature summaries 227

8.2 Developing the linear optimization framework 229

Explanation of linear equations and inequalities 230 Data definition 230 ▪ Objective function 232 Constraints 233 ▪ Decision variable bounds 236 ▪ Solving the linear programming problem 236 ▪ Result evaluation 239

9 Running Monte Carlo simulations 242

9.1 Applications and benefits of Monte Carlo simulations 243

9.2 Step-by-step process 244

9.3 Hands-on approach 246

Establishing a probability distribution (step 1) 246 ▪ Computing a cumulative probability distribution (step 2) 248 ▪ Establishing an interval of random numbers for each variable (step 3) 250 Generating random numbers (step 4) 252 ▪ Simulating a series of trials (step 5) 253 ▪ Analyzing the results (step 6) 254

9.4 Automating simulations on discrete data 255

Plotting and analyzing the results 257

9.5 Automating simulations on continuous data 259

Predicting stock prices with Monte Carlo simulations 259 Analyzing historical data (step 1) 261 ▪ Calculating log returns (step 2) 262 ▪ Computing statistical parameters (step 3) 264 Generating random daily returns (step 4) 265 ▪ Simulating prices (step 5) 266 ▪ Simulating multiple trials (step 6) 267 Analyzing the results (step 7) 268

10 Building and plotting a decision tree 271

10.1 Decision-making without probabilities 272

Maximax method 273 ▪ Maximin method 276 ▪ Minimax Regret method 277 ▪ Expected Value method 279

    10.2   Decision trees   282
               Creating the schema 283 ▪ *Plotting the tree 289*

11   *Predicting future states with Markov analysis* 294

    11.1   Understanding the mechanics of Markov analysis   295

    11.2   States and state probabilities   296
               Understanding the vector of state probabilities for multistate systems 297 ▪ *Matrix of transition probabilities 300*

    11.3   Equilibrium conditions   307
               Predicting equilibrium conditions programmatically 308

    11.4   Absorbing states   311
               Obtaining the fundamental matrix 313 ▪ *Predicting absorbing states 315* ▪ *Predicting absorbing states programmatically 316*

12   *Examining and testing naturally occurring number sequences* 319

    12.1   Benford's law explained   320

    12.2   Naturally occurring number sequences   324

    12.3   Uniform and random distributions   325
               Uniform distribution 325 ▪ *Random distribution 327* *Plotted distributions 328*

    12.4   Examples   330
               Street addresses 330 ▪ *World population figures 333* *Payment amounts 336*

    12.5   Validating Benford's law   337
               Chi-square test 338 ▪ *Mean absolute deviation 341* *Distortion factor and z-statistic 343* ▪ *Mantissa statistics 344*

13   *Managing projects* 349

    13.1   Creating a work breakdown structure   350

    13.2   Estimating activity times with PERT   354

    13.3   Finding the critical path   357
               Earliest times 357 ▪ *Latest times 359* ▪ *Slack 360* *Finding the critical path programmatically 362*

    13.4   Estimating the probability of project completion   369

    13.5   Crashing the project   374

14 Visualizing quality control 378

14.1 Quality control measures 380

Upper control limit and lower control limit 380 ▪ Mean and center line 381 ▪ Standard deviation 381 ▪ Range 382 ▪ Sample size 383 ▪ Proportion defective 383 ▪ Number of defective items 384 ▪ Number of defects 385 ▪ Defects per unit 385 Moving range 386 ▪ z-score 386 ▪ Process capability indices 387

14.2 Control charts for attributes 388

p-charts 388 ▪ np-charts 392 ▪ c-charts 394 ▪ g-charts 396

14.3 Control charts for variables 398

x-bar charts 400 ▪ r-charts 401 ▪ s-charts 403 ▪ I-MR charts 405 ▪ EWMA charts 407

index 411

preface

Data-driven decision-making has become a cornerstone of modern business, technology, and scientific research. Whether predicting financial trends, detecting potentially fraudulent activity, or managing large-scale projects, quantitative methods provide the foundation for solving complex problems with confidence. Yet, too often, critical decisions are made without using these powerful techniques, relying instead on intuition, tradition, or incomplete analysis. This needs to change. The ability to apply statistical reasoning and optimization methods is no longer a specialized skill: it is an essential competency for professionals in every data-driven field.

This book was born out of a need to bridge the gap between theoretical statistics and practical implementation—particularly for those who work with data but may not have a formal background in statistical modeling. My career has revolved around using statistical and analytical techniques to drive business intelligence and operational improvements. Over the years, I have seen firsthand how programmers, analysts, and professionals in various fields benefit from a deeper understanding of statistics—not just as a theoretical discipline but as a toolkit for solving real-world problems. Yet many resources either focus too heavily on mathematical derivations without application or provide code without sufficient explanation of the underlying principles. This book aims to strike a balance, offering both the "how" and the "why" behind each technique.

The idea for this book took shape as I noticed the increasing demand for statistical and machine learning techniques in business, finance, and engineering. Companies were hiring data scientists and analysts in record numbers, but many professionals found themselves needing to apply advanced methods without a structured way to learn them. More and more, I have seen practitioners who can write Python scripts and present results to leadership but lack a deep understanding of what is happening under the hood. This superficial knowledge can lead to misinterpretations, poor model assumptions, and flawed decision-making. Knowing how to apply statistical methods is important—but understanding when, why, and under what conditions they work is critical.

The book covers a range of topics essential for any data-driven professional, beginning with foundational probability theory and moving through regression analysis, decision trees, Monte Carlo simulations, and Markov chains. Later chapters explore project management and quality control—areas where quantitative methods play a crucial role in ensuring efficiency and reliability. Although Python is used throughout the book as a computational tool, this is not just a Python book; it is a guide to using quantitative methods effectively, providing reusable code alongside clear explanations to ensure that you understand the concepts behind the calculations.

A key focus of this book is demonstrating how these techniques are applied in practice. For instance, you will learn how to fit predictive models, optimize decisions using constrained optimization, simulate outcomes with Monte Carlo methods, and analyze patterns in naturally occurring number sequences. The book also emphasizes the importance of statistical rigor, showing when and how to validate results to avoid misleading conclusions.

Whether you are a programmer looking to enhance your statistical knowledge, a business professional making data-driven decisions, or a student seeking a structured way to approach quantitative methods, I hope this book serves as a valuable resource. By the time you finish, you will not only know how to apply these techniques but also have a deeper appreciation for the mathematical principles that underpin them. More importantly, you will gain the ability to make data-driven decisions with confidence—ensuring that complex problems are approached with the clarity and precision they deserve.

acknowledgments

This book, like any meaningful project, was not the work of one person alone. I'm grateful to the many collaborators, reviewers, and supporters who contributed their wisdom, time, and encouragement throughout this journey.

First and foremost, I'm deeply grateful to my development editor, Ian Hough, whose insight, candor, and steady guidance shaped this book at almost every stage. I was fortunate to work with him on my first book and even more so this time around.

I'm thankful to Marjan Bace, Manning's publisher, and Andy Waldron, acquisitions editor, for giving me the opportunity to write a second book and apply the many lessons I learned from the first.

A special thank you to my technical editor, Rohit Goswami, a Software Engineer (II) at Quansight Labs and a Rannis-funded doctoral researcher at the Science Institute of the University of Iceland, whose sharp eye and deep expertise helped ensure that every technical detail was sound and every explanation accessible.

Thanks to Aleks Dragosavljevic, who coordinated the peer review process and no doubt handled countless other behind-the-scenes tasks that helped moved this book forward.

Huge thanks to the production team—especially Azra Dedic, Angelina Lazukić, Marija Tudor, Keri Hales, Tiffany Taylor, and Jason Everett—for their expert handling of the many moving parts involved in bringing this book to life. Copyediting, typesetting, and proofreading a manuscript filled with code, equations, and plots is no small feat, and their attention to detail made all the difference.

I'm sincerely grateful to the peer reviewers who dedicated many hours to reading the manuscript and offering thoughtful, constructive feedback: Aastha Joshi, Aditi Godbole, Ajay Tanikonda, Akshay Phadke, Alireza Aghamohammadi, Anmolika

Singh, Anupam Samanta, Ariel Andres, Arun Moorthy, Christian Sutton, Clemens Baader, Edgar Hassler, Eduardo Rienzi, Georg Sommer, Jatinder Singh, Ken W. Alger, Kevin Middleton, Krishna Gandhi, Mahima Bansod, Marius Radu, Monisha Athi Kesavan Premalatha, Pankaj Verma, Praveen Gupta Sanka, Purva Bangad, Steven Fernandez, Su Liu, Swati Tyagi, and Tony Dubitsky. Your suggestions helped make this a better book.

And finally, I want to thank my wife, Liane, who once again tolerated the wide variance in my mood swings while I wrote—and while I overthought what to write. Her patience remains unmatched.

about this book

This book is designed to provide you with a strong foundation in statistics and the practical application of quantitative techniques for real-world problem-solving. At its core, the book is about equipping you to make data-driven decisions in complex scenarios where resources are limited and choices carry significant consequences. By blending theoretical underpinnings with hands-on Python implementations, the text demystifies essential statistical and computational methods while helping you understand when and why to apply each technique. Through carefully constructed chapters on regression and other models, optimization, simulation, and more, the book ensures that you gain not only the tools to solve quantitative problems but also the intuition to select the right approach for the right challenge.

What sets this book apart is its commitment to a dual focus on theory and practice. Unlike texts that focus exclusively on statistical formulas or coding recipes, this book bridges the gap, explaining the "nuts and bolts" behind each method and providing reusable Python code that uses popular libraries like pandas, NumPy, Scikit-learn, statsmodels, SciPy, Matplotlib, and more. It caters to practitioners and college students with prior exposure to statistics who are eager to deepen their understanding of quantitative techniques and their applications. You will learn to automate tasks like running regressions or Monte Carlo simulations as you develop a critical understanding of the algorithms.

Who should read this book

This book is designed for professionals and students who want to develop a strong foundation in statistics and quantitative methods while using Python for implementation. Whether you're an analyst, data scientist, project manager, or researcher, this book provides the essential techniques needed to make data-driven decisions, solve complex optimization problems, and implement predictive models.

A background in Python is helpful but not required. Although familiarity with Python will certainly make it easier to follow along with the code examples, the book does not assume advanced programming skills. Every code snippet is accompanied by explanations that clarify not only how to implement a technique but also why and how it works. If you're new to Python, you can still benefit from the statistical and quantitative concepts presented, as long as you're willing to experiment with the code and explore Python as you progress.

Some prior exposure to statistics and basic quantitative methods is beneficial. The book assumes a basic understanding of concepts like means, variances, probability, and simple regression, but it reinforces and builds on these foundations. If you've taken an introductory statistics course or have experience analyzing data, you'll find this book a practical guide to applying and extending those skills.

This book is particularly well-suited for *business analysts and data scientists* looking to enhance their statistical modeling and decision-making skills with Python; *engineers, researchers, and finance professionals* who need quantitative methods to optimize processes, forecast trends, or assess risks; *project managers and operations specialists* who want to incorporate data-driven decision-making into their planning, resource allocation, and risk management strategies; *students in business analytics, operations research, data science, and applied mathematics* who seek a structured way to learn and apply statistical and quantitative techniques; and *anyone transitioning into a data-driven role* who wants to gain practical experience with statistical modeling, simulation techniques, and optimization methods.

The book covers a wide array of topics, including probability distributions, regression analysis, Monte Carlo simulations, Markov chains, decision trees, and constrained optimization. It also explores practical applications such as detecting fraud with Benford's law, improving project scheduling with PERT and CPM, and assessing quality control using statistical charts.

For the most part, there is a one-to-one relationship between chapters and Python scripts, allowing you to download and execute code easily. Whether you're following the book sequentially or jumping to a specific topic of interest, you'll have access to well-structured Python scripts that support the concepts discussed. By the end of this book, you will not only have gained proficiency in implementing quantitative techniques with Python but also developed a deeper understanding of the mathematical principles behind them, ensuring that your analyses are both technically sound and practically impactful.

How this book is organized: A road map

This book is structured into 14 chapters, each designed to provide a focused exploration of a specific quantitative technique. For the most part, each technique is introduced, explained, and applied within a single chapter, ensuring that concepts are presented in a self-contained manner. This approach allows you to systematically build your knowledge while also giving you the flexibility to jump directly to topics of interest without needing to cross-reference multiple sections. Whether you're learning about regression analysis, Monte Carlo simulations, or Markov chains, each chapter delivers a complete learning experience, combining theoretical foundations with practical Python implementations.

Here is a chapter-by-chapter breakdown:

- *Chapter 1* provides an essential foundation for understanding the statistical and quantitative methods covered throughout the book. It introduces the book's approach, explaining the balance between theory and practice, the role of Python as a computational tool, and the structure of individual chapters. You will gain insight into why Python was chosen for implementation, how different decision-making techniques will be explored, and the benefits of developing both technical proficiency and critical thinking skills in data analysis.
- *Chapter 2* covers fundamental probability concepts and counting principles essential for statistical analysis. It introduces different types of probability, key counting rules, and the distinction between permutations and combinations. The chapter also explains random variables, probability density functions (PDFs), and cumulative distribution functions (CDFs), providing a foundation for understanding probability distributions in later chapters.
- *Chapter 3* explores key probability distributions, including normal, binomial, uniform, and Poisson, which are essential for statistical analysis and decision-making. The chapter explains how these distributions model real-world phenomena, how probabilities are computed, and the role of conditional probability. By understanding these concepts, you will be better equipped to analyze uncertainty and apply probabilistic reasoning in various scenarios. Although the content in chapters 2 and 3 stands on its own merit, many of the concepts introduced in these chapters will serve you well in many of the remaining chapters.
- *Chapter 4* explores linear regression, a fundamental statistical method used to model the relationship between independent and dependent variables. The chapter covers key concepts such as model fitting, evaluation, assumption testing, and techniques for detecting outliers and testing for normality. You will learn how to assess model performance, interpret key regression metrics, and ensure model reliability through assumption checks. These foundational concepts will provide a strong basis for more advanced modeling techniques in later chapters.
- *Chapter 5* introduces logistic regression, a classification technique used to predict binary outcomes based on one or more independent variables. The chapter explains how logistic regression estimates probabilities using the logistic (sigmoid) function. You will learn how to fit and evaluate a logistic regression

model, interpret its coefficients, and assess its predictive power using classification metrics. Although distinct from linear regression, many concepts from chapter 4 carry over, reinforcing the importance of model evaluation and variable selection.

- *Chapter 6* introduces decision trees and random forests, two widely used machine learning techniques for classification and regression tasks. It explains the mechanics of decision tree construction, including how splits are determined using Gini impurity and information gain. The chapter then expands on random forests, highlighting their ability to improve model accuracy and reduce overfitting through ensemble learning. You will also explore model evaluation, interpretation, and feature importance, gaining practical insights into how these models can enhance predictive analysis.

- *Chapter 7* introduces time series analysis, a fundamental technique for forecasting sequential data points over time. The chapter covers key methods—ARIMA models and exponential smoothing—explaining how they capture temporal dependencies, trends, and seasonality. Practical applications, such as forecasting stock prices, are explored to illustrate model implementation and evaluation. By the end, you will have the necessary tools to build and assess time series forecasting models for various domains.

- *Chapter 8* introduces linear programming as a powerful optimization tool for decision-making in resource-limited environments. It covers the fundamentals of constrained optimization, focusing on defining objective functions and constraints to maximize efficiency or minimize costs. The chapter presents a real-world application, project prioritization, and demonstrates how linear programming can systematically allocate resources within budgetary and strategic constraints. You will gain insight into translating decision problems into mathematical models, ensuring optimal outcomes while adhering to predefined limitations.

- *Chapter 9* explores Monte Carlo simulations, a powerful technique for modeling uncertainty and variability in complex systems. The chapter introduces the mathematical foundations of Monte Carlo methods and demonstrates their application to both discrete and continuous random variables. You will learn how to generate and interpret simulation results, gaining insights into probability distributions and risk assessment. These concepts provide a robust framework for decision-making under uncertainty, complementing topics covered in earlier chapters.

- *Chapter 10* explores various decision-making methods, emphasizing both probability-based and non-probability-based approaches. It introduces the Maximax, Maximin, and Minimax Regret methods, each suited to different risk tolerances and levels of uncertainty. The chapter then transitions to the Expected Value method, which incorporates probabilities to assess potential outcomes more systematically. Decision trees are introduced as a visual representation of decision-making processes, illustrating how probabilities and payoffs can guide optimal choices. These techniques equip you with structured approaches to navigating complex decisions in both business and personal contexts.

- *Chapter 11* explores Markov analysis, a statistical technique used to predict the future states of a system based on its current state and transition probabilities. The chapter introduces key concepts such as state probabilities, transition matrixes, equilibrium conditions, and absorbing states, demonstrating how Markov chains can model dynamic processes in various fields. You will learn to construct and manipulate transition matrices, predict future states, and identify steady-state distributions, gaining valuable insights into long-term system behavior.

- *Chapter 12* explores Benford's law, a mathematical principle stating that in many naturally occurring numerical data sets, smaller leading digits appear more frequently than larger ones. The chapter explains where Benford's law applies and its significance in fraud detection, data integrity, and forensic analysis. It also demonstrates statistical tests—such as the chi-square test, mean absolute deviation, and Mantissa statistics—to evaluate whether a data set follows a Benford distribution, reinforcing the importance of rigorous validation when analyzing numerical data.

- *Chapter 13* explores the role of quantitative methods in project management, covering essential techniques for planning and execution. Topics include creating a work breakdown structure (WBS) to organize tasks, using the program evaluation and review technique (PERT) for time estimation, and applying the critical path method (CPM) to determine the shortest project duration. The chapter also addresses calculating the probability of on-time completion and strategies for project crashing to accelerate timelines while managing costs. Effective project management requires structured planning, data-driven decision-making, and rigorous statistical analysis to mitigate risks and ensure project success.

- *Chapter 14* explores statistical quality control, focusing on methods used to monitor and improve process stability and product consistency. It introduces key quality control measures, such as control limits and standard deviation, before examining control charts for both attribute and variable data. Attribute-based charts track defects and proportions, whereas variable-based charts assess process variation and consistency. By using visualization techniques, the chapter emphasizes how control charts provide valuable insights for maintaining and improving quality standards.

This structured approach ensures that each chapter provides a self-contained exploration of a specific quantitative technique while contributing to a broader understanding of data-driven decision-making. Whether analyzing uncertainty, optimizing processes, or modeling complex systems, the book offers a balanced mix of theoretical foundations and hands-on applications. To support this learning experience, the book includes extensive Python code implementations throughout.

About the code

This book contains reusable Python code throughout, integrated seamlessly with the explanatory text. All of the statistical and quantitative techniques discussed are accompanied by Python implementations that you can adapt for your own projects. Some sections include plots to visually complement the concepts being discussed. Although all of these plots are printed in grayscale, you will notice that the corresponding code often includes color specifications. These are there so you can easily customize and run the visualizations in full color for your own use. However, not every plot is explicitly demonstrated in the code, particularly for straightforward visualizations such as the sigmoid function (a mathematical function used in logistic regression and other binary classification problems; see chapter 5) and the beta probability distribution (a continuous probability distribution used to model uncertainty in project activity durations; see chapter 13), where the focus is on interpretation rather than on the mechanics of generating the plot. When visualizations add significant value to the learning process—such as a line chart for time series data or a quality control chart for monitoring process performance—the book includes the full Python code along with a detailed explanation of each step.

The methods used in this book rely on specific Python libraries such as pandas, NumPy, Scikit-learn, and Matplotlib. Every effort has been made throughout to clearly identify in advance which libraries are needed, and the corresponding `import` statements are always included. For instance, if `pandas` is required for data manipulation, it must first be imported into the script, like so:

```
import pandas as pd
df = pd.read_csv('data.csv')
```

By ensuring that all necessary imports are explicitly provided, you can seamlessly follow along with the examples and apply the techniques to your own data sets without the risk of encountering import errors or missing dependencies in your scripts.

This book contains many examples of source code, both in snippets and in line with normal text. In both cases, source code is formatted in a `fixed-width font like this` to separate it from ordinary text. Sometimes code is also **`in bold`** to highlight code that has changed from previous steps in the chapter, such as when a new feature adds to an existing line of code. Additionally, comments in the source code have often been removed from the listings when the code is described in the text. Code annotations accompany many of the listings, highlighting important concepts.

You can get executable snippets of code from the liveBook (online) version of this book at https://livebook.manning.com/book/statistics-every-programmer-needs. All the Python scripts, which contain code included and not included in the text, as well as the .csv files imported into a subset of these same scripts, can be downloaded from the

Manning website at https://www.manning.com/books/statistics-every-programmer-needs and from GitHub at https://github.com/garysutton/quant. There is, for the most part, a one-to-one relationship between scripts and chapters, allowing you to easily follow along and apply the concepts to your own analyses.

liveBook discussion forum

Purchase of *Statistics Every Programmer Needs* includes free access to liveBook, Manning's online reading platform. Using liveBook's exclusive discussion features, you can attach comments to the book globally or to specific sections or paragraphs. It's a snap to make notes for yourself, ask and answer technical questions, and receive help from the author and other users. To access the forum, go to https://livebook.manning.com/book/statistics-every-programmer-needs/discussion. You can also learn more about Manning's forums and the rules of conduct at https://livebook.manning.com/discussion.

Manning's commitment to our readers is to provide a venue where a meaningful dialogue between individual readers and between readers and the author can take place. It is not a commitment to any specific amount of participation on the part of the author, whose contribution to the forum remains voluntary (and unpaid). We suggest you try asking the author some challenging questions lest his interest stray! The forum and the archives of previous discussions will be accessible from the publisher's website as long as the book is in print.

about the author

 **GARY SUTTON** is a business intelligence and analytics leader and the author of *Statistics Slam Dunk: Statistical analysis with R on real NBA data*, also published by Manning. Mr. Sutton earned his undergraduate degree from the University of Southern California and his master's degrees from George Washington University and Northwestern University.

about the cover illustration

The figure on the cover of *Statistics Every Programmer Needs* is "Cafetzy," or "A coffee vendor," taken from the *Album of Turkish costume paintings*, a part of George Arents Collection. In those days, it was easy to identify where people lived and what their trade or station in life was just by their dress. Manning celebrates the inventiveness and initiative of the computer business with book covers based on the rich diversity of regional culture centuries ago, brought back to life by pictures from collections such as this one.

Laying the groundwork

This chapter covers
- Python's strengths as a tool for statistical computing and quantitative analysis
- Choosing Python IDEs to support readable, testable code
- Combining conceptual understanding with hands-on implementations
- Laying the groundwork for real-world modeling and decision-making

In today's data-driven landscape, mastering statistics and quantitative techniques is crucial for making informed decisions. These methodologies can transform complex data into actionable insights across industries and functions—from predicting stock trends and customer behavior to detecting anomalies and optimizing resource allocation. Python serves as the analytical engine throughout, offering flexibility, speed, and a rich ecosystem of tools for everything from exploratory analysis to simulation modeling.

Statistical thinking begins with core concepts like probability, variation, and inference—tools for understanding uncertainty and drawing conclusions from data. But meaningful analysis doesn't end with computation; it also requires clear reasoning, careful interpretation, and a firm grasp of both the assumptions and limitations behind each method. To that end, the techniques introduced here are paired with reusable, annotated Python code designed to both illustrate and reinforce practical implementation.

What follows sets the stage for deeper exploration of methods such as regression, classification, simulation, and optimization. These aren't just abstract academic ideas—they're everyday tools for analysts, data scientists, and business leaders seeking clarity in an uncertain world. With the right foundation, it becomes possible to build not only accurate models but also better questions, sharper intuition, and more confident decisions.

1.1 Stats and quant

In an era defined by digital information, vast volumes of data are generated and then stored every second—by systems, users, and machines. Making sense of this scale and complexity requires more than intuition; it calls for structured techniques that reveal patterns, test relationships, and support confident decision-making. That's the role of statistics and quantitative methods. Although outcomes in real-world settings are often uncertain, the methods used to analyze them are grounded in rigor and repeatability. With so much data now available, applying these techniques is not just useful—it's essential for drawing meaningful conclusions and enabling fast, efficient, and defensible decisions.

1.1.1 Understanding the basics

Statistics is the discipline that allows us to make sense of uncertainty. It involves collecting, analyzing, interpreting, and presenting data in a way that reveals meaningful patterns, even when the underlying information is incomplete, noisy, or variable. By applying statistical methods, it's possible to draw reliable inferences and identify trends that would otherwise remain hidden in raw data.

Quantitative techniques extend this foundation by introducing mathematical models to support structured decision-making. These methods are used to optimize outcomes, forecast future behavior, and simulate complex systems. For example, linear programming helps allocate limited resources across competing priorities, and Monte Carlo simulations explore a wide range of possible outcomes to quantify risk and opportunity. Together, statistics and quantitative methods—stats and quant—form a practical, complementary toolkit for solving real-world problems with clarity and precision.

1.1.2 Why they matter

Statistics and quantitative techniques are essential because they turn data into clarity—and ultimately, into better decisions. In high-stakes environments, intuition alone isn't enough; what's needed are systematic methods to uncover patterns, assess uncertainty, and optimize outcomes.

Consider a data solutions provider tasked with prioritizing projects under tight budgetary and resource constraints. Statistical methods can reveal which projects align most closely with performance goals, and linear programming helps allocate limited resources in a way that maximizes overall strategic effect.

Or take the case of a financial analyst forecasting stock performance. Using Monte Carlo simulations, the analyst can model thousands of possible outcomes to evaluate risk exposure and opportunity under different market conditions—delivering a more complete picture of what the future might hold.

These examples reflect the real power of stats and quant: they don't just describe what has happened—they offer frameworks for understanding what could happen and for making the best possible decision in the face of complexity and uncertainty.

1.1.3 The broader effect

Statistics and quantitative methods are indispensable across a wide range of industries. In marketing, models like Markov chains help track customer behavior over time—estimating the likelihood of brand switching, retention, or churn. In finance, Monte Carlo simulations are used to evaluate investment risk by modeling thousands of potential market outcomes. In operations, linear programming supports strategic resource allocation under tight budgetary and logistical constraints.

Mastering these techniques enables programmers, analysts, and decision-makers to build systems that are not only technically sound but also strategically aligned. The ability to convert complex data into clear, actionable insight is what makes stats and quant more than just analytical tools—they are foundational to innovation, efficiency, and informed decision-making in forward-looking and innovative organizations.

1.1.4 Diving deeper: Core concepts

Effectively applying statistics and quantitative techniques starts with a strong understanding of a few essential concepts. These foundational ideas form the backbone of everything from basic analysis to advanced modeling.

Descriptive statistics provide a summary view of a data set, using metrics like mean, median, standard deviation, and range to quickly convey the shape, spread, and central tendency of continuous data, or other metrics like frequency counts and proportions to describe the distribution of values for categorical data. They're often the first step in understanding what the data shows and where deeper investigation may be needed.

Inferential statistics allow conclusions to extend beyond the immediate data set. By using samples to make generalizations about larger populations, inferential tools like confidence intervals, p-values, and hypothesis tests quantify uncertainty and guide evidence-based decisions.

Probability lies at the heart of both statistical inference and many quantitative models. It provides a structured way to quantify uncertainty and evaluate the likelihood of future outcomes based on current information.

Regression analysis explores relationships between variables—how one variable changes in response to another. This is a core tool for modeling trends, forecasting future outcomes, and identifying key drivers of behavior.

Optimization focuses on finding the best possible solution under a set of constraints. Linear programming is a classic example, commonly used to allocate resources or maximize efficiency when trade-offs are involved.

Simulation, particularly through methods like Monte Carlo simulations, models complex or uncertain systems by generating thousands of potential outcomes. This technique is widely used in finance, operations, and risk analysis to evaluate possible futures and make decisions under uncertainty.

Machine learning builds on many of these principles, using algorithms that learn from data to make increasingly accurate predictions or classifications. Although it may include familiar tools like linear or logistic regression, machine learning extends well beyond traditional statistical models—often relying on large data sets, nonlinear relationships, and iterative model training. Techniques such as decision trees and random forests enable flexible modeling in complex environments where patterns may be too subtle or dynamic for conventional approaches. Despite its modern scope, machine learning shares statistical roots and is grounded in core ideas like probability, optimization, and generalization. Together, these concepts make up the practical and theoretical core of modern data analysis—and serve as the launching point for more specialized techniques covered throughout the book.

1.2 *Why Python?*

Although not the primary focus, Python is central to applying the statistical and quantitative methods covered here. Its readable syntax, powerful libraries, and versatility make it ideal for translating concepts into practice.

Python bridges the gap between theory and implementation: beginners can follow the logic easily, and experienced users can tackle advanced tasks with speed and clarity. Rather than relying on dense equations, methods are explained through clear narratives and annotated code—from basic analysis to complex simulations.

Given its widespread use in data science, finance, and machine learning, using Python is a future-proof skill. Hands-on coding strengthens both understanding and practical fluency, opening doors across industries.

Python is used throughout the book to prepare data, fit models, visualize results, and simulate outcomes. Next, we'll explore why Python excels in these tasks and how to set up your coding environment effectively.

1.2.1 *Rich ecosystem*

Python's extensive ecosystem of libraries is a major reason it excels in data analysis and quantitative work. Tasks like data manipulation, visualization, and statistical modeling become efficient and intuitive, letting you focus on problem-solving rather than technical complexity.

Key libraries include the following:

- pandas for filtering, aggregating, and cleaning data
- NumPy and SciPy for fast numerical computations
- Matplotlib and seaborn for creating clear, informative visualizations
- scikit-learn and statsmodels for implementing machine learning and statistical models

These tools are actively maintained by a global community and regularly updated with new capabilities. Python also integrates well with other languages, databases, and platforms, thereby making it a flexible choice for end-to-end analysis. Together, these libraries support the full analytics pipeline, from exploration to modeling and presentation, with both power and simplicity.

1.2.2 Ease of learning

Python's clear, readable syntax makes it one of the most beginner-friendly programming languages—ideal for those learning statistics and quantitative methods. Its structure mirrors natural language, helping users grasp code quickly, even without prior experience.

Simple tasks like fitting a linear regression can be done in just a few lines. This simplicity reduces cognitive load, allowing you to focus on the concepts rather than the syntax.

Python also supports rapid development through a consistent, modular design. Whether you're building a quick prototype or refining a complex model, the workflow remains efficient. This combination of accessibility and power makes Python equally useful for newcomers and experienced analysts working at speed and scale.

1.2.3 Online support and community

Python's widespread popularity is backed by one of the most active global communities of developers and analysts. From tutorials to forums, support is readily available for everything from debugging to exploring new libraries.

Platforms like Stack Overflow provide answers to common challenges, and GitHub offers thousands of open source projects showcasing Python's use in data analysis and machine learning. This shared knowledge accelerates learning and fosters collaboration.

Comprehensive documentation—like that for pandas—includes examples that make it easier to apply library functions effectively. Ongoing community contributions also keep Python's ecosystem current and innovative. With such strong support, learning Python becomes a collaborative process, helping users solve problems quickly and build robust analytical solutions.

1.2.4 Industry adoption

Python's dominance in data science, statistics, and quantitative analysis is reinforced by its widespread use across industries—from tech giants to finance, healthcare, and academia. Its versatility makes it essential for tasks like machine learning, forecasting, and optimization.

One reason for this popularity is Python's seamless integration with other technologies, enabling full-scale solutions—from demand forecasting to dashboard visualization. Its flexibility supports everything from automation to advanced modeling.

This broad adoption drives strong demand for Python skills. Employers value its blend of simplicity and power, making Python proficiency a key asset in roles involving analytics, machine learning, and research. Mastering Python equips you to meet real-world challenges while staying aligned with industry needs in a rapidly evolving job market.

1.2.5 Versatility

Python's versatility extends far beyond statistics and analytics. It's used across domains like web development, data engineering, automation, and even creative fields like game design and digital art.

A data scientist might build predictive models while automating data pipelines, and a web developer can embed machine learning into interactive apps—all with the same language. Python's flexibility allows seamless transitions between disciplines without switching tools.

Skills like data manipulation, visualization, and modeling are transferable across industries, making Python a smart long-term investment. Whether shifting from analytics to cloud computing or research to software engineering, Python remains relevant.

Its adaptability also fuels rapid innovation. From prototyping to deployment, Python empowers users to solve diverse technical challenges with speed and creativity.

1.3 Python IDEs

An integrated development environment (IDE) lets you write, test, debug, and run code efficiently. Although Python includes a basic IDE (Integrated Development and Learning Environment [IDLE]), many others offer features tailored to different needs, helping streamline workflows and boost productivity.

Choosing the right IDE depends on your goals, technical needs, and project complexity. Lightweight tools like IDLE work well for quick tests or small scripts. For larger or more advanced work—like simulations, regression modeling, or collaborative projects—robust IDEs such as PyCharm and Jupyter Notebook offer features like code completion, debugging, and version control. The following sections highlight several popular IDEs, outlining their strengths and helping you select the one best suited to your analytical workflow.

1.3.1 IDLE: A starting point

IDLE is a simple, accessible tool bundled with Python—ideal for beginners or small projects. It requires no setup, allowing code to be written and run immediately after installation. Its lightweight design reduces distractions, and the interactive shell is useful for testing calculations, trying out algorithms, or exploring statistical ideas in real time.

However, IDLE lacks advanced features like debugging, version control, and project management. As projects become more complex—such as running simulations or analyzing large datasets—more robust IDEs may be preferable. Still, IDLE remains a practical option for learning, quick experiments, and reinforcing core statistical concepts before moving on to full-featured tools.

1.3.2 *PyCharm: A professional tool*

PyCharm is a robust IDE well-suited for statistical and quantitative workflows involving regression models, simulations, and advanced data analysis. It offers features like intelligent code completion, integrated Git support, and powerful debugging—ideal for use with libraries such as pandas, NumPy, and statsmodels.

The IDE supports both standalone scripts and Jupyter Notebooks, making it adaptable for exploratory and production workflows. Available in Community (free) and Professional (paid) Editions, PyCharm also supports virtual environments and scales effectively with project complexity. Despite a steeper learning curve than simpler tools like IDLE, PyCharm's functionality makes it a valuable choice for those seeking speed, structure, and efficiency in development.

> **NOTE** All examples in this book were developed using PyCharm 2023.3.3 (Community Edition) on a MacBook Air running macOS Sonoma 14.2.1. The Python interpreter was set to version 3.12.12, with the necessary libraries installed via pip.

1.3.3 *Other popular IDEs*

Beyond IDLE and PyCharm, several other Python IDEs support different workflows and user needs:

- *Jupyter Notebook* is widely used in data science and education for its interactive, cell-based format. It enables code execution alongside explanatory text, ideal for data exploration, machine learning, and teaching.
- *Spyder*, often called the "scientific Python development environment," resembles MATLAB and includes a variable explorer and integrated console, making it well-suited for users handling arrays, data frames, and real-time computation.
- *PyDev*, built on Eclipse, supports complex, multilanguage projects and offers strong debugging and modular capabilities, making it a good fit for professional development teams.
- *Visual Studio Code (VS Code)* is a lightweight yet powerful editor that becomes a full IDE with Python extensions. It supports intelligent code completion, Git integration, and customization through a vast extension library.

Each IDE offers distinct advantages: Jupyter for exploration, Spyder for scientific computing, PyDev for multilanguage environments, and VS Code for flexible, fast development. Although all the examples in this book were created in PyCharm, exploring multiple IDEs can expand your adaptability and effectiveness across varied project types.

1.4 Benefits and learning approach

This book is crafted to provide an unparalleled blend of theoretical knowledge and practical application, ensuring that you not only understand advanced statistical and quantitative techniques but also know how to apply them effectively in real-world scenarios. It addresses a critical challenge faced by many students and professionals: bridging the gap between abstract concepts and practical implementation. By combining a rigorous exploration of the underlying principles with hands-on Python examples, this book empowers you to develop both technical proficiency and the critical thinking skills necessary to make data-driven decisions in high-stakes environments.

Imagine sitting in a technical interview and being asked to define the coefficient of determination, commonly known as R-squared (R^2). Many candidates might be able to state that it quantifies the proportion of variance in the dependent variable explained by the independent variables in a linear regression. However, when asked to derive it mathematically, most stumble. This book ensures that you can confidently answer both the "what" and the "how." For example, you'll learn that R^2 can be derived by dividing the regression sum of squares (SSR) by the total sum of squares (SST) or, alternatively, by subtracting the proportion of variance attributed to residuals from 1. This level of understanding demonstrates not just theoretical knowledge but practical mastery, setting you apart in interviews, classrooms, and professional settings. (Don't be concerned if this seems complex right now—chapter 4 will guide you through linear regression in detail, thereby making these measures easy to understand.)

The benefits extend far beyond theoretical understanding. For instance, instead of relying solely on visual inspections like histograms to assess the normality of a numeric data series, you'll learn how to apply formal statistical tests such as the Shapiro–Wilk test. These techniques ensure that your analyses are precise, defensible, and aligned with professional standards. This approach fosters not just confidence but competence, equipping you to handle complex tasks with clarity and precision.

The learning methodology balances conceptual clarity with actionable outcomes. Each chapter begins by laying a solid theoretical foundation, ensuring that you understand the mechanics and assumptions of a given method. This is followed by practical, hands-on examples, often using real-world data to solve meaningful problems. The Python code snippets provided are not merely functional: they are annotated and explained in detail, enabling you to adapt them to your own projects. From building a time series model to simulating Monte Carlo scenarios, every example is designed to solidify your grasp of the subject matter while showcasing its applicability.

Whether you are a novice seeking to build foundational knowledge or an experienced practitioner aiming to refine your expertise, this book offers a structured, accessible, and engaging approach to learning. By the end, you'll have developed a versatile toolkit that empowers you to approach problems with confidence, creativity, and critical insight. This dual focus on theory and application ensures that the skills you acquire are not only technically sound but also practically impactful.

1.4.1 From statistical measures to real-world application

The knowledge gained extends far beyond theoretical discussions—it is designed to be actionable in both academic and professional settings. The concepts and techniques covered here directly address challenges you are likely to encounter in real-world scenarios, ensuring that your skills are both relevant and adaptable.

Consider, for example, the task of building a linear regression model to solve a business problem. Suppose you've developed a model, only to find that it yields a low R^2 value, indicating that the model explains very little of the variance in the dependent variable. Instead of arbitrarily adding more predictors to inflate R^2—a practice that can introduce complexity and multicollinearity—you'll learn how to dissect the sum of squares. A step-by-step breakdown of concepts like SSR and SST helps identify meaningful opportunities to improve your model while maintaining interpretability and statistical integrity.

Now imagine being tasked with leading a dual role on a high-stakes project: both contributing as a technical resource and serving as the project manager. You might be responsible for implementing an automated reporting solution while simultaneously managing timelines, deliverables, and stakeholder expectations. This book prepares you for such multifaceted roles by blending technical depth with practical project management strategies. You'll learn not only how to execute statistical analyses but also how to structure and manage projects effectively, enabling you to succeed both as a technical expert and as a strategic leader.

The techniques demonstrated also enhance your ability to communicate insights to nontechnical stakeholders. For instance, when discussing the results of a chi-square test or a time series analysis, you'll have the tools to explain both the statistical outcomes and their practical implications. This capability is crucial in bridging the gap between raw data and actionable recommendations, making your work more impactful and easier for others to understand.

By emphasizing real-world applications, this book ensures that you're equipped to navigate the complexities of modern data analysis with confidence. Whether you're optimizing business operations, improving predictive models, or exploring innovative solutions to emerging challenges, the skills you develop here will enable you to tackle these tasks effectively and thoughtfully.

1.4.2 Expanding beyond traditional techniques

In the modern landscape of data science and analytics, traditional statistical techniques—such as linear regression and basic hypothesis testing—often serve as foundational tools. However, many real-world problems require more advanced methods to address their inherent complexity. The content is designed to equip you with those advanced techniques, allowing you to tackle challenges that go beyond the capabilities of traditional approaches.

Imagine being tasked with forecasting stock prices over a volatile market period. A linear regression model might provide some insights, but its assumptions and limitations can make it less suitable for capturing the stochastic nature of financial markets.

Instead, Monte Carlo simulations—one of the techniques explored in this book—offer a way to model uncertainty and variability by generating thousands of potential price trajectories. These simulations provide a probabilistic view of the future, enabling better risk assessment and decision-making.

Consider another scenario: analyzing customer behavior using Markov chains. Whereas traditional models might track individual metrics like purchase frequency, a Markov chain enables you to understand the likelihood of transitions between states—such as moving from a loyal customer to a churn risk. This structured probabilistic approach helps businesses predict and influence long-term customer behaviors, making it an invaluable tool in marketing and operations. (Once more, you don't need to grasp any details just yet—chapters 9 and 11 will walk you through Monte Carlo simulations and Markov chains, respectively, and show exactly how they're applied in practice.)

Optimization techniques like linear programming are also introduced, allowing you to effectively allocate resources under constraints. For example, you might be asked to prioritize projects within a fixed budget while maximizing their effect. Linear programming provides a systematic way to determine the best allocation of resources, ensuring that strategic objectives are met efficiently.

By breaking down these advanced methods into digestible steps and providing annotated Python code, this book empowers you to implement them with clarity and confidence. Each technique is paired with practical examples that demonstrate its relevance and application across industries, from finance and healthcare to logistics and marketing. Moreover, the emphasis on understanding the "why" behind each method ensures that you're not just following a recipe but are fully equipped to adapt these tools to new and unique challenges.

Expanding your analytical toolkit with these advanced techniques will prepare you to solve problems that demand more sophisticated solutions. Whether simulating complex systems, optimizing decision-making processes, or analyzing probabilistic models, the skills you develop here will enable you to address a broader range of scenarios with confidence and precision.

1.4.3 A balanced approach to theory and practice

One of the central goals of this book is to strike a meaningful balance between theoretical understanding and practical application. Many texts lean heavily on abstract mathematical principles or, conversely, focus solely on coding shortcuts, but this book bridges the gap, providing a dual focus to ensure that you not only learn how to execute techniques but also comprehend why they work.

Each chapter begins by laying down the theoretical foundations of a particular method. For instance, before diving into Python code for linear regression, we explore key concepts such as assumptions, coefficients, and goodness-of-fit measures. Similarly, when we discuss Monte Carlo simulations, we first establish the principles of randomness and probability distributions that underpin this method. This foundational approach equips you with the knowledge to make informed decisions when applying these techniques to real-world problems.

Chapters 2 and 3 establish the groundwork for the statistical and quantitative methods explored throughout the book. Chapter 2 introduces the essential principles of probability and counting, ranging from basic probabilities to combinations and permutations, and culminates with an exploration of continuous and discrete random variables. This broad foundation equips you with the tools needed to quantify uncertainty and structure problem-solving approaches. Chapter 3 then builds on this by examining four fundamental probability distributions—normal, binomial, uniform, and Poisson—while also tackling probability computations and conditional probabilities. Together, these chapters provide you with a solid conceptual and computational base, enabling a confident transition to more advanced topics in subsequent chapters.

Once the theoretical groundwork is established, the focus shifts to hands-on implementation. Python serves as the medium for translating abstract concepts into actionable solutions, with reusable and well-annotated code provided throughout. For example, you'll learn how to use pandas to preprocess data, NumPy to perform arithmetic computations, and scikit-learn to develop predictive models. But more than just showing you how to write code, the book explains the purpose behind each step, fostering a deeper connection between theory and practice.

This integrated approach is especially important for tackling complex challenges that require critical thinking. Consider a scenario where a predictive model produces unexpected results: by understanding the statistical assumptions behind the method, you'll be better equipped to diagnose and address issues such as multicollinearity and data outliers. Similarly, if you're designing a decision tree, knowing how the algorithm splits data at each node allows you to fine-tune its performance for greater accuracy.

Moreover, this balance extends to the way results are interpreted and communicated. Statistical outcomes, such as p-values and regression coefficients, are contextualized to ensure their relevance to the problem at hand. Graphical outputs, whether scatterplots or simulation trajectories, are analyzed with a focus on deriving actionable insights rather than just presenting visuals.

By combining theoretical rigor with practical application, the book ensures that you develop both the technical skills and critical thinking abilities required to solve real-world problems effectively. The emphasis on understanding not just the "how" but also the "why" enables you to adapt techniques to a variety of challenges, making you a more versatile and confident analyst. Chapters 2 and 3 provide a solid foundation, and subsequent chapters build on that base, empowering you to produce solutions that are not only technically sound but also impactful and meaningful.

1.5 How this book works

The content is designed to provide a seamless learning experience, combining theoretical insights with practical applications across its chapters. Each chapter is self-contained, focusing on a specific statistical or quantitative technique, and is structured to guide you step by step through the essential concepts, their practical implementation, and their interpretation in real-world contexts. This modular design allows you to engage with topics independently, making it easy to explore specific methods or follow the chapters in sequence for a comprehensive learning journey.

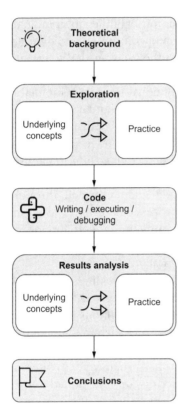

Figure 1.1 A process map that depicts how you should expect most of the subsequent chapters to flow. The linear component closely aligns with a typical statistical or quantitative problem at work or in the classroom, especially if we were to change out the theoretical background in favor of an opening problem definition. But there is also some nonlinearity due to mixing the underlying concepts with practice where and when it makes sense.

To facilitate this journey, the chapters are structured to align closely with how statistical and quantitative problems are tackled in real-world scenarios. Starting with theoretical foundations, you'll progress into exploratory data analysis and hands-on Python implementations, followed by in-depth evaluation and interpretation of results. This blend ensures not only an understanding of "how" to use these tools but also a grasp of the "why" behind them.

Chapters 2 and 3 serve as foundational pillars for the rest of the book, equipping you with critical knowledge of probability principles, counting methods, and probability distributions. These chapters are designed to give you a strong start, providing the statistical groundwork needed to tackle the more advanced techniques explored in later chapters. From Chapter 4 onward, the book moves into specialized topics, including linear and logistic regressions, decision trees and random forests, time series models, constrained optimization, Monte Carlo simulations, and Markov chains, each addressed with both rigor and practicality. This structured approach is visually captured in the process map in figure 1.1.

Although most chapters follow a linear progression—mirroring the steps of a typical statistical or quantitative project—the book also incorporates nonlinear elements to intersperse conceptual learning with practice where it's most effective. By design, this method ensures that you build not only technical proficiency but also the critical thinking skills needed to apply these tools to diverse and complex problems.

1.5.1 Foundational learning with exploration and practice

The approach to learning begins by establishing a strong theoretical foundation for each technique before diving into hands-on applications. This balance ensures that you understand the underlying principles while also gaining practical skills to apply these techniques effectively. Whether exploring basic statistical concepts like regression or delving into advanced methods like Markov chains, each chapter combines conceptual clarity with actionable insights.

For instance, chapter 4 focuses on linear regression, a cornerstone of statistical analysis. It introduces regression assumptions, key measures, and statistical properties, providing a solid theoretical framework. From there, the chapter transitions into a real-world application: predicting ultramarathon split times from historical race data. Similarly, chapter 12, which examines Benford's law, begins by exploring the theoretical underpinnings of naturally occurring number sequences before applying these insights to evaluate real-world data sets like global population distributions.

Exploration is another critical component of the book's overall learning methodology. Each analysis starts with an exploratory phase to assess the data's structure and quality. For example, before fitting a regression model, you'll identify outliers, test for normality, and examine the relationships between variables through correlation matrices and scatterplots. Similarly, when analyzing a data set for adherence to Benford's law, you'll first visualize its distribution and compare it to a perfect Benford curve. This exploratory stage ensures that subsequent analyses are grounded in a comprehensive understanding of the data, leading to more robust and meaningful conclusions.

By integrating exploration and theory, the book fosters a methodical learning process that builds confidence and competence. Theoretical insights help you understand why certain techniques are appropriate, and exploration ensures that your analyses are based on solid foundations. This dual emphasis strengthens your ability to address complexity thoughtfully and effectively, thereby enabling you to draw meaningful conclusions and apply your findings with purpose in real-world settings.

1.5.2 Using Python for precision and efficiency

Python serves as the book's computational backbone, enabling efficient implementation of statistical and quantitative methods across diverse applications. Its rich ecosystem of libraries allows you to transition seamlessly from theory to practice, ensuring that your analyses are not only accurate but also efficiently executed. Throughout subsequent chapters, Python's capabilities are demonstrated through annotated code examples designed to enhance understanding and usability.

For instance, in chapter 4, we use Python to fit a linear regression model, compute regression and residual sums of squares, and generate detailed regression tables. Chapter 9 applies Python's NumPy library to run Monte Carlo simulations, demonstrating how randomness can be modeled and analyzed to make predictions under uncertainty. In chapter 11, Python facilitates the construction and analysis of Markov chains, enabling the modeling of state transitions and long-term system behaviors. Each chapter integrates Python into its methodology, providing reusable code snippets that you can adapt for your own projects.

Beyond implementation, Python's libraries simplify complex tasks, allowing you to focus on interpretation and decision-making. For example, visualizations created with

Matplotlib and seaborn provide intuitive insights into data distributions, and scikit-learn and statsmodels streamline machine learning and statistical modeling processes. These tools not only enhance productivity but also make it easier to communicate results effectively, whether through detailed plots or succinct summaries.

This integration of Python into the learning process ensures that you develop both technical proficiency and a deeper understanding of the methods you apply. The code is not presented as a black box but as a transparent tool that reveals the mechanics behind each calculation. Whether you are optimizing a linear program, analyzing time series data, or testing adherence to theoretical distributions, Python empowers you to work with precision and confidence, making it an indispensable part of your analytical toolkit.

1.5.3 Adaptable learning for diverse skill levels

This book is designed to cater to a broad audience, from beginners taking their first steps in statistics and quantitative techniques to experienced professionals looking to refine and expand their skill sets. Its structured approach, clear explanations, and practical examples ensure that learners at any level can engage with the material meaningfully.

For those new to the field, the book offers a gradual introduction to fundamental concepts like probability, regression modeling, and data visualization, presented in an accessible and straightforward manner. Python code is introduced progressively, with annotations and explanations that demystify its use, allowing beginners to gain confidence in applying computational methods.

For seasoned practitioners, the book dives into advanced techniques such as Monte Carlo simulations, Markov chains, and optimization methods, exploring their theoretical underpinnings and practical implementations. By including reusable Python code and illustrating its application with real-world scenarios, the book ensures that experienced readers can quickly grasp complex methodologies and apply them to their own analytical challenges.

The adaptability of the material extends beyond skill levels to learning preferences. Each chapter is self-contained, enabling readers to follow the content sequentially or skip to specific topics of interest. This modular design allows professionals to focus on areas most relevant to their work while providing newcomers with a comprehensive roadmap to mastering statistical and quantitative techniques. By bridging gaps in both knowledge and application, the book empowers you to tackle analytical problems with clarity, creativity, and confidence.

1.6 What this book does not cover

The book's focus is on teaching statistical and quantitative techniques using Python, assuming you already have Python installed along with your preferred IDE. Although we briefly discuss IDE options to enhance your productivity, we do not provide detailed installation instructions or a comparative review of tools like PyCharm and Jupyter Notebook.

Additionally, this is not a Python programming tutorial. Instead, the book emphasizes the application of Python to implement statistical methods and solve analytical problems. Readers seeking an introduction to Python's syntax or general-purpose programming concepts are encouraged to explore resources dedicated to those topics before diving into this book. Here, the focus remains on empowering you to apply quantitative techniques effectively and confidently.

Summary

- Statistics and quantitative methods guide decision-making by solving everyday, business-critical problems through structured analysis and insight.
- Statistics provides tools to summarize, model, and infer from data, and quantitative methods offer mathematical frameworks for solving structured decision problems.
- These techniques are valuable because they offer systematic ways to uncover patterns, evaluate uncertainty, and support high-stakes decision-making.
- Methods such as Monte Carlo simulations, Markov chains, and linear programming illustrate how the combination of stats and quant applies across finance, marketing, operations, and other verticals.
- Descriptive and inferential statistics, probability, regression, simulation, optimization, and machine learning form the conceptual foundation for the techniques used throughout.
- Python stands out for its clarity, efficiency, and robust ecosystem of libraries that support everything from data preparation to model evaluation.
- Libraries such as pandas, NumPy, statsmodels, scikit-learn, and Matplotlib enable powerful and flexible statistical analysis in Python.
- Python's simple syntax, broad community support, and real-world adoption make it an ideal language for applying statistical and quantitative techniques.
- IDEs like IDLE, PyCharm, Jupyter Notebook, Spyder, and VS Code offer development environments that support varied workflows and project complexity.
- Going forward, the book's learning approach combines theoretical explanations with practical Python implementations to build both fluency and confidence.
- Techniques are introduced in a way that encourages critical thinking, helping you not just compute results but also interpret and apply them in real-world scenarios.
- The goal is to equip you with a flexible, reusable toolkit for tackling uncertainty, drawing insight from data, and making better decisions in practice.

Exploring probability and counting

This chapter covers
- Basic probabilities
- Counting rules
- Combinations versus permutations
- Continuous random variables
- Discrete random variables

Our combined purpose in this chapter and chapter 3 is to explore the fascinating world of probabilities from several different angles—from the very basics to more advanced topics like conditional probabilities. Probabilities are the cornerstone of statistical analysis and many other quantitative techniques, so it makes perfect sense to start here and paint the subject of probabilities with a broad brush before tackling more specific topics in subsequent chapters.

Probability theory is not just some mathematical abstraction; on the contrary, it is a powerful tool for making informed decisions across almost any professional field—and in our personal lives. By understanding probabilities, we can quantify uncertainty, assess risks, and make informed predictions from data. Mastering probability concepts not only establishes a solid foundation from which to approach the techniques covered in the rest of this book but also opens up a world of possibilities around analyzing data, making predictions, and drawing meaningful and actionable insights.

Our journey in chapter 2 starts small with the basics of probabilities and odds and finishes big with conditional probability calculations. In between, we'll examine fundamental counting rules, evaluate the distinctions between combinations and permutations, and explore the properties of continuous and discrete random variables. Then, in chapter 3, we'll inspect four probability distributions—normal, binomial, uniform, and Poisson—that are foundational in statistical and quantitative analysis, and review the fundamental principles underlying probability computations. Let's begin by getting grounded in the basics.

2.1 Basic probabilities

In everyday life, numerous events unfold as a result of randomness or chance, ranging from the mundane to the consequential. Consider the simple act of flipping a coin, where the outcome—heads or tails—is beyond our influence. Similarly, when rolling a pair of dice, the probability of rolling a 7—an outcome more likely than any other possible result—is still subject to chance. Or think about selecting a single card from a standard deck of 52 cards, which are equally divided into four suits and further split into three types of face cards and 10 numbered cards; the probabilities of selecting *any* face card or *any* numbered card still exist in a state of unpredictability.

However, when we know the total number of possible outcomes and can identify how many of those lead to a successful event, we can calculate the probability by comparing the number of successful outcomes to the total possible outcomes. This enables us to make probability-based decisions grounded in the ratio of favorable outcomes to all potential outcomes. In fact, when we think about probabilities, we are really focusing on the likelihood of a specific event occurring, such as getting heads on a coin flip after calling heads. Therefore, the probability of a successful event can be expressed as follows:

$$\text{Probability(Event)} = \frac{\text{total number of potential outcomes that are successful}}{\text{total number of possible outcomes}}$$

or more simply

$$\text{Probability(Event)} = \frac{\text{number of successes}}{\text{number of outcomes}}$$

Two prerequisites are absolutely critical: we need to get the denominator right, and there must be agreement about what qualifies as a success. Getting the denominator right is easy when flipping a two-sided coin. But it's not as easy when rolling two six-sided dice or selecting cards from a deck without replacement. Likewise, agreement about what constitutes a success is easy when we call heads on a coin flip and get heads, but we also might want to qualify a product malfunction as a "success" if such malfunctions are rare and therefore easy to track.

Let's explore some simple and straightforward probabilities together. When we flip a fair coin with two sides, there are two potential outcomes, heads or tails, that are equally likely. If we call heads, and therefore heads is the successful outcome, the probability of success is

$$\frac{1}{2}$$

When we roll two six-sided dice, there are 6 × 6 = 36 possible outcomes. There's only one way of getting double 6s, if that's what we're hoping for; so, the probability of success is

$$\frac{1}{36}$$

And when selecting a card from a standard deck of 52 cards, the probability of selecting a face card—that is, a King, Queen, or Jack—regardless of suit is

$$\frac{12}{52} = \frac{6}{26} = \frac{3}{13}$$

Let's now assume we've flipped a coin and it came up heads. The probability that the same coin will come up heads on the next flip is

$$\frac{1}{2}$$

The probability is the same because these are independent events. Just because the first flip came up heads doesn't increase the likelihood that the next flip will result in the other potential outcome. Or consider 35 rolls of two six-sided dice, none of which resulted in double 6s. The probability that the next roll will result in a pair of 6s is still

$$\frac{1}{36}$$

In fact, it will always be the same probability—the number of potential outcomes doesn't change, nor does the number of ways to get a successful outcome change.

Or consider selecting a face card. As long as each selected card is then returned to the deck, the probability of getting a face card will always be equal to

$$\frac{3}{13}$$

The probability of a successful event is independent of the outcomes of previous like events. Although we should expect, for instance, the counts of heads and tails to converge after hundreds, or thousands, of coin flips—this is the essence of the law of large numbers, by the way—this phenomenon is completely separate and unrelated to the next flip of the coin.

So far, we've been discussing *theoretical probabilities*. That's because flipping coins, rolling dice, and selecting cards are based on a theoretical or assumed understanding of equally likely outcomes in a fixed and controlled environment. But there are other types of probabilities, which we'll discuss next.

2.1.1 Probability types

We have covered one type of probability already: what we call *theoretical probabilities*. Let's consider two other types of probability: empirical and subjective.

Empirical probabilities are derived from trials or real-world observations. The probability of success is therefore expressed this way:

$$\text{Probability(Event)} = \frac{\text{number of successes observed}}{\text{number of observations made}}$$

For instance, consider the probability of rainfall in Cincinnati, Ohio. Suppose meteorologists have been collecting data on rainfall for several years. They've recorded whether it rains or not each day and have otherwise kept a running tally of rainy days versus the number of days overall. Empirical probability in this context would involve calculating the probability of rainfall based on the observed data. So, if the denominator equals 365 days and the numerator equals 75 (because it's previously rained 75 times over that span), then the empirical probability of rainfall on any given day would be calculated as

$$\text{Probability(rainfall)} = \frac{\text{number of rainy days}}{\text{total number of days}}$$

or

$$\text{Probability(rainfall)} = \frac{75}{365}$$

And then there's subjective probability. *Subjective probability* is based on personal judgment, opinions, or beliefs rather than on observed data or mathematical calculations; it can therefore vary from person to person and may be influenced by individual experiences, biases, or perceptions. For example, a person's subjective probability of winning a chess match may be higher if they feel confident in their skill and experience, even if the theoretical probability of winning is lower due to objective factors.

2.1.2 Converting and measuring probabilities

Probabilities are frequently converted to percentages and odds and then presented in these terms. Let's first demonstrate how probabilities are converted to percentages by using Python as a calculator.

The following snippet of code calculates the probability of getting heads in a single coin flip, converts the probability to a percentage by multiplying the result by 100, and prints the result by combining a character string with the percentage probability:

```
>>> probability_heads = 1 / 2
>>> probability_heads_percent = probability_heads * 100
>>> print(f'The probability of success equals: '
    f'{probability_heads_percent}%')
The probability of success equals: 50.0%
```

NOTE A few notes about this snippet of code and many others to follow: first, lines of Python code are always preceded by >>>, whereas the results copied and pasted from the Python Console are not. Second, the backslash character (\) is frequently used to cleanly split long lines of Python code into multiple lines. And third, single or double quotation marks are equally acceptable in Python, but consistency is required for each character string, or Python will throw an error.

The following snippets of code perform similar operations with respect to getting double 6s or selecting a face card:

```
>>> probability_double_sixes = 1 / 36
>>> probability_double_sixes_percent = probability_double_sixes * 100
>>> print(f'The probability of success equals: '
>>>     f'{probability_double_sixes_percent}%')
The probability of success equals: 2.7777777777777777%

>>> probability_face_card = 12 / 52
>>> probability_face_card_percent = probability_face_card * 100
>>> print(f'The probability of success equals: '
>>>     f'{probability_face_card_percent}%')
The probability of success equals: 23.076923076923077%
```

There is thus a 50% chance of getting heads on a coin flip, an almost 3% chance of getting double 6s from a pair of dice, and a 23% chance of selecting a face card from a standard deck of 52 cards.

Odds, meanwhile, are expressed as the ratio between successes and failures, whereas probability represents the ratio of successes to total possible outcomes:

$$\text{Odds} = \frac{\text{number of potential successes}}{\text{number of potential failures}}$$

Although related, odds and probabilities are clearly not the same and should not be used interchangeably.

The odds of selecting a face card are

$$\text{Odds(face card)} = \frac{\text{number of potential successes}}{\text{number of potential failures}}$$

or
$$\text{Odds(face card)} = \frac{12}{40}$$

The numerator and denominator, when added together, equal the total number of possible outcomes. Simplifying the previous fraction, we get

$$\text{Odds(face card)} = \frac{3}{10}$$

or

$$\text{Odds(face card)} = 0.3$$

Alternatively, rather than assigning the number of successes to the numerator and the number of failures to the denominator, we can instead assign the probabilities of success and failure, which must sum to 1, to get the same result:

$$\text{Odds(face card)} = \frac{0.23}{0.77}$$

or

$$\text{Odds(face card)} = 0.3$$

And incidentally, we can go in reverse; that is, we can derive the probability of selecting a face card from the odds of doing the same. We simply insert the odds into the following formula:

$$\text{Probability(Event)} = \frac{\text{Odds}}{\text{Odds} + 1}$$

So that

$$\text{Probability(face card)} = \frac{0.3}{0.3 + 1}$$

or

$$\text{Probability(face card)} = \frac{0.3}{1.3}$$

All this returns us to a 23% probability of selecting a face card from a standard deck of 52 cards when the fractional result is converted to a percentage.

We previously mentioned that it can sometimes be challenging to compute the number of potential outcomes. Such challenges can be resolved by understanding fundamental counting rules, the differences between combinations and permutations, and the concepts of replacement and without replacement. We'll look at this topic next.

2.2 Counting rules

In probability and combinatorics (the study of counting, arrangement, and combination of objects), understanding how to count the number of possible outcomes is paramount. A pair of fundamental principles are our guides: the multiplication rule and the addition rule. These two rules are the very foundation for calculating the total number of outcomes when dealing with multiple events or scenarios. The multiplication rule is a method for determining the total number of potential outcomes when events are simultaneous or sequential, and the addition rule is a method for determining the same result when events are mutually exclusive. Together, they are powerful tools for analyzing various probability scenarios and uncovering the myriad ways in which events can unfold.

2.2.1 Multiplication rule

The multiplication rule states that if there are i choices to be made, with n_1 possibilities for the first choice, n_2 possibilities for the second choice, and so forth, then the aggregate number of potential outcomes equals the product of the individual choices, denoted as $n_1 \times n_2 \times \ldots n_i$. To illustrate, when rolling a pair of six-sided dice, we used the multiplication rule (rolling two dice consists of two simultaneous events, after all) to compute the number of possible outcomes, arriving at 36 by multiplying 6 by itself. It's easy to envision so many possible outcomes when you realize that getting 3 on the first die and 2 on the second die is not the same outcome as getting 2 on the first die and 3 on the second. Let's explore a pair of other examples where the multiplication rule applies:

- If a license plate contains three letters followed by three numerals (e.g., ABC123), applying the multiplication rule returns the total number of possible outcomes. There are 26 letters in the alphabet and 10 single-digit numerals; therefore, the number of possible outcomes equals $26 \times 26 \times 26 \times 10 \times 10 \times 10$, or 17,576,000 unique license plates.
- Similarly, in the case of a briefcase featuring a three-digit lock, where each digit is any number between 0 and 9, the total number of possible outcomes amounts to $10 \times 10 \times 10$, or 1,000 unique outcomes.

The multiplication rule applies when the outcomes of two or more events are independent of each other, meaning that the occurrence of one event does not influence the occurrence of the other event(s). It allows us to calculate the total number of outcomes for the *combined* events by multiplying the number of outcomes for each individual event.

2.2.2 Addition rule

In situations where events are mutually exclusive, the addition rule is applied to calculate the probability of either event occurring. The addition rule states that the total probability of one or another of the mutually exclusive events occurring is the sum of their individual probabilities. It's important to note that this rule applies specifically to events that cannot happen simultaneously.

For example, consider a scenario where you have the option to either flip a coin or roll a die. The outcomes of these events are mutually exclusive because you can only do one of the actions at a time. If you choose to flip the coin, there are two possible outcomes (heads or tails), and if you choose to roll the die, there are six possible outcomes. According to the addition rule, the total number of potential outcomes is 2 + 6 = 8, assuming you choose to perform only one of these actions.

However, if the events are independent (i.e., the outcome of one event does not affect the outcome of another), the addition rule does not apply. Instead, the multiplication rule is used to calculate the total number of possible outcomes. For instance, if you were to flip a coin, roll a die, and select a card from a standard deck, the number of possible outcomes would be calculated as 2 × 6 × 52 = 624, reflecting all possible combinations of these independent events.

Here are some additional examples to clarify the application of the addition rule:

- If you choose to read 1 of 12 classic novels or 1 of 14 data science manuals (but not both), the number of possible outcomes is 12 + 14 = 26.
- If you have three interstate routes and two backroad routes to travel from Cincinnati to Nashville, and you can only choose one of these routes, the total number of possible routes is 3 + 2 = 5.

It is essential to distinguish between when to apply the addition rule versus the multiplication rule, as each rule applies to different types of events. The addition rule is used when calculating the total number of outcomes for mutually exclusive events, and the multiplication rule is used when dealing with independent events. Understanding the correct application of these rules is crucial for accurately computing probabilities.

2.2.3 Combinations and permutations

We've been chewing on a mix of combinations and permutations. In spite of the fact that *combination* is frequently used as a euphemism for combinations and permutations, the two are actually quite different; and because they are different, the methods by which they are mathematically derived are unalike. And then there's *replacement* and *without replacement*, both of which apply to combinations and permutations, which further complicates matters.

We'll remove the haze, but for now, bear in mind that when the order doesn't matter, it's a combination; but when the order does matter, it's a permutation. When a public address announcer introduces the five starting players before a basketball game, that's a combination, because the sequence of introductions is immaterial; the starting lineup remains unchanged regardless of the order in which the players were introduced. Conversely, consider the three-digit lock on a briefcase, such as 3-7-4. This is a permutation because the specific sequence matters significantly: only 3-7-4 will unlock the briefcase, whereas other arrangements of the same numerals won't work.

PERMUTATIONS WITH REPLACEMENT

Permutations with replacement are relatively simple and straightforward, at least mathematically. A permutation with replacement involves selecting items from a set in a specific order and, after each selection, returning the chosen item to the set before the next selection is made, thereby making the chosen item eligible to be selected again.

For instance, if the three-digit lock on a briefcase can be set as 3-3-4, that's a permutation with replacement because the order matters and reusing digits is allowed. And because the digits are immediately replaced once they're used, the number of choices remains unchanged throughout; it's not decremented by one immediately following each selection. Decrementing by one occurs when replacement is not allowed, meaning each choice reduces the number of available options.

Setting a three-digit lock on a briefcase involves selecting a sequence of single-digit numerals to secure the contents. The process is akin to selecting a password for access, where the order of the numerals matters. When setting the first digit of the lock, we have 10 numerals, 0 through 9, from which to choose. Because the digits can be reused, we then have the same 10 choices when setting the second digit and again when setting the third and final digit.

Thus, the formula to get the number of potential outcomes when the order matters and replacement is allowed is simply

$$n^r$$

where

- n is the number of distinct items (*events* or *choices* could be substituted for *items*).
- r is the number of selections made.
- n^r represents the total number of permutations allowing for replacement after each selection. It is a "take" on the multiplication rule in that both concepts involve the number of outcomes from independent, yet simultaneous or sequential, events.

So, there are 10^3 or $10 \times 10 \times 10 = 1,000$ unique outcomes, just as we previously mentioned.

To demonstrate how to calculate the number of permutations with replacement in Python, let's say n equals 5 and r equals 3, which is to say we have five choices for each selection and three choices to be made:

```
>>> n = 5
>>> r = 3
```

In Python, one method of raising a number, like n, to the power of another, such as r, is to call the asterisk (**) twice, like so:

```
>>> num_permutations = n ** r
>>> print(f'Number of permutations with replacement: {num_permutations}')
Number of permutations with replacement: 125
```

Alternatively, we can pass n and r to the `pow()` method to get the same result; `pow()` raises the first argument it takes to the power of the second argument:

```
>>> num_permutations = pow(n, r)
>>> print(f'Number of permutations with replacement: {num_permutations}')
Number of permutations with replacement: 125
```

That was simple and straightforward enough, but permutations are more complicated when replacement is not allowed.

PERMUTATIONS WITHOUT REPLACEMENT

A permutation without replacement means that although the order remains relevant, we have to reduce the number of available choices for each successive selection. Let's say we have five choices for the first selection and a total of three choices to be made. So, we again set n to equal 5 and r to equal 3:

```
>>> n = 5
>>> r = 3
```

But this time, we apply the factorial function (!) to n and r to get the total number of potential outcomes. When we apply the factorial function, we are merely multiplying a series of incrementally descending natural numbers, with the effect of successively decrementing available options. Here are a couple of examples:

- $5! = 5 \times 4 \times 3 \times 2 \times 1 = 120$
- $3! = 3 \times 2 \times 1 = 6$

The formula to calculate the number of potential outcomes when the order matters and replacement is not allowed is given by

$$\frac{n!}{(n-r)!}$$

This formula is derived from the concept that for each position in a sequence, you have one fewer option as each item is used up. Initially, there are n choices for the first position, $n-1$ choices for the second, and so on, until you've made r selections. The factorial in the denominator, $(n-r)!$, accounts for the reduction in available choices as each item is selected, reflecting the fact that replacement is not allowed.

So, when n is 5 and r is 3, the number of potential outcomes is equal to

$$\frac{5!}{(5-3)!}$$

or

$$\frac{120}{12}$$

which, of course, is equal to 60. So, if any three runners out of five can qualify for a medal, there are 60 first-, second-, and third-place permutations possible.

In Python, we call the `factorial()` method from the `math` library to get the same result:

```
>>> import math
>>> permutations = math.factorial(n) / math.factorial(n - r)
>>> print(f'Number of permutations without replacement: '
>>>       f'{permutations}')
Number of permutations without replacement: 60
```

Or we can instead pass `n` and `r` to the `math.perm()` method, which inserts the assignments for `n` and `r` and then runs the permutations without replacement formula:

```
>>> permutations = math.perm(n, r)
>>> print(f'Number of permutations without replacement: '
>>>       f'{permutations}')
Number of permutations without replacement: 60
```

We get the same result, incidentally, by simply multiplying the three digits, $5 \times 4 \times 3$, that are greater than the denominator. This method offers a quick and intuitive mathematical shortcut to calculate the number of permutations without replacement, bypassing the need to apply the full factorial formula while still arriving at the correct answer. It works because $n! / (n - r)!$ effectively *removes* the unnecessary tail end of the factorial—that is, everything from $(n - r)!$ downward—leaving just the first r descending terms, which is exactly what you get by multiplying $n \times (n - 1) \times \ldots \times (n - r + 1)$. It's a handy trick that underscores the elegance and efficiency of mathematical thinking.

COMBINATIONS WITHOUT REPLACEMENT

Most lotteries are examples of combinations without replacement—numbers are drawn one at a time (and can't be drawn again), but like the introduction of players at the start of a basketball game, the order in which the numbers are selected has no meaning. Maybe the easiest and most logical way to think about combinations without replacement is to first think about permutations without replacement and then insert an adjustment to eliminate the significance of order.

Let's walk through this together, where n (the number of distinct items) once more equals 5 and r (the number of items to be selected) again equals 3. We already know, from our prior example, that the number of permutations without replacement equals 60. However, when the order no longer matters, the number of distinct outcomes is significantly reduced. For example, the sequences 123, 132, 213, 231, 312, and 321 are all considered different when the order matters; but when the order doesn't matter, these six sequences are treated as identical, leaving only one relevant outcome. To find the number of ways three digits can be sequenced when the order matters, we apply the factorial function, like so:

$$3! = 3 \times 2 \times 1 = 6$$

This means permutations without replacement have six times as many possible outcomes as combinations without replacement when n and r equal 5 and 3, respectively.

Consequently, we adjust the permutations without replacement formula to reduce it by an order of magnitude equal to the number that was just calculated, because we no longer care about the order. Thus, the number of combinations without replacement can be derived by plugging the values for n and r into the following equation:

$$\frac{n!}{(n-r)!} \times \frac{1}{r!} = \frac{n!}{r!(n-r)!}$$

or simply

$$\frac{n!}{r!(n-r)!}$$

or

$$\frac{5!}{3!(5-3)!}$$

or

$$\frac{120}{12}$$

This, of course, equals 10. So when n is 5 and r is 3, the number of permutations without replacement is, indeed, exactly six times more than the number of combinations without replacement. Another, much more interesting, method of getting the same result is to use Pascal's Triangle.

PASCAL'S TRIANGLE

Pascal's triangle is a geometric arrangement of numbers in a triangular shape. The triangle is named after the French mathematician Blaise Pascal, although it was known long before his time. It's commonly used in algebra, probability theory, and combinatorics. Here's how it works.

The triangle is built from the top down: it starts with the single number 1 at the top, and each row below it is constructed by adding the two numbers immediately above it. So, for example, the fourth row in the triangle contains two instances of the number 3—the first instance is obtained by adding the 1 and the 2 immediately above it, and the second instance is obtained by adding the same 2 and a different 1 just above it.

It turns out that each row begins and ends with the number 1. And as you progress downward in Pascal's triangle, the sum of the numbers in each row doubles compared to the sum in the row above it.

More significantly for our purposes, each number in Pascal's triangle corresponds to the combination of choosing r items out of n possibilities, typically denoted as "n choose r" or, when n equals 5 and r equals 3, "5 choose 3." The number of potential outcomes can be found at the $(n+1)$th row and the $(r+1)$th position in the triangle (see figure 2.1). So, given 5 and 3 for n and r, respectively, we get the number of potential outcomes by referencing the value found at the intersection of the sixth row and the fourth position in that row.

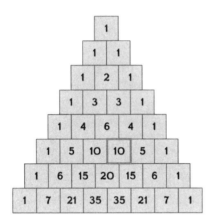

Figure 2.1 The top of Pascal's triangle. The triangle is constructed from the top down, where numbers are derived by adding the two numbers immediately above. It so happens that the sum of numbers for each row is twice the sum of numbers from the row above. The number of combinations without replacement can be found at the intersection of the (n + 1)th row and the (r + 1)th position in that row. When n equals 5 (sixth row down) and r equals 3 (fourth position from the left), the number of combinations without replacement equals 10.

In Python, we can achieve the same result in two ways: either by performing an arithmetic operation using the factorial() method with n and r, or by utilizing the math.comb() method with n and r as arguments:

```
>>> n = 5
>>> r = 3

>>> combinations = (math.factorial(n) / \
>>>                 (math.factorial(r) * math.factorial(n - r)))
>>> print(f'Number of combinations without replacement: '
>>>       f'{combinations}')
Number of combinations without replacement: 10.0

>>> combinations = math.comb(n, r)
>>> print(f'Number of combinations without replacement: '
>>>       f'{combinations}')
Number of combinations without replacement: 10
```

This brings us to combinations with replacement—maybe the most complex of all these counting rules.

COMBINATIONS WITH REPLACEMENT

A combination with replacement involves selecting items from a set where any item can potentially be selected multiple times, and the order of selection doesn't matter. Imagine purchasing a pizza topped with three out of five available ingredients. Because replacement is allowed, it's possible, for instance, to purchase extra pepperoni with mushrooms rather than pepperoni, mushrooms, and sausage. And it doesn't matter in what order these selections are made, because the pizza will be the same regardless.

The formula for calculating the number of potential combinations with replacement is actually derived from the formula for counting combinations without replacement:

$$\frac{n!}{r!\,(n-r)!}$$

When replacement is allowed, we still choose r items from a set of n distinct items, but we allow any item to be selected multiple times. To then derive the formula for combinations with replacement, we'll introduce the concept of *dummy* items.

Imagine adding $r-1$ dummy items to the set before making selections. These are not actual items, but rather are placeholders to separate different groups of selections. By doing this, we ensure that each selection can be made independently, as the dummy items create clear divisions between groups, allowing us to account for all possible combinations, including those where some items are chosen multiple times. So, effectively, we have $n + (r-1)$ items from which to choose; thus, $n + (r-1))!$ becomes our numerator in lieu of $n!$ and $r!((n+(r-1))-r)!$ becomes our denominator in place of $r!(n-1)!$, like so:

$$\frac{(n+(r-1))!}{r!\,((n+(r-1))-r)!}$$

or simply

$$\frac{(n+r-1)!}{r!\,(n-1)!}$$

So, if n equals 5 available ingredients and r equals 3 total selections, the number of possible combinations with replacement equals

$$\frac{(5+3-1)!}{3!\,(5-1)!}$$

or

$$\frac{7!}{3! \times 4!}$$

or

$$\frac{5,040}{6 \times 24}$$

which equals 35 possible combinations.

One way of getting Python to do the heavy lifting is to again utilize the `factorial()` method with n and r as part of an arithmetic operation that mirrors the combinations with replacement formula:

```
>>> n = 5
>>> r = 3
>>> combinations = (math.factorial(n + r - 1) / \
>>>                 (math.factorial(r) * math.factorial(n - 1)))
>>> print(f'Number of combinations with replacement: '
>>>       f'{combinations}')
Number of combinations with replacement: 35.0
```

Or, even better, we can combine n and r with the math.comb() method:

```
>>> combinations = math.comb(n + r - 1, r)
>>> print(f'Number of combinations with replacement: '
>>>       f'{combinations}')
Number of combinations with replacement: 35
```

Now, let's shift our focus from counting rules to exploring continuous and discrete random variables.

2.3 Continuous random variables

A *random variable* is a mathematical concept that assigns a numerical value to each possible outcome of a random experiment or process. It represents uncertain quantities or events in probabilistic models, allowing for the analysis of probabilities with different outcomes. A *continuous random variable* is a variable that can take any value within a certain range or interval, including both integers (whole numbers like –8, 0, and 24) and non-integers (decimals, fractions, and mixed numbers). Unlike *discrete random variables*, which can only take on specific, countable values, continuous random variables can assume an infinite number of values within a continuous range.

Continuous random variables are characterized by their infinite precision; for instance, whereas units of time are typically measured in discrete intervals such as seconds, minutes, and hours, time itself is continuous and can therefore be measured in milliseconds, microseconds, nanoseconds, and so on. No matter how small the interval may be, there are an infinite number of possible values the variable can take on. And every possible value has a nonzero probability of occurrence.

The range of possible values for a continuous random variable is typically denoted by an interval such as $[a, b]$, where a and b represent the lower and upper bounds of the interval, respectively. For instance, the interval for the Boston Marathon is $[2, 6]$, because the fastest runners in the world can't complete the course in less than 2 hours, and 6 hours is the cutoff time. Although every possible value between 2 and 6 hours has some probability of occurrence, it doesn't necessarily mean they have equal probabilities of occurrence. In fact, the average Boston Marathon finish time is around 4 hours, which is to say that more runners will complete the course in about 4 hours, plus or minus, but very few runners will do so in just over 2 hours or barely less than 6 hours.

Understanding continuous phenomena is essential for comprehending and predicting real-world events that occur across a spectrum of values without distinct boundaries. We'll demonstrate how to measure probabilistic behavior in many continuous phenomena, how to analyze the likelihood of different outcomes occurring, and how these probabilities accumulate across a range of values.

2.3.1 Examples

Time might be the most obvious example, but in fact, continuous random variables are used to model numerous real-world phenomena, including the following:

- Temperature measurements, whether in Celsius, Fahrenheit, or Kelvin, are continuous random variables. Temperature can take on any real value within a specified range, with infinite precision. For instance, although temperature readings of 21 °C and 72 °F are absolutely possible, so are 21.511 °C and 72.5111 °F, thereby demonstrating the continuous nature of temperature.
- Measurements of distance or length, such as the length of a road, the height of a building, or the width of a river, are continuous random variables. Distance can take on any real value within a specified range, with infinite precision. For instance, the length of a road is typically measured in kilometers or miles, but it can also be measured in fractions of a meter, millimeters, or even smaller units.
- Speed measurements, such as the speed of a vehicle or the velocity of an object, are continuous random variables. The speedometer in a car might display speeds such as 85 kilometers per hour or 55 miles per hour, and a speed gun may record the velocity of a pitched ball in a baseball game at 88 miles per hour, but speed actually takes on any real value within a specified range, with infinite precision, because speed can also be measured in fractions of kilometers or miles per hour.
- Measurements of volume or capacity, such as the volume of a container or the capacity of a reservoir, are continuous random variables. The volume of a container, for instance, may be measured in liters or gallons, but it can also be measured in fractions of a milliliter or cubic centimeter.
- Stock prices in financial markets are yet another example of continuous random variables. Any given stock may be priced at $45.00 per share, or $45.51 per share, or even $45.511 per share.

These examples are but a small subset of continuous random variables that occupy our everyday lives, whether we're aware of this simple fact or not. Although many of these and other like measurements may be presented discretely for practical purposes, it's important to acknowledge their underlying continuous nature.

2.3.2 Probability density function

The *probability density function* (PDF) is a mathematical function that quantifies the likelihood of a continuous random variable falling within a specific range of values. It is typically denoted as $f(x)$ or $p(x)$, where x represents the value of the random variable. It also provides the relative likelihood—that is, the likelihood compared to other possible values—of the random variable taking on a specific value or falling within a specific interval. So, if the interval happens to be [2, 6], meaning the lower bound is 2 and the upper bound is 6, $f(3.2)$ is the relative likelihood of observing 3.2 as the continuous random variable between 2 and 6.

The PDF is typically illustrated using a graph, where the *x* axis, or horizontal axis, represents the possible values of the random variable, and the *y* axis, or vertical axis, represents the likelihood or probability density of each value. The PDF curve is a smooth line—how smooth or not so smooth usually depends on the sample size—that exhibits different shapes depending on the specific distribution.

That is to say, the PDF is not one size fits all; the PDF formula varies depending on the specific probability distribution being modeled. Different probability distributions, such as the normal distribution versus the uniform distribution, have their own unique PDFs and therefore their own characteristics and shapes. (The uniform distribution, by the way, can represent discrete phenomena, as well; see chapter 3.)

No doubt the most common continuous probability distribution is the normal distribution, due to its prevalence among natural phenomena. In the worlds of data science and statistics, the normal distribution is predominant due to its pivotal role in a multitude of statistical techniques, including hypothesis testing and regression analysis. Thus, it only makes sense to draw a normal distribution to help further explain the PDF (see figure 2.2).

The normal distribution is a bell-shaped probability distribution characterized by its symmetric shape centered around the mean. In this particular instance—where the lower and upper bounds equal 2 and 6, respectively; the mean, or the average value, equals 4; and the standard deviation, the dispersion or spread of all values, equals 1—the distribution reveals several key properties.

For starters, the area under the PDF curve represents the probability of the continuous random variable falling within the interval [2, 6]. It illustrates the relative likelihood of observing values within the specified range.

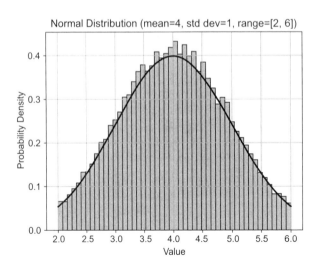

Figure 2.2 The normal distribution illustrates where the interval, or range of possible values—which runs along the *x* axis—equals [2, 6]. The probability density, which runs along the *y* axis, peaks at the mean and typically tops out at approximately 0.399. The probability density for any value can therefore be estimated merely by observation. When the value equals 3.2, the probability density appears to be equal to approximately 0.30.

Secondly, notice how the probability density is greater than 0 throughout. It peaks at the mean and approaches 0 at both tails, but it stops short of taking on a non-positive value. This guarantees that the likelihood of observing any particular value is never negative.

And finally, the integral of the PDF—that is, the total probability of all possible outcomes—is equal to the area under the curve and always sums to 1. In short, the PDF provides a method for quantifying the likelihood of different outcomes for a continuous random variable by providing insights into the distribution of probabilities across a predefined range of possible values.

Next, we'll explore the PDF's counterpart, the cumulative distribution function. It provides insights into the cumulative probability distribution of continuous random variables by integrating probabilities over a range of values.

2.3.3 Cumulative distribution function

The *cumulative distribution function* (CDF) is a function that gives the probability that a random variable takes on a value up to and including the given value x. The CDF is derived by adding up the probabilities given by the PDF. Therefore, much like the PDF, the CDF can be given as an equation and illustrated with a graph.

The CDF, typically denoted as $F(x)$ or $P(X \leq x)$, gives the probability that a continuous random variable X takes on a value less than or equal to a given point x. It represents the cumulative probability distribution of the random variable.

CDFs for continuous random variables possess many important properties. For a CDF $F(x)$ associated with the random variable X and values a and b, the following are true:

- The function $F(x)$ is nondecreasing (also called *monotonically increasing*); that is, as x increases, the probability $P(X \leq x)$ does not decrease. It will either increase or stabilize; but as a CDF, it does not and cannot ever decrease. So, if $a < b$, then $F(a) \leq F(b)$.
- The value of $F(x)$, as a probability, is always equal to some value between 0 and 1; therefore, $0 \leq F(x) \leq 1$.
- To find the probability that the random variable X takes on a value within the interval $[a, b]$, we can use the formula $P\{a < X \leq b\} = F(b) - F(a)$.
- To compute the value $F(a)$, assuming we know the PDF, we find the area under the PDF between 0 and a.

The shape of the CDF is intimately connected to that of the PDF. As the PDF changes according to the distribution being modeled, the CDF adapts accordingly, exhibiting diverse characteristics and shapes reflective of the underlying distribution. When the probability density is normally distributed, the CDF takes on an S-shaped curve (as we will see shortly).

When plotting the CDF for a normal distribution, several notable features emerge:

- The CDF starts at 0 and tops out at 1. This property actually holds true regardless of the underlying distribution.

- The CDF remains relatively flat near the tails, or when the value of the random variable is close to the lower or upper bounds of the range [2, 6]. This flatness indicates that the probabilities at the tails, as provided by the PDF, are small and contribute insignificantly to the overall CDF.
- Probabilities accumulate at a much faster rate at or around the mean. The opposite effects at the tails versus the inflection point at the mean is what gives the CDF for a normal distribution its S-shaped appearance. (It shares similarities with the sigmoid function, which will be discussed in chapter 5 during the process of fitting a logistic regression model.)
- The area under the CDF curve represents the cumulative probability. For instance, in our example, when the random variable equals 4.5, the cumulative probability—that is, the sum of probabilities given by the PDF—is approximately 70%. This means the probability of the random variable being less than 4.5 is about 70%.

All this leads to the graph in figure 2.3, where the continuous random variable is plotted along the *x* axis and the cumulative probability is plotted along the *y* axis.

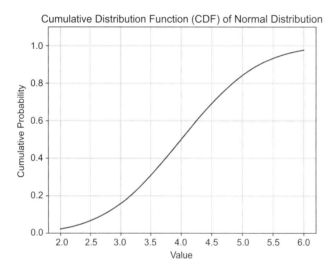

Figure 2.3 The CDF for the normal distribution when the lower and upper bounds equal 2 and 6, respectively, the mean equals 4, and the standard deviation equals 1. The shape of the CDF will vary depending on the PDF being modeled; regardless, it will always start at 0 and top out at 1.

Chapter 3 includes a more detailed discussion of the normal distribution and computing actual probabilities. For now, our focus shifts to discrete random variables.

2.4 Discrete random variables

Discrete random variables represent outcomes with distinct, countable values. For instance, when rolling a six-sided die, the whole numbers 1, 2, 3, 4, 5, and 6 represent the only possible outcomes; fractional or other "outcomes" such as 2.78 or 5.111 are impossible. This one property is what mostly differentiates discrete random variables from continuous random variables, but there are also other differences:

- Discrete random variables have a probability mass function (PMF) for calculating probabilities, whereas continuous random variables, of course, have a PDF. The PDF describes the relative likelihood of outcomes within a continuous range, whereas the PMF provides the probability of each individual outcome for a discrete random variable. Put differently, the PMF returns the actual probability of getting each specific outcome for discrete variables. The PMF for rolling a fair six-sided die assigns a probability of 1/6, or roughly 16.7%, to each possible outcome. In fact, the PMF is most commonly associated with the uniform distribution, where it assigns equal probabilities to each possible outcome within a finite range, like rolling a fair die. However, the PMF also applies to other discrete probability distributions; similar to the PDF for continuous random variables, the PMF is not one size fits all.
- The CDF for discrete random variables is a step function, increasing only at specific values, whereas the CDF for continuous random variables is instead a smooth, continuous curve. When plotted, the CDF might resemble a flight of stairs, where the height of each step represents the cumulative probability up to that outcome. For instance, where six discrete outcomes are possible and the probability is constant throughout, the cumulative probability after the first two values equals 1/6 + 1/6, or 16.7% + 16.7%, or about 33.3%.

Understanding discrete random variables is essential in probability theory and statistics, as they form the foundation for modeling discrete events, designing experiments, and making informed predictions from discrete data sets, providing valuable insights into a wide range of real-world phenomena.

2.4.1 Examples

Rolling a fair six-sided die is just one of several examples of discrete random variables. Here are a few others:

- Selecting a card from a standard deck of 52 cards. Because each card has an equal probability of being selected, 1/52, it is similar to rolling a fair die; in fact, both of these discrete random variables follow a uniform probability distribution.
- Any binomial experiment where each trial has only two possible outcomes: success or failure. For instance, this could involve counting the number of heads in a series of coin flips, where obtaining heads is deemed a success and tails a failure. Alternatively, it might entail tallying the number of defective units from a sample of items manufactured on a production line, where a defect is considered a success due to its (presumably) relative rarity compared to nondefective units.
- Scenarios where events are tallied within a set timeframe or area, like tracking the count of vehicles passing through a tollgate in an hour or the number of typographical errors found on a single page of text. In such instances, the random variable represents the frequency of (occasionally rare) events transpiring within a defined timeframe or spatial region.

- Counting the number of black marbles drawn from a bag without replacement, where the bag contains a mix of black and white marbles and a finite number of draws are allowed; or recording the number of successful applicants selected for a job from a pool of candidates, where a fixed number of candidates are selected without replacement.

These examples illustrate how discrete random variables arise in various contexts and follow different probability distributions depending on the nature of the random experiment or process being modeled.

2.4.2 Probability mass function

The PMF is to discrete random variables as the PDF is to continuous random variables. But that does not mean the PMF and PDF are otherwise alike. Formally, the PMF is denoted as $P(X = x)$, where X is the random variable and x represents its possible values. The specific formula depends on the probability distribution being modeled. Different probability distributions—binomial versus uniform versus Poisson—have their own unique PMFs, each with distinct formulas and properties. The PMF assigns an actual probability, rather than a relative likelihood, to each specific value of the random variable, which indicates the likelihood of that value occurring. Mathematically, it satisfies the following two properties:

- *Nonnegativity*—The PMF assigns nonnegative probabilities to each possible outcome, thereby ensuring that all probabilities are greater than or equal to zero.
- *Summation*—The sum of all probabilities for all possible outcomes of the random variable is equal to 1. In other words, $\Sigma P(X = x) = 1$, where the sum is taken over all possible values of x.

To illustrate, let's plot the PMF for rolling a pair of six-sided dice; see figure 2.4.

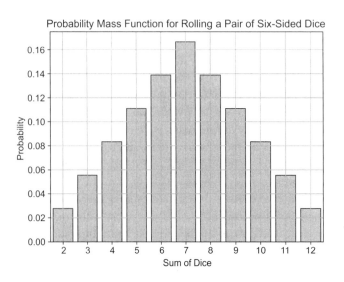

Figure 2.4 The PMF for rolling a pair of six-sided dice, where the discrete random variable and its possible values, which are equal to the whole numbers between 2 and 12, are plotted along the x axis, and their respective probabilities of occurrence are plotted along the y axis. The y axis represents their actual probabilities, not their relative likelihood of occurrence. All probabilities are equal to or greater than zero.

The discrete random variable and its possible values—that is, every possible outcome from rolling a pair of six-sided dice, which are and must be in the form of integers or whole numbers—are plotted along the x axis. Their respective probabilities—not their relative likelihood of occurrence—are plotted along the y axis. Every individual probability is, and must be, equal to or greater than zero.

For instance, out of 36 possible outcomes, there is only one way to get a pair of six-sided dice to total 2, so

$$P(X = 2) = \frac{1}{36}$$

or

$$P(X = 2) = 0.0278$$

But there are two ways to get a pair of six-sided dice to total 3: a 1 from one die and a 2 from the other, or vice versa. So

$$P(X = 3) = \frac{2}{36}$$

or

$$P(X = 3) = 0.0556$$

And there are exactly three ways of getting the same dice to total 4, so

$$P(X = 4) = \frac{3}{36}$$

or

$$P(X = 4) = 0.0833$$

To reiterate, these values represent actual probabilities. The PDF for continuous random variables returns relative likelihoods, but the PMF for discrete random variables returns actual probabilities of occurrence for each possible value.

2.4.3 Cumulative distribution function

The CDF of a discrete random variable X, typically denoted as $F(x)$, is defined as the probability that X is less than or equal to a certain value x. It is more formally expressed as $F(x) = P(X \leq x)$.

It assumes the following properties:

- *Nondecreasing*—The CDF is nondecreasing, meaning that as the value of x increases, the cumulative probability either increases or at least remains constant. It will not and cannot ever decrease.
- *Bounded*—The CDF is bounded between 0 and 1, inclusive. This reflects the fact that probabilities always range from 0 to 1.
- *Right-continuous*—The CDF is typically right-continuous, meaning that the cumulative probability jumps at each value of x, reflecting the total probability up to and including that point, with no jumps or increases between values of x.

The CDF is calculated by simply summing the probabilities of all possible values less than or equal to a specific value of x. So, $F(x) = P(X \le x) = \Sigma P(X = k)$, where the sum is taken over all possible values of k that are less than or equal to x.

Consider the cumulative probabilities of rolling a pair of six-sided dice. The probability of getting 4 or less is equal to the probability of getting 2 plus the probability of getting 3 plus the probability of getting 4:

$$P(X = 2) = .0278$$
$$+$$
$$P(X = 3) = .0556$$
$$+$$
$$P(X = 4) = .0833$$
$$=$$
$$F(4) = 0.167$$

Thus, the probability of getting 4 or less from rolling a pair of six-sided dice equals 16.7%.

As mentioned previously, the CDF is typically represented in graphical format using a step function (see figure 2.5). The plot consists of horizontal line segments connecting consecutive values for x, with each segment representing the cumulative probability up to that point.

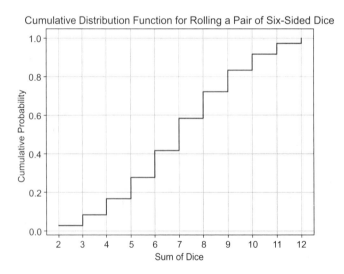

Figure 2.5 The CDF for rolling a pair of six-sided dice. The shape of the distribution resembles a two-dimensional flight of stairs in which the horizontal line segments represent consecutive values for x and the vertical lines represent their respective probabilities.

To further explain, the probability of getting 2 equals 0.0278, which is exactly where the horizontal line segment connecting 2 and 3 is drawn. The probability of getting 3 equals 0.0556; rather than it being drawn from 0, it is instead drawn from where the horizontal line segment ends. Therefore, the point at which the vertical line ends is the cumulative probability of getting 3 or less. This process of adding each probability to the previous cumulative value is repeated for each successive outcome until we reach the last possible outcome, and the cumulative probability at that point equals 1.

As we conclude this chapter and prepare for the next, let's quickly reflect on all the content we packed into these pages and briefly summarize what we've learned. We learned how to compute a theoretical probability based on mathematical principles and assumptions and then how to compute an empirical probability derived from observed data and real-world experiments. We discovered the fundamental principles of the multiplication and addition rules of counting, equipping us with the knowledge of their precise applications and significance across various probability scenarios. We explored the intricacies of combinations and permutations, including how to set them apart, and we are now familiar with the concepts of replacement and without replacement, and specifically how one leads to a greater number of combinations or permutations than the other. And we examined the characteristics of both continuous and discrete random variables, shedding light on their unique properties and applications.

This sets us up well for chapter 3. The next chapter picks up right where we are about to leave off: with a discussion of various probability distributions.

Summary

- Theoretical probabilities are equal to the number of successes divided by the total number of possible outcomes.
- Empirical probabilities are derived from trials or real-world observations. Such probabilities are equal to the number of successes observed (however a "success" might be defined) divided by the number of observations made.
- The multiplication rule states that the probability of two or more events occurring is equal to the product of their individual probabilities. This rule applies to independent events that occur simultaneously or sequentially.
- The addition rule states that the probability of two or more mutually exclusive events occurring is equal to the sum of their individual probabilities. This rule applies when the events cannot occur simultaneously.
- Combinations and permutations are not the same. A combination refers to the selection of items where the order does not matter, whereas a permutation involves arrangements where the order means everything. Combinations apply to scenarios like choosing a group of students to sit on a committee, and permutations apply to situations like arranging a sequence of numbers or letters.
- A permutation with replacement is a method of arranging items from a set where each item can be chosen multiple times for each position in the

arrangement. This allows for the repetition of items in the arrangement, resulting in a larger number of possible permutations compared to permutations without replacement.
- A permutation without replacement is a method of arranging items from a set where each item can be chosen only once for each position in the arrangement. This ensures that each item appears no more than once in the final arrangement, leading to fewer permutations compared to permutations with replacement.
- A combination without replacement is a selection of items from a set where each item can be selected no more than once, and the order of selection does not matter. This ensures that each item is selected maybe once for the combination, leading to a unique subset of items from the original set.
- A combination with replacement is a selection of items from a set where each item can be chosen multiple times, and the order of selection does not matter. This allows for the repetition of items in the combination, resulting in a larger number of possible combinations compared to combinations without replacement.
- A continuous random variable is a type of random variable that can take on any value within a certain range, often representing measurements or quantities that can be infinitely subdivided.
- A discrete random variable is a type of random variable that can take on only a countable number of distinct values, often representing outcomes of experiments or events that result in a finite or countably infinite set of possible outcomes. Unlike continuous random variables, which can assume any value within a range, discrete random variables have specific and separate values with no intermediate possibilities.

Exploring probability distributions and conditional probabilities

This chapter covers
- Probability distributions
- Probability computations
- Conditional probabilities

In statistics and especially probability theory, understanding the behavior of random variables is just the beginning of a fascinating journey into the worlds of uncertainty and prediction. As we dive deeper into this subject, we arrive at a crucial inflection point: the exploration of probability distributions and conditional probability computations.

This chapter builds on the foundation established in chapter 2, where we introduced the concept of random variables and their properties. With this groundwork in place, we now embark on an in-depth exploration of four common probability distributions: normal, binomial, uniform, and Poisson.

Random variables serve as the bedrock on which probability distributions are constructed, allowing us to model and analyze the likelihood of various outcomes in a systematic manner. By examining specific probability distributions such as the normal distribution, which describes continuous phenomena like heights and weights, and the binomial distribution, which deals with discrete events like coin flips, we gain a deeper appreciation for the diverse ways in which uncertainty manifests itself in the real world.

Furthermore, this chapter not only focuses on describing probability distributions but also explores the practical aspect of probability computations, including a final discussion around understanding and applying conditional probabilities. We will therefore study the interplay between prior and future events, thereby offering a more nuanced understanding of uncertainty and inference. When you reach the end of this journey, you will not only have a solid grasp of common probability distributions, but also the tools and techniques to navigate complex probabilistic scenarios with confidence and clarity.

3.1 Probability distributions

Probability distributions are foundational concepts in probability theory and statistics; they provide systematic methods and graphical techniques to quantify or illustrate the likelihood of different outcomes or events in the haze of uncertain and random phenomena. Understanding probability distributions is imperative because they form the backbone of statistical inference and decision-making processes in various fields, including finance, engineering, biology, and the social sciences. Mastery of probability distributions makes it possible to not only analyze and model complex real-world phenomena but also assess risk, forecast outcomes, and optimize strategies.

Our plan is to explore the four probability distributions—normal, binomial, uniform, and Poisson—that are most common when practicing data science. Each of these probability distributions assumes a unique set of properties and is therefore "designed" to handle specific, and different, types of random variables and phenomena. Our goal is to provide the twin benefits of theoretical understanding mixed with practical applications so as to establish a solid footing for effective probability analysis.

3.1.1 Normal distribution

The normal distribution—sometimes called a Gaussian distribution in honor of the mathematician Carl Friedrich Gauss, who contributed significantly to its study and application—is best characterized by its bell-like shape. We caught a glimpse of the normal distribution in chapter 2 when introducing continuous random variables. Many real-world phenomena follow the normal distribution, including heights and weights of adults, IQ scores, measurement errors, test scores, weights of products, residuals in regression analysis (see chapter 4), and daily stock returns.

PROPERTIES

The probability density function (PDF) of the normal distribution—that is, the *relative* likelihood of observing a continuous random variable at a particular value—is given by the following equation:

$$(x|\mu, \sigma) = \frac{1}{\sigma\sqrt{2\pi}} \times e^{-\frac{(x-\mu)^2}{2\sigma^2}}$$

where

- $f(x|\mu, \sigma)$ represents the PDF of a given value x, mean μ, and standard deviation σ.
- μ (mu) is the mean, or average, of the distribution.
- σ (sigma) is the standard deviation, which measures the spread or dispersion of the distribution.
- e is the base of the natural logarithm, approximately equal to 2.72.
- π is the mathematical constant pi, approximately equal to 3.14.

Remember an important takeaway from the previous chapter: *the PDF isn't defined by a single equation; rather, it varies depending on the specific distribution under consideration.* So, this specific probability density equation applies exclusively to the normal distribution.

Let's examine, by visual inspection, a 2 × 2 grid of normal distributions where the mean is held constant at 0 but the standard deviation (abbreviated Std Dev) equals a range of values between 5 and 20 (see figure 3.1).

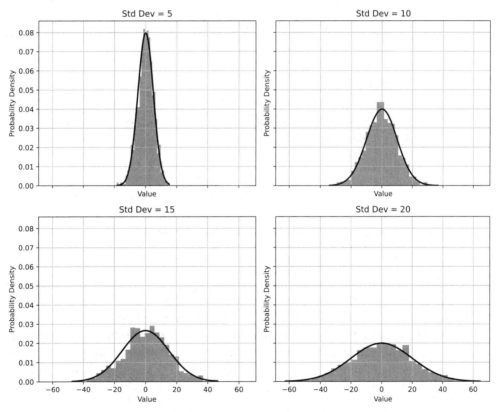

Figure 3.1 A 2 × 2 grid of normal distributions where each plot shares the same x-axis and y-axis scales. The mean equals 0 throughout, and the standard deviation equals 5, 10, 15, or 20. Increases in the standard deviation translate to greater dispersion from the mean, flatter distributions, and wider tails. In other words, the PDF becomes more dispersed across a larger range of values, and the distribution is broader and less peaked around the mean. The bell-like shape applies throughout, however, where the values are distributed symmetrically around the mean.

This grid of histograms reveals several important features about the normal distribution:

- The distribution is symmetrical around its center, or mean. This is to say that the probability of observing a value greater than the mean is equal to 0.5, and the probability of observing another value less than the mean is also equal to 0.5.
- Due to its symmetrical and unimodal nature, the normal distribution takes on a bell-shaped curve, with a single peak at the mean. This shape indicates that values closer to the mean are more likely to be observed than values further away.
- Assuming a normal distribution, a pair of parameters—the mean and standard deviation—are key. The mean is equal to the sum of all values in a numeric data series divided by the record count; when the same data is normally distributed, the mean is at the center of the distribution. The standard deviation, meanwhile, shapes the distribution by determining its spread around the mean. Although the normal distribution inherently assumes a bell-like shape, the standard deviation indicates the extent to which the distribution is thin or flat. The standard deviation can be estimated by dividing 0.399—which represents the maximum probability density function from a standard normal distribution, where the mean is 0 and the standard deviation is 1—by the maximum PDF associated with the normal distribution under observation. So, for instance, 0.399 divided by .080 returns an estimated standard deviation equal to 4.99 (see the upper-left histogram, where the actual standard deviation is equal to 5).
- The PDF achieves its maximum when the value for x is the mean, regardless of the standard deviation.

When working with the normal distribution, it's important to always remember what is commonly called the *68–95–99 rule*. This rule, also known as the *three-sigma rule* (for three standard deviations), states that approximately 68% of the data in the normal distribution is within one standard deviation of the mean, that approximately 95% of the data is within two standard deviations of the mean, and up to 99.7% of the data is within three standard deviations of the mean. It's important to be aware of this rule because it provides valuable, and fairly precise, insights into normally distributed data—helping analysts quickly assess how likely an outcome is, estimate the probability of extreme values, and set reasonable expectations around what constitutes normal variation. These characteristics make the normal distribution a popular assumption in many fields, as it offers predictable guidelines for interpreting data variability.

Let's repeatedly test the 68–95–99 rule by generating 10,000 random samples from a normal distribution with mean `0` and standard deviation `1` using the `np.random.normal()` method from the `numpy` library:

```
>>> mean = 0
>>> std_dev = 1

>>> import numpy as np
>>> samples = np.random.normal(mean, std_dev, 10000)
```

3.1 Probability distributions

In the next line of Python code,

- `np.abs(samples - mean)` calculates the absolute differences between each sample in the `samples` array and the mean. We want the absolute differences, rather than a mix of positive and negative differences, to prevent the final calculations from canceling each other.
- `< std_dev` checks whether each absolute difference is less than the standard deviation; it creates a Boolean array where `True` indicates the absolute difference is less than the standard deviation and `False` otherwise.
- `np.sum(...)` sums the Boolean array where `True` is equivalent to 1 and `False` is equivalent to 0, thereby providing a count of samples within one standard deviation of the mean.
- `within_1_std` is a variable that stores the results.

In summary, the following line of code calculates the number of samples from 10,000 random samples that are within one standard deviation of the mean:

```
>>> within_1_std = np.sum(np.abs(samples - mean) < std_dev)
```

The next two lines of code calculate the number of samples that are within two or three standard deviations of the mean.

```
>>> within_2_std = np.sum(np.abs(samples - mean) < 2 * std_dev)
>>> within_3_std = np.sum(np.abs(samples - mean) < 3 * std_dev)
```

And from the next snippet of code, we get the percentage of samples within one, two, or three standard deviations of the mean. Percentages are obtained by dividing the sample counts by `100`; results are then printed as formatted strings:

```
>>> print(f'Percent within 1 standard deviation: {within_1_std / 100}%')
Percent within 1 standard deviation: 66.89%

>>> print(f'Percent within 2 standard deviations: {within_2_std / 100}%')
Percent within 2 standard deviations: 95.13%

>>> print(f'Percent within 3 standard deviations: {within_3_std / 100}%')
Percent within 3 standard deviations: 99.69%
```

These results are obviously consistent with the 68–95–99 rule. But let's run the same code two more times and then compare the results:

```
>>> mean = 0
>>> std_dev = 1

>>> samples = np.random.normal(mean, std_dev, 10000)

>>> within_1_std = np.sum(np.abs(samples - mean) < std_dev)
>>> within_2_std = np.sum(np.abs(samples - mean) < 2 * std_dev)
>>> within_3_std = np.sum(np.abs(samples - mean) < 3 * std_dev)

>>> print(f'Percent within 1 standard deviation: {within_1_std / 100}%')
>>> print(f'Percent within 2 standard deviations: {within_2_std / 100}%')
```

```
>>> print(f'Percent within 3 standard deviations: {within_3_std / 100}%')
Percent within 1 standard deviation: 68.3%
Percent within 2 standard deviations: 95.45%
Percent within 3 standard deviations: 99.75%

>>> mean = 0
>>> std_dev = 1

>>> samples = np.random.normal(mean, std_dev, 10000)

>>> within_1_std = np.sum(np.abs(samples - mean) < std_dev)
>>> within_2_std = np.sum(np.abs(samples - mean) < 2 * std_dev)
>>> within_3_std = np.sum(np.abs(samples - mean) < 3 * std_dev)

>>> print(f'Percent within 1 standard deviation: {within_1_std / 100}%')
>>> print(f'Percent within 2 standard deviations: {within_2_std / 100}%')
>>> print(f'Percent within 3 standard deviations: {within_3_std / 100}%')
Percent within 1 standard deviation: 68.31%
Percent within 2 standard deviations: 95.46%
Percent within 3 standard deviations: 99.78%
```

The results may never be exactly alike, no matter how many times we run and rerun the same code. But they won't ever deviate in any meaningful way from the 68–95–99 rule.

PROBABILITY DENSITY FUNCTION

To effectively compute (and explain) probabilities from the normal distribution, it's essential to have a visual reference. Rather than reusing one or more of the normal distributions from our 2 × 2 grid, we'll instead draw a standard normal distribution, where the mean equals 0 and the standard deviation equals 1 (see figure 3.2). In the standard normal distribution, the raw data has been transformed, or standardized, so that the values along the *x* axis represent the number of standard deviations they are below or above the mean.

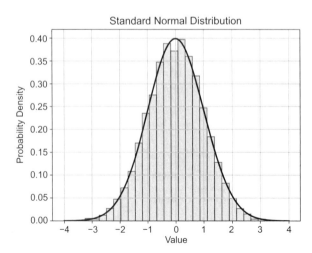

Figure 3.2 A standard normal distribution is a normal distribution where the mean is equal to 0, the standard deviation is equal to 1, and the values have been standardized from their raw form. The PDF typically peaks at or around 0.399.

We want to find the PDF of a transformed continuous random variable from the standard normal distribution. When the mean equals 0 and the standard deviation equals 1, the random variable is actually denoted as z rather than x (why will be clear in a bit).

There are two ways of going about this in Python. One way is to plug values for `mu` (the mean), `sigma` (the standard deviation), and `z` (the continuous random variable that has since been standardized from its raw form) into an arithmetic operation based on the PDF.

The first step is to initialize these three variables:

```
>>> mu = 0
>>> sigma = 1
>>> z = 1
```

The second step is to write and execute a snippet of code that calculates the PDF for z when the mean equals 0 and the standard deviation equals 1:

```
>>> pdf_value = ((1 / (sigma * math.sqrt(2 * math.pi))) * \
>>>             math.exp(-((z - mu) ** 2) / (2 * sigma ** 2)))
```

And the third and final step is to print the results:

```
>>> print(f'PDF at {z} = {pdf_value}')
PDF at 1 = 0.24197072451914337
```

Another (easier) way is to pass the same variables to the `norm.pdf()` method from the `norm` module in the `scipy` library:

```
>>> mu = 0
>>> sigma = 1
>>> z = 1

>>> from scipy.stats import norm
>>> pdf_value = norm.pdf(z, loc = mu, scale = sigma)
>>> print(f'PDF at {z} = {pdf_value}')
PDF at 1 = 0.24197072451914337
```

A PDF equal to 24% is relatively high when you consider that the maximum PDF for the standard normal distribution is just less than 40%. To be clear, the PDF does *not* represent the probability of observing a continuous random variable at a particular standardized value. So, it would be incorrect to conclude that when the mean is equal to 0 and the standard deviation is equal to 1, the probability of observing a continuous random variable standardized to 1 is approximately 24%. Rather, it would be correct to infer that when z equals 1, we can expect a higher density of probabilities at that value compared to other values for z in the same distribution. However, there are methods we can use to get a true probability.

COMPUTING PROBABILITIES

One way—maybe the old-school way—is to use a z-score table. If the raw data hasn't yet been transformed, we first need to convert the values to their corresponding z-scores. A *z-score*, also known as a *standard score*, is a statistical measure that indicates how many standard deviations a particular value is from the mean. It is calculated using the following formula:

$$z = \frac{x - \mu}{\sigma}$$

where

- z is the z-score.
- x is an individual data point.
- μ is the mean of the distribution.
- σ is the standard deviation of the distribution.

A positive z-score indicates that the data point, or a particular value, is above the mean, whereas a negative z-score indicates that it is below the mean. The magnitude of the z-score reflects how many standard deviations the value is from the mean—a larger absolute value means the point is farther from the average. By converting raw data to standardized scores, we can then compare values from different data sets or even different variables from the same data set that were originally on different scales. Standardized scores are commonly used in hypothesis testing, statistical analysis, and data normalization. From a data series that follows the standard normal distribution, z-scores are used to determine probabilities.

If we set z to equal 1, it signifies that a specific raw value, on standardization, corresponds to a z-score of 1, thereby indicating that it is one standard deviation above the mean of the distribution. With the z-score determined, we can then obtain the probability associated with it from a z-score table (see figure 3.3).

z	.00	.01	.02	.03	.04	.05	.06	.07	.08	.09
0.0	.5000	.5040	.5080	.5120	.5160	.5199	.5239	.5279	.5319	.5359
0.1	.5398	.5438	.5478	.5517	.5557	.5596	.5636	.5675	.5714	.5753
0.2	.5793	.5832	.5871	.5910	.5948	.5987	.6026	.6064	.6103	.6141
0.3	.6179	.6217	.6255	.6293	.6331	.6368	.6406	.6443	.6480	.6517
0.4	.6554	.6591	.6628	.6664	.6700	.6736	.6772	.6808	.6844	.6879
0.5	.6915	.6950	.6985	.7019	.7054	.7088	.7123	.7157	.7190	.7224
0.6	.7257	.7291	.7324	.7357	.7389	.7422	.7454	.7486	.7517	.7549
0.7	.7580	.7611	.7642	.7673	.7704	.7734	.7764	.7794	.7823	.7852
0.8	.7881	.7910	.7939	.7967	.7995	.8023	.8051	.8078	.8106	.8133
0.9	.8159	.8186	.8212	.8238	.8264	.8289	.8315	.8340	.8365	.8389
1.0	.8413	.8438	.8461	.8485	.8508	.8531	.8554	.8577	.8599	.8621
1.1	.8643	.8665	.8686	.8708	.8729	.8749	.8770	.8790	.8810	.8830
1.2	.8849	.8869	.8888	.8907	.8925	.8944	.8962	.8980	.8997	.9015
1.3	.9032	.9049	.9066	.9082	.9099	.9115	.9131	.9147	.9162	.9177
1.4	.9192	.9207	.9222	.9236	.9251	.9265	.9279	.9292	.9306	.9319
1.5	.9332	.9345	.9357	.9370	.9382	.9394	.9406	.9418	.9429	.9441
1.6	.9452	.9463	.9474	.9484	.9495	.9505	.9515	.9525	.9535	.9545
1.7	.9554	.9564	.9573	.9582	.9591	.9599	.9608	.9616	.9625	.9633
1.8	.9641	.9649	.9656	.9664	.9671	.9678	.9686	.9693	.9699	.9706
1.9	.9713	.9719	.9726	.9732	.9738	.9744	.9750	.9756	.9761	.9767
2.0	.9772	.9778	.9783	.9788	.9793	.9798	.9803	.9808	.9812	.9817

Figure 3.3 The top of a typical z-score table. The probability (or area to the right of a particular value that has been standardized) is found where the integer and remaining fractional parts of the value intersect.

The probability is where the first two digits of the z-score, located in the far-left column of the table, intersect with the next two digits of the z-score, located along the top row. A z-score of 1, for instance, is the equivalent of 1.000. The corresponding probability is therefore equal to .8413, or 84.13%, which is where 1.0 and .00 intersect. This figure also represents the area to the left of the z-score in the standard normal distribution, where the area left of the mean equals 0.5 and the area between the mean and one standard deviation above it equals .3413—these probabilities (or areas) when added together sum to 84.13%.

To further explain, imagine a statistics class of 30 students taking their final exam. The exams are graded and the scores standardized. One student achieved a score one standard deviation above the class mean. That student thus scored in the 84th percentile, or performed better than 25 of the 30 students in the class—derived by multiplying 30 students times .8413 and rounding the product down to the nearest whole number.

Finally, we can use the z-score table to get the probability of a particular value falling within some range along the standard normal distribution. For instance, if we were curious about the probability of some value being equal to or greater than 1.000 but less than 1.500, we could subtract their respective probabilities (.9332 − .8413) and apply the difference (.0919) to get the probability (roughly 9%).

Another way is to write a short snippet of Python code. We initialize a z-score value of 1; pass that to the `norm.cdf()` method, which calculates the cumulative probability (or area) under the standard normal distribution curve up to the value of one standard deviation above the mean and stores the result in a variable called `first_probability`; and then print the results in the form of a percentage by multiplying the fractional output by `100`:

```
>>> z = 1
>>> first_probability = norm.cdf(z)
>>> print(f'Probability (area): {first_probability * 100}%')
Probability (area): 84.1344746068543%
```

We can even use Python to get the probability (or area) between a pair of standardized scores, like 1.000 and 1.500.

First we make a second call to the `norm.cdf()` method, this time with z initialized to `1.5`. `norm.cdf()` calculates the cumulative probability (or area) up to 1.5 standard deviations above the distribution mean and stores the results in a variable called `second_probability`:

```
>>> z = 1.5
>>> second_probability = norm.cdf(z)
>>> print(f'Probability (area): {second_probability * 100}%')
Probability (area): 93.3192798731142%
```

Then we subtract `first_probability` from `second_probability` to get the probability (or area) of some value falling between the standardized scores of 1 and 1.5:

```
>>> range_probability = second_probability - first_probability
>>> print(f'Probability (area) between '
```

```
        f'1.0 and 1.5: {range_probability * 100}%')
Probability (area) between 1.0 and 1.5: 9.184805266259898%
```

From continuous random variables and the normal distribution, we now shift our focus to discrete outcomes and the binomial distribution. At first glance, this so-called shift may appear to be substantial, but in reality the normal distribution is the result of many continuous trials of the binomial distribution.

KEY TAKEAWAYS

The normal distribution, often referred to as the Gaussian distribution, is a continuous probability distribution characterized by its symmetric bell-shaped curve centered around the mean. This distribution is unique due to its symmetry and is entirely defined by its mean and standard deviation. The PDF of a normal distribution describes the relative likelihood of different outcomes, providing insights into the distribution's shape and spread without yielding actual probabilities. To compute actual probabilities from a *standard* normal distribution, we must use the cumulative distribution function, which can be done manually using a z-table or programmatically using Python methods. Demonstrating these computations both manually and programmatically is crucial for a thorough understanding of the underlying mechanics and ensures that we can accurately interpret and implement statistical analyses in various contexts.

3.1.2 Binomial distribution

A binomial experiment is a statistical experiment in which a binomial random variable represents the number of successes in a fixed number of repeatable trials, where the probability of success is consistent throughout. The binomial distribution is a probability distribution that describes the likelihood of observing a specific number of successes from a series of trials where each trial has only two potential outcomes: success or failure. The following conditions must prevail:

- The trials are independent. That means each trial is unaffected by previous trials and does not then influence the outcomes of subsequent trials. Independence between trials is a fundamental assumption in many statistical analyses and probability models, including the binomial distribution. For instance, when flipping a fair coin multiple times, each flip is considered an independent trial because the outcome of one flip has no bearing on the outcome of any other flip.
- Each trial can be classified as either success or failure, where p equals the probability of success and $1 - p$ equals the probability of failure.
- The number of trials is fixed and determined in advance.
- The probability of success is consistent across trials. Thus, the trials must not only be independent, but they must also be alike in order to hold the probability of success constant.

Quality control inspections that result in pass or fail, medical tests that return positive or negative results, surveys featuring binary responses—these are just a few examples of binomial distributions in everyday life. Binomial distributions are important to understand because they provide a framework for quantifying probabilities of binary outcomes in repeated trials across various domains, including manufacturing, healthcare, and market research.

PROPERTIES

The probability mass function (PMF) is a function that assigns probabilities to discrete random variables that represent the likelihood of each possible outcome. In the context of binomial distributions, the PMF calculates the probability of observing a specific number of successes (or failures) in a fixed number of independent trials, each with two possible outcomes.

The PMF for a binomial distribution is given by the following equation:

$$p(x = k) = \binom{n}{k} \times p^k \times (1-p)^{n-k}$$

where

- $p(x = k)$ represents the probability of observing k successes in n trials.
- n over k is the binomial coefficient, also known as "n choose k," which represents the number of ways to choose k successes from n trials.
- p is the probability of success on any individual trial.
- $1 - p$ represents the probability of failure on any individual trial.
- n is the total number of trials.
- k is the number of successes.

The PMF for a binomial distribution is a property that characterizes the distribution and allows us to determine the probabilities associated with different numbers of successes. By evaluating the PMF at different values of k, we can obtain the probability distribution for the binomial random variable, thereby providing insights into the likelihood of various outcomes in a binomial experiment.

Let's examine two pairs of plotted binomial distributions (see figures 3.4 and 3.5), where

- The number of trials equals 20 throughout.
- Therefore, the number of potential successes ranges from 0 to 20.
- The probability of success iterates from 0.20 and 0.50 in the first two plots to 0.75 and 0.90 in the next pair.

We initialize n, k, and p like so: the `np.arrange()` method creates an array of evenly spaced values starting at 0 and ending at n (inclusive), where each value is incremented by 1. The second argument passed to the `np.arrange()` method, n + 1, ensures that the endpoint n is included in the array.

For now, p equals a list containing just two probabilities of success, because we intend to apply different methods to create each pair of plots:

```
>>> n = 20
>>> k = np.arange(0, n + 1)
>>> p = [0.20, 0.50]
```

These values are passed to a snippet of Python code that mirrors the PMF equation; it specifically calculates the PMF for a binomial distribution for each possible number of successes j in n trials, given the parameters n and p[i] and the array k.

Here's the complete breakdown of the code:

- `pmf = [...for j in k]` is a list comprehension that iterates over each value j in the array k, which represents the possible number of successes in n trials.
- `np.math.comb(n, j)` calculates the binomial coefficient, which represents the number of ways to choose j successes from n trials.
- `(p[i] ** j)` calculates the probability of obtaining j successes, raised to the power of j, using the value p[i], where p is assumed to be an array or list of probabilities indexed by i.
- `((1 - p[i]) ** (n - j))` calculates the probability of getting n – j failures, raised to the power of n – j, assuming failure probability 1 - p[i] for each trial.

And here's the code:

```
>>> pmf = [(np.math.comb(n, j) * (p[i] ** j) * \
>>>         ((1 - p[i]) ** (n - j))) for j in k]
```

This, when combined with a chunk of Matplotlib code, returns the graphical output shown in figure 3.4. (Matplotlib is a popular Python plotting library that we began using in the prior chapter.)

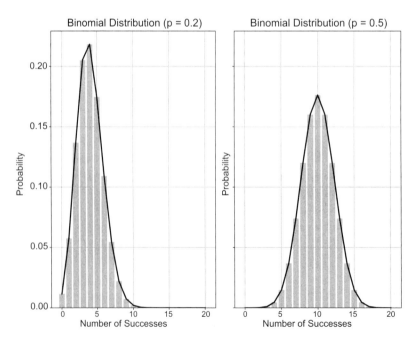

Figure 3.4 **A first pair of binomial distributions where the probability of success equals 0.20 (on the left) and 0.50 (on the right), given 20 independent trials. Although the distributions are binomial, the data is nonetheless distributed normally.**

3.1 Probability distributions

For our next pair of plots, instead of supplying the number of trials, the count of potential successes, and a fresh list of success probabilities to a single arithmetic operation, we will make a call to the `binom.pmf()` method for this purpose. But first, we reinitialize n and k and assign new probabilities to p:

```
>>> n = 20
>>> k = np.arange(0, n + 1)
>>> p = [0.75, 0.90]
```

The `binom.pmf()` method, which requires the `binom` module from `scipy.stats`, twice calculates the PMF for a binomial distribution—in this instance, the number of trials again equals `20`, the number of potential successes therefore also equals `20`, and the probabilities of success now equal `0.75` and then `0.90`:

```
>>> from scipy.stats import binom
>>> pmf = binom.pmf(k, n, p[i])
```

When the `binom.pmf()` method is mixed with another chunk of Matplotlib code, we get the plots shown in figure 3.5.

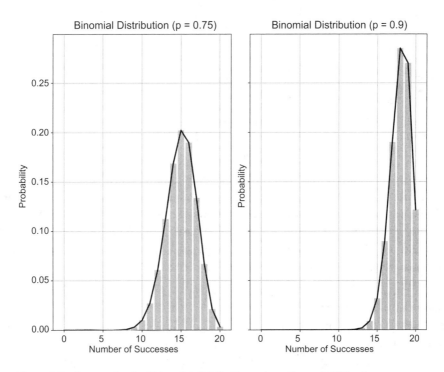

Figure 3.5 A second pair of binomial distributions where the probability of success equals 0.75 (on the left) and 0.90 (on the right), given 20 independent trials. Regardless of the probability of success, although the distribution mean shifts as a result, the binomial distributions maintain their normal distribution look.

The primary observation from examining these plots is that binomial outcomes exhibit characteristics resembling a normal distribution. Variations in the probability of success bring about corresponding changes in the distribution mean, but the distributions nevertheless consistently retain their symmetrical shapes, with binomial outcomes equally centered around the mean. Hence, although it may seem somewhat evident, it's worth emphasizing that the distribution mean is derived by multiplying the fixed trial count by the probability of success:

$$\mu = np$$

where

- μ is the binomial distribution mean.
- n is the number of independent trials.
- p is the probability of success.

So, for instance, when the number of independent trials equals 20 and the probability of success in each of them equals 0.20, the mean number of successes equals 20 × 0.2 = 4. This coincides with the point where the PMF reaches its maximum value.

The standard deviation of a binomial distribution is derived by taking the square root of the product of the distribution mean and the probability of failure:

$$\sigma = \sqrt{np(1-p)}$$

where

- σ represents the standard deviation.
- n is the number of independent trials.
- p is the probability of success.
- $1 - p$ is the inverse of p and therefore equals the number of failures.

Therefore, the standard deviation is relatively low when the probabilities of success are either low or high; alternatively, the standard deviation is relatively high, or higher, when the probability of success equals something like 0.50 or 0.75. Another glimpse at our histograms illustrates what we can derive mathematically: low and high probabilities of success, like 0.20 and 0.90, respectively, translate to thinner and taller binomial distributions, whereas "average" probabilities of success render just the opposite.

COMPUTING PROBABILITIES

Let's say we want to know the probability of getting heads 7 times from 20 flips of a fair coin. Or maybe we want to know the probability of discovering 7 defective products from a batch of 20. Although the probabilities of these outcomes might be very different, both are nevertheless examples of a binomial experiment.

There are at least two ways to derive the probability of a specific binomial outcome in Python. We'll demonstrate the first way by simulating 20 coin flips. So, we initialize `n` to equal `20`, `k` to equal `7`, and `p` to equal `0.5`:

```
>>> n = 20
>>> k = 7
>>> p = 0.5
```

Then we calculate the binomial coefficient by applying the formula for counting combinations without replacement:

$$\binom{n}{k} = \frac{n!}{k!\,(n-k)!}$$

The binomial coefficient and the number of combinations without replacement share the same formula because both calculate the number of ways to choose a specific number of objects from a fixed set without considering the order of selection. We replicate this formula in Python by passing our three parameters to the `math.factorial()` method:

```
>>> binomial_coefficient = (math.factorial(n) / \
>>>                        (math.factorial(k) * math.factorial(n - k)))
>>> print(binomial_coefficient)
77520.0
```

Finally, we obtain the probability of getting heads exactly 7 times from 20 coin flips by inputting this result into the PMF equation:

```
>>> probability = binomial_coefficient * (p ** k) * ((1 - p) ** (n - k))
>>> print(f'Probability: {probability * 100}%')
Probability: 7.39288330078125%
```

This result perfectly corresponds to the binomial distribution displayed on the right side of figure 3.4, where the probability of success was set at 0.5.

The more efficient way is to instead pass n, k, and p to the `binom.pmf()` method. Let's change p to equal 0.2 but keep n and k constant:

```
>>> n = 20
>>> k = 7
>>> p = 0.2
```

This time around, we want the probability of observing exactly 7 successes in 20 independent trials when the probability of success equals 0.2. The `binom.pmf()` method automatically calculates the binomial coefficient and subsequently applies the result to the PMF equation:

```
>>> probability = binom.pmf(k, n, p)
>>> print(f"Probability: {probability * 100}%")
Probability: 5.454985048652523%
```

This result is perfectly in sync with the binomial distribution displayed on the left side of figure 3.4, where the probability of success was established at 0.2.

Having explored the intricacies of binomial distributions and their application in modeling discrete random phenomena, we now direct our attention to uniform distributions as the next step in our exploration of probability analysis.

KEY TAKEAWAYS

The binomial distribution is a discrete probability distribution that models the number of successes in a fixed number of independent trials, each with the same probability of success. It is defined by two parameters: the number of trials and the probability of success in each trial. The binomial PMF describes the probability of obtaining a specific number of successes, providing insight into the distribution's shape and the likelihood of different outcomes. To compute actual probabilities from a binomial distribution, we typically use the binomial formula or use Python methods for computational efficiency. Once again, understanding how to calculate these probabilities both manually and programmatically is essential for gaining a solid grasp of the binomial distribution's behavior and applying it correctly in statistical analysis, especially in scenarios involving binary outcomes like pass/fail or yes/no events.

3.1.3 *Discrete uniform distribution*

The discrete uniform distribution is a probability distribution with a constant probability; that is, every value, or every discrete random variable, within a predefined range has an equal probability of occurring. When flipping a fair coin, for instance, heads and tails both have probabilities equal to 50%; or when rolling a fair six-sided die, each possible outcome has an equal probability of 1/6, or 16.7%. Consequently, the discrete uniform distribution is sometimes called a *rectangular distribution* because, when plotted, the distribution takes on a rectangular shape. It is typically denoted as $X \sim U(a, b)$, where a and b represent, respectively, the lower and upper bounds of possible values.

Thus:

- Each outcome within the range $[a, b]$ must have the same probability of occurrence.
- The distribution only applies to a finite set of values within the specified range.
- The sum of all probabilities within the range must therefore equal 1.
- Each outcome is independent of the others.

The discrete random distribution applies to a wide array of contexts, ranging from modeling coin flips, dice rolls, and card selections to generating random numbers for simulations, test and control assignments, and numerical experiments; creating random keys and nonces (numbers used once) for cryptographic applications; and randomly selecting items from a fixed set or population. This is why discrete uniform distributions, despite their relative simplicity, still deserve our attention.

PROPERTIES

The PMF of a discrete uniform distribution is defined as

$$f(x) = \frac{1}{b - a + 1}$$

where

- a represents the lower bound of the distribution.
- b represents the upper bound of the distribution.

- $f(x)$ is the PMF, representing the probability of obtaining a specific value x within the range $[a, b]$.

Any and all specific values must be discrete random variables, or a countable set of distinct values, typically integers or whole numbers. Otherwise, the PMF simply defines the lower and upper boundaries of possible values and assigns an equal probability of occurrence to all values equal to or greater than a and equal to or less than b. So, for instance, if a is equal to 1 and b is equal to 6, the denominator, which represents the range of possible outcomes, is equal to 6. By adding 1 to the difference between b and a, the PMF ensures that the range of possible outcomes is inclusive of the lower and upper bounds. When we assign a to 1 and b to 6 and embed the PMF equation in a chunk of Matplotlib code, we obtain a typical plot illustrating the discrete uniform distribution (see figure 3.6).

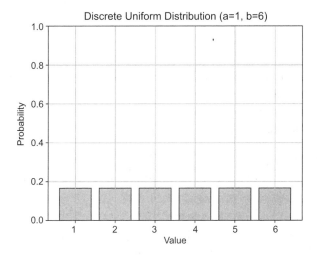

Figure 3.6 A typical discrete uniform distribution, where each discrete random variable has the same probability of occurrence. It doesn't matter what the lower and upper bounds are; the discrete uniform distribution will always assume this rectangular shape.

Why the discrete uniform distribution is sometimes referred to as the rectangular distribution is now evident. Regardless of the two values designated as a and b, respectively, the discrete uniform distribution consistently maintains this rectangular shape.

> **Continuous uniform distribution**
>
> There are actually two types of uniform distributions. In addition to the discrete uniform distribution, there is also a continuous uniform distribution, which represents a scenario where any value within a specified range has an equal probability of occurring. Unlike the discrete uniform distribution, which deals with countable outcomes (typically integers or whole numbers only), the continuous uniform distribution applies to an uncountably infinite set of values within the range (which might include fractional numbers). However, our sole focus on the discrete type of uniform distribution makes sense due to its simplicity in modeling scenarios with finite and equally probable outcomes, offering clarity and practicality in various real-world applications.

It's important to emphasize a couple of related points. First, probabilities do not guarantee specific outcomes; in other words, when rolling a fair six-sided die six times, it's improbable that each possible outcome will occur exactly once in those six attempts. When sample sizes are relatively low, actual outcomes will not necessarily align with theoretical distributions. And second, equal probabilities absolutely do not guarantee equal outcomes. We would anticipate convergence with larger sample sizes, such as 10,000 or more. However, even with such sample sizes, there is still no promise of achieving a distribution where each of, let's say, six discrete random variables is observed between 16% and 17% of the time.

COMPUTING PROBABILITIES

In Python, one approach to computing the probabilities of observing a range of discrete random variables is by writing an arithmetic operation based on the PMF. We start by defining the values for a and b, representing the lower and upper bounds of the range, respectively:

```
>>> a = 1
>>> b = 6
```

These assignments represent the parameters of the discrete uniform distribution.

Next, we write a line of code that evaluates the total number of possible outcomes within the predefined range, inclusive of both the lower and upper bounds, and stores the result in a variable called `total_outcomes`:

```
>>> total_outcomes = b - a + 1
```

Of course, we already know that when the lower and upper bounds are equal to 1 and 6, there are six possible outcomes.

Then we create another variable, `pmf_values`, where

- `1/total_outcomes` computes the probability for each individual outcome, which is equal to the reciprocal of the total number of outcomes; this ensures that the probabilities sum to 1.
- `[1/total_outcomes] * total_outcomes` creates a list where the computed probability value is repeated `total_outcomes` times; this ensures that each outcome has the same probability value.

The list of six common probabilities is stored in the variable `pmf_values`:

```
>>> pmf_values = [1 / total_outcomes] * total_outcomes
```

And finally, we write a snippet of Python code that jointly iterates through each possible value within the specified range and the corresponding probability value stored in `pmf_values`. For each value, it prints the probability of that value occurring, formatted as a percentage.

Here's the breakdown:

- `zip(range(a, b + 1), pmf_values)` pairs each value from the range a to b with its corresponding probability value stored in the variable `pmf_values`.

3.1 Probability distributions

- `for value, probability in...` iterates through each value and probability pair.
- `print(f'p(x = {value}) = {probability * 100}%')` prints each discrete random variable and its probability, formatted as a percentage. The probabilities are converted from decimals to percentages by multiplying the results by `100`.

And here's the snippet of code, followed by the results:

```
>>> for value, probability in zip(range(a, b + 1), pmf_values):
>>>     print(f'p(x = {value}) = {probability * 100}%')
p(x = 1) = 16.666666666666664%
p(x = 2) = 16.666666666666664%
p(x = 3) = 16.666666666666664%
p(x = 4) = 16.666666666666664%
p(x = 5) = 16.666666666666664%
p(x = 6) = 16.666666666666664%
```

But, of course, there is a Python method that simplifies this operation.

Once more, let's define the lower and upper bounds as `1` and `6`, respectively:

```
>>> a = 1
>>> b = 6
```

Then we create a discrete uniform distribution object, called `uniform_dist`, by making a call to the `stats.radint()` method from the `scipy` library.

```
>>> import scipy.stats as stats
>>> uniform_dist = stats.randint(a, b + 1)
```

The `stats.randint()` method constructs a discrete uniform distribution object, which generates random variates within a specified range. It's important to note that a *random variate*, distinct from a *random variable*, refers to a specified observed value of the random variable. The `stats.randint()` method requires two arguments: the lower and upper bounds, incremented by 1 to ensure inclusivity. The returned object facilitates various calculations, including PMFs.

Then we instruct Python to iterate over each value in the specified range, calculate the PMF for each value using `uniform_dist.pmf(value)`, and return the results as percentages rather than decimals. This operation requires the `uniform` module from `scipy.stats`:

```
>>> from scipy.stats import uniform
>>> for value in range(a, b + 1):
>>>     probability = uniform_dist.pmf(value)
>>>     print(f'p(x = {value}) = {probability * 100}%')
p(x = 1) = 16.666666666666664%
p(x = 2) = 16.666666666666664%
p(x = 3) = 16.666666666666664%
p(x = 4) = 16.666666666666664%
p(x = 5) = 16.666666666666664%
p(x = 6) = 16.666666666666664%
```

Just a different path to get the exact same results as before.

Last, but certainly not least, we have Poisson distributions—yet another fundamental concept in probability theory and statistics. Poisson distributions are used to model the frequency of events occurring within a fixed interval of time or space. This distribution is particularly useful in scenarios where events happen independently at a constant average rate and the probability of multiple occurrences within a short interval is low.

KEY TAKEAWAYS

The discrete uniform distribution is a simple yet pervasive probability distribution where each outcome in a finite set of equally likely outcomes has the same probability. Its straightforward nature makes it a fundamental concept in probability theory and statistics, and it's often used in real-world applications like games of chance, random sampling, and simulations. The equal likelihood of outcomes in a discrete uniform distribution provides a clear and intuitive framework for understanding randomness and fairness in various contexts.

3.1.4 Poisson distribution

The Poisson distribution is a discrete probability distribution used to model the likelihood of a specific number of events occurring within a fixed interval of time or space. Its shape varies based on the frequency of events, ranging from right-skewed to approaching normal as occurrences become more frequent. This means the following:

- Because Poisson distributions are inherently discrete, they are used exclusively to model countable events.
- This entails that only nonnegative integers are applicable, as countable events cannot, of course, be negative.
- These events are typically fixed within a predefined interval of time or space, such as the number of arrivals *within an hour* or the count of typographical errors *per page*.

The Poisson distribution is named after the French mathematician Simeon-Denis Poisson, who introduced it in the early 19th century. One of the earliest recorded applications of the Poisson distribution was by a statistician named Ladislaus Bortkiewicz, who used it to model the annual rate of accidental deaths in the Prussian army caused by horse kicks. Today, the Poisson distribution can be applied to various scenarios. It can model the annual occurrences of meteor showers, the diagnosis count of measles within a year, daily text message traffic, hourly customer purchases, accidents at a specific intersection during peak hours, or the hourly inbound call volume received by a customer service center.

PROPERTIES

The PMF of the Poisson distribution is given by the following equation:

$$P(X = k) = \frac{e^{-\lambda} \lambda^x}{x!}$$

where

- $P(X = k)$ is the probability of observing k events.
- e is the base of the natural logarithm, approximately equal to 2.72.
- λ (lambda) is the average rate of occurrence (also known as the rate parameter).
- k is the number of events.

It's often observed that the PMF for the Poisson distribution includes the mean (μ) rather than the rate parameter (λ). However, this discrepancy is inconsequential because in the Poisson distribution, both the mean and the variance (σ^2) are equal to the rate parameter, so

$$\mu = \sigma^2 = \lambda$$

In essence, then, the PMF for the Poisson distribution models the probability of observing a specific number of events within a fixed interval of time or space, given the average rate at which those events occur. It uses the frequency of recorded events to estimate the rate at which the same events should occur in a future interval of time or space. Yet the Poisson distribution is memoryless. That is to say, although the Poisson distribution does utilize past event frequencies to estimate future rates of occurrence, its memoryless property explicitly refers to the probability of an event happening at a *specific* time in the future. This property therefore implies that the *distribution* of future events remains the same regardless of when the previous like events occurred, given the overall average rate of occurrence.

Previously, we noted that the Poisson distribution is discrete and nonnegative. As the rate parameter increases, the distribution becomes more symmetric and eventually resembles a normal distribution. Let's look at this phenomenon (see figure 3.7).

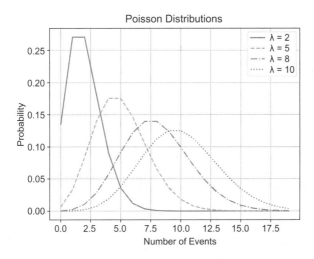

Figure 3.7 Four Poisson distributions, distinguished by their rate parameters, plotted in a single graph. As the rate parameter increases, the distribution mutates from right-skewed to normal.

We've embedded the PMF for the Poisson distribution in a chunk of Matplotlib code to create a single graph that plots four Poisson distributions distinguished only by their respective rate parameters. When the rate parameter is relatively low—that is, the rate at which an event occurs is relatively rare—the distribution takes on a right-skewed shape, where the tail on the right-hand side of the distribution is noticeably longer than the tail on the left-hand side. This is to say that, when the frequency of past occurrences is low, the PMF returns a distribution that estimates a high probability for a small number of events and low or zero probabilities for a larger number of events.

As the rate parameter (λ) increases, the Poisson distribution gradually becomes more symmetrical, resembling a normal distribution when λ reaches a sufficiently high value. This symmetry implies that the PMF then estimates nearly equal probabilities for the number of events to be either less than or greater than the given rate parameter (or the mean). Notably, the Poisson distribution can be seen as a limiting case of the binomial distribution when the number of trials is large and the probability of each event is small. This connection underscores why the Poisson distribution approximates a normal shape at high values of λ, much like how a binomial distribution also becomes approximately normal under similar conditions.

COMPUTING PROBABILITIES

Let's begin by setting two parameters: the rate parameter, denoted as lambda (`lam`), is set to 2, and the number of events, denoted as `k`, is set to 4. Essentially, this means the estimated number of events within a fixed period of time, based on historical rates of occurrence, is two, and we're interested in calculating the probability of observing four events:

```
>>> lam = 2
>>> k = 4
```

In Python, there are two methods for obtaining the probability. The first is to pass the values for `lam` and `k` to an arithmetic operation derived from the PMF for Poisson distributions, like so:

```
>>> probability_formula = ((np.exp(-lam) * lam ** k) / \
>>>                        math.factorial(k))
```

Then we print the probability—converted from a decimal to a percentage by multiplying the result by 100—as a formatted string:

```
>>> print(f'Probability (using PMF formula): '
>>>       f'{probability_formula * 100}%')
Probability (using PMF formula): 9.02235221577418%
```

The second method is to pass the same values to `poisson.pmf()`, which automatically calls the PMF and returns the same result. This operation first requires the `poisson` module from `scipy.stats`:

```
>>> from scipy.stats import poisson
>>> probability_python = poisson.pmf(k, lam)
```

```
>>> print(f'Probability (using Python method): '
>>>       f'{probability_formula * 100}%')
Probability (using Python method): 9.02235221577418%
```

So, when the estimated number of events is two, the probability of actually observing four events is about 9%. We can revisit figure 3.7, particularly focusing on the Poisson distribution with a rate parameter of 2, for comparison. Our computed probability aligns closely with the graph.

Before moving on to probability computations, let's repeat these exercises, but with different values for lambda (`lam`) and `k`:

```
>>> lam = 10
>>> k = 8

>>> probability_formula = ((np.exp(-lam) * lam ** k) / \
>>>                         math.factorial(k))
>>> print(f'Probability (using PMF formula): '
>>>       f'{probability_formula * 100}%')
Probability (using PMF formula): 11.259903214901998%

>>> probability_python = poisson.pmf(k, lam)
>>> print(f'Probability (using Python method): '
>>>       f'{probability_formula * 100}%')
Probability (using Python method): 11.259903214901998%
```

Regardless of which method is used, we get a roughly 11% probability of observing 8 events when the estimated number of events is 10. These results, too, align well with the Poisson distribution from figure 3.7, where the parameter rate is 10.

KEY TAKEAWAYS

The Poisson distribution is unique in that it seamlessly integrates empirical data with theoretical probabilities, offering a practical tool for modeling real-world events that occur independently over a fixed interval. Unlike other probability distributions that are more theoretical, the Poisson distribution directly connects with observed data, making it invaluable for applications like traffic flow analysis, call center management, and biological processes. One of its defining features is the way its shape can dramatically change with variations in the rate parameter, shifting from a highly skewed form for low rates to a more symmetric shape as the rate increases. Notably, the Poisson distribution can be seen as an approximation of the binomial distribution when the number of trials is large and the probability of each event is small. This adaptability makes the Poisson distribution a versatile and essential concept in both theoretical and applied statistics.

3.2 Probability problems

Having explored several probability and counting rules in the prior chapter—mostly from a theoretical perspective—we now intend to apply them empirically, demonstrating along the way that solving real-world problems typically requires some combination of these same rules. In chapter 2, we discovered that the probability of a (successful) event can be determined by dividing the number of favorable outcomes by the total number of possible outcomes. For instance, when rolling a six-sided die and aiming for an even number, out of the six possible outcomes, three would qualify as successes. Thus, the probability of success is calculated as three out of six, or 50%.

Then we demonstrated how to convert probabilities to odds—by dividing the number of potential successes by the number of potential failures or, alternatively, by dividing the probability of success by the probability of failure. So, when again rolling a six-sided die, the probability of getting a 4 is one out of six, or about 16.7%. This means the odds of getting a 4 are derived by dividing 1 by 5, or rather 0.167 by its inverse, 0.833. Either way, we get 0.2, or 20%, as a result.

Furthermore, we explored the multiplication and addition rules and discussed where and when each of these rules apply. According to the multiplication rule, the probability of two or more events occurring is equal to the product of their individual probabilities. So, if we roll a pair of six-sided dice, the probability of getting a pair of 4s is equal to the probability of rolling one 4 multiplied by the probability of rolling another 4, or 16.7% times 16.7%: less than 3%.

Although the multiplication rule applies to two or more independent events occurring simultaneously, the addition rule, by contrast, is used to calculate the probability of at least one of two mutually exclusive events happening. Consider once more the event of rolling a single six-sided die. The addition rule can be applied to find the probability of rolling either a 4 or a 5. The probability of rolling a 4 is 16.7%, and the probability of rolling a 5 is also 16.7%. Using the addition rule, we sum the probabilities of these two mutually exclusive events—16.7% plus 16.7%—to get the probability of rolling a 4 or a 5 on a single die: 33%.

We concluded our exploration of basic probabilities with an in-depth look into the intricacies of combinations and permutations. We isolated the key differentiator between the two: permutations account for arrangements where the order matters, and combinations do not. Furthermore, we provided step-by-step instructions for computing combinations and permutations, broken down by scenarios involving replacement and without replacement.

Our purpose here is not to belabor these concepts but rather to present them in compact formats for the twin purposes of easy reference and deeper appreciation and understanding. To achieve these goals, we'll construct a single table—a quick reference guide—that neatly organizes these concepts into their own rows, featuring concise definitions, formulas, and, where applicable, short snippets of Python code. Then we'll present a series of probability problems and demonstrate that solving them typically requires the combined use of multiple probability concepts and counting rules. The reference guide will be a valuable resource, eliminating the need to revisit chapter 2 and navigate through its content. But first, a discussion of the complement rule for probability is in order.

3.2.1 Complement rule for probability

Sometimes it's much easier to find the probability of an event *not* happening than it is to find the probability that the same event *will* happen. The complement rule is a fundamental principle in probability theory that states that the probability of the complement of an event is equal to 1 minus the probability of the event itself. In simpler terms, if we denote the event of interest as A, then the complement of A, typically denoted as A^C, represents all outcomes that are not in A. Mathematically, this can be expressed as $P(A^C) = 1 - P(A)$. By using the complement rule, we can often quickly and easily calculate the probability of an event not occurring by subtracting the probability of an event from 1. This rule is particularly useful when dealing with scenarios where it is easier to determine the probability of the complement, or inverse, rather than the event itself, allowing for more efficient probability computations and problem-solving strategies.

Let's demonstrate the complement rule with a pair of examples. We want to find the probability of getting a 4 on at least one of two dice rolls; thus, we need to consider the following three scenarios:

1. Getting a 4 on the first die and any number other than 4 on the second die
2. Getting a number other than 4 on the first die and a 4 on the second die
3. Getting a 4 on both dice

We can calculate the probabilities of these three scenarios by repeatedly applying the multiplication rule. With respect to the first and second scenarios, the probability of getting a 4 on one die is 1/6, and the probability of getting any number other than 4 on the other die is 5/6; therefore, the probability is equal to 1/6 × 5/6, or 5/36, or about 14%.

The probability of getting a 4 on both dice is 1/6 × 1/6, or 1/36, or less than 3%. Then we can apply the addition rule once to get the total probability: 5/36 + 5/36 + 1/36 = 11/36. This is to say that, out of 36 total possible outcomes, 11 of them, or about 31%, result in getting a 4 at least once.

That was rather cumbersome. The complement of getting at least one 4 from two dice rolls is twice getting any number other than 4. This, by again applying the multiplication rule, is equal to 5/6 × 5/6, or 25/36, or about 69%; thus, the probability of getting the inverse is 1 minus this result, or about 31%.

We can get the exact same result with just a few lines of Python code. In the first line of code, the variable `probability_not_4` equals 5/6 and therefore represents the probability of rolling a six-sided die and getting some number other than 4:

```
>>> probability_not_4 = 5/6
```

In the next line of code, the variable `probability_not_4_both` equals the probability of getting any number other than 4 from a pair of dice rolls. The `pow()` method is used to compute the power of a number. It takes two arguments: the base and the exponent. In this line of code, `pow()` raises the variable `probability_not_4` to the power of 2. In other words, it essentially applies the multiplication rule to compute the probability of not getting a 4 from either die roll and assigns the result to `probability_not_4_both`:

```
>>> probability_not_4_both = pow(probability_not_4, 2)
```

Then we instruct Python to print the result as a percentage, rather than as a decimal, in the form of a printed string:

```
>>> print(f'Probability of NOT getting at least one 4: '
>>>       f'{probability_not_4_both * 100}%')
Probability of NOT getting at least one 4: 69.44444444444446%
```

Let's look at one more example. This time, we want the probability of getting heads (H) at least one time when flipping three coins, versus all tails (T). By applying the multiplication rule, we get a total of eight possible outcomes:

1. HHH
2. HHT
3. HTH
4. HTT
5. THH
6. THT
7. TTH
8. TTT

Of these eight outcomes, seven include at least one coin that is heads. So, the probability of getting at least one heads from three coin flips is 7/8, or almost 88%.

Not bad. However, combining the multiplication rule with the complement rule to derive this same outcome is still the most efficient alternative.

The complement of getting heads at least once is not getting heads at all, or getting tails on all three coin flips. We can use the multiplication rule to calculate the probability of getting all tails. Because each coin flip is independent, the probability of getting tails on a single coin flip is 1/2. Therefore, the probability of getting tails on all three coin flips is $(1/2)^3$, or 1/8, which is equal to about 12%. Subtracting this result from 1 gets us the inverse, or the probability of getting heads at least once, which of course is 88%.

3.2.2 Quick reference guide

Now that the complement rule for probability is in our rearview mirror, it's time to unveil the quick but comprehensive reference guide in table 3.1. It is a snapshot of the probabilities and counting rules covered so far in this chapter and chapter 2; it includes short definitions, formulas, and snippets of Python code, packed into a single table. So, if you're tackling, let's say, a problem involving permutations without replacement, and you require just the formula and a snippet of code, there's no need to sift through lengthy explanations, now or in the future; instead, table 3.1 puts that information right at your fingertips.

Table 3.1 Quick reference guide for probabilities, odds, and counting rules

Theoretical probability Theoretical ratio of successes to outcomes	**Empirical probability** Ratio of observed success to observations
Formula	**Formula**
$P(\text{Event}) = \dfrac{\text{number of successes}}{\text{number of outcomes}}$	$P(\text{Event}) = \dfrac{\text{number of successes observed}}{\text{number of observations made}}$
colspan **Complement rule** Inverse probability of an event occurring or the probability of an event not occurring	
colspan **Formula**	
colspan $P(A^C) = 1 - P(A)$	
colspan **Odds** Ratio of successes to failures or the probability of success to the probability of failure	
colspan **Formulas**	
colspan $\text{Odds} = \dfrac{\text{number of potential successes}}{\text{number of potential failures}}$ or $\text{Odds} = \dfrac{\text{probability of success}}{\text{probability of failure}}$	
Multiplication rule Applies to simultaneous or sequential events	**Addition rule** Applies to mutually exclusive events
Formula	**Formula**
$n_1 \times n_2 \times \ldots n_k$	$n_1 + n_2 + \ldots n_k$
colspan **Permutations with replacement:** order matters; repetition allowed	
Formula	**Python code**
n^r	`pow(n, r)`
colspan **Permutations without replacement:** order matters; no repetition allowed	
Formula	**Python code**
$\dfrac{n!}{(n-r)!}$	`math.perm(n, r)`

Table 3.1 Quick reference guide for probabilities, odds, and counting rules *(continued)*

Combinations without replacement: order irrelevant; no repetition allowed

Formula	Python code
$\dfrac{n!}{r!\,(n-r)!}$	`math.comb(n, r)`

Combinations with replacement: order irrelevant; repetition allowed

Formula	Python code
$\dfrac{(n+r-1)!}{r!\,(n-1)!}$	`math.comb(n + r - 1, r)`

Keep in mind that *n* typically refers to the total number of items in a set, and *r* usually represents the number of items chosen or selected from that set.

3.2.3 Applied probability: Examples and solutions

The upcoming probability problems (and their solutions) feature scenarios involving rolling dice, flipping coins, and selecting cards from a standard deck. We will present several probability problems to showcase the combined application of the many probability and counting rules introduced thus far.

A typical die has six sides or faces, numbered 1 through 6. We always assume an equal probability of getting any of these outcomes when rolling a die, regardless of any previous results. Of course, when playing craps, backgammon, or many other games, two dice are rolled together. When that is the case, we write (3, 4) to represent getting 3 on the first die and 4 on the second, which is a different outcome from (4, 3), or getting 4 on the first die and 3 on the second die.

When a fair coin is flipped, we assume equal probabilities of getting heads (H) or tails (T), independent of previous coin flips. So, the probability of heads and the probability of tails always equal 0.5. Although many scenarios involve flipping just a single coin once, there are other scenarios where multiple coins are flipped simultaneously or a single coin is flipped multiple times in succession.

Selecting cards from a standard playing deck of 52 cards can potentially result in millions of combinations or permutations. The 52 cards are equally divided into four suits: hearts, diamonds, clubs, and spades. Within each suit, the cards are numbered between 1 and 10; plus, there is a King, a Queen, and a Jack for each suit. Cards numbered 1 are typically referred to as Aces. That all being said, let's get started.

PROBLEM 1

Problem: Two dice are rolled together. What is the probability of getting 1, 2, or 3 on the first die and 4, 5 or 6 on the second die?

Solution: We first use the multiplication rule to get the denominator, or the total number of possible outcomes. There are six possible outcomes when rolling a single six-sided die, so there must be 6 × 6, or 36, possible outcomes when rolling a pair of six-sided dice together. We get the numerator by again applying the multiplication rule. There are three successful outcomes from the first die and three successful outcomes from the second die; so, there must be 3 × 3, or nine, possible successes. Therefore, the probability of getting 1, 2, or 3 on the first die and 4, 5, or 6 on the second die is 9/36, or 25%, when we convert the result from a fraction to a percentage.

PROBLEM 2

Problem: Two dice are rolled together. What are the odds of getting 1, 2, or 3 on the first die and 4, 5, or 6 on the second die?

Solution: We know that the probability of success is equal to 0.25; therefore, the probability of failure must be the inverse of that, or 0.75. So, the odds of getting 1, 2, or 3 on one die and 4, 5, or 6 on the other are 0.25/0.75, or 33%.

PROBLEM 3

Problem: Two dice are rolled together. What is the probability of getting a sum of 7 or a sum of 11?

Solution: Six possible outcomes sum to 7: (1, 6), (2, 5), (3, 4), (4, 3), (5, 2), and (6, 1). There are, of course, 36 total outcomes when rolling a pair of six-sided dice, so the probability of rolling a sum of 7 is equal to 6/36, or 16.7%. Only two possible outcomes sum to 11: (5, 6) and (6, 5). So, the probability that two dice sum to 11 is 2/36, or between 5% and 6%. Because these are mutually exclusive events, we then apply the addition rule to get the probability that two dice will sum to 7 or 11: 6/36 + 2/36 = 8/36, or 22.2%.

PROBLEM 4

Problem: Two dice are rolled together. What is the probability of getting a sum equal to or greater than 2 and equal to or less than 11?

Solution: Rather than calculating the probabilities for all sums between 2 and 11 and then again applying the addition rule to get the total probability, the quickest, easiest, and surest method is to utilize the complementary rule. This of course entails computing the probability of the complementary event—rolling a sum of 12—and then subtracting that probability from 1 to obtain the probability of the desired outcome. The likelihood of rolling double 6s, the only way a pair of dice can sum to 12, is 1 in 36, or approximately 3%. Consequently, the probability of obtaining any other outcome is the complement of that, which is 1 − 1/36, or equivalently, 36/36 − 1/36, resulting in a probability of about 97% when expressed as a percentage.

PROBLEM 5

Problem: A single coin is flipped five times. What is the probability of getting heads on all five flips?

Solution: The probability of getting heads from just one flip is 1/2. We then apply the multiplication rule to get the probability of getting the same result four more times. So, the probability of getting heads on five out of five coin flips is equal to $(1/2)^5$, or 1/2 multiplied by itself five times. This equals 1/32, or approximately 3%.

Problem 6

Problem: A single coin is flipped five times. What is the probability of getting the following sequence: HTHHT?

Solution: The probability of getting heads on the first flip is 1/2. The probability of getting tails on the second flips is also 1/2, and so forth. So, the probability of getting this sequence, or any specific sequence from five flips, is equal to $(1/2)^5$, or roughly 3%.

Problem 7

Problem: A single coin is about to be flipped five times. How many different sequences are there?

Solution: If any random sequence has a roughly 3% probability of occurring, it stands to reason that there must be 32 or 33 possible sequences. There are two possible outcomes from any coin flip. Because each flip is independent of every other flip, we can use the multiplication rule to get the exact number of possible sequences. So, two possible outcomes from five flips means there are 2^5 or 32 possible sequences of heads and tails.

Problem 8

Problem: A single coin is flipped five times. What is the probability of getting exactly two heads and three tails, in any order?

Solution: We just learned there are 32 possible sequences of heads and tails, so that's our denominator. To find the numerator, we utilize the combinations-without-replacement counting rule. That's because the order of flips doesn't matter, but once we've achieved two heads, further replacement isn't allowed. We can therefore pass 5 and 2 to the `math.comb()` method; `math.comb()` assigns these two parameters as n and r, respectively, runs the combinations-without-replacement formula, and returns 10 as the numerator. Thus, there is a 10 in 32 chance of getting exactly two heads and three tails from five coin flips, or an approximate probability of 31%.

Problem 9

Problem: A single card is to be selected from a standard deck. What is the probability of selecting a face card?

Solution: There are four suits and three face cards per suit, so 12 of the 52 cards are face cards. Thus, there is a 12/52 chance, or 23% probability, of selecting a face card.

Problem 10

Problem: Two cards are to be selected from a standard deck. What is the probability of selecting two face cards if the first card is not returned to the deck?

Solution: We know the probability of selecting one face card. The probability of then selecting a second face card is not 12/52, but rather 11/51, because the first card was permanently removed from the deck. To find the probability of two consecutive successes, we apply the multiplication rule, where $12/52 \times 11/51 = 132/2{,}652$, which is roughly equal to 5%. So, there is about a 5% probability of consecutively selecting two face cards from a standard deck without replacement.

PROBLEM 11

Problem: Five cards are selected (or dealt) at random for a game of poker. How many different poker hands are possible?

Solution: This is another example of a combination-without-replacement problem. We therefore pass 52 and 5 to the math.comb() method, which returns a result of 2,598,960 possible hands.

PROBLEM 12

Problem: Now we're playing bridge; 13 cards are selected (or dealt) at random. How many different bridge hands are possible?

Solution: This time, we pass 52 and 13 to the math.comb() method, which returns a result of 635,013,559,600 possible hands.

PROBLEM 13

Problem: Five cards are to be selected from a standard deck. What is the number of ways to arrange the cards in a specific order, without replacement?

Solution: Because the order is now significant, this becomes a permutations-without-replacement problem. We therefore pass 52 as the total number of items (n) and 5 as the number of items to be selected (r) to Python's math.perm() method; math.perm() computes the number of ways to select and arrange 5 items from a set of 52 items without the possibility of replacement, which equals 311,875,200 possible permutations.

PROBLEM 14

Problem: Five cards are to be selected from a standard deck. What is the number of possible combinations if replacement is allowed?

Solution: In this instance, whenever a card is selected, it is then returned to the deck to potentially be selected again. This is therefore a combination-with-replacement problem, because the order doesn't matter. So, we pass 56 and 5 to the math.comb() method, which returns the combinations count by computing the number of ways to choose 5 items from 56 options. The result is 3,819,816 possible combinations.

The preceding series of probability problems aimed to offer a comprehensive set of examples with varying levels of complexity. The goal was to ensure a solid understanding of how to apply different probability concepts and counting rules in practical contexts, highlighting the need to combine these methods to solve complex probability problems.

As we conclude our exploration of probability computations, it's worth acknowledging that probabilities often extend beyond simple or straightforward events to more complex scenarios, where outcomes may depend on prior conditions or events, which leads us to conditional probabilities. Conditional probabilities allow us to calculate the likelihood of an event occurring given that another event has already occurred. This concept is critical in many real-world applications, from weather forecasting to medical diagnosis. By exploring conditional probabilities, we gain a deeper understanding of probabilistic reasoning and its practical implications in decision-making and problem-solving.

3.3 Conditional probabilities

Conditional probabilities refer to the likelihood of an event occurring given that another event has already happened or is known, or at least assumed, to be true. Rather than quantifying probabilities in isolation, we assess them within a context where additional information shapes our expectations. From a mathematical perspective, known or presumed information typically triggers a change in the denominator, representing the number of possibilities, without necessarily any modification to the numerator, representing the number of successes.

From a more practical perspective, it affects the size of the sample space: that is, the set of all possible outcomes or events that could occur in a given experiment or situation. Understanding conditional probabilities enables us to navigate uncertainty more effectively, as it allows for nuanced decision-making based on available and relevant information. By recognizing how the probability of an event changes with additional data points, we gain a more comprehensive understanding of the changing dynamics across various scenarios, from risk assessment to strategic planning. A few examples should help.

3.3.1 Examples

The following examples, deliberately chosen for their relative simplicity, are provided to reinforce our fundamental understanding of conditional probabilities before we explore their mathematical intricacies and other properties.

WEATHER FORECASTING

- *Without additional information:* The probability of rain tomorrow, based on historical record-keeping, might be 30%.
- *With additional information* (dark clouds gathering, rainy conditions in neighboring states): The probability of rain might increase to 70%.

The denominator, or sample space, is reduced from all possible weather conditions to cloudy and rainy conditions. By reducing the denominator but keeping the numerator constant, the probability of rain increases.

MEDICAL TESTING

- *Without additional information:* The probability of having a noninfectious disease might be 5%, based on general population statistics.
- *With additional information* (positive test result): The probability of having a noninfectious disease might increase to 80%.

In this case, the sample space changes from the entire population to only those individuals who test positive, significantly altering the probability.

TRAFFIC

- *Without additional information:* The probability of heavy traffic during rush hour might be 60%, based on prior commutes.

- *With additional information* (accident reported ahead): The probability of heavy traffic might increase to as high as 90%.

The denominator changes from all possible traffic conditions to only those affected by the reported accident.

BASKETBALL GAME

- *Without additional information:* The probability of a professional basketball team advancing in the playoffs might be 50%.
- *With additional information* (leading scorer/rebounder is injured): The probability of the team winning their current series and advancing to the next round of the playoffs might drop to 25%.

In this scenario, the sample space changes from all possible outcomes to only those where the team's leading scorer/rebounder is injured and therefore unable to play.

FINANCIAL INVESTMENT

- *Without additional information:* The probability of a stock price increasing in value might be 70%, based on recent market trends.
- *With additional information* (company reports strong earnings): The probability of the stock increasing might rise to 90%.

Here, the denominator is reduced from all possible market movements to only those influenced by the company's earnings report, leading to a higher probability of an increase (and likely more investments).

In each of these scenarios, the likelihood of one event has a legitimate and viable influence on the probability of another event; in other words, there is some sort of dependency between the two. But let's briefly discuss the inverse of this: when two events are instead independent of each other.

3.3.2 Conditional probabilities and independence

Imagine rolling a six-sided die and getting a 6 on one roll. Your intuition might suggest that the chance of rolling another 6 is less than the probability of rolling any other number. However, this outcome doesn't influence the probability of getting a 6, or any other outcome for that matter, on the next roll of the same die. These events are independent, meaning past results have no bearing on future ones. The roll of a single die always follows a discrete uniform distribution, regardless of previous outcomes.

Or consider five successive flips of the same fair coin, all of which resulted in heads. In no way should this prior information be used to predict the result of the next coin flip. The previous results do not change the probability of getting heads or tails on the next flip. That's because coin flips are independent events, where prior outcomes have no bearing on future outcomes. Although we should expect coin flips, or any other binomial experiment, to normalize after several flips, that's separate from the probability of getting heads (or tails) on the very next flip.

Likewise, if the queen of diamonds is selected from a standard deck of 52 cards and then immediately returned to the deck, in no way does that affect the probability of then selecting the same card when the next selection is made. The probability of again selecting the queen of diamonds is exactly the same, 1 in 52, as selecting any other card.

So, it's important to distinguish independent events from dependent events: conditional probabilities apply to the latter but not to the former. Even events that appear dependent require assessment to determine the extent of their interdependence. Rain in Oregon may or may not be a leading indicator of rain in California. Similarly, market trends in one sector of the economy may or may not influence future performance in other sectors. Now that we've clarified the contexts in which conditional probabilities are relevant and where they aren't, let's explore two methods for solving the same conditional probability problem.

3.3.3 Intuitive approach to conditional probability

Once more, conditional probability is the likelihood of an event occurring given that another event has already happened or is known to be true. It is given by the following equation:

$$P(A|B) = \frac{P(A \text{ and } B)}{P(B)}$$

where

- $P(A|B)$ denotes the conditional probability of event A occurring with the knowledge that event B has already occurred.
- $P(A \text{ and } B)$ is the probability of both events A and B occurring.
- $P(B)$ is the probability of event B occurring.

However, let's set aside the conditional probability formula *for the moment*; we'll first demonstrate how to solve a conditional probability problem not by plugging numbers into a formula but rather through a more intuitive method.

We'll start by constructing a contingency table containing the data for our analysis. A *contingency table*—sometimes referred to as a *cross-tabulation* or a *two-way table*—is a tabular representation of two categorical variables. It organizes the data into rows and columns, where each cell in the table represents the frequency or count of occurrences for a particular combination of classes from the two variables. More specifically,

- Each row in the contingency table corresponds to a distinct class of one categorical variable.
- Each column corresponds to a distinct class of the other categorical variable.
- Each cell contains a count or frequency of occurrences that align to a combination of classes from each categorical variable.

The following snippet of Python code creates a categorical variable called `test_results` containing illustrative data that initializes our contingency table.

test_results contains two classes, Negative and Positive, which represent the two possible outcomes of a medical test:

```
>>> test_results = {'Negative': [860, 10],
>>>                 'Positive': [90, 40]}
```

The values assigned to each class represent counts or frequencies. The Negative class contains 860 instances where the test result was negative and 10 instances where the test result was positive. Similarly, the Positive class contains 90 instances where the test result was negative and 40 instances where the test result was positive. Negative and Positive are intended to be our column labels.

Our next line of code initializes a new categorical variable called symptoms, which consists of two classes. In this context, No signifies the absence of symptoms, and Yes signifies their presence:

```
>>> symptoms = ['No', 'Yes']
```

No and Yes will serve as our row labels.

The last piece of code constructs the contingency table and displays it in the Python console. This requires the pd.DataFrame() method from the pandas library. The pandas library contains several methods for creating and manipulating data structures; pd.DataFrame() creates a two-dimensional, labeled data structure similar to a table in a database or an Excel spreadsheet. We pass the categorical variables test_results (as the data) and symptoms (as the index) to pd.DataFrame() to create an object called contingency_table:

```
>>> import pandas as pd
>>> contingency_table = pd.DataFrame(test_results, index = symptoms)
>>> print(contingency_table)
     Negative  Positive
No        860        90
Yes        10        40
```

Now that we have our contingency table, we can write other snippets of code to extract values from it and perform arithmetic operations, such as conditional probability calculations. To demonstrate, the following line of code uses the .iloc attribute to extract the value from contingency_table where the second row and second column intersect (Python indices begin at 0 rather than 1):

```
>>> contingency_table.iloc[1, 1]
40
```

We then want to find the probability of getting a positive test result, knowing in advance the presence of symptoms, which can be expressed this way:

$$P(\text{positive test result} \mid \text{presence of symptoms})$$

This is derived by dividing the number of instances where the test result was positive and there was the presence of symptoms (*A* and *B*) by the sum of those instances and the number of instances where the test result was negative and there was the presence of symptoms (B):

```
>>> P = (contingency_table.iloc[1, 1] / \
>>>      (contingency_table.iloc[1, 1] + contingency_table.iloc[1, 0]))
>>> print(f'Conditional probability: {P * 100}%')
Conditional probability: 80.0%
```

This is equivalent to the quotient between 40 and 50 converted from a decimal to a percentage.

From the same contingency table, we can also find the reverse—that is, the probability that the symptoms are correct given a positive test result—simply by switching A and B. It can be expressed this way:

$$P(\text{presence of symptoms} \mid \text{positive test result})$$

The numerator remains unchanged. To get the denominator, we extract the two values from the second column and add them together:

```
>>> P = (contingency_table.iloc[1, 1] / \
>>>      (contingency_table.iloc[0, 1] + contingency_table.iloc[1, 1]))
>>> print(f'Conditional probability: {P * 100}%')
Conditional probability: 30.76923076923077%
```

In both instances, we computed higher, and yet more accurate, probabilities by reducing the sample space. This triggers very different action plans than if there had been no additional information in advance.

3.3.4 Formulaic approach to conditional probability

We get the exact same results by instead plugging numbers into the conditional probability formula. Here's how.

STEP 1: DEFINE THE EVENTS

- A represents a positive test result.
- B represents the presence of symptoms.

STEP 2: FIND P(A AND B)

- $P(A) = 130$ (total number of positive test results).
- $P(B) = 50$ (total number of instances with the presence of symptoms).
- $P(A \text{ and } B) = 40$ (total number of instances where both A and B occur.

Thus,

$$P(A \text{ and } B) = \frac{40}{1,000} = 0.04$$

STEP 3: FIND P(B)

- There are 50 instances with the presence of symptoms and 1,000 observations, so

$$P(B) = \frac{50}{1,000} = 0.05$$

STEP 4: CALCULATE $P(A \mid B)$

- $P(A \text{ and } B) = 0.04$.
- $P(B) = 0.05$.

Thus

$$P(A|B) = \frac{P(A \text{ and } B)}{P(B)} = \frac{0.04}{0.05} = 0.8$$

Just like the intuitive approach, the formulaic approach returns an 80% probability of a positive test result given the presence of symptoms.

To calculate the probability of the symptoms being correct given a positive test result, we switch A and B and divide the same numerator—after all, the probability of A and B is the same as the probability of B and A—by $P(A)$ rather than by $P(B)$:

$$P(B|A) = \frac{P(B \text{ and } A)}{P(A)} = \frac{0.04}{0.13} = 0.31$$

This again returns a 31% probability (rounded) of the symptoms being correct given a positive test result.

The intuitive approach is likely easier to understand and to carry forward than the formulaic approach. But as demonstrated here, both methods return the same results, so you should apply whichever works best for you.

We've packed a wealth of knowledge on probabilities and counting rules into just two chapters. These learnings will prove invaluable as we move forward into more specific subject matters, starting with linear regression models.

Summary

- The normal distribution is a probability distribution symmetric around the mean so that, when plotted, it assumes a bell-like shape. It is defined by two parameters: the mean, which, of course, determines the center of the distribution, and the standard deviation, which determines the spread.
- A standard normal distribution is a special case of the normal distribution with a mean of 0 and a standard deviation of 1. The raw data has been transformed, or standardized, so that the values represent the number of standard deviations they are below or above the mean.
- The binomial distribution describes the probability of a specific number of successes in a fixed number of independent trials, where each trial has but two outcomes and the probabilities of those outcomes remain constant throughout. It is characterized by two parameters: the number of trials and the probability of success. Regardless of those parameters, binomial outcomes are normally distributed.
- The discrete uniform distribution is a probability distribution where all outcomes in a finite set of values have an equal probability of occurring. It is characterized by two parameters: the number of possible outcomes and the range of values in the set.

- The Poisson distribution is a probability distribution that describes the number of events occurring in a fixed interval of time or space, given a known average rate of occurrence and assuming independence between events. It is characterized by a single parameter: the rate of occurrence.
- When computing probabilities, it's essential to use a combination of various probabilities and counting rules to accurately assess the likelihood of events occurring.
- In some scenarios, it can be simpler to compute the inverse, or complement, of an event's occurrence, thereby providing an alternative approach to understanding its probability.
- Conditional probabilities represent the likelihood of an event occurring given that another event has already occurred, thereby allowing for a deeper understanding of how events relate to each other. They are calculated by adjusting the probability of the event of interest based on additional information provided by the occurrence of another event. In other words, the sample space is reduced by decreasing the denominator and maybe the numerator as well, which can significantly influence the dynamics of subsequent decision-making and risk assessment.

Fitting a linear regression

This chapter covers
- Model fitting
- Model evaluation
- Model assumption tests
- Data exploration, testing for normality, and detecting outliers

Linear regression is a supervised learning method, meaning it uses labeled data—where the input features and corresponding outputs are known for a subset of data—to predict a quantitative response from one or more independent variables. This model is then applied to make predictions on new, unknown data. Although linear regression might now lack the spark of random forests (see chapter 5) and other more contemporary methods, it's still an "implement" at or near the top of every data scientist's toolbox. Furthermore, linear regression is a foundational model that is easy both to understand and to implement, with virtually endless use cases. Here are just a few examples:

- Marketing organizations predicting sales revenues based on advertising expenditures across multiple channels

- Buyers and lenders predicting future home prices based on size and square footage, number of bedrooms and bathrooms, age and condition of the property, architectural design, and lot size
- University admissions officers predicting student performance based on high school GPAs and standardized test scores
- Retailers predicting product demand based on historical sales figures

Any relationship between independent and dependent variables—that is, between predictors that explain change and the outcomes they affect—that shows a linear pattern in the given feature space can be modeled with linear regression. Although more complex methods can transform data to model nonlinear relationships, linear regression is designed to capture relationships that align well with a straight line through the data. When fitting a linear regression, we are attempting, at minimum, to answer the following questions:

- *Is there a meaningful relationship between independent variables, also known as explanatory variables or predictors, and a dependent variable, known as the target or response variable?* Linear regression models the relationship between independent and dependent variables under the assumption that the relationship is linear, allowing us to test for statistical significance in the strength of this association.
- *What is the nature of the relationship?* Linear regression reveals if the relationship between variables is either positive or negative—positive if they change in the same direction, negative if they change in opposite directions.
- *How strong is the relationship?* Linear regression returns measures from which we can quantify the degree of association between variables, although these measures are most accurate when the independent variables are truly independent—a condition that is not always satisfied in real-world data.
- *Can we estimate changes in a dependent variable from variances in the independent variables?* Linear regression provides coefficients that represent the estimated effect of each predictor on the dependent variable, allowing us to model expected outcomes under the assumption that the observed relationships are consistent.
- *When fitting a multiple linear regression, where a response variable is modeled against two or more predictors, which predictors have a statistically significant influence on changes in the response variable?* Linear regression helps identify which predictors are statistically significant, although this significance can be affected by factors like collinearity and other model assumptions.
- *How well does the model fit the data?* Linear regression estimates the goodness of fit, indicating how well the model explains and predicts variances in the response variable under the assumption of linearity.
- *Have model assumptions been met?* Model integrity (the internal soundness of the model) and reliability (its consistency in returning valid results) are predicated on several assumptions being true. Tests and other checks are available to establish whether or not these assumptions have been satisfied.

We intend to answer all these questions and more. Our path forward will be broadly divided into two parts. Section 4.1 focuses on the theoretical: understanding the relationship between variables, simple versus multiple regressions, conditions that must prevail for linear regression to best fit the data, coefficients, constants, regression lines, and residuals. Section 4.2 is way more practical: we'll import a real data set and demonstrate how to fit a simple linear regression in Python, evaluate the results, and test model assumptions.

4.1 Primer on linear regression

Linear regression, one more time, is a popular and practical supervised learning method for predictions—when the response variable is numeric. You should never fit a linear regression when attempting to solve a classification problem, which involves predicting categorical outcomes such as labels or group membership. Linear regression is a method used to model the relationship between a numeric dependent variable and one or more independent variables, which may or may not also be numeric. It assumes a linear relationship between variables. Our purpose here is to get you thoroughly grounded in all things linear regression before fitting a model to a real data set.

4.1.1 Linear equation

The purpose of linear regression is to measure the correlation between independent and dependent variables by finding the line of best fit that models the relationship under the assumption of linearity. The so-called *regression line*, which represents the predicted values of the dependent variable, is determined by estimating the coefficients and the intercept in a way that minimizes the differences between it and the observed data.

The equation for a simple linear regression, where the dependent variable is regressed against just one independent variable, or predictor, is typically represented as follows:

$$y = \beta_0 + \beta_1 x + \epsilon$$

This formulation reflects the underlying population model, where

- y is the observed dependent variable (also called the *response* or *target variable*).
- x is the independent variable (also known as the *predictor* or *explanatory variable*).
- β_0 is the intercept, or the value of the response variable when x equals 0.
- β_1 is the slope or the change in the response variable for every one-unit change in x.
- ϵ is the error term, capturing the deviation of the observed values from the regression line.

When making predictions, the model is often expressed in terms of the predicted value, $\hat{y}$ (or *yhat*), omitting the error term:

$$\hat{y} = \beta_0 + \beta_1 x$$

Here, $\hat{y}$ distinguishes the predicted response from the actual observed response. The error term, ϵ, is still present conceptually but not explicitly included in the predictive formula.

The equation for a multiple linear regression, where the dependent variable is regressed against, let's say, three predictors, is expressed this way:

$$y = \beta_0 + \beta_1 x_1 + \beta_2 x_2 + \beta_3 x_3 + \epsilon$$

Or, for prediction purposes,

$$\hat{y} = \beta_0 + \beta_1 x_1 + \beta_2 x_2 + \beta_3 x_3$$

where

- x_1, x_2, and x_3 represent the three predictors.
- β_1, β_2, and β_3 are the regression coefficients (slopes) associated with each independent variable.

Let's explain further with the aid of an illustration: see figure 4.1.

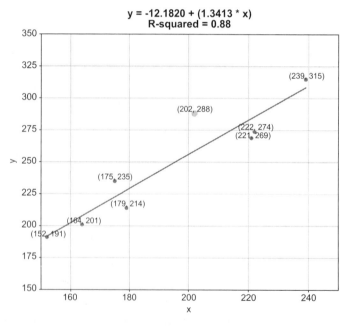

Figure 4.1 A scatter plot that displays eight data points, their respective x and y coordinates, and a regression line. The data points represent the observed data (for instance, when x equals 202, y equals 288, which has been highlighted and magnified). The regression line ties back to a simple linear regression that was fit on the data, where a response variable called y, which runs along the y axis, was regressed against a predictor called x, which runs along the x axis. It represents the linear equation at the top that can be derived from the model output, which is to say, it is also a representation of the predictions for y given x. R-squared is one of several metrics contained in the model output; it represents the percentage of variance in the response variable that can be explained by changes in the predictor.

This scatter plot was created with Matplotlib. A scatter plot visualizes the relationship between a pair of numeric variables on a two-dimensional plane, where each point represents a single observation in the data. Scatter plots have many uses, including

- Identifying patterns or trends in the relationship between two variables
- Assessing the strength and direction of the relationship between variables
- Detecting outliers or other potentially anomalous observations in the data
- Evaluating the fit of linear modeling

We'll demonstrate later how to create a similar plot using a series of methods from the Matplotlib library, but in the meantime, let's review what's shown in figure 4.1.

The horizontal axis (or x axis) represents the independent variable, labeled x, and the vertical axis (or y axis) represents the dependent variable, labeled y. Although it's conventional to place the predictor on the x axis and the response on the y axis, the linear relationship itself is symmetric and does not inherently depend on this orientation.

Each of the eight dots, or data points, corresponds to a pair of values from the same row in an 8 × 2 data frame. Consider, for example, the one data point we've intentionally magnified: the data contains one record where x equals 202 and y equals 288. The points, therefore, represent the observed values from the data. A printout of the data source is provided here for cross-referencing purposes:

```
     x    y
0  152  191
1  175  235
2  179  214
3  222  274
4  202  288
5  221  269
6  239  315
7  164  201
```

The relationship between x and y—that is, between our independent and dependent variables—is positive, because as x increases, so does y. The relationship is negative when increases in the independent variable correspond to decreases in the dependent variable (see figure 4.2). Linear regression may be a good fit for the data either way, as long as the total difference between observed and predicted values (the residual error) is kept to a minimum. However, even if the residual error is low, a near-zero slope would suggest a weak or statistically insignificant relationship between the variables.

Alternatively, the relationship is considered neutral when changes in the independent variable appear to have little or no effect on the dependent variable (see figure 4.3). In such cases, linear regression may yield a best-fit line with a near-zero slope, indicating a weak or nonexistent relationship rather than a meaningful predictive model.

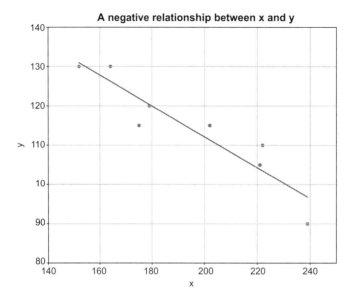

Figure 4.2 A scatter plot that shows a negative relationship between variables. The relationship is negative because the variables move in opposite directions: as the independent variable x increases, the dependent variable y decreases.

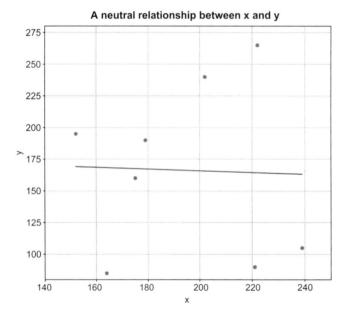

Figure 4.3 A scatter plot that shows a neutral relationship between variables. The relationship is neutral because changes in the independent variable x appear to have almost no effect on the dependent variable y.

4.1.2 Goodness of fit

The *regression line*, or *line of best fit*, is a straight line that represents the relationship between the independent variable x and the dependent variable y from a simple linear model. It is determined by estimating the values of the intercept and slope coefficients that best minimize the sum of squared residuals, which is a measure of the overall difference between the actual values of y and the predicted values of y. The lower the sum of squared residuals, the better the regression line fits the data, and vice versa. In multiple linear regression, where there are two or more predictors, the regression line becomes a hyperplane in a multidimensional space, but the concept of modeling the relationship between variables is unchanged.

Goodness of fit is most typically measured by a single statistic called R-squared. R-squared (or R^2), formally known as the coefficient of determination, is a statistical measure that indicates the proportion of variance in the dependent variable that is explained by the one predictor in a simple linear regression or by the two or more predictors in a multiple regression; it is used to assess the goodness of fit of the regression model to the observed data. Because it's a squared measure, R^2 will always equal some number between 0 and 1; the higher the coefficient of determination, the better the predictor(s) account for changes in the dependent variable, and vice versa.

When fitting a simple regression, R^2 represents the square of the correlation coefficient between the same dependent and independent variables (it's less straightforward when fitting a multiple regression). R^2 is a commonly used metric for assessing model fit, but it has important limitations that must be acknowledged. As a single-point measure, R^2 doesn't capture all aspects of model quality, and thorough model evaluation also requires checking the underlying data distribution and other diagnostic measures. Additionally, R^2 naturally increases when other predictors are added to a regression, even if those variables have little to no true relationship with the dependent variable; this can lead to overfitting. An overfitted model is overly tailored to the data it was trained on, capturing noise rather than general patterns. As a result, it may perform poorly when applied to new data, failing to generalize effectively.

Also, R^2 doesn't indicate the direction or causal relationship between variables; it simply tells you how well the model variables fit together. The direction must be inferred from other metrics or observed by plotting the data. We will talk much more about R^2 and other metrics when we fit a simple regression on real data.

4.1.3 Conditions for best fit

One more point: linear regression provides the best fit when the variables are normally distributed—forming a bell-shaped curve—and are free of outliers. Non-normal data should be transformed to normal distributions before fitting a linear regression. However, applying transformations to achieve normality changes the assumed relationship between dependent and independent variables, as the fitted model then describes associations on the transformed scale rather than the original scale. Transforming data can help meet the assumptions of a linear model, but it's essential to exercise caution, as this approach may overlook other modeling options that could better capture complex, nonlinear relationships in the data.

A variable called x from a data frame named df can be normalized, depending on its original distribution, by applying one of the following transformation methods:

- Logarithmic transformation (requires numpy, a common Python library for scientific computing):

  ```
  df['x'] = np.log(df['x'])
  ```

  or

  ```
  df['x'] = np.log10(df['x'])
  ```

  Apply when the data spans several orders of magnitude or is right-skewed, as this transformation compresses the range and can normalize distributions.

- Reciprocal transformation:

  ```
  df['x'] = 1/df.x
  ```

  Use when dealing with data that is heavily right-skewed or when large values need to be compressed and small values expanded. Be cautious with zeros or negative values, as they require special handling.

- Square root transformation (also requires numpy):

  ```
  df['x'] = np.sqrt(df.x)
  ```

  Best applied to moderate right-skewed data or when the variance of the data increases with the mean. It's useful for stabilizing variance and making the data more normal.

- Exponential transformation:

  ```
  df['x'] = df.x**(1/1.2)
  ```

  This transformation can be applied when you need to reverse the effect of a power transformation or slightly reduce the range of variability in data. It's effective for moderately skewed data.

But the larger point to be discussed—and demonstrated—is the effect of outliers. *Outliers* are data points that differ significantly from other observations in the same set of data. (Incidentally, removing outliers is yet another method by which to normalize a data series.) One way of detecting outliers, although not necessarily the most accurate, is to plot the data in a scatter plot. Let's revisit our first scatter plot in figure 4.1, specifically the magnified data point where the x and y coordinates equal 202 and 288, respectively.

For the sake of this demonstration, let's assume (or pretend) it qualifies as the one outlier in the data. After all, the distance between it and the fitted regression line is clearly greater than the distance between any other observed data point and the corresponding prediction for y. Because linear regression draws a straight line through the data that minimizes the total distance between it and the observed data, this one outlier, which might actually be a measurement error or the representation of a rare or anomalous event, has undue influence on the model. Let's then remove that one record from the data, rerun our regression, and plot the results (see figure 4.4).

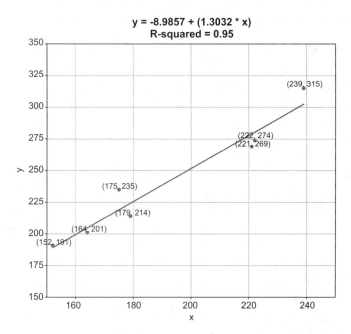

Figure 4.4 A scatter plot that displays seven data points rather than eight. The one presumed outlier was removed, and another regression was fit. The coefficient of determination, which was previously equal to 0.88, is now 0.95. By removing one outlier, we've made a strong model even stronger.

By removing one outlier from the data, we've minimized the residuals and—based just on the coefficient of determination (R^2), which increased from 0.88 to 0.95—improved the predictive power of our model. The independent variable x now explains 95% of the variance in the dependent variable y. However, be aware that removing outliers can sometimes lead to overfitting, as it may cause the model to fit too closely to the remaining data and reduce its generalizability to new data.

Now that we've covered many of the fundamentals of linear regression—goodness of fit measures, conditions for best fit, and other underlying assumptions—we'll import a real data set, demonstrate how to fit a simple linear regression on it, evaluate the key measures and show how they're derived, and test model assumptions.

4.2 Simple linear regression

Our plan is to do the following:

1. Import a real data set that contains 20 records and a pair of numeric variables.
2. Demonstrate how to perform a basic data exploration exercise.
3. Regress one of those variables against the other, print the results, and evaluate the key measures.

4   Provide instructions for how to run a series of tests and other checks to determine how well, or not so well, model assumptions have been met.

Data exploration is the process of analyzing data to reveal patterns, trends, and relationships that can influence statistical methods. When preparing to fit a linear regression, we should at least test for normality, determine whether the data contains any outliers that might weigh on our model, and take corrective action as necessary.

4.2.1 Importing and exploring the data

The *Marathon des Sables* (French for "Marathon of the Sands") is an ultramarathon that has been held every year since 1986 in the Sahara Desert. The race is divided into six stages over seven days; the total distance is 250 kilometers, or about 160 miles, roughly equivalent to six marathons. Daytime temperatures can sometimes reach 50° Celsius, or about 130° Fahrenheit. Runners are responsible for carrying their own supplies, like food and water, extra shoes and socks, etc.

Our data set contains the Stage 1 and Stage 2 split times for the top 20 male finishers from the 2021 race. The split times are in minutes, rounded to the nearest whole number. We import the data, a .csv file stored in our working directory, by passing the full filename, bounded by opening and closing quotation marks, to the `pd.read_csv()` method; `pd.read_csv()` directly accesses the working directory and, in this instance, imports a file called mds.csv. If mds.csv were stored elsewhere, we would need to pass the file's path—either the full path or a relative path—to `pd.read_csv()`.

The contents of mds.contents are read into a data frame called mds. But to prevent `pd.read_csv()` from throwing an error, we must first import the pandas library, a powerful Python library for data analysis and data manipulation:

```
>>> import pandas as pd
>>> mds = pd.read_csv('mds.csv')
```

Note that, by default, the `pd.read_csv()` method assumes that the first row of the file contains column headers. Now that we have imported our data, we can next call other methods to get a thorough understanding of it.

UNDERSTANDING THE DATA

The `info()` method in pandas returns a concise summary of the mds data frame. It's an easy and logical first data-exploration step:

```
>>> print(mds.info())
<class 'pandas.core.frame.DataFrame'>
RangeIndex: 20 entries, 0 to 19
Data columns (total 2 columns):
 #   Column  Non-Null Count  Dtype
---  ------  --------------  -----
 0   stage1  20 non-null     int64
 1   stage2  20 non-null     int64
dtypes: int64(2)
memory usage: 452.0 bytes
None
```

More specifically, `info()` returns the following information:

- *The number of rows, or entries, in the data frame.* The `info()` method excludes the header and therefore returns just the number of entries that contain data. The `mds` data frame contains 20 rows of data. Python indexes the row count starting from 0 rather than 1.
- *The number of columns, listed from left to right.* Python also indexes columns starting at 0. The `mds` data frame contains two columns, `stage1` and `stage2`.
- *The number of non-null values in each column.* The sum of non-null values in both `stage1` and `stage2` equals 20; because the count of non-null values equals the `mds` record count, our data therefore contains no null values to worry about.
- *The data type of each column.* Both `stage1` and `stage2` are of type `int64` (short for integer).

Of course, it's always helpful to see the contents of a data frame instead of just being aware of its dimension and other properties. Next we'll show how to do that.

VIEWING THE DATA

There are several ways to get a glimpse of the data. If `mds` were a much longer data frame, we would likely call the `head()` and `tail()` methods in pandas to print the first few and last few records. But because `mds` is just 20 records long, we'll pass it as an argument to the `print()` method, which returns the entire data frame:

```
>>> print(mds)
    stage1  stage2
0      152     191
1      162     184
2      165     193
3      163     191
4      166     193
5      187     292
6      175     235
7      202     226
8      179     214
9      222     274
10     184     300
11     193     242
12     255     279
13     202     288
14     221     269
15     207     329
16     227     268
17     239     315
18     164     201
19     226     345
```

Seeing the data, even if it is just a small subset of records, piques our curiosity. We naturally want to know the size and shape of every variable. Even when the data comprises only 20 records, it's difficult or impossible to draw meaningful conclusions merely by observation.

COMPUTING BASIC STATISTICS

The `describe()` method in pandas interrogates the data and returns a series of *descriptive* statistics, provided the data is numeric, including the record count (`count`), mean (`mean`), standard deviation (`std`), minimum (`min`) and maximum (`max`) values, and three quartiles (`25%`, `50%`, and `75%`). When the data is categorical—that is, when the data represents categories or labels and therefore does not contain a natural numerical value—the `describe()` method instead returns *summary* statistics, such as the number of unique groups and the record count for each:

```
>>> print(mds.describe())
            stage1       stage2
count    20.000000    20.000000
mean    194.550000   251.450000
std      29.623026    51.112338
min     152.000000   184.000000
25%     165.750000   199.000000
50%     190.000000   255.000000
75%     221.250000   289.000000
max     255.000000   345.000000
```

Let's review these.

The *mean*, also known as the *average*, is a measure of central tendency that represents the sum of all values divided by the number of records; it is commonly used to describe the "typical" value in a set of numeric data. Another common measure of central tendency is the *median*, which represents the middle value in a sorted data set and can be more robust against outliers than the mean. When working with data stored in columns (a columnar format), you can apply these calculations across each column using methods like `apply()` and `median()`, available in pandas.

The *standard deviation* is a measure that quantifies the amount of variation, or dispersion, from the mean. A low standard deviation indicates that most of the data is close to the mean; a high standard deviation suggests longer tails and therefore more dispersion in the data. The standard deviation is obtained by calculating the square root of the variance, which is the average of the squared differences between each data point and the mean.

The *minimum* and *maximum* represent the smallest and largest values, respectively. From a more statistical perspective, they equal the lower and upper bounds of a numeric data series.

The second quartile (Q2) is `50%` and therefore equals the median, which is to say it divides the data into two equal halves. The first, or lower, quartile (Q1) is `25%`; it marks the boundary line below which lies the lowest 25% of the data. And `75%` is the third, or upper, quartile (Q3); it marks the boundary line above which lies the highest 75% of the data. By any of these measures, Stage 2 is clearly longer in distance, or at least more challenging, than Stage 1.

TESTING FOR NORMALITY

Linear regression assumes that the residuals—that is, the differences between the observed and predicted values—are normally distributed. We'll demonstrate how to test this assumption after fitting our model, but for now, we want to know whether the variables themselves are normally distributed. That's because if the single predictor in a simple regression is normally distributed, the residuals are likely to be as well.

We can draw a histogram or density plot for each variable and determine from observation whether the data is or is not normally distributed. But that is a very imprecise method. Data that appears to be distributed normally (it resembles a bell shape) may in fact not be normal. And the reverse can also be true—data that looks non-normal may actually meet the standard for normality, which is why we'll refrain from drawing any plots and instead run a pair of Shapiro–Wilk tests.

> **Statistical testing and the 5% threshold for significance**
>
> Statistical tests are tools used to determine whether the results observed in data are likely due to a true effect or merely to random chance. These tests return a p-value, which quantifies the probability that the observed results could have occurred under the null hypothesis (assuming no real effect). Researchers often compare this p-value to a significance threshold to decide whether to reject or fail to reject the null hypothesis. The 5% significance level ($p < 0.05$) is a widely accepted threshold, where results are deemed statistically significant if there is less than a 5% probability they could occur under the null hypothesis; when that is the case, the null hypothesis is rejected. However, the choice of 5% is somewhat arbitrary; it's not derived from a universal principle but rather has become standard due to historical and practical reasons, making it a convenient convention in many fields.
>
> Although 5% is not inherently special, it offers a balanced approach to controlling the risk of both Type I errors (false positives) and Type II errors (false negatives). This threshold provides a reasonably low probability of mistakenly rejecting the null hypothesis while maintaining sensitivity to detect real effects. Importantly, having a clear threshold—whether 5%, 1%, or any other predetermined value—is essential because it gives researchers a consistent, objective criterion for decision-making. Without such a threshold, interpreting statistical tests would become subjective, making it difficult to compare studies or replicate results.
>
> The 5% significance level strikes a practical balance, helping maintain scientific rigor while allowing for the detection of meaningful results in data. The 5% significance threshold does not tell us the probability that the null hypothesis is true or false; it only indicates the likelihood of observing the data (or more extreme results) if the null hypothesis were true. Additionally, it does not measure the effect size or practical significance of the results.

A Shapiro–Wilk test is a statistical test that, based on the returned p-value, tells us whether a set of numeric data is normally distributed. The null hypothesis of a Shapiro–Wilk test is that the data is, in fact, normally distributed. We therefore require a really low p-value—less than 5%—to reject that null hypothesis and conclude the data is non-normal. But if a Shapiro–Wilk test instead returns a p-value greater than 5%, we will fail to reject that same null hypothesis and conclude that the data is normally distributed.

To run a pair of Shapiro–Wilk tests, one for each `mds` variable, we import the `stats` module from the `scipy` library, which contains various statistical functions for scientific computing, and then pass `stage1` and `stage2` to the `shapiro()` method:

```
>>> from scipy import stats

>>> print(stats.shapiro(mds.stage1))
ShapiroResult(statistic=0.9446673217389622, pvalue=0.29328758849732417)

>>> print(stats.shapiro(mds.stage2))
ShapiroResult(statistic=0.9290259439587454, pvalue=0.1478907551379664)
```

Because the p-values are above the 5% threshold, we should twice fail to reject the null hypothesis. So, according to our two Shapiro–Wilk tests, the `mds` variables `stage1` and `stage2` are both normally distributed.

DETECTING OUTLIERS

There are many ways to detect outliers in data. Statistical tests in this space have serious limitations, however. Boxplots display outliers, if there are any, as individual data points above and below the whiskers, but they don't actually tell us which records contain those outliers.

Let's first define an outlier as any data point that falls beyond three standard deviations from the mean, plus or minus, which is quite common. And of course we know the `stage1` and `stage2` means and standard deviations; we obtained these, along with other measures, when we called the `describe()` method.

So, a `stage1` outlier is any data point beyond the `stage1` mean plus or minus the product of 3 and the `stage1` standard deviation. We can define these, respectively, as `upper_threshold` and `lower_threshold`, where `194.55` is the mean and `29.62` is the standard deviation:

```
>>> upper_threshold = 194.55 + (3 * 29.62)
>>> lower_threshold = 194.55 - (3 * 29.62)
```

The following snippet of code subsets the `mds` data frame on those records that exceed either the `upper_threshold` or `lower_threshold`; the | operator means OR, so that only one condition must be satisfied. Python then returns a reduced data frame, `exceed_threshold`, or an empty data frame if `mds` contains zero records that meet either condition. Note the use of the backslash (\), which is used as a line continuation character in Python code:

```
>>> exceed_threshold = mds[(mds['stage1'] > upper_threshold) | \
>>>                        (mds['stage1'] < lower_threshold)]
>>> print(exceed_threshold)
Empty DataFrame
Columns: [stage1, stage2]
Index: []
```

The variable `stage1` does not contain any outliers, at least according to our criteria. We get the same results for `stage2`, in fact, after changing our parameters and rerunning the same snippet of code:

```
>>> upper_threshold = 251.45 + (3 * 51.11)
>>> lower_threshold = 251.45 - (3 * 51.11)
>>> exceed_threshold = mds[(mds['stage2'] > upper_threshold) | \
>>>                        (mds['stage2'] < lower_threshold)]
>>> print(exceed_threshold)
Empty DataFrame
Columns: [stage1, stage2]
Index: []
```

If either `stage1` or `stage2` contained any outliers, we would at least consider taking corrective action by removing them. One method is to transform the data to a different distribution; this might be a good option if `stage1` or `stage2` were not already normally distributed. We could then, of course, solve two problems with one operation. Another method is to simply remove outliers from the data. Although this may solve one problem, it can also introduce new issues—especially for short data frames like `mds`. Yet another method is to winsorize the outlying data points. *Winsorization* is the process of replacing extreme values with less extreme values. A data point more than three standard deviations from the mean can be modified so that it then falls within a specified percentile range.

There is no right way or best way of treating outliers; it depends on the circumstances. However, there is absolutely a right or best *process*: carefully consider the implications of each alternative, and always document your thought process for the purposes of transparency and reproducibility. Now let's fit our linear regression.

4.2.2 Fitting the model

We'll fit a simple linear regression by calling the `OLS()` method from the `statsmodels` library; `stage2` will be our dependent variable, and `stage1` will be our independent variable. We are therefore regressing `stage2` against `stage1` to estimate Stage 2 split times from Stage 1 split times.

> **NOTE** OLS is short for *ordinary least squares*. That's because linear regression minimizes the distances between the observed and predicted values of the dependent variable by estimating the sum of the squared differences between them. The method of estimation is known as "ordinary" to distinguish it from other regression techniques and "least squares" because, once more, it minimizes the squared differences.

Our first order of business is to import the `statsmodels` library and define our response variable, y:

```
>>> import statsmodels.api as sm
>>> y = mds['stage2']
```

Then we define our predictor variable, x:

```
>>> x = mds['stage1']
```

If we were instead fitting a multiple linear regression with a total of two predictors, stage1 and, let's say, second_variable, we would define x this way (note the extra set of brackets):

```
>>> x = mds[['stage1', 'second_variable']]
```

Next we add a constant to x, known as the *intercept*:

```
>>> x = sm.add_constant(x)
```

We can now fit our model, lm, and print the results:

- sm.OLS(y, x) initializes the regression using x (stage1) as the only independent variable and y (stage2) as the dependent variable. Because we previously *added* the constant to x, we only need to pass y and x; the constant is already accounted for.
- fit() fits the initialized model to the mds data frame and estimates the coefficients of the linear regression that minimizes the sum of squared differences between the observed and predicted values of y. These results and other meaningful statistics are read into an object called lm.
- print() returns the lm content in the form of what's called a *regression table*.

It takes just two lines of Python code to fit the regression and print the model output:

```
>>> lm = sm.OLS(y, x).fit()
>>> print(lm.summary())
                            OLS Regression Results
==============================================================================
Dep. Variable:                 stage2   R-squared:                       0.575
Model:                            OLS   Adj. R-squared:                  0.551
Method:                 Least Squares   F-statistic:                     24.35
Date:                Mon, 11 Mar 2024   Prob (F-statistic):           0.000107
Time:                        14:06:15   Log-Likelihood:                -97.991
No. Observations:                  20   AIC:                             200.0
Df Residuals:                      18   BIC:                             202.0
Df Model:                           1
Covariance Type:            nonrobust
==============================================================================
                 coef    std err          t      P>|t|      [0.025      0.975]
------------------------------------------------------------------------------
const         -3.0778     52.150     -0.059      0.954    -112.640     106.485
stage1         1.3083      0.265      4.934      0.000       0.751       1.865
==============================================================================
Omnibus:                        2.616   Durbin-Watson:                   2.326
Prob(Omnibus):                  0.270   Jarque-Bera (JB):                2.150
Skew:                           0.749   Prob(JB):                        0.341
Kurtosis:                       2.420   Cond. No.                     1.34e+03
==============================================================================
```

Notes:
[1] Standard Errors assume that the covariance matrix of the errors is correctly specified.
[2] The condition number is large, 1.34e+03. This might indicate that there are strong multicollinearity or other numerical problems.

It will take much more effort to review and evaluate these results and apply them.

4.2.3 Interpreting and evaluating the results

The statsmodels library returns regression results in tabular form, not as a scatter plot with a fitted regression line, because it prioritizes numerical analysis and statistical summaries over graphical representations. This makes sense for a couple of reasons. Although scatter plots can be useful for visualizing simple regressions with a single predictor, they aren't practical for models with multiple predictors, which require multidimensional plots that are difficult to display. For starters, we should be more interested in measures of predictive power, statistical significance, and the like, which we only get from a regression table. And in any event, scatter plots are derived from just a subset of these same results, so it only makes sense to first evaluate the raw data and then have the flexibility to create a plot over it. That being said, let's unpack these results by interpreting and evaluating the most critical measures one by one.

COEF

In the model output, under coef, the intercept (β_0) equals -3.0778, and the slope (β_1) equals 1.3083. We therefore get the fitted regression by plugging these two values into the linear equation:

$$\hat{y} = -3.0778 + 1.3083(x)$$

or

$$stage2 = -3.0778 + 1.3083(stage1)$$

So, if a runner's Stage 1 split time was 193 minutes, we would then predict his Stage 2 split time to equal

$$stage2 = -3.0778 + 1.3083(193)$$

or 249 minutes (rounded to the nearest whole number).

Let's illustrate these same results with a Matplotlib scatter plot that contains the observed values for stage1 and stage2 overlayed with the fitted regression line. Here's the snippet of code:

```
>>> import matplotlib.pyplot as plt
>>> plt.scatter(mds['stage1'], mds['stage2'])
>>> plt.xlim(150, 260)
```

- `import matplotlib.pyplot as plt` — Imports the matplotlib library
- `plt.scatter(mds['stage1'], mds['stage2'])` — Draws a scatter plot with stage1 data on the x axis and stage2 data on the y axis
- `plt.xlim(150, 260)` — Establishes the minimum and maximum values of the x axis

```
>>> plt.ylim(150, 350)              ⟵┘ Establishes the minimum and
>>> yhat = -3.078 + (1.3083 * x)       maximum values of the y axis         Calculates the predicted
>>> plt.plot(x, yhat, linewidth = 2,                                        values from the simple
>>>          color = 'red')                                              ⟵┘ linear regression equation
>>> plt.title('2021 Marathon Des Sables - Top 20 Male Finishers\n'      Plots the regression line
>>>           'y = -3.078 + (1.3083 * x)\n'                          ⟵┘ and defines the aesthetics
>>>           'R-squared = 0.575',                  ⟵┐ Sets the
>>>           fontweight = 'bold')                     title        ⟵┐ Sets the
>>> plt.xlabel('Stage 1 Running Time (min)')                           x axis label
>>> plt.ylabel('Stage 2 Running Time (min)')       ⟵┐ Sets the
>>> plt.grid()              ⟵┐ Adds vertical and      y axis label
>>> plt.show()        ⟵┐      horizontal grid
                 Displays     lines to the plot
                 the plot
```

Figure 4.5 shows our scatter plot, where each point represents the observed `stage1` and `stage2` values from a row in the `mds` data frame, and the fitted regression line represents the predictions for `stage2`. It's especially important to understand how the slope and intercept are derived. Although other measures are critical for evaluating fit, the coefficient estimates represent the cornerstone of regression analysis by quantifying the relationship between variables and calculating predictions that drive decision-making.

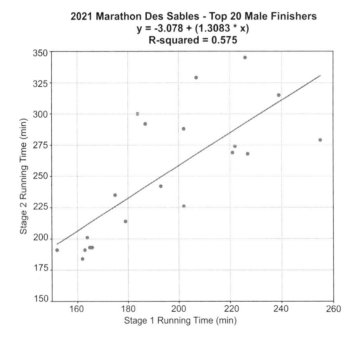

Figure 4.5 A scatter plot that displays the observed `stage1` and `stage2` values from the `mds` data frame, their respective x and y coordinates, and a regression line that represents the predictions for `stage2` from a simple linear regression where `stage2` was regressed against `stage1`. The regression line is drawn by applying the linear equation at the top of the plot. R-squared is one of several metrics contained in the model output; it represents the percentage of variance in `stage2` that can be explained by changes in `stage1`.

Let's begin by revisiting the linear equation for a simple regression:

$$y = \beta_0 + \beta_1 x + \epsilon$$

We require the means and totals for `stage1` and `stage2` to calculate the intercept and slope. The `stage1` and `stage2` means equal `194.55` and `251.45`, respectively; these were obtained when we passed the `mds` data frame to the `describe()` method. The `stage1` and `stage2` sums can be derived by multiplying their means by the `mds` record count or, better yet, making a pair of calls to the `sum()` method:

```
>>> stage1_sum = mds['stage1'].sum()
>>> print(stage1_sum)
3891

>>> stage2_sum = mds['stage2'].sum()
>>> print(stage2_sum)
5029
```

The slope represents the rate of change in the dependent variable for a one-unit change in the independent variable; it therefore quantifies the strength and direction of the linear relationship between variables. It can be calculated by plugging the `stage1` and `stage2` totals (x and y) and the `stage1` and `stage2` means ($\bar{x}$ and $\bar{y}$) into the following formula (see table 4.1 for reference):

$$\beta_1 = \frac{\sum (x - \bar{x})(y - \bar{y})}{\sum (x - \bar{x})^2}$$

or

$$\beta_1 = \frac{21813.05}{16672.95} = 1.308$$

The intercept, meanwhile, represents the value of the dependent variable when the independent variable (or variables) is equal to zero; it therefore indicates the point where the regression line intersects the y axis. It can be calculated by adding the slope and the `stage1` and `stage2` means to the following formula:

$$\beta_0 = \bar{y} - \beta_1 \bar{x}$$

or

$$\beta_0 = 251.45 - 1.308\,(194.55) = -3.0778$$

The coefficient estimates represent the most significant output from regression analysis. They help us understand and quantify the association between independent and dependent variables. By regressing `stage2` against `stage1`, we've discovered that for every one-unit (or one-minute) increase in `stage1`, we should expect `stage2` to increase by 1.3083. The other measures worth evaluating have much less to do with quantifying the association between variables and more to do with assessing goodness of fit.

Table 4.1 Totals to help derive slope estimates. Fractional numbers are rounded to two decimal places. The first two columns, from left to right, represent the observed split times. The slope is derived by dividing the total in the last column by the total in the third column, but these totals can only be derived by first computing the same for each observation in the data.

x	y	$(x - \bar{x})^2$	$(x - \bar{x})(y - \bar{y})$
152	191	$(152 - 194.55)^2 = 1{,}810.50$	$(152 - 194.55)(191 - 251.45) = 2{,}572.15$
162	184	$(162 - 194.55)^2 = 1{,}059.50$	$(152 - 194.55)(184 - 251.45) = 2{,}195.50$
165	193	$(165 - 194.55)^2 = 873.20$	$(152 - 194.55)(193 - 251.45) = 1{,}727.20$
163	191	$(163 - 194.55)^2 = 995.40$	$(152 - 194.55)(191 - 251.45) = 1{,}907.20$
166	193	$(166 - 194.55)^2 = 815.10$	$(152 - 194.55)(193 - 251.45) = 1{,}668.75$
187	292	$(187 - 194.55)^2 = 57.00$	$(152 - 194.55)(292 - 251.45) = -306.15$
175	235	$(175 - 194.55)^2 = 382.20$	$(152 - 194.55)(235 - 251.45) = 321.60$
202	226	$(202 - 194.55)^2 = 55.50$	$(152 - 194.55)(226 - 251.45) = -189.60$
179	214	$(179 - 194.55)^2 = 241.80$	$(152 - 194.55)(214 - 251.45) = 582.35$
222	274	$(222 - 194.55)^2 = 753.50$	$(152 - 194.55)(274 - 251.45) = 618.00$
184	300	$(184 - 194.55)^2 = 111.30$	$(152 - 194.55)(300 - 251.45) = -512.20$
193	242	$(193 - 194.55)^2 = 2.40$	$(152 - 194.55)(242 - 251.45) = 14.65$
255	279	$(255 - 194.55)^2 = 3{,}654.20$	$(152 - 194.55)(279 - 251.45) = 1{,}665.40$
202	288	$(202 - 194.55)^2 = 55.50$	$(152 - 194.55)(288 - 251.45) = 272.30$
221	269	$(221 - 194.55)^2 = 699.60$	$(152 - 194.55)(269 - 251.45) = 464.20$
207	329	$(207 - 194.55)^2 = 155.00$	$(152 - 194.55)(329 - 251.45) = 965.50$
227	268	$(227 - 194.55)^2 = 1{,}053.00$	$(152 - 194.55)(268 - 251.45) = 537.05$
239	315	$(239 - 194.55)^2 = 1{,}975.80$	$(152 - 194.55)(315 - 251.45) = 2{,}824.80$
164	201	$(164 - 194.55)^2 = 933.30$	$(152 - 194.55)(201 - 251.45) = 1{,}541.25$
226	345	$(226 - 194.55)^2 = 989.10$	$(152 - 194.55)(345 - 251.45) = 2{,}942.15$
3891	5,029	16,672.95	21,813.05

R-SQUARED

In the model output, R-squared is equal to 0.575. R-squared (R^2), the coefficient of determination, equals the percentage of the variance in the response variable that can be explained by the independent variable. So, 57.5% of the variance in Stage 2 split times from the top 20 male finishers in the 2021 Marathon des Sables can be explained by their Stage 1 split times. R^2 is a fundamental and significant measure of fit for regression analysis—either fixed to just one model or even to compare different models fitted to the same data. Because it's a squared number and represents the percentage of the variance in the response variable caused by the one predictor in a simple regression or the two or more predictors in a multiple regression, R^2 will always equal a number between 0 and 1. In order for R^2 to equal 1, every data point must lie on the regression line, which is rare.

Adding independent variables typically produces increases in R^2, even when those additional variables are statistically insignificant and therefore don't help to further explain variances in the response variable. When that's the case, R^2 and Adjusted R^2, which are typically aligned in a simple regression, diverge. That's because Adjusted R^2 adds a penalty for including unnecessary predictors; it therefore attempts to balance model complexity with explanatory power. When R^2 and Adjusted R^2 differ significantly, Adjusted R^2 should be prioritized for quantifying model fit. In such cases, it's advisable to perform model reduction by systematically removing insignificant predictors to improve the model's accuracy and interpretability.

The most direct way of deriving R^2 is to divide the sum of squares regression (SSR) by the sum of squares total (SST):

$$R^2 = \frac{\text{SSR}}{\text{SST}}$$

The SST is a measure of the total variability in the dependent variable without consideration of any predictors (this and other measures are squared to prevent positive and negative results from potentially canceling each other out). Mathematically, it is equal to the sum of the squared differences between the observed values of the dependent variable and the overall mean of the dependent variable:

$$\text{SST} = \sum (y - \bar{y})^2$$

Thus, observed values far from the stage2 mean will return a high sum of squares, and observed values close to the mean will return a low sum of squares. A pair of examples with the aid of a table should provide all the further transparency we need (see table 4.2). Consider just the second and third columns from the left: the stage2 column contains the observed values from the mds variable stage2, and the SST column equals their respective sum of squares, or the variability of each observed value relative to the stage2 mean. Where the stage2 column value is 184, which of course is distant from the stage2 mean of 251.45, the sum of squares equals 4,549.50, or the product of (184 − 251.45) and (184 − 251.45), or simply (184 − 251.45)^2. Where the stage2 column value instead equals 242, a value much closer to the stage2 mean, the sum of squares equals just 89.30, or (242 − 251.45)^2. Adding the individual sum of squares returns the SST, 49,636.95.

Table 4.2 The sum of squares summary for the fitted linear regression. The stage1 and stage2 columns represent, respectively, the observed values from the two mds variables. SST equals the sum of squares total, or the total variability in the dependent variable without the consideration of any predictors. The yhat column contains the predictions for the response variable from the fitted regression. SSE equals the sum of squares error, or the portion of the SST that can't be explained by the regression; and SSR equals the sum of squares regression, or the percentage of the variance in the dependent variable explained by the model.

x stage1	y stage2	$(y - \bar{y})^2$ SST	$\hat{y}$ yhat	$(y - \hat{y})^2$ SSE	$(\hat{y} - \bar{y})^2$ SSR
152	191	3,654.20	195.78	22.88	3098.73
162	184	4,549.50	208.87	618.36	1813.33
165	193	3,416.40	212.79	391.71	1494.46
163	191	3,654.20	210.18	367.68	1,703.62
166	193	3,416.40	214.10	445.21	1,395.02
187	292	1,644.30	241.57	2,542.75	97.53
175	235	270.60	225.87	83.27	654.10
202	226	647.70	261.20	1,238.96	95.04
179	214	1,402.50	231.11	292.68	413.80
222	274	508.50	287.36	178.62	1,289.87
184	300	2,357.10	237.65	3,887.60	190.46
193	242	89.30	249.42	55.12	4.10
255	279	759.00	330.54	2,656.24	6,255.02
202	288	1,335.90	261.20	718.30	95.04
221	269	308.00	286.06	290.92	1,197.61
207	329	6,014.00	267.74	3,752.75	265.37
227	268	273.90	293.91	671.14	1,802.54
239	315	4,038.60	309.61	29.10	3,382.11
164	201	2,545.20	211.48	109.90	1,597.33
226	345	8,751.60	292.60	2,745.97	1,693.16
		49,636.95		21,099.16	28,538.24

It's much easier to use Python as a calculator to get this result. In the following snippet of code, which requires numpy, ** is the exponential operator. When coupled with the numeral 2, it means we're raising the result contained within the parentheses by the power of 2:

```
>>> import numpy as np
>>> SST = np.sum((mds['stage2'] - np.mean(mds['stage2'])) ** 2)
```

```
>>> print(SST)
49636.950000000004
```

The SSR, meanwhile, quantifies the variability in the dependent variable explained by the regression model. It represents the sum of squared differences between the predicted values of the dependent variable and the mean of those values:

$$\text{SSR} = \sum (\hat{y} - \bar{y})^2$$

So, predictions far removed from the stage2 mean will return a high sum of squares, whereas other predictions close to the mean will return a low sum of squares. Now consider the yhat and SSR columns in table 4.2: yhat represents the predicted values for the dependent variable from our regression model, and SSR equals the sum of squares, or the variability of our model's predictions for stage2 relative to the stage2 mean. With respect to the top record in our table, the sum of squares equals 3,098.73, which in turn is the product of (195.78 − 251.45) and (195.78 − 251.45), or (195 − 251.45)^2. By adding the individual sum of squares, we get the SSR, 28,538.24.

We get the same result by plugging the SSR equation into Python—that is, by squaring the differences between the predicted values for stage2 and the mean of stage2 and summing the results—as long as we ignore the rounding differences:

```
>>> SSR = np.sum((lm.predict(x) - np.mean(mds['stage2'])) ** 2)
>>> print(SSR)
28537.790271217757
```

The object we created when fitting our regression, lm, contains a variable called fittedvalues, which holds the predictions for the dependent variable stage2. Whereas yhat represents predictions that were more or less calculated offline by plugging the coefficients into the linear equation, fittedvalues contains the actual predictions for stage2 from the fitted regression. They are slightly different paths to the same destination:

```
>>> print(lm.fittedvalues)
0     195.782270
1     208.865168
2     212.790037
3     210.173458
4     214.098327
5     241.572412
6     225.872935
7     261.196759
8     231.106094
9     287.362554
10    237.647543
11    249.422151
12    330.536117
13    261.196759
14    286.054265
```

```
15     267.738208
16     293.904003
17     309.603480
18     211.481747
19     292.595713
dtype: float64
```

Now that we have the SSR and the SST, we can divide one by the other and get the coefficient of determination for our linear regression:

$$R^2 = \frac{\text{SSR}}{\text{SST}} = \frac{28537.79}{49636.95} = 0.575$$

In Python, it's like so:

```
>>> R2 = SSR / SST
>>> print(R2)
0.5749303748763321
```

The SSE, or the sum of squares error, sometimes referred to as the sum of squared residuals, represents that portion of the SST that the SSR fails to explain. It therefore equals the difference between the SST and the SSR:

$$\text{SSE} = \text{SST} - \text{SSR} = 21099.16$$

This means the SST equals the sum of the SSR and the SSE:

$$\text{SST} = \text{SSR} + \text{SSE} = 49636.95$$

We can confirm both by again using Python as a calculator:

```
>>> SSE = SST - SSR
>>> print(SSE)
21099.159728782248

>>> SST_new = SSR + SSE
>>> print(SST_new)
49636.950000000004
```

The SSE represents the sum of the squared differences between the observed and predicted values for the dependent variable:

$$\text{SSE} = \sum (y - \hat{y})^2$$

In Python, we sum and square the residuals, like so:

```
>>> SSE = np.sum(lm.resid ** 2)
>>> print(SSE)
21099.159728782255
```

Let's return to table 4.2 one last time. The 20 individual values listed in the SSE column equal the squared differences between the observed and predicted values for `stage2`. Thus, the SSE for the top record equals 22.88, which is equal to $(191 - 195.78)^2$. The SSE, 21,099.16, is then obtained by adding the results of the 20 sum of squares.

Now that we have the SSE, we can next demonstrate a second way of deriving R^2. Because the SSE represents the portion of the SST that the SSR fails to account for, we can derive R^2 by dividing the SSE by the SST and subtracting the quotient from 1:

$$R^2 = 1 - \frac{\text{SSE}}{\text{SST}} = 1 - \frac{21099.16}{49636.95} = 0.575$$

The following are a few notes about R^2:

- R^2 represents the percentage of variation in the dependent variable explained by the one predictor in a simple regression and the two or more predictors in a multiple regression.
- R^2 will always equal a number between 0 and 1, where 0 means the predictors don't explain any of the variance in the response variable and 1 means the predictors explain all of the variability.
- R^2 is a critical goodness of fit measure for one model or for competing models fit to the same data.

Although R^2 is paramount among goodness of fit measures, model strength must be evaluated by considering other measures as well.

F-STATISTIC

The `F-statistic`, equal to `24.35`, is a measure of the overall significance of a regression. It evaluates whether the model explains a statistically significant amount of the variance in the dependent variable compared to a model with just an intercept and therefore no predictors. The formula for the F-statistic is

$$F = \frac{\frac{\text{SSR}}{p}}{\frac{\text{SSE}}{n-p-1}}$$

where

- SSR is the sum of squares regression.
- SSE is the sum of squares error.
- n is the number of observations.
- p is the number of predictors.

This means

$$F = \frac{\frac{25838.24}{1}}{\frac{21099.16}{20-1-1}} = \frac{25838.24}{1172.17} = 24.35$$

104   CHAPTER 4 *Fitting a linear regression*

To interpret the F-statistic, we need to bump it against the critical value in an F-table; it doesn't have any immediate meaning by itself. If the F-statistic is greater than the critical value (see figure 4.6), we can then conclude that the model explains a statistically significant amount of the variance in the response variable.

The critical value is located by first selecting a significance level (5% is most common) and then cross-referencing the number of independent variables in the regression with the number of observations in the data minus 1. The rows represent the former (1), and the columns represent the latter (19). Because the F-statistic is greater than the critical value of 4.38, we conclude that a statistically significant amount of the variance in `stage2` is explained by our simple linear regression.

	F-table of Critical Values of α = 0.05 for F(df1, df2)																	
	DF1=1	2	3	4	5	6	7	8	9	10	12	15	20	24	30	40	60	120	∞
DF2=1	161.45	199.50	215.71	224.58	230.16	233.99	236.77	238.88	240.54	241.88	243.91	245.95	248.01	249.05	250.10	251.14	252.20	253.25	254.31
2	18.51	19.00	19.16	19.25	19.30	19.33	19.35	19.37	19.38	19.40	19.41	19.43	19.45	19.45	19.46	19.47	19.48	19.49	19.50
3	10.13	9.55	9.28	9.12	9.01	8.94	8.89	8.85	8.81	8.79	8.74	8.70	8.66	8.64	8.62	8.59	8.57	8.55	8.53
4	7.71	6.94	6.59	6.39	6.26	6.16	6.09	6.04	6.00	5.96	5.91	5.86	5.80	5.77	5.75	5.72	5.69	5.66	5.63
5	6.61	5.79	5.41	5.19	5.05	4.95	4.88	4.82	4.77	4.74	4.68	4.62	4.56	4.53	4.50	4.46	4.43	4.40	4.37
6	5.99	5.14	4.76	4.53	4.39	4.28	4.21	4.15	4.10	4.06	4.00	3.94	3.87	3.84	3.81	3.77	3.74	3.70	3.67
7	5.59	4.74	4.35	4.12	3.97	3.87	3.79	3.73	3.68	3.64	3.57	3.51	3.44	3.41	3.38	3.34	3.30	3.27	3.23
8	5.32	4.46	4.07	3.84	3.69	3.58	3.50	3.44	3.39	3.35	3.28	3.22	3.15	3.12	3.08	3.04	3.01	2.97	2.93
9	5.12	4.26	3.86	3.63	3.48	3.37	3.29	3.23	3.18	3.14	3.07	3.01	2.94	2.90	2.86	2.83	2.79	2.75	2.71
10	4.96	4.10	3.71	3.48	3.33	3.22	3.14	3.07	3.02	2.98	2.91	2.85	2.77	2.74	2.70	2.66	2.62	2.58	2.54
11	4.84	3.98	3.59	3.36	3.20	3.09	3.01	2.95	2.90	2.85	2.79	2.72	2.65	2.61	2.57	2.53	2.49	2.45	2.40
12	4.75	3.89	3.49	3.26	3.11	3.00	2.91	2.85	2.80	2.75	2.69	2.62	2.54	2.51	2.47	2.43	2.38	2.34	2.30
13	4.67	3.81	3.41	3.18	3.03	2.92	2.83	2.77	2.71	2.67	2.60	2.53	2.46	2.42	2.38	2.34	2.30	2.25	2.21
14	4.60	3.74	3.34	3.11	2.96	2.85	2.76	2.70	2.65	2.60	2.53	2.46	2.39	2.35	2.31	2.27	2.22	2.18	2.13
15	4.54	3.68	3.29	3.06	2.90	2.79	2.71	2.64	2.59	2.54	2.48	2.40	2.33	2.29	2.25	2.20	2.16	2.11	2.07
16	4.49	3.63	3.24	3.01	2.85	2.74	2.66	2.59	2.54	2.49	2.42	2.35	2.28	2.24	2.19	2.15	2.11	2.06	2.01
17	4.45	3.59	3.20	2.96	2.81	2.70	2.61	2.55	2.49	2.45	2.38	2.31	2.23	2.19	2.15	2.10	2.06	2.01	1.96
18	4.41	3.55	3.16	2.93	2.77	2.66	2.58	2.51	2.46	2.41	2.34	2.27	2.19	2.15	2.11	2.06	2.02	1.97	1.92
19	**4.38**	3.52	3.13	2.90	2.74	2.63	2.54	2.48	2.42	2.38	2.31	2.23	2.16	2.11	2.07	2.03	1.98	1.93	1.88
20	4.35	3.49	3.10	2.87	2.71	2.60	2.51	2.45	2.39	2.35	2.28	2.20	2.12	2.08	2.04	1.99	1.95	1.90	1.84
21	4.32	3.47	3.07	2.84	2.68	2.57	2.49	2.42	2.37	2.32	2.25	2.18	2.10	2.05	2.01	1.96	1.92	1.87	1.81
22	4.30	3.44	3.05	2.82	2.66	2.55	2.46	2.40	2.34	2.30	2.23	2.15	2.07	2.03	1.98	1.94	1.89	1.84	1.78
23	4.28	3.42	3.03	2.80	2.64	2.53	2.44	2.37	2.32	2.27	2.20	2.13	2.05	2.01	1.96	1.91	1.86	1.81	1.76
24	4.26	3.40	3.01	2.78	2.62	2.51	2.42	2.36	2.30	2.25	2.18	2.11	2.03	1.98	1.94	1.89	1.84	1.79	1.73

Figure 4.6   A snippet from a typical F-table where the selected significance level equals 5%. The critical value is located at the intersection of the predictor count (1) and the observation count minus 1 (19). Because the F-statistic is greater than the critical value, the model explains a statistically significant amount of the variance in the response variable.

However, we don't reject or fail to reject a null hypothesis based on the F-statistic. We do so by evaluating the p-value associated with the F-statistic.

PROB (F-STATISTIC)
`Prob (F-statistic)`, which is equal to `0.000107`, represents the p-value associated with the F-statistic. It indicates the probability of observing an F-statistic as extreme, or

even more extreme, than the one calculated from the data, under the assumption that the null hypothesis is true.

When modeling a linear relationship between variables, the null hypothesis states that all regression coefficients except the intercept are equal to zero, and therefore the independent variables have no effect whatsoever on the dependent variable. However, when the p-value from the F-statistic is less than the 5% threshold for significance, as it is here, we should reject that null hypothesis and conclude that at least one predictor in the regression has a statistically significant effect on the dependent variable. On the other hand, a p-value above that same 5% threshold would suggest the regression as a whole is not statistically significant, and therefore we should fail to reject the same null hypothesis.

In a simple linear regression, a p-value less than 5% indicates that the single predictor is statistically significant at the commonly used 5% significance level, meaning there's less than a 5% chance that the observed association is due to random variation. The 5% threshold is an arbitrary convention, often chosen for convenience, and can be applied in either a one-tailed or a two-tailed test depending on the hypothesis. However, in regression analysis, two-tailed tests are typically used because we are often testing whether a coefficient is significantly different from zero in either direction. In multiple regression, a model with a p-value below 5% suggests that at least one predictor is statistically significant, although others may not be. In this case, model reduction—removing statistically insignificant predictors—can help simplify the model and improve interpretability.

P>|T|

`P>|t|` represents the p-value for each predictor. The p-value for `stage1` equals `0.000`, so it is therefore statistically significant. Had we instead fit a multiple regression with a mix of significant and insignificant predictors, we would need to balance model complexity with explanatory power. The preferred approach in this case is to fit a reduced model that includes only the statistically significant predictors, simplifying the model while retaining its most meaningful explanatory variables.

We've fit our model and assessed its most critical outputs. Now it's important to determine whether our conclusions are valid by testing the underlying model assumptions.

4.2.4 *Testing model assumptions*

Once a regression has been fit and the key measures interpreted and evaluated, a series of tests should then be run to (hopefully) confirm that the regression results are reliable. Our trust in the model output should be temporarily paused until we've determined that all linear regression assumptions have been tested and validated.

ASSUMPTION #1: LINEARITY BETWEEN VARIABLES

There must be a linear relationship between the independent and dependent variables. In other words, the relationship is assumed to be adequately represented by a straight line so that changes in the predictor cause proportional changes, positive or negative, in the response variable. Although R^2 measures the proportion of variance in the dependent variable explained by the model, it doesn't confirm whether the relationship between variables is actually linear. A high R^2 value could still occur in cases where a nonlinear relationship exists, making it essential to use visual methods instead.

The best method of checking this assumption is to draw a residuals plot, or a scatter plot that displays the fitted values against the residual values, and evaluate the results. Once again, we'll use Matplotlib. Here's the snippet of code:

```
>>> plt.scatter(lm.fittedvalues, lm.resid)
>>> plt.axhline(y = 0, color = 'red',
>>>             linestyle = '--')
>>> plt.title('Residuals Plot')
>>> plt.xlabel('Fitted Values')
>>> plt.ylabel('Residuals')
>>> plt.show()
```

- `plt.scatter(...)` Draws a scatter plot with fittedvalues and lm.resid (the residuals) on the y axis
- `plt.title(...)` Sets the title
- `plt.axhline(...)` Draws a red and dashed horizontal line where y = 0
- `plt.xlabel(...)` Sets the x-axis label
- `plt.ylabel(...)` Sets the y-axis label
- `plt.show()` Displays the plot

Figure 4.7 shows the result: a scatter plot where the fitted values from the linear regression are plotted along the x axis and the residuals are plotted along the y axis. We should conclude that the assumption of linearity between variables is met when the residuals appear randomly scattered around the horizontal axis, as they do here. This randomness indicates that the model has successfully captured the systematic (linear) component of the relationship between the predictor and response variables. If a nonlinear pattern were present, such as a curve or funnel shape, it would suggest that a linear model was insufficient and that some structure in the data remained unexplained. But in this case, the absence of such a pattern supports the validity of the linearity assumption.

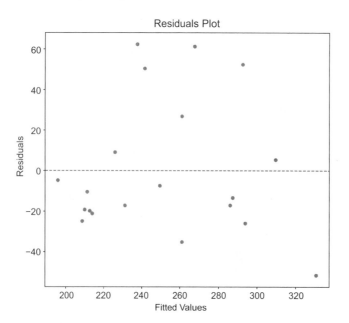

Figure 4.7 A residuals plot that displays the fitted values from a linear regression on the x axis and the residuals from the same model on the y axis. Linearity between variables is confirmed when the data points do not follow any obvious pattern or trend.

ASSUMPTION #2: INDEPENDENCE OF RESIDUALS

The residuals are assumed to be independent of one another; in other words, it's assumed that there is no correlation between them. Correlation between the residuals specifically refers to the degree to which the errors from the linear regression are related to each other. A meaningful correlation between the residuals might be an indication that the regression model failed to detect some systematic pattern in the data.

The Durbin–Watson test is a statistical method used to detect correlation in the residuals of a regression model. It provides a test statistic ranging from 0 to 4, which helps determine whether we should reject the null hypothesis of no correlation. When the test statistic falls between 1.5 and 2.5, we generally fail to reject the null hypothesis, indicating that the assumption of independent residuals is likely satisfied. If the statistic falls outside this range, we may reject the null hypothesis, suggesting potential correlation in the residuals. The closer the test statistic is to the extremes (0 or 4), the stronger the evidence for positive or negative correlation, respectively.

The Durbin–Watson test statistic is calculated as the ratio of the squared differences between successive residuals (numerator) to the total sum of squared residuals (denominator). In the regression table, the Durbin–Watson statistic is given as 2.326, which allows us to conclude that we should fail to reject the null hypothesis and that the assumption of independence in the residuals is satisfied. Alternatively, you can calculate it by importing the `statstools` module from the `statsmodels.stats` package and passing the residuals of the regression (e.g., `lm.resid`) to the `durbin_watson()` method:

```
>>> from statsmodels.stats.stattools import durbin_watson
>>> print(durbin_watson(lm.resid))
2.3264601831112186
```

So far, so good, but we have two more assumptions to test.

ASSUMPTION #3: HOMOSCEDASTICITY OF RESIDUALS

The residuals are also assumed to be homoscedastic and thus not heteroscedastic. Homoscedasticity refers to the expectation that the variability, or spread, of the residuals is consistent across all levels of the predictors; that is, the spread of the residuals should not increase or decrease as the values of the predictors change. This assumption is important because heteroscedasticity can lead to inefficient estimates and biased standard errors, which in turn can distort hypothesis tests and confidence intervals. If the variance of residuals increases or decreases systematically, it undermines the reliability of the model's inferences—making it more likely to incorrectly accept or reject statistical significance. Ensuring homoscedasticity, therefore, strengthens the validity of any conclusions drawn from the model.

The Breusch–Pagan test is a statistical method for detecting heteroscedasticity in the residuals of a regression model or, alternatively, whether the residuals have constant variance (homoscedasticity) across observations. The test works by assessing whether the variance of the residuals depends systematically on the values of the independent variables. The null hypothesis is that the residuals are homoscedastic. If the test returns a p-value less than 5%, we reject the null hypothesis and conclude that the residuals exhibit heteroscedasticity. Conversely, if the p-value is greater than 5%, we conclude that the residuals are homoscedastic, meaning the assumption of constant variance holds.

The Breusch–Pagan test statistic is calculated by regressing the squared residuals from the original regression model on the independent variables and examining the explained variance in this auxiliary regression. The test statistic is proportional to the explained variance in this second regression, where a high value indicates that variance in residuals may depend on predictor values, suggesting heteroscedasticity.

To perform a Breusch–Pagan test, first import the `het_breuschpagan` function from the `statsmodels.stats.diagnostic` module:

```
>>> from statsmodels.stats.diagnostic import het_breuschpagan
```

Then pass the residuals (`lm.resid`) and the independent variables (`lm.model.exog`) from the fitted regression model to the `het_breuschpagan()` method:

```
>>> lm_BreuschPagan = het_breuschpagan(lm.resid, lm.model.exog)
```

The `het_breuschpagan()` method calculates the test statistic, the p-value, and additional test details, returning them as a tuple. Because we are mainly interested in the p-value to assess the presence of heteroscedasticity, we can use `print()` to display only the second element of the tuple, which is the p-value:

```
>>> print(lm_BreuschPagan[1])
0.181071316321208
```

In this case, the p-value is greater than 5%, so we fail to reject the null hypothesis and conclude that the assumption of homoscedasticity (constant variance in residuals) has been satisfied.

ASSUMPTION #4: NORMALITY OF RESIDUALS

Finally, *the residuals are assumed to be normally distributed*. If this assumption is violated, it may affect the integrity of the coefficient estimates and the significance of the predictors. There are two main approaches to testing this: a visual, subjective method and a more precise statistical test.

One of the most common methods for assessing normality is to create a Quantile–Quantile (Q–Q) plot. In a Q–Q plot, the residuals are represented by points and are compared to a perfectly normal distribution, represented by a dashed line at a 45-degree angle. If the residuals follow a normal distribution, the points should roughly align along this line. Minor deviations may be acceptable depending on the context, but significant departures suggest a potential violation of the normality assumption. Here's a simple way to create a Q–Q plot using Matplotlib:

```
>>> stats.probplot(lm.resid,
>>>                dist = 'norm', plot = plt)
```
⟵ Creates the Q-Q plot and compares the distribution of the residuals to a normal distribution

4.2 Simple linear regression

```
>>> plt.gca().get_lines()[1].set_linestyle('--')    ← Adds aesthetics to the plot
>>> plt.title('Q-Q Plot')    ← Sets the title
>>> plt.show()    ← Displays the plot
```

After running this code, you'll see the Q–Q plot in figure 4.8, which visually indicates the degree of normality in the residuals. In this example, the Q–Q plot shows that the residuals deviate from the line of normality, especially at the tails, suggesting that they may not be normally distributed and may, in fact, have heavier tails or some degree of skewness. Although the Q–Q plot is a useful first check, interpreting it can be subjective. For a more definitive answer, we can apply a Jarque–Bera test, which provides a statistical basis for assessing normality.

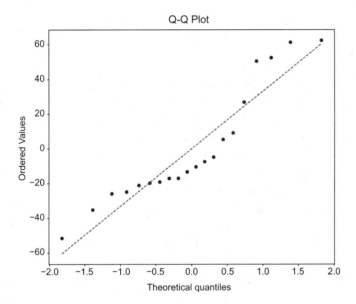

Figure 4.8 A Q–Q plot that displays the distribution of the residuals (points) versus a normal distribution (dashed line). Linear regression assumes that the residuals are normally distributed; however, our Q–Q plot might suggest otherwise.

The Jarque–Bera test calculates its statistic by measuring skewness and kurtosis (i.e., symmetry and tail thickness) in the distribution of the residuals. The null hypothesis is that the data is normally distributed. If the test returns a p-value less than 5%, we reject the null hypothesis and conclude that the residuals are not normally distributed. Here's how to calculate it directly from the residuals:

```
>>> from statsmodels.stats.stattools import jarque_bera
>>> print(jarque_bera(lm.resid))
SignificanceResult(statistic=2.150037983280995, pvalue=0.34129127355827205)
```

In this example, the p-value is 0.341, which of course is above the 5% threshold, allowing us to conclude that the residuals are likely normally distributed—even if the Q–Q plot might have suggested otherwise. Although the Q–Q plot gives a visual overview, the Jarque–Bera test provides a more rigorous measure of normality.

Finally, it's worth noting that if we were fitting a multiple linear regression, we would need to test an additional assumption: that the predictors are not highly correlated with each other, known as *multicollinearity*. Excessive multicollinearity can lead to overfitting, so reducing the model by removing redundant predictors may be necessary. We'll explore this concept further in the next chapter.

We've demonstrated linear regression in theory and in practice. But just as significantly, we've (hopefully) established a solid foundation for learning other modeling techniques. We'll pivot toward logistic regression next to solve a classification problem.

Summary

- Linear regression is a statistical method used to model the relationship between a numeric dependent variable and one or more independent variables by fitting a linear equation to observed data. It assumes a linear relationship between the independent and dependent variables, with the goal of estimating the parameters of the linear equation to minimize the overall difference between observed and predicted values. Linear regression is commonly used to predict and understand the relationship between variables across multiple domains, including economics, finance, and the social sciences.
- Goodness of fit should be evaluated from multiple measures. R^2, or the coefficient of determination, which equals a number between 0 and 1 that specifies the proportion of variance in the dependent variable explained by the regression, might be the most meaningful measure, but hardly the only measure that matters. Overall fit is determined by the F-statistic. Significance (and insignificance) are fixed by the p-values for the individual coefficients as well as the p-value for the model.
- Testing for model assumptions—linearity between variables, independence, homoscedasticity, and normality of the residuals—warrants the reliability and validity of regression results and therefore further facilitates interpretation and decision-making.
- Applying best practices along the way, like testing for normality in the predictors and removing any and all outliers from the data, contributes considerably to getting the best possible fit and guaranteeing positive results in post-regression tests.

Fitting a logistic regression

This chapter covers
- Model fitting
- Model interpretation and evaluation
- Classification metrics
- Data exploration through histograms and correlation heat maps

Logistic regression is a supervised learning method for predicting a binary response from one or more independent variables. It's commonly used for classification tasks where the dependent variable represents two possible categories or classes (e.g., pass or fail, presence or absence). It estimates the probability that a given instance belongs to a particular category based on the values of the independent variables, or predictors, using the logistic function (also known as the sigmoid function) that maps the output to a range between 0 and 1. We'll see how the value between 0 and 1 translates to binary outcomes in section 5.1.

The use cases are infinite. Here is just a small sample of problems that can be solved with logistic regression:

- Banks predicting whether a loan applicant will default, using factors such as credit score, credit history, income, and (if allowed) demographic data
- Wireless carriers predicting the likelihood of customers canceling their service, based on usage patterns and satisfaction scores
- Political scientists predicting election outcomes by analyzing survey data
- Meteorologists predicting the probability of rain from a mix of satellite and radar data, atmospheric humidity, cloud cover, and other factors

The results are immediately actionable. Banks, for instance, will reject a loan application if the probability of defaulting is greater than 50% or, alternatively, extend an amount of credit if that same probability is less than 50%.

When fitting a logistic regression, we are attempting to answer a series of questions previously applied to linear regression in chapter 4, but specifically focused on predicting binary outcomes:

- *Can it predict the probability of a dependent variable equaling yes (e.g., a customer will churn, a patient has heart disease)?* Logistic regression returns coefficients that can be plugged into an equation to predict binary outcomes.
- *Is there a meaningful relationship between the dependent variable and the one or more independent variables?* Logistic regression identifies which predictors have, and don't have, a statistically significant effect on the probability of a binary outcome.
- *How can it measure the relationship between predictors and outcomes?* Logistic regression provides quantitative insights into how changes in the predictors affect the probability of the binary outcome.
- *How does it assess the strength and direction of associations between variables?* The returned coefficient estimates measure the relationships between predictors and the log odds of the binary outcome.

Our journey will be very similar to the path blazed in the previous chapter. We'll get into the nuts and bolts of logistic regression, sometimes by comparing and contrasting it to linear modeling; we'll import a real data set and immediately go about analyzing and visualizing it, variable by variable; and then we'll demonstrate how to fit a multiple logistic regression, interpret and evaluate the results, apply the coefficient estimates to make binary predictions, and compute a set of classification metrics to further evaluate the predictive power of the model.

We'll be attempting to solve a rather innocuous classification problem: correctly predicting the variety of raisins from a set of physical properties. However, the methods demonstrated throughout this chapter can be applied to *any* problem, on *any* data set, across *any* domain—as long as the dependent variable is binary. Let's begin our journey with a deep dive into all things logistic regression.

5.1 Logistic regression vs. linear regression

Logistic regression is a supervised learning method used to model the relationship between a binary dependent variable and one or more independent variables, or predictors. A simple logistic regression is when the binary dependent variable is regressed against just one predictor, which can be numeric or categorical; a multiple logistic regression, on the other hand, is when the dependent variable is regressed against two or more predictors. In the previous chapter, we fit a simple regression; this time, we'll demonstrate how to fit a multiple regression.

In logistic regression, the dependent variable, which is typically coded as 0 or 1, is modeled as a function of the independent variables using the *logistic function*, also known as the *sigmoid function*. This function transforms the linear combination of the predictors into a probability for each record in the data that equals some value between 0 and 1. When the probability equals 50% or greater, the model is predicting the binary outcome to equal 1; conversely, when the probability is less than 50%, the model is instead predicting the binary outcome to equal 0.

The sigmoid function is typically written in its standard form as

$$\sigma(x) = \frac{1}{1 + e^{-x}}$$

This formulation is useful for visualizing the S-shaped curve, as shown in figure 5.1, where x is treated as a single continuous variable.

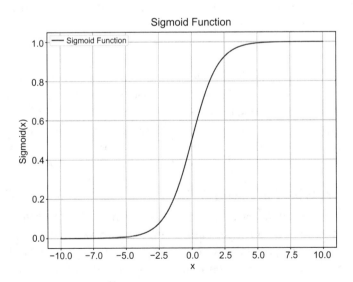

Figure 5.1 A graphical illustration of the sigmoid function. The sigmoid function is characterized by its S-shaped curve, compared to a linear function, which is characterized by a straight line.

We get probabilities by plugging the predictors and their coefficient estimates into this function, where the input is replaced by a linear combination of predictors:

$$P(Y = 1|X) = \frac{1}{1 + e^{-(\beta_0 + \beta_1 X_1 + \beta_2 X_2 + \beta_3 X_3)}}$$

where

- $P(Y = 1|X)$ is the probability of the outcome variable, designated as Y, being 1 given the predictor variables X.
- e is the base of the natural logarithm, equal to 2.72.
- β_0 is the intercept term.
- β_1, β_2, and β_3 are the coefficients of the predictor variables.
- $X1$, $X2$, and $X3$ are the predictor variables.

In linear regression we are trying to predict changes in a numeric dependent variable given the predictors; but in logistic regression, we are instead applying the sigmoid function to predict the probability of a binary dependent variable coded as 0 or 1 to be 1 from a single predictor in a simple regression or from two or more predictors in a multiple regression. Whereas the coefficients in linear modeling represent the change in the dependent variable for a one-unit change in the independent variable, the coefficient estimates in logistic regression represent the change in the log odds of the binary outcome for a one-unit change in the independent variable.

The sigmoid function, usually denoted as $\sigma(x)$, is a mathematical function that maps any real number to a value between 0 and 1. When the input x is large, either positive or negative, the value of e^{-x} approaches 0, causing the denominator of the fraction to become large, thereby resulting in $\sigma(x)$ being close to 1. Conversely, when x is large in the negative direction, e^{-x} subsequently becomes large, causing $\sigma(x)$ to approach 0.

Now that we have a good theoretical understanding of logistic regression and are aware of the differences between it and linear regression, we are prepared to take the next steps. We'll import a real data set, explore it, demonstrate how to fit a multiple logistic regression, explain how to interpret and evaluate and apply the model output, and show how to compute classification metrics to assess the model's accuracy and predictive power.

5.2 *Multiple logistic regression*

Our plan is to import a real data set that is both longer and wider than the data we worked with in the previous chapter. It contains a single binary variable (which will be our dependent variable) and several numeric variables (which will be our predictors). As mentioned earlier, our data set deals with raisins. Two varieties of raisins are grown in Turkey: Kecimen and Besni. Our data contains the morphological features for 450 Kecimen raisins and 450 Besni raisins. Morphological features typically refer to the size, shape, and other physical qualities of objects or other entities, usually in the context of image processing. In fact, the numeric variables are measured in pixels or derived from the pixel count (pixels represent the smallest unit of measurement in digital imaging). We'll discover that Kecimen and Besni raisins have several distinguishing qualities, which provides some hope that a logistic regression can accurately predict which raisin is of what variety given their morphological features.

Once we have imported the data, we'll analyze it in ways that go above and beyond the exploratory data analysis performed in chapter 4. Then we'll demonstrate how to fit a logistic regression model, how to digest the output, and how to calculate other measures that go a long way toward quantifying model accuracy and predictive power.

Data exploration is an exercise that typically involves a mix of basic statistical and visualization techniques to reveal patterns, trends, and relationships that might influence the scope and direction of more advanced methods. When preparing to fit a regression model, linear or logistic, exploratory data analysis helps us understand basic properties of each variable, such as counts for categorical variables or distributions for numeric variables; identify missing values and detect outliers; reveal relationships between variables; and even drive variable selection. Because we intend to fit a logistic regression with a binary dependent variable and numeric predictors, our preliminary analysis of the data will mostly focus on understanding the similarities and differences in the characteristics of every predictor segmented by category.

5.2.1 Importing and exploring the data

Our data set is a .csv file stored in our working directory. We read it into Python by importing the pandas library and then making a call to the pd.read_csv() method. The following line of code imports raisin_dataset.csv into a data frame called raisins:

```
>>> import pandas as pd
>>> raisins = pd.read_csv('raisin_dataset.csv')
```

Now that we've imported our data, we can call other methods to analyze and visualize it.

UNDERSTANDING THE DATA

The info() method in pandas returns a concise summary of the raisins data frame. A call to info() is a quick, easy, and logical starting point for any data exploration exercise:

```
>>> print(raisins.info())
<class 'pandas.core.frame.DataFrame'>
RangeIndex: 900 entries, 0 to 899
Data columns (total 8 columns):
 #   Column           Non-Null Count   Dtype
---  ------           --------------   -----
 0   Area             900 non-null     int64
 1   MajorAxisLength  900 non-null     float64
 2   MinorAxisLength  900 non-null     float64
 3   Eccentricity     900 non-null     float64
 4   ConvexArea       900 non-null     float64
```

```
5   Extent            900 non-null    float64
6   Perimeter         900 non-null    float64
7   Class             900 non-null    object
dtypes: float64(6), int64(1), object(1)
memory usage: 56.4+ KB
None
```

This tells us the following about the data:

- *The dimensions*—It's 900 × 8, or 900 rows by 8 columns.
- *The column names and types*—The morphological features are represented by seven integers and floats, and the one binary variable is Class.
- *The number of non-null values by variable*—This equals 0 across the width of the data frame.

The morphological features are defined as follows:

- *Area* represents the number of pixels within the boundary of each raisin.
- *Major axis length* is the length of the main axis, which is the longest line that can be drawn on the raisin grain.
- *Minor axis length* is the length of the small axis, which is the shortest line that can be drawn on the raisin grain.
- *Eccentricity* is a measure of how elongated or stretched a raisin grain is compared to an ellipse.
- *Convex area* represents the number of pixels within the total area enclosed by the outer perimeter of the raisin grain.
- *Extent* gives the ratio of the region formed by the raisin grain to the total pixels in the bounding box.
- *Perimeter* is a measure of the distance between the boundaries of the raisin grain and the pixels around it.

Of course, it's always helpful to view at least some of the content instead of just being aware of its dimensions and other properties; we'll next show how to best go about doing that, considering the length and width of the data.

VIEWING THE DATA

In the prior chapter, because we were working with a data frame that was just 20 rows long and 2 columns wide, it was practical to print the whole object. That's no longer an option. We first make a call to the set_option() method from the pandas library to instruct Python to print every column in the console, rather than just a few, for easy fit:

```
>>> pd.set_option('display.max_columns', None)
```

Then we pass our data frame to the head() and tail() methods, which return the first three and last three records, respectively. The head() and tail() methods will print whatever number of records are passed (although 10 or fewer should be sufficient for most use cases):

```
>>> print(raisins.head(n = 3))
    Area  MajorAxisLength  MinorAxisLength  Eccentricity  ConvexArea  Extent
0  87524           442.25           253.29          0.82     90546.0    0.76
1  75166           406.69           243.03          0.80     78789.0    0.68
2  90856           442.27           266.33          0.80     93717.0    0.64
   Perimeter    Class
0    1184.04  Kecimen
1    1121.79  Kecimen
2    1208.58  Kecimen

>>> print(raisins.tail(n = 3))
      Area  MajorAxisLength  MinorAxisLength  Eccentricity  ConvexArea
897  99657           431.71           298.84          0.72    106264.0
898  93523           476.34           254.18          0.85     97653.0
899  85609           512.08           215.27          0.91     89197.0
     Extent  Perimeter  Class
897    0.74    1292.83  Besni
898    0.66    1258.55  Besni
```

As previously mentioned, the binary dependent variable is typically coded as 0 or 1 before regressing it against one or more predictors. However, it's unlikely the raw data will ever be coded that way. So, you absolutely need to know how to transform the values, in this case from Kecimen and Besni, to 0 and 1. It doesn't matter which is which—as long as you keep in mind that when we fit our logistic regression, we're predicting the probability of the binary outcome equaling 1.

Transforming the original values requires just two lines of Python code. In the first, we map the categorical labels Kecimen and Besni to numerical form to subsequently convert them to equal 0 and 1, respectively:

```
>>> class_mapping = {'Kecimen': 0, 'Besni': 1}
```

In the second line of code, we call the map() method to map the values in the variable Class using the previously defined mapping dictionary. This line then replaces the original class labels, Kecimen and Besni, with their corresponding numerical values, 0 and 1, effectively converting the variable Class from categorical to numerical (but still binary):

```
>>> raisins['Class'] = raisins['Class'].map(class_mapping)
```

Let's confirm the success of this operation by rerunning the head() and tail() methods. This time, however, we add instructions to both methods so that head() and tail() return just a subset of the raisins variables. It's not necessary, after all, to again view the entire width of the raisins data frame; we merely want to confirm that the variable Class is now in numeric form:

```
>>> print(raisins[['Area', 'MajorAxisLength', 'Class']].head(n = 3))
    Area  MajorAxisLength  Class
0  87524           442.25      0
1  75166           406.69      0
2  90856           442.27      0
```

```
>>> print(raisins[['Area', 'MajorAxisLength', 'Class']].tail(n = 3))
      Area  MajorAxisLength  Class
897  99657           431.71      1
898  93523           476.34      1
899  85609           512.08      1
```

And it is—where `Class` equaled `Kecimen`, it now equals `0`, and where `Class` equaled `Besni`, it now equals `1`.

COMPUTING BASIC STATISTICS

In the previous chapter, we called the `describe()` method to return a series of descriptive statistics on two numeric variables. But now it makes much more sense to pull some of those same statistics divided by `Kecimen` versus `Besni`, or `0` versus `1`. So, rather than make another call to `describe()`, we instead call the `agg()` and `groupby()` methods to return the minimum (`min`), maximum (`max`), mean, median, standard deviation (`std`), and variance (`var`) from the numeric variables, grouped by the variable `Class`. Instructions are then provided to limit the results to two decimal places. Although `round(2)` is applied to limit results to two decimal places, large values may nevertheless appear in scientific notation due to `pandas` display defaults:

```
>>> basic_statistics = (raisins.groupby('Class') \
>>>                      .agg(['min', 'max', 'mean', 'median',
>>>                            'std', 'var']))
>>> print(basic_statistics.round(2))
        Area
          min     max       mean    median       std           var
Class
0       25387  180898   63413.47   61420.0  17727.77  3.142738e+08
1       40702  235047  112194.79  104426.5  39229.90  1.538985e+09
        MajorAxisLength
                   min     max    mean  median     std       var
Class
0               225.63  843.96  352.86  350.24   59.61   3553.54
1               274.17  997.29  509.00  493.19  105.77  11187.53
        MinorAxisLength
                   min     max    mean  median    std      var
Class
0               143.71  326.90  229.35  228.62  34.06  1159.96
1               172.51  492.28  279.62  273.36  50.76  2576.98
        Eccentricity
                 min   max  mean  median   std   var
Class
0               0.35  0.92  0.74    0.77  0.09  0.01
1               0.50  0.96  0.82    0.83  0.07  0.00
        ConvexArea
             min        max       mean    median       std           var
Class
0        26139.0   221396.0   65696.36   63826.5  19005.89  3.612239e+08
1        41924.0   278217.0  116675.82  108062.5  40797.07  1.664401e+09
```

```
        Extent
          min    max   mean   median    std     var
Class
0         0.45   0.84   0.71    0.71    0.04    0.0
1         0.38   0.83   0.69    0.70    0.06    0.0

        Perimeter
          min      max      mean    median     std       var
Class
0         619.07   2253.56   983.69   977.93   150.31   22591.74
1         771.80   2697.75  1348.13  1305.80   246.80   60912.53
```

Let's briefly review these measures:

- The *minimum* is the smallest observed value.
- The *maximum* is the largest observed value.
- The *mean* represents the sum of all values divided by the number of records.
- The *median* represents the middle value when the data is sorted in ascending order. When the number of observations equals an even number, the median is derived by taking the average, or mean, of the two middle values. It is equivalent to the second quartile.
- The *standard deviation* quantifies the amount of variation, or dispersion, from the mean.
- So does the *variance*; it can be derived by squaring the standard deviation.

From these descriptive statistics, we can gather that Kecimen and Besni raisins generally have very different physical qualities: Kecimen raisins tend to be smaller and rounder compared to the Besni variety, whereas Besni raisins are larger and more elongated. These distinguishable qualities suggest that at least some of these variables might be good predictors of class labels. However, if the variances in these same measures are significant enough to negate some of the distinguishing characteristics that separate the two varieties of raisins, it could be an indication that the segmentation is far from perfect, which might result in misclassifications. We'll make a best attempt to flush out these similarities and dissimilarities by drawing a series of histograms.

HISTOGRAMS

A *histogram* is a graphical representation of the shape, central tendency, and dispersion of numeric data. It contains a series of adjacent bars, where the width of each bar corresponds to a specific range of values, represented on the *x* axis, and the height of each bar corresponds to the number of occurrences, represented on the *y* axis. A paired histogram displays two distributions—the same numeric data series, but split by class—so that their respective shapes can be readily compared and contrasted.

If Kecimen and Besni raisins have variances that indicate partial similarities in their respective distributions across the morphological features in our data, those will be revealed by drawing a series of paired histograms (see figure 5.2). Rather than create seven paired histograms from seven similar snippets of code, we'll create a matplotlib grid of paired histograms by iterating through each numeric variable in the raisins data frame:

```
>>> import matplotlib.pyplot as plt          ◁─┐ Libraries and modules must be
>>> fig, ((ax1, ax2, ax3), (ax4, ax5, ax6),     imported (once per script)
>>>       (ax7, ax8, ax9)) = plt.subplots(nrows = 3,   before running subsequent code.
>>>                                       ncols = 3,     ◁─ Creates a 3 × 3 grid of subplots
>>>                                       figsize = (8, 10))  ax1 through ax9 that, when
                                                              displayed, will be 8 × 10 in size
>>> axes = [ax1, ax2, ax3, ax4, ax5,          ◁─ Creates a list of subplots
>>>         ax6, ax7, ax8, ax9]                  ax1 through ax9
>>> columns = ['Area', 'MajorAxisLength', 'MinorAxisLength',   ◁─ Creates a list of
>>>            'Eccentricity', 'ConvexArea',                       column names
>>>            'Extent', 'Perimeter']                              to be plotted
>>> for i, column in enumerate(columns):      ◁─ Initiates a loop that iterates
>>>     for class_label,                        over each column name
>>>     data in raisins.groupby('Class'): \   ◁─ Initiates a loop that iterates
>>>         data[column] \                      over each unique value in Class
>>>         .hist(alpha = 0.5,
>>>         label = class_label,              ◁─ Plots the paired histograms, which are configured
>>>         ax = axes[i])                        to be transparent to show overlapping shapes
>>>     axes[i].set_title(f'{column}')        ◁─ Sets the title for each histogram
>>>     axes[i].set_xlabel(column)               to equal the column name
>>>     axes[i].set_ylabel('Frequency')       ◁─ Sets the x-axis label for each histogram
>>>     axes[i].legend(labels = ['Kecimen',      to also equal the column name
>>>                              'Besni'])    ◁─ Sets the y-axis label for each histogram
>>> for ax in [ax8, ax9]:                     ◁─ Establishes a common
>>>     ax.axis('off')       ◁─ Hides subplots ax8   legend across histograms
                                and ax9; otherwise,
>>> plt.tight_layout()   ◁─   the 3 × 3 grid          Initiates a loop over plots ax8 and
>>> plt.show()           ◁─   would contain           ax9 (which actually don't exist)
                              two empty plots
          Displays the grid
                              Provides vertical separation between adjacent
                              plots to prevent elements from overlapping
```

Figure 5.2 shows the result.

Drawing paired histograms, especially in preparation for fitting a logistic regression model, provides an opportunity to visually inspect the distributions of the predictors across both classes. By comparing the distributions side by side, we can immediately assess whether there are similarities or differences in the respective distributions between classes. They could reveal which of the variables might be statistically significant predictors for predicting one binary outcome versus the other and therefore guide the variable selection process. Furthermore, paired histograms reveal separation, overlap, or some combination thereof between classes, which is crucial for understanding the potential discriminatory power of the variables and the feasibility of classification through logistic regression.

5.2 *Multiple logistic regression* 121

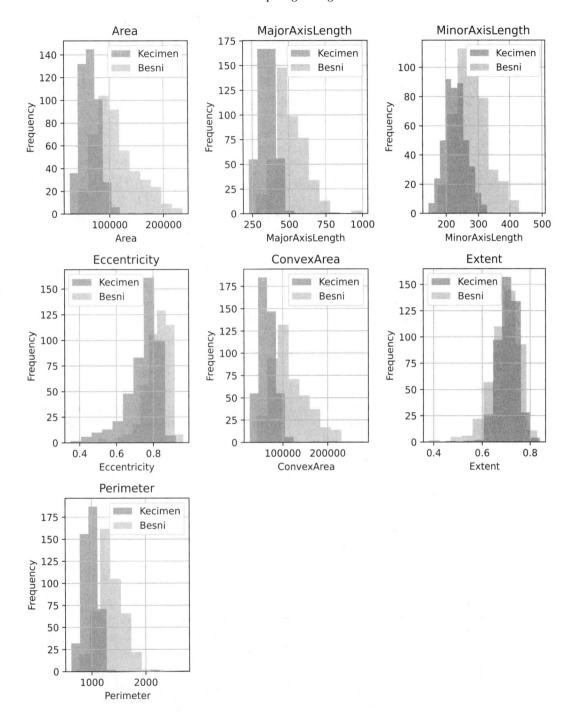

Figure 5.2 A grid of histograms that displays the data distributions of each numeric variable in the `raisins` data frame, further segmented by the binary variable `Class`.

Our plots show a mix of opportunities and challenges. Take `MajorAxisLength` and `Perimeter`, for instance: because their respective distributions between classes are mostly (although not entirely) distinct, their potential value as predictors is substantial. But also consider `Eccentricity` and `Extent`: because their respective distributions between classes are more similar than dissimilar, we may be better off excluding them as predictors.

CORRELATION HEAT MAPS

A *correlation heat map* is a graphical representation of the pairwise correlations between numeric variables. It uses color coding to indicate both the strength and the direction of the correlations. Typically, darker colors, usually deep shades of red and blue, represent strong correlations, whereas lighter shades of the same colors indicate weaker or no correlations. The correlation coefficients are usually added by default. The correlation coefficient between a pair of numeric variables will always equal some number between –1 and +1; the closer the coefficient is to –1 or +1, the stronger the relationship. Two variables are positively correlated when they both move in the same direction, up or down, whereas a pair of variables are negatively correlated when they move in opposite directions.

When fitting a multiple linear regression, understanding the correlations between the predictors and the numeric dependent variable could drive variable selection; that's because independent variables strongly correlated with the response variable, positively or negatively, are the most promising predictors. It's also important to understand the correlation coefficients between the independent variables; strong correlations between potential predictors might be a leading indicator of multicollinearity and therefore a potential loss in predictive power. This is because multicollinearity makes it difficult to isolate the individual effect of each predictor: if two variables are highly correlated, the model can't determine which one is truly influencing the outcome, which inflates standard errors and reduces the statistical significance of meaningful predictors.

In logistic regression, because the dependent variable is binary and not numeric, we can't be concerned about its relationships with the other variables, at least from a correlation perspective. However, we can, and should, be curious about the correlation coefficients between the independent variables. Multicollinearity is a potential issue in logistic regression, just as it is in linear regression. Multicollinearity occurs when independent variables in a regression model are strongly correlated with each other, which can cause difficulties in isolating the effects of individual predictors on the dependent variable and even reduce the predictive power of the model.

That all being said, as a final analysis step before fitting our logistic regression, we'll demonstrate how to create a Matplotlib correlation heat map—actually two maps, one where the data is subset on the variable `Class` equaling `0` and another where the data is subset on `Class` equaling `1`. These will be displayed as one object, printed vertically.

5.2 Multiple logistic regression

Because we intend to create two correlation heat maps rather than just one, we first split the `raisins` data frame into two equal halves: one where `Class` equals 0 and the other where `Class` equals 1. `class_0_data` contains those observations from `raisins` where the variety of raisin is Kecimen, and `class_1_data` contains the remaining `raisins` observations where the variety of raisin is Besni. Splitting the data by class makes it possible to perform separate, but equal, analyses on the data:

```
>>> class_0_data = raisins[raisins['Class'] == 0]
>>> class_1_data = raisins[raisins['Class'] == 1]
```

Then we pass our two splits in the data to the `corr()` method, which computes the correlation coefficients between every pair of variables. This method measures only linear relationships, thereby indicating how strongly each pair of variables is linearly related, but it won't capture nonlinear associations:

```
>>> correlation_matrix_class_0 = class_0_data.corr()
>>> correlation_matrix_class_1 = class_1_data.corr()
```

Our pair of correlation heat maps (see figure 5.3) requires `matplotlib` (already imported) and another Python data visualization library called `seaborn`:

```
>>> import seaborn as sns
>>> fig, axs = plt.subplots(2, 1,
>>>                         figsize = (8, 10))
>>> sns.heatmap(correlation_matrix_class_0,
>>>             annot = True,
>>>             cmap = 'coolwarm',
>>>             ax = axs[0])
>>> axs[0].set_title('Correlation Heatmap - \
>>>             Kecimen Variety')
>>> sns.heatmap(correlation_matrix_class_1,
>>>             annot = True,
>>>             cmap = 'coolwarm',
>>>             ax = axs[1])
>>> axs[1].set_title('Correlation Heatmap - \
>>>             Besni Variety')
>>> plt.tight_layout()
>>> plt.show()
```

- Imports one of the two required libraries
- Creates a single figure with two subplots arranged vertically (two rows, one column)
- Creates a correlation heat map for the Kecimen variety
- Adds the correlation coefficients as annotations to each cell and sets the color map
- Sets the title for the first subplot
- Creates a correlation heat map for the Besni variety
- Adds the correlation coefficients as annotations to each cell and sets the color map
- Sets the title for the second subplot
- Adjusts the layout to prevent any overlap between subplot
- Displays one figure with two heat maps

Figure 5.3 shows the result.

To get the correlation coefficient between any two variables, identify the row and column corresponding to each and then locate where they intersect. So, for instance, where the raisin variety equals Kecimen, the correlation coefficient between `MajorAxisLength` and `MinorAxisLength` equals 0.58; where the raisin variety is Besni, the correlation coefficient between these same two variables equals 0.62.

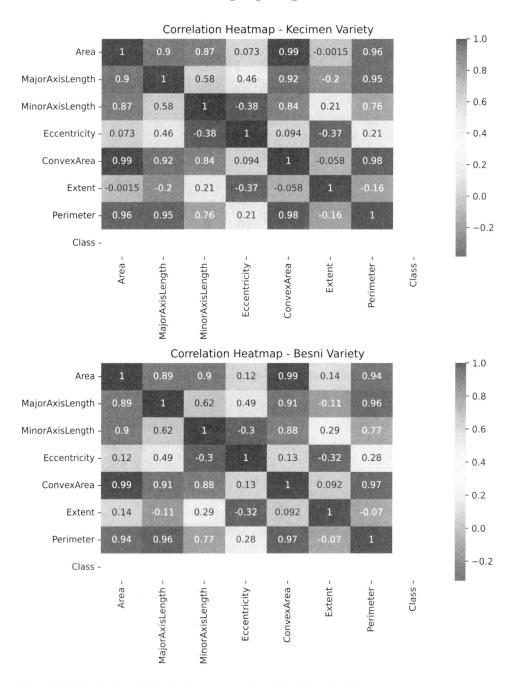

Figure 5.3 A pair of correlation heat maps, one for each variety of raisin

The correlation heat maps show that we might have a multicollinearity issue; that's because there are strong correlations between several pairs of variables. We'll demonstrate how to test for multicollinearity and discuss how to handle it during model development.

5.2.2 Fitting the model

We'll fit a multiple logistic regression by calling the `logit()` method from Python's `statsmodels` library; `Class` will be our dependent variable, whereas `Area`, `MajorAxisLength`, `MinorAxisLength`, `Eccentricity`, `ConvexArea`, `Extent`, and `Perimeter` will be our independent variables. We are regressing `Class` against all the morphological features in the `raisins` data frame to predict the variety of raisin.

We import the `statsmodels` library and then fit our regression, `log_model`:

- `smf.logit(…)` specifies the logistic regression and assigns `Class` as the dependent variable and the remaining variables as predictors.
- `fit()` fits the initialized model to the `raisins` data frame and estimates the parameters of the regression using the specified data.
- `summary()` returns a regression table that contains the coefficient estimates, p-values, and goodness of fit statistics.

Here's the code and the model output:

```
>>> import statsmodels.formula.api as smf
>>> log_model = smf.logit('Class ~ Area + '
>>>                       'MajorAxisLength + '
>>>                       'MinorAxisLength + '
>>>                       'Eccentricity + '
>>>                       'ConvexArea + '
>>>                       'Extent + '
>>>                       'Perimeter', data = raisins).fit()
>>> print(log_model.summary())
Optimization terminated successfully.
         Current function value: 0.338384
         Iterations 9
                           Logit Regression Results
==============================================================================
Dep. Variable:                  Class   No. Observations:                  900
Model:                          Logit   Df Residuals:                      892
Method:                           MLE   Df Model:                            7
Date:                Wed, 27 Mar 2024   Pseudo R-squ.:                  0.5118
Time:                        15:03:56   Log-Likelihood:                -304.55
converged:                       True   LL-Null:                       -623.83
Covariance Type:            nonrobust   LLR p-value:                 1.196e-133
==============================================================================
                     coef    std err          z      P>|z|      [0.025      0.975]
------------------------------------------------------------------------------
Intercept         -2.6642      7.028     -0.379      0.705     -16.439      11.111
Area               0.0005      0.000      4.027      0.000       0.000       0.001
MajorAxisLength
                  -0.0447      0.016     -2.801      0.005      -0.076      -0.013
MinorAxisLength
                  -0.0899      0.027     -3.342      0.001      -0.143      -0.037
```

```
Eccentricity
          -3.5248    4.909   -0.718   0.473  -13.147    6.097
ConvexArea
          -0.0004    0.000   -3.446   0.001   -0.001   -0.000
Extent    -0.6051    2.697   -0.224   0.822   -5.891    4.681
Perimeter  0.0361    0.007    5.464   0.000    0.023    0.049
```

The null hypothesis for a logistic regression is that the predictors have no effect on distinguishing one class from another. So, if the p-value for the model is greater than the 5% threshold for significance, we will fail to reject the null hypothesis. But if the p-value is less than 5%, we should instead reject the null hypothesis and conclude that the morphological features of raisins can be used to detect one variety from the other. The log-likelihood ratio (LLR) p-value, which more or less equals the p-value in the F-statistic from a linear regression, is equal to 0; therefore, the null hypothesis should be rejected.

However, not every predictor is statistically significant; `Eccentricity` has a p-value equal to `0.473`, and `Extent` has a p-value equal to `0.822`. Rather than further evaluating this model, we will instead fit a reduced model that excludes, at a minimum, those two variables. But first, we'll demonstrate how to test for multicollinearity, evaluate the results, and weigh alternative courses of action. The easiest way of treating multicollinearity is to discard the offending variables. So, we may decide to reduce our next regression by more than two predictors. (The intercept's p-value is `0.705`, indicating that it is also not statistically significant—but because intercepts are generally less critical for interpretation and prediction, we typically don't exclude them.)

Multicollinearity in regression analysis is measured by a statistic called the variance inflation factor (VIF). It assesses how much the variance of an estimated regression coefficient is increased—or inflated—due to multicollinearity among the predictors. Multicollinearity is present when at least one of the predictors has a VIF equal to or greater than 1. However, some form of remediation is required only when one or more of the predictors has a VIF equal to or greater than 10.

The formula to calculate the VIF for a single predictor X_j is

$$\text{VIF}_j = \frac{1}{1 - R_j^2}$$

We get R^2 by fitting a linear regression in which one of the predictors is regressed against the remaining predictors. For instance, to get the VIF for `MinorAxisLength`, we would regress that variable against the other predictors in our multiple logistic model, get the R^2 statistic, and then plug that value into the VIF formula. Let's demonstrate.

We first define our dependent variable, independent variable, and constant:

```
>>> y = raisins['MinorAxisLength']
>>> x = raisins[['Area', 'MajorAxisLength', 'ConvexArea', 'Extent', \
        'Eccentricity', 'Perimeter']]
>>> x = sm.add_constant(x)
```

5.2 Multiple logistic regression

Then we fit our linear regression by making a call to the `OLS()` method from the `statsmodels` library:

```
>>> import statsmodels.api as sm
>>> multicollinearity_test = sm.OLS(y, x).fit()
```

And finally, rather than instruct Python to return a regression table, we instead write two short lines of code to get just the R^2 statistic:

```
>>> r2 = multicollinearity_test.rsquared
>>> print(r2)
0.9751270231122477
```

So, the VIF for `MinorAxisLength` is

$$\text{VIF}_{\text{MinorAxisLength}} = \frac{1}{1 - 0.97513}$$

This comes to 40.21.

Fortunately, it's not necessary to repeat this exercise by fitting a linear model for every predictor in our multiple logistic regression. The following snippet of code automatically returns the VIF for every predictor:

```
>>> from patsy import dmatrices
>>> from statsmodels.stats.outliers_influence
>>> import variance_inflation_factor

>>> y, X = dmatrices('Class ~ Area + '
>>>                   'MajorAxisLength + '
>>>                   'MinorAxisLength + '
>>>                   'ConvexArea + '
>>>                   'Extent + '
>>>                   'Eccentricity + '
>>>                   'Perimeter',
>>>                   data = raisins,
>>>                   return_type = 'dataframe')

>>> vif_df = pd.DataFrame()
>>> vif_df['variable'] = X.columns

>>> vif_df['VIF'] = [variance_inflation_factor(X.values, i) \
>>>                  for i in range(X.shape[1])]

>>> print(vif_df)
         variable          VIF
0       Intercept  1117.154039
1            Area   404.773424
2 MajorAxisLength   129.289901
3 MinorAxisLength    40.204275
4      ConvexArea   446.016527
```

```
5          Extent     1.600679
6     Eccentricity    5.194067
7        Perimeter  184.388548
```

So, as we suspected might be the case once we examined the correlation heat maps, we have a serious multicollinearity issue. Only the statistically insignificant predictors `Extent` and `Eccentricity`, have VIFs below 10.

Multicollinearity can be remediated by combining predictors or by fitting a different type of model to the data. However, the most common method is to simply fit a reduced model. We previously decided to fit a second logistic regression without `Extent` and `Eccentricity` because, according to our first regression, neither of those predictors has a statistically significant effect on detecting one variety of raisin versus the other. We will next regress `Class` against `MinorAxisLength` and `Perimeter` only—although this doesn't entirely resolve our multicollinearity issue, it mitigates the effect and, at the same time, furthers our commitment to fit and evaluate a multiple logistic regression.

So, once more, we make a call to the `logit()` method:

```
>>> reduced_model = smf.logit('Class ~ MinorAxisLength + Perimeter', \
>>>                            data = raisins).fit()
>>> print(reduced_model.summary())
Optimization terminated successfully.
         Current function value: 0.346417
         Iterations 8
                           Logit Regression Results
==============================================================================
Dep. Variable:                  Class   No. Observations:                  900
Model:                          Logit   Df Residuals:                      897
Method:                           MLE   Df Model:                            2
Date:                Thu, 28 Mar 2024   Pseudo R-squ.:                  0.5002
Time:                        19:06:19   Log-Likelihood:                -311.78
converged:                       True   LL-Null:                       -623.83
Covariance Type:            nonrobust   LLR p-value:                 2.987e-136
==============================================================================
                    coef    std err          z      P>|z|      [0.025      0.975]
------------------------------------------------------------------------------
Intercept        -11.8048      0.878    -13.442      0.000     -13.526     -10.084
MinorAxisLength   -0.0244      0.004     -5.586      0.000      -0.033      -0.016
Perimeter          0.0159      0.001     13.333      0.000       0.014       0.018
==============================================================================
```

Now we have a model that is worthy of a full evaluation.

5.2.3 Interpreting and evaluating the results

Our intent here is to pull the key measures from the regression table and demonstrate how they should be interpreted and evaluated. In this section, we will provide instructions on deriving, evaluating, and even visualizing classification metrics that are used to measure the performance of a regression in predicting binary outcomes.

PSEUDO R-SQUARED

In logistic regression, pseudo R^2 is a measure used to assess the model's goodness of fit. Unlike in linear regression, where R^2 represents the proportion of variance explained by the predictors, pseudo R^2 represents the model's ability to explain variation in the binary dependent variable.

There are actually several pseudo R^2 measures common to logistic regression; the statsmodels library returns what's called McFadden's pseudo R^2, which is the most popular. McFadden's R^2 is equal to 1 minus the quotient between the log-likelihood of the model and the log-likelihood of a model with just an intercept term and no predictors:

$$\text{McFadden's } R^2 = 1 - \frac{L_{\text{model}}}{L_{\text{null}}}$$

It therefore measures the added value of the independent variables in predicting binary outcomes; so, the higher McFadden's R^2, the better the model fits the data. The log-likelihoods are stored as attributes in the fitted model object and are printed to the regression table.

This means

$$\text{McFadden's } R^2 = 1 - \frac{-311.78}{-623.83} = 0.5002$$

Log-likelihood is a measure of how well a statistical model, including logistic regression, fits the observed data. Specifically, it represents the logarithm of the likelihood function, which is the probability of observing the data given the parameters of the model. The log-likelihood of the null model is a baseline of sorts, and the log-likelihood of the model is the predictive value of the independent variables above that baseline. Therefore, the greater the difference between the log-likelihoods of the model and the null model, the higher McFadden's R^2, and the better the model fits the data.

Log-likelihoods are difficult to interpret in isolation, but they can readily be compared to like measures from competing models fitted to the same data. Therefore, McFadden's R^2, which of course is derived from the log-likelihoods, is also a valuable metric for the purposes of model comparison. But unlike the log-likelihoods, McFadden's R^2 is easy to evaluate and interpret against the fitted model. It will always equal some number between 0 and 1, where values as "low" as 0.40 correspond to an excellent fit. Thus, a McFadden's R^2 equal to 0.50 suggests that `MinorAxisLength` and `Perimeter` are accurate predictors for distinguishing one variety of raisin from the other.

LLR P-VALUE AND P>|z|

Because the reduced model excluded statistically insignificant predictors from the full model and other predictors with high multicollinearity, it's not surprising that we again get a p-value equal to 0. We've simplified the model without making a sacrifice in statistical significance. So, regressing `Class` against just `MinorAxisLength` and

Perimeter leads us to the same conclusion as did regressing Class against the full complement of morphological features: because the p-value for the model is less than 5%, we should again reject the null hypothesis and now conclude that MinorAxisLength and Perimeter, which both have p-values also equal to 0, are useful for detecting one variety of raisin versus the other.

COEF

The intercept (β_0) equals -11.8048, the coefficient estimate for MinorAxisLength (β_1) is equal to -0.0244, and the same for Perimeter (β_2) is equal to 0.0159. We therefore get the fitted regression by plugging these three values into the logistic equation:

$$P(Y = 1|X) = \frac{1}{1 + e^{-(-11.8048 + -0.0244(X_1) + 0.0159(X_2))}}$$

or

$$P(\text{Besni}) = \frac{1}{1 + 2.72^{-(-11.8048 + -0.0244(\text{MinorAxisLength}) + 0.0159(\text{Perimeter}))}}$$

Once more, the purpose of logistic regression is to predict the probability of the dependent variable being equal to 1. And because we previously coded Kecimen raisins as 0 and Besni raisins as 1, we are therefore predicting the probability of the raisin variety equaling Besni.

Let's create a subset of the raisins data frame that contains just the variables MinorAxisLength, Perimeter, and Class:

```
>>> raisins_subset = raisins[['MinorAxisLength', 'Perimeter', 'Class']]
```

After all, only these three variables from our original data frame now factor into our analysis, so it makes sense to subset the data by removing unnecessary variables and thus retain only what is needed.

Next we create a new raisins_subset variable called probability that corresponds to the coefficient estimates and their place in the logistic equation. This operation first requires that we import the math library:

```
>>> import math
>>> raisins_subset['probability'] = 1 / (1 + 2.72**(-(-11.8048 +
>>>                 (-.0244 * raisins_subset['MinorAxisLength']) +
>>>                 (.0159 * raisins_subset['Perimeter']))))
```

Let's get a glimpse—two glimpses, actually—of the raisins_subset data frame by making successive calls to the head() and tail() methods:

```
>>> print(raisins_subset.head(n = 3))
   MinorAxisLength  Perimeter  Class  probability
0           253.29    1184.04      0     0.698821
1           243.03    1121.79      0     0.525426
2           266.33    1208.58      0     0.713766
```

```
>>> print(raisins_subset.tail(n = 3))
     MinorAxisLength  Perimeter  Class  probability
897           298.84    1292.83      1     0.811597
898           254.18    1258.55      1     0.881365
899           215.27    1272.86      1     0.960193
```

Take a look at the first and last observations in the data. When `MinorAxisLength` equals `253.29` and `Perimeter` equals `1184.04`, our logistic regression gives a 70% probability that `Class` equals `1`; when `MinorAxisLength` equals `215.27` and `Perimeter` equals `1272.86`, our model gives a 96% probability of `Class` equaling `1`.

This was just an interim step, however. We now need to mutate the values in `probability` to binary predictions that coincide with the observed outcomes. The following snippet of code mutates the values in `probability` to either `0` or `1` and stores the results in a new variable called `prediction`: `0` if the `probability` is less than 0.50 or `1` otherwise. This operation requires the `pandas` and `numpy` libraries. Although 0.5 is a common default cutoff—meaning we predict a 1 when the probability is at least 50%—this threshold can be adjusted depending on the context. For instance, in situations where false positives are more costly than false negatives (or vice versa), a higher or lower cutoff might be more appropriate to optimize the model's performance:

```
>>> import numpy as np
>>> raisins_subset['prediction'] = (raisins_subset['probability'] \
>>>                                 .apply(lambda x: 0 if x < 0.5 else 1))
```

Successive calls to the `head()` and `tail()` methods display the top three and bottom three observations in the `raisins_subset` data frame:

```
>>> print(raisins_subset.head(n = 3))
   MinorAxisLength  Perimeter  Class  probability  prediction
0           253.29    1184.04      0     0.698821           1
1           243.03    1121.79      0     0.525426           1
2           266.33    1208.58      0     0.713766           1

>>> print(raisins_subset.tail(n = 3))
     MinorAxisLength  Perimeter  Class  probability  prediction
897           298.84    1292.83      1     0.811597           1
898           254.18    1258.55      1     0.881365           1
899           215.27    1272.86      1     0.960193           1
```

Now that we have a binary outcome variable and a binary prediction variable, we can calculate a series of classification metrics to further evaluate the predictive power of our logistic regression.

5.2.4 Calculating and evaluating classification metrics

Classification metrics are used to evaluate the performance of a binary classification model, including logistic regression. These metrics provide insights into how well, or not so well, the model is able to classify instances into their correct classes.

CONFUSION MATRIX

A *confusion matrix* is a table that is typically used to describe the performance of a classification model like logistic regression. It neatly visualizes the performance of an algorithm by comparing actual classes (from our data set) with predicted classes. The matrix consists of four main components: true positives (tp), false positives (fp), true negatives (tn), and false negatives (fn).

These components represent the counts of correct and incorrect predictions made by the model. By analyzing the confusion matrix, we can intelligently and quantitatively evaluate the performance of our logistic regression. The confusion matrix with respect to our classification of Turkish raisins is shown in table 5.1.

Table 5.1 Confusion matrix for raisin classification. A confusion matrix stores classification metrics from a regression with actual and predicted binary outcomes.

		Predicted	
		Kecimen (0)	Besni (1)
Actual	Kecimen (0)	tn	fp
	Besni (1)	fn	tp

The following snippet of code returns the number of records in the `raisins_subset` data frame where `Class` and `prediction` both equal 0; this is therefore the count of true negatives, or the number of instances where `Class` equals 0 and was then predicted to equal 0. The `len()` method typically returns the number of items in an object:

```
>>> count = len(raisins_subset[(raisins_subset['Class'] == 0) &
>>>                            (raisins_subset['prediction'] == 0)])
>>> print(count)
397
```

So, out of the 450 observations where the variety of raisin equals Kecimen, our model correctly predicted the outcome 397 times.

The next snippet of code returns the inverse of that, or the number of instances where Kecimen raisins were incorrectly predicted to be of the Besni variety. This is the count of false positives:

```
>>> count = len(raisins_subset[(raisins_subset['Class'] == 0) &
>>>                            (raisins_subset['prediction'] == 1)])
>>> print(count)
53
```

The number of observations where `Class` equals 1 and `prediction` equals 1 represents the number of times the model correctly predicted the variety of raisin to equal Besni, which is the count of true positives:

```
>>> count = len(raisins_subset[(raisins_subset['Class'] == 1) &
>>>                            (raisins_subset['prediction'] == 1)])
print(count)
384
```

Thus, from the 450 observations where the variety of raisin equals Besni, our logistic regression correctly predicted that outcome 384 times.

And finally, we get the inverse of the true positives, the false negatives, by counting the number of instances where Class equals 1 but prediction equals 0:

```
>>> count = len(raisins_subset[(raisins_subset['Class'] == 1) &
>>>                             (raisins_subset['prediction'] == 0)])
>>> print(count)
66
```

We get a populated confusion matrix by passing the raisins_subset variables Class and prediction to the pd.crosstab() method:

```
>>> confusion_matrix = pd.crosstab(raisins_subset['Class'], \
>>>                                 raisins_subset['prediction'])
>>> print(confusion_matrix)
prediction    0    1
Class
0           397   53
66          384
```

Thus:

$$tn = 397$$
$$fp = 53$$
$$tp = 384$$
$$fn = 66$$
$$n = 900$$

where

- tn equals the number of true negatives.
- fp equals the number of false positives.
- tp equals the number of true positives.
- tn equals the number of false negatives.
- n equals the total record count, which, again, is evenly divided between Kecimen and Besni raisins; it also equals the total number of predictions.

We'll plug these values into other formulas to get additional classification metrics that help us further evaluate the predictive power of our model.

SENSITIVITY

Sensitivity is the true positive rate (*tpr*); it equals the number of true positives divided by the sum of true positives and false negatives. The quotient is then multiplied by 100 to get a percentage:

$$\text{sensitivity} = \left(\frac{tp}{tp + fn}\right) 100$$

or

$$\text{sensitivity} = \left(\frac{384}{384 + 66}\right) 100$$

There are two ways to get the true positive rate. We can use Python as a calculator:

```
>>> sensitivity = (tp / (tp + fn)) * 100
>>> print(sensitivity)
85.33333333333334
```

Or we can pass the `raisins_subset` variables `Class` and `prediction` to the `recall_score()` method from the scikit-learn (`sklearn`) library:

```
>>> from sklearn.metrics import recall_score
>>> tpr = recall_score(raisins_subset['Class'], \
>>>                    raisins_subset['prediction'])
>>> print(tpr * 100)
85.33333333333334
```

Either way, we get a true positive rate of 85.33%. In other words, our logistic regression correctly identified positive instances 85% of the time, which is pretty good.

SPECIFICITY

Specificity is the true negative rate (tnr); it equals the number of true negatives divided by the sum of true negatives and false positives. The quotient is then transformed to a percentage by multiplying it by 100:

$$\text{specificity} = \left(\frac{tn}{tn + fp}\right) 100$$

or

$$\text{specificity} = \left(\frac{397}{397 + 53}\right) 100$$

Once more, we can get the true negative rate by performing another simple arithmetic operation:

```
>>> specificity = (tn / (tn + fp)) * 100
>>> print(specificity)
88.22222222222223
```

Or we can again call the `recall_score` method(). In addition to passing the variables `Class` and `prediction`, we must also pass a third argument this time, `pos_label = 0`, which instructs `recall_score()` to fix its computations on the negative class:

```
>>> tnr = recall_score(raisins_subset['Class'], \
>>>                    raisins_subset['prediction'], pos_label = 0)
>>> print(tnr * 100)
88.22222222222223
```

So, the true negative rate, or the proportion of negative instances correctly predicted by our logistic regression, is 88.22%, which is also good. Thus, our model performs (almost) equally well across classes.

FALSE POSITIVE RATE

The false positive rate (*fpr*) measures the proportion of actual negatives incorrectly classified as positives by the logistic regression. It equals the number of false positives divided by the sum of false positives and true negatives, which is then multiplied by 100 to get a percentage:

$$tnr = \left(\frac{fp}{fp + tn}\right)100$$

or

$$tnr = \left(\frac{53}{53 + 397}\right)100$$

There's no function available to get the false positive rate, but of course, we can again use Python as a calculator to determine it. It is the inverse of the true negative rate:

```
>>> false_positive_rate = (fp / (fp + tn)) * 100
>>> print(false_positive_rate)
11.777777777777777
```

Our model incorrectly classified the negative instances less than 12% of the time.

FALSE NEGATIVE RATE

The false negative rate (*fnr*) measures the proportion of actual positives incorrectly classified as negatives by our model. We get the false negative rate by dividing the number of false negatives by the sum of false negatives and true positives, and then, of course, multiplying that result by 100 to get a percentage of records that meet this criterion:

$$fnr = \left(\frac{fn}{fn + tp}\right)100$$

or

$$fnr = \left(\frac{66}{66 + 384}\right)100$$

We can get the result in Python just as before. It is the inverse of the true positive rate:

```
>>> false_negative_rate = (fn / (tp + fn)) * 100
>>> print(false_negative_rate)
14.666666666666666
```

So, our model missed on just 15% of the actual positives.

> **False positive rates vs. false negative rates**
>
> Depending on the scenario, false positives and false negatives are not equally severe. Consider, for instance, airport security screening. False positives, or false alarms, are the result of incorrectly identifying harmless objects as potential threats, which of course inconveniences passengers and creates potential delays. But those consequences are not nearly as severe as what might occur, such as a security breach or even a terrorist attack, if the false negatives were high.
>
> Or consider medical diagnoses for life-threatening diseases. Incorrectly flagging healthy individuals for medical care is not as consequential as missing the true positives, which result in undiagnosed cases and delays in treatment.
>
> We can also consider the incarceration of innocent individuals. These false positives are absolutely more severe than providing freedom to those who are actually guilty.

ACCURACY

Model *accuracy* is the ratio of correct predictions to the total number of predictions. Mathematically, it is the sum of true positives and true negatives divided by the number of records in the data (assuming that a prediction was applied to each observation), multiplied by 100:

$$\text{accuracy} = \left(\frac{tp + tn}{n}\right) 100$$

or

$$\text{accuracy} = \left(\frac{384 + 397}{900}\right) 100$$

We can naturally get the same result by performing yet another arithmetic operation in Python:

```
>>> accuracy = ((tp + tn) / n) * 100
>>> print(accuracy)
86.7777777777777
```

Of course, the closer the model accuracy is to 100%, the better. Our logistic regression isn't quite there, but an 87% accuracy rate is fairly impressive.

MISCLASSIFICATION RATE

The *misclassification rate* is the opposite, or inverse, of model accuracy. It is the proportion of false predictions to the record count, multiplied by 100:

$$\text{misclassification rate} = \left(\frac{fp + fn}{n}\right) 100$$

or

$$\text{misclassification rate} = \left(\frac{53 + 66}{900}\right) 100$$

This should be approximately 13%:

```
>>> misclassification_rate = ((fp + fn) / n) * 100
>>> print(misclassification_rate)
13.222222222222221
```

So, our model falsely, or incorrectly, predicted the variety of raisin just 13% of the time.

AREA UNDER THE ROC CURVE

The *area under the ROC curve* (AUC) is a measure that quantifies the overall performance of a classification problem, including logistic regression, across all possible classification thresholds. The `roc_auc_score()` method from the `sklearn` library compares the predictions against the true binary labels and returns a statistic between 0 and 1.

The AUC may or may not align with the model accuracy rate. Whereas model accuracy calculates the ratio of correct predictions to the total number of predictions, AUC measures the ability of the model to effectively discriminate between positive and negative classes. The difference might seem subtle, but consider an imbalanced data set where one class is predominant over the other. For example, consider a data set where 90 students pass an exam and 10 fail: accuracy may be high if the model predicts the dominant class correctly most of the time, but the AUC may be lower than the accuracy rate if the model struggles to effectively distinguish between the classes.

When the data is evenly divided between classes (remember, we have 450 Kecimen raisins and 450 Besni raisins in our data), and if the model performs equally well across classes, the AUC statistic should align well with model accuracy:

```
>>> from sklearn.metrics import roc_auc_score
>>> auc = roc_auc_score(raisins_subset['Class'], \
>>>                     raisins_subset['prediction'])
>>> print(auc)
0.8677777777777779
```

And it does. In fact, the AUC and the model accuracy rate are exactly the same.

In general, an AUC close to 1 indicates very good model performance, thereby suggesting that our logistic regression has high discriminatory power; if the AUC were instead close to 0.5, it would suggest that model performance was no better than random guessing. But more specifically, what qualifies as a "good" AUC statistic depends to a large degree on the context and the problem at hand. When the problem is innocuous, like distinguishing one variety of raisin from the other, an AUC equal to 87% is considered excellent; but if one variety happened to be poisonous, 87% might be unsatisfactory.

ROC CURVE

A *receiver operating characteristic* (ROC) curve is a graphical representation of the AUC. It plots the false positive rate along the *x* axis and the true positive rate along the *y* axis. It illustrates the potential trade-off between the false and true positive rates across different threshold values. A ROC curve that hugs the upper-left quadrant of the plot indicates strong model performance whereby the true positives are maximized while the true negatives are minimized (see figure 5.4); this increases the area under it, driving the AUC statistic closer to 1.

Here's the snippet of Python code:

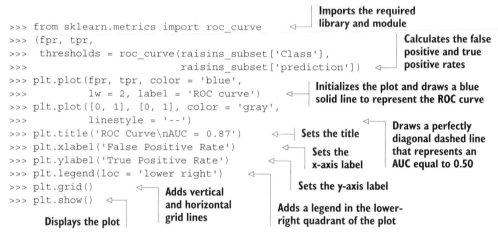

Figure 5.4 shows the plot.

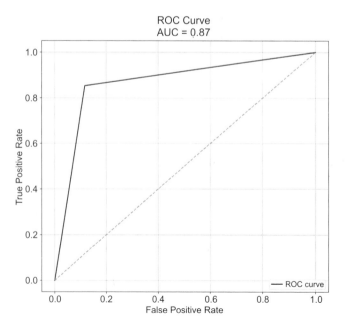

Figure 5.4 A ROC curve. The false positive rate is plotted along the *x* axis, and the true positive rate is plotted along the *y* axis. When the curve, represented by the solid line, hugs the upper-left quadrant of the plot, as it does here, it increases the area under the curve. The dashed line represents an AUC equal to 0.5, or the equivalent of random guessing.

We learned how logistic regression can effectively solve a real-world classification problem, but the journey to get there was a bit of a crooked path. Our preliminary analysis of the data showed that a full model—where the binary dependent variable is regressed against every other variable in the data—might cause a multicollinearity issue. We demonstrated how to fit a multiple logistic regression and then how to test for multicollinearity, which led us to fit a reduced model where the same dependent variable was then regressed against a subset of our original predictors. We showed how to interpret and evaluate goodness of fit measures and other model outputs, how to apply the coefficient estimates with some data wrangling to make predictions, and how to compute classification metrics that are typically used to measure model performance. In the next chapter, we will solve another classification problem, but with very different modeling techniques.

Summary

- Logistic regression is a statistical method used to model the relationship between a binary outcome variable and one or more predictors. Unlike linear regression, which predicts continuous outcomes, logistic regression predicts the probability that an observation belongs to one class versus the other. Logistic regression applies the logistic function, or sigmoid function, to transform the linear combination of predictors into probabilities, which are then used to make binary predictions. Logistic regression models are regularly fit in many fields, including medicine, finance, marketing, and the social sciences.
- Goodness of fit should be evaluated from at least a trio of measures: McFadden's pseudo R^2, which represents a model's ability to explain variation in the binary dependent variable above and beyond a null model that contains just an intercept term; the LLR p-value, which measures a model's statistical significance; and the p-values for the individual predictors, which indicate whether the relationship between a predictor and the binary outcome variable is statistically significant.
- Classification metrics—true and false positive rates, true and false negative rates, accuracy and misclassification rates, and the area under the receiver operating characteristic curve—are essential for evaluating the performance of a logistic regression and its ability to accurately predict binary outcomes. By analyzing these metrics, you can draw conclusions about a model's strengths and weaknesses, identify opportunities for improvement, and make informed decisions about model optimization and deployment.
- Data exploration, which typically involves a mix of computing basic statistics and creating graphical displays of the data, should scale with the length and width of the data set. The value proposition of data exploration, when done correctly and thoroughly, lies in its ability to identify patterns, outliers, and potential issues with the data that could drive variable selection and other model development decisions.

Fitting a decision tree and a random forest

This chapter covers
- Decision trees and random forests
- Model interpretation and evaluation
- Mathematical foundations
- Data exploration through grouped bar charts and histograms
- Common data wrangling techniques

In the previous chapter, we solved a classification problem using logistic regression, achieving 87% accuracy in predicting the variety of Turkish raisins based on their morphological features. In this chapter, we will approach a similar classification problem using two powerful modeling techniques: decision trees and random forests.

A *decision tree* is a simple, intuitive model that makes decisions by recursively splitting the data into subsets based on the most significant feature at each step. It operates like a flowchart, where each internal node represents a decision based on a feature, each branch represents the outcome of that decision, and each leaf node represents a class label or a regression value. Decision trees are easy to interpret and visualize, making them a popular choice for both classification and regression tasks.

A *random forest*, on the other hand, is an ensemble learning method that constructs multiple decision trees during training. For classification problems, the random forest outputs the class that is selected by the majority of the trees (a process known as *majority vote*), whereas for regression tasks, it averages the predictions of the individual trees. Random forests are particularly effective because they combine the predictions of many trees, which reduces the risk of overfitting and improves model robustness and accuracy.

6.1 Understanding decision trees and random forests

Building a decision tree involves selecting the best features to split the data at each node. The algorithm evaluates various splits and chooses the one that best separates the classes, typically using metrics such as Gini impurity (which measures misclassification) and information gain (which quantifies reduction in uncertainty) for classification tasks. For regression tasks, the algorithm evaluates splits using criteria such as mean squared error (MSE) and mean absolute error (MAE), both of which measure how well the split reduces the variability in the continuous target variable. The tree continues to grow by adding branches until it reaches a stopping criterion, such as a maximum depth or a minimum number of samples per leaf. The resulting tree is then used to make predictions by following the path from the root to a leaf node.

A random forest takes this process a step further. It is an ensemble technique that constructs multiple decision trees using different subsets of the data, which are randomly selected with replacement through a process called *bagging* (bootstrap aggregating). Each tree is trained on a slightly different data set, leading to variations in the trees. Additionally, random forests introduce randomness by selecting a random subset of features to consider at each split, ensuring that the trees are diverse and not overly correlated. This diversity among the trees strengthens the overall model, making it more resistant to overfitting and enhancing its generalization ability. Furthermore, random forests provide an importance ranking of features based on how often each feature is selected across trees and its effect on reducing impurity, offering valuable insights into which predictors contribute most to the model.

> **Ensemble techniques**
>
> Ensemble techniques, such as combining logistic regression with decision trees or using random forests, use multiple models to enhance prediction accuracy and robustness. By aggregating predictions from diverse models, ensemble methods reduce the risk of overfitting and increase the generalizability of the prediction.
>
> For example, in a random forest, numerous decision trees operate on slightly different subsets of the data and/or features, each contributing a prediction. The final output is typically the majority vote or the average of these predictions, smoothing out anomalies and errors that individual models might make. Similarly, combining fundamentally different models such as logistic regression and decision trees allows the

> *(continued)*
> strengths of one model to compensate for the weaknesses of another, offering a more balanced and reliable prediction across various scenarios. This synergy effectively harnesses the unique capabilities of each model type, leading to more accurate and stable outcomes.

For classification tasks, the final prediction of a random forest is determined by a majority vote among the trees, whereas for regression tasks, it is the average prediction of all the trees. This approach results in a model that is typically more accurate and robust than a single decision tree. Furthermore, random forests have the advantage of requiring less preprocessing than regression models, because they are not sensitive to the scale or distribution of the input variables and can naturally handle both numerical and categorical data without requiring normalization or transformation. They are typically faster to fit in high-dimensional settings due to their randomized approach. After training, feature importance can be easily estimated and visualized, providing insights into which variables have the most significant effect on the predictions.

We will first demonstrate how to build a single decision tree, interpret its structure, and evaluate its performance. Following that, we will explore how to construct and use the power of a random forest to solve our classification problem, showing the benefits of random forests and the ease with which they can be implemented and interpreted.

But before exploring the nuts and bolts of decision trees and random forests, we will introduce the classification problem we'll be solving: predicting whether an American football team will successfully convert a fourth-down attempt. To solve this problem, we'll begin by importing a real data set, demonstrating common data wrangling techniques to prepare the data for analysis, and then exploring the data by computing basic statistics and creating graphical content to reveal leading insights.

6.2 Importing, wrangling, and exploring the data

American football is a game of strategy and skill that evolved from English rugby and soccer—although nowadays, nobody would mistake one for the others. Players use their hands to control the ball, not their feet, and teams take turns in possession of the ball. The game is played with 11 players on each side. The team on offense attempts to advance the ball downfield to score 3 points by kicking a field goal between the goal posts or 7 points by running or passing the ball into their opponent's end zone—and then converting the extra point. The team on defense tries to stop them.

Teams must advance the ball against their opponent's defense at least 10 yards at a time over three successive plays, also known as downs, to maintain possession and get a new set of downs. Fourth down is the critical down. If out of range for a field goal attempt, most teams choose to punt the ball and relinquish possession to their opponent. However, depending on the situation, teams sometimes go for it: that is, rather than punting, they call a run or pass play in an attempt to gain the required yardage for a new set of downs. They convert the fourth down or they don't. It's a classic risk-and-reward scenario with binary outcomes: if successful, teams maintain possession of the ball and keep alive their chances for a score, but if unsuccessful, their opponent gains possession where the fourth down failed.

We will attempt to predict whether a professional football team converts a fourth-down play by fitting a decision tree and then a random forest to a data frame containing play-by-play data from the 2023 National Football League (NFL) regular season and postseason. Our data set is a .csv file stored in our working directory. We typically read .csv files into Python by passing the filename (including the .csv extension) to the `pd.read_csv()` method from the `pandas` library. However, in this instance, it makes sense to add the `usecols` parameter to our code to specify which variables, or columns, to import rather than the entire data set. Using `usecols` is often preferred over importing everything and then subsetting, as it reduces memory usage and speeds up data loading, particularly when working with large data sets that contain many irrelevant variables. This approach helps streamline the data import process by bringing in only the columns essential to our analysis:

```
>>> import pandas as pd
>>> nfl_pbp = pd.read_csv('nfl_pbp.csv',
>>>                 usecols = ['QUARTER',
>>>                            'DOWN',
>>>                            'TO_GO',
>>>                            'OFFENSIVE_TEAM_VENUE',
>>>                            'SCORE_DIFFERENTIAL',
>>>                            'PLAY_TYPE',
>>>                            'YARDS_GAINED'])
```

Let's review these variables one by one.

6.2.1 Understanding the data

Even if you're well-acquainted with American football, some of the `nfl_pbp` variables may not be immediately intuitive. Each observation in the data corresponds to a single play:

- QUARTER represents the period in which a play occurred. Games are typically divided into four quarters, so QUARTER is an integer that, for most observations, equals 1, 2, 3, or 4. However, some games end in a tie, and then an overtime period is played to determine a winner. For those plays that occurred in overtime, QUARTER equals 5.
- DOWN is an integer that represents the play's down number, with a value equal to 1, 2, 3, or 4 corresponding to a first-down, second-down, third-down, or fourth-down play, respectively.
- TO_GO is an integer that equals the number of yards remaining for a first down; it therefore equals any whole number equal to or greater than 1.

- OFFENSIVE_TEAM_VENUE is a character string that can be either Road or Home. When the visiting team is in possession of the ball, OFFENSIVE_TEAM_VENUE is set to Road; otherwise, it is set to Home.
- SCORE_DIFFERENTIAL is an integer that equals the number of accumulated points scored by the home team minus the number of accumulated points scored by the road team. It can therefore be a negative number if the road team has accumulated more points, a positive number if the home team has accumulated more points, or zero if both teams have accumulated an equal number of points.
- PLAY_TYPE is a character string that represents the category of play that occurred. For instance, if the team on offense executed a running play, PLAY_TYPE equals Run; if a field goal was attempted, PLAY_TYPE equals Field Goal.
- YARDS_GAINED is an integer that represents the number of yards gained on a play; it can be positive, negative, or zero.

Unfortunately, our data is not plug-and-play ready for the type of problem we intend to solve, which means it requires some wrangling before we can fit a decision tree or a random forest to it.

6.2.2 Wrangling the data

Data wrangling is the process of transforming and preparing raw data into a clean and usable format for analysis. This may involve one or more of the following steps: reshaping the data by gathering columns into rows or spreading rows into columns, extracting observations that meet a logical criterion, selecting variables by name, transforming data types, correcting errors or inconsistencies, handling missing values, or joining data from other sources. The goal of data wrangling is to ensure the data is accurate, complete, and properly formatted to avoid a "garbage in, garbage out" problem. Wrangling data doesn't do much toward demonstrating how to fit a decision tree or a random forest, but it is typically required as a prerequisite to fitting any type of model or performing any sort of analysis.

DATA FILTERING

Data filtering is the process of subsetting a data frame based on specific logical criteria. Our data frame, nfl_pbp, now contains every play from the 2023 NFL season, including the postseason. However, we only need fourth-down plays that involve a run or pass; we don't need plays from other downs, nor do we need fourth-down plays that included a punt or a field-goal attempt. So, we filter nfl_pbp where the variable DOWN equals 4 and where the variable PLAY_TYPE equals Pass or Run:

```
>>> nfl_pbp = nfl_pbp[(nfl_pbp['DOWN'] == 4) & \
>>>                   (nfl_pbp['PLAY_TYPE'].isin(['Pass', 'Run']))]
```

The code creates a pair of Boolean series that each resolve to TRUE when the specified logical criteria are met. The bitwise AND operator combines the two Boolean series to create a final Boolean series that resolves to TRUE only if both conditions are met.

6.2 Importing, wrangling, and exploring the data

MISSING VALUES

The variable YARDS_GAINED contains several NaN values, which is short for "Not a Number." NaN is a special floating-point value that typically represents undefined or unrepresentable numerical results, which makes sense for those plays—a timeout, for instance—where there were no yards to be gained. Although we've stripped those observations from the nfl_pbp data frame, YARDS_GAINED also equals NaN rather than 0 when a passing or running play gained no yards.

This is a minor inconvenience that we can quickly and easily fix. In the following line of code, we call the fillna() method to replace every instance of NaN in YARDS_GAINED with 0:

```
>>> nfl_pbp['YARDS_GAINED'] = nfl_pbp['YARDS_GAINED'].fillna(0)
```

This common fix addresses a frequent problem, thereby preventing errors and inaccuracies when the data is subjected to analysis. Although replacing NaN values with 0 is appropriate in this case, it's important to note that this approach may not be suitable in all situations. Imputing missing data can significantly affect model predictions, potentially leading to unintended patterns, such as an excess of zeros or distorted minima. Carefully consider the implications and context of the data before choosing an imputation method.

DATA TRANSFORMATION

Let's say the home team has accumulated 24 points and the road team has accumulated 17 points. The variable SCORE_DIFFERENTIAL therefore equals 7, because it is derived by subtracting the number of points accumulated by the road team from the number of points accumulated by the home team. If the variable OFFENSIVE_TEAM_VENUE equals Home, it indicates that the home team has a 7-point advantage over the road team, which is what we want. But if OFFENSIVE_TEAM_VENUE instead equals Road, SCORE_DIFFERENTIAL should equal −7 rather than 7; after all, the road team is *trailing* by 7 points.

The following line of code inverts the sign of the SCORE_DIFFERENTIAL values where OFFENSIVE_TEAM_VENUE equals Road by multiplying the raw data by -1:

```
>>> nfl_pbp.loc[nfl_pbp['OFFENSIVE_TEAM_VENUE'] == \
>>>             'Road', 'SCORE_DIFFERENTIAL'] *= -1
```

The net effect of this operation is that positive numbers are flipped to negative and negative numbers are flipped to positive, but only when the variable OFFENSIVE_TEAM_VENUE is equal to Road. Where SCORE_DIFFERENTIAL equals 0, the data remains unchanged, of course, because multiplying 0 by any number still results in 0.

DATA TYPE CONVERSION

Machine learning models, including decision trees and random forests, require numeric inputs; so, converting categorical string data to numeric data types makes the data frame fully compatible with machine learning algorithms. The following snippets of code convert the values in OFFENSIVE_TEAM_VENUE and PLAY_TYPE from strings to integers (0 and 1):

```
>>> OFFENSIVE_TEAM_VENUE_mapping = {'Road': 0, 'Home': 1}
>>> nfl_pbp['OFFENSIVE_TEAM_VENUE'] = \
>>>     nfl_pbp['OFFENSIVE_TEAM_VENUE'].map(OFFENSIVE_TEAM_VENUE_mapping)

>>> PLAY_TYPE_mapping = {'Run': 0, 'Pass': 1}
>>> nfl_pbp['PLAY_TYPE'] = \
>>>     nfl_pbp['PLAY_TYPE'].map(PLAY_TYPE_mapping)
```

We have simply converted the string values of both variables to integers. For OFFENSIVE_TEAM_VENUE, Road has been mapped to 0 and Home to 1; similarly, for PLAY_TYPE, Run has been mapped to 0 and Pass to 1.

DERIVED VARIABLE

Decision tree and random forest algorithms use a categorical target variable—binary or otherwise—during training to build and optimize each decision tree, whether as part of an ensemble or as a standalone model. It might go without saying, but our data frame does not contain a binary variable indicating whether a professional football team converted a fourth-down play; so, we need to create a new feature, or attribute, from existing nfl_pbp data through a mathematical operation and assign it as our target variable.

From the variable TO_GO, we know the number of yards needed to convert a fourth down and get a new set of downs; and from the variable YARDS_GAINED, we know the number of yards gained on the play. So if YARDS_GAINED is less than TO_GO, then our derived variable, CONVERT, should equal 0, indicating failure; otherwise it should equal 1, indicating success.

The following snippet of code creates a new variable called CONVERT and appends it to the nfl_pbp data frame. It compares the values from TO_GO and YARDS_GAINED and assigns a value of 0 or 1 to the new variable:

```
>>> nfl_pbp['CONVERT'] = np.where(nfl_pbp['YARDS_GAINED'] < \
>>>                               nfl_pbp['TO_GO'], 0, 1)
```

When the number of yards gained is less than the number of yards needed to earn a new set of downs, it's assumed the fourth-down attempt failed, and a value of 0 is assigned to the derived variable CONVERT. Alternatively, when the number of yards gained is equal to or greater than the yards needed, we're assuming the fourth-down attempt was successful, and a value of 1 is assigned to CONVERT.

SUMMARY

Now that we have our data frame in order, let's summarize it. The info() method returns a concise summary of the nfl_pbp data frame:

```
>>> print(nfl_pbp.info())
<class 'pandas.core.frame.DataFrame'>
Index: 883 entries, 16 to 52381
```

6.2 Importing, wrangling, and exploring the data

```
Data columns (total 8 columns):
 #   Column                Non-Null Count  Dtype
---  ------                --------------  -----
 0   QUARTER               883 non-null    int64
 1   DOWN                  883 non-null    float64
 2   TO_GO                 883 non-null    float64
 3   OFFENSIVE_TEAM_VENUE  881 non-null    float64
 4   SCORE_DIFFERENTIAL    883 non-null    int64
 5   PLAY_TYPE             883 non-null    int64
 6   YARDS_GAINED          883 non-null    float64
 7   CONVERT               883 non-null    int64
dtypes: float64(4), int64(4)
memory usage: 62.1 KB
None
```

This tells us the following about our data:

- There are 883 observations (rows) and 8 variables (columns) in `nfl_pbp`. So, during the 2023 NFL regular season and postseason, there were 883 instances where teams ran a play from scrimmage—that is, a running play or a passing play—in an attempt to convert a fourth down.
- There are no remaining null values. We effectively eliminated them by converting every `NaN` in `YARDS_GAINED` to 0.
- Every variable is now numeric because we converted the character strings of `OFFENSIVE_TEAM_VENUE` and `PLAY_TYPE` (int or float makes no difference).

To get an overview of the `nfl_pbp` data frame, we can call the `head()` method to print the first 10 observations. However, before doing so, we should instruct Python to display all columns by using the `pd.set_option()` method. By default, Python limits the number of columns shown in a data frame's output to avoid overwhelming the display, which can be problematic when there are many columns and we need to see all of them without truncation:

```
>>> pd.set_option('display.max_columns', None)
>>> print(nfl_pbp.head(10))
     QUARTER  DOWN  TO_GO  OFFENSIVE_TEAM_VENUE  SCORE_DIFFERENTIAL  \
16         1   4.0    2.0                   0.0                   0
85         2   4.0   10.0                   0.0                  -7
162        4   4.0    2.0                   0.0                   1
168        4   4.0   25.0                   1.0                  -1
500        4   4.0    1.0                   0.0                   0
536        1   4.0    1.0                   0.0                   0
636        3   4.0    1.0                   0.0                  -9
696        4   4.0   13.0                   0.0                 -16
709        4   4.0    3.0                   0.0                 -16
857        4   4.0    4.0                   0.0                 -13
     PLAY_TYPE  YARDS_GAINED  CONVERT
16           0           3.0        1
85           1           0.0        0
162          1           0.0        0
168          1           0.0        0
500          0           1.0        1
```

```
536        1          -11.0        0
636        0            0.0        0
696        1            0.0        0
709        1           12.0        1
857        1          -13.0        0
```

Seeing the data is one thing, but getting insights from it is another.

6.2.3 Exploring the data

In our exploration of the data, we will be laser-focused on identifying which features might be the most significant for predicting the derived variable CONVERT. By examining these relationships, we aim to uncover key indicators and logical splits within the variables that will inform our decision tree model. This analysis is essential for understanding the data's structure and ensuring that our model is built on a solid foundation of relevant features. Along the way, we will demonstrate how to compute basic statistics and how to plot grouped bar charts and paired histograms. We will take a variable-by-variable approach, starting with QUARTER.

QUARTER

We already know that nfl_pbp contains 883 observations, and we know there is a one-to-one relationship between observations and fourth-down attempts. But we don't yet know the observation counts between the two CONVERT class labels. In the snippet of code that follows, the value_counts() method counts the number of times each unique value appears in the CONVERT column from the nfl_pbp data frame:

```
>>> convert_counts = nfl_pbp['CONVERT'].value_counts()
>>> print(convert_counts)
CONVERT
1    462
0    421
Name: count, dtype: int64
```

So, teams were successful more times than not on fourth-down attempts during the 2023 NFL regular season and postseason—although not by much. Let's group these totals by QUARTER and plot the results in a Matplotlib grouped bar chart. A grouped bar chart is a type of bar chart that displays multiple bars grouped together for each category, thereby allowing a comparison of subcategories within each main category:

```
>>> import matplotlib.pyplot as plt        ⟵ Library must be imported
                                             before running subsequent
>>> grouped_data = (nfl_pbp.groupby(['QUARTER', 'CONVERT']) \
>>>         .size().unstack(fill_value = 0))
>>> grouped_data.plot(kind = 'bar')        ⟵ Creates a grouped
                                             bar chart
```

Groups the data by QUARTER and CONVERT and then reshapes it so each CONVERT value becomes a column; unstack() enables grouped bar plotting by aligning categories side-by-side; fill_value = 0 passed to unstack() replaces any NaNs

```
>>> for p in ax.patches:
>>>     ax.annotate(str(p.get_height()),
>>>                 (p.get_x() + p.get_width() / 2., p.get_height()),
>>>                 ha = 'center', va = 'bottom',
>>>                 fontweight = 'bold',
>>>                 color = 'black')
>>> plt.title('Observation Counts by Quarter')    ⟵ Sets the title
>>> plt.xlabel('Quarter')                          ⟵ Sets the x-axis label
>>> plt.ylabel('Count')    ⟵ Sets the y-axis label
>>> plt.xticks(rotation = 0)
>>> plt.legend(title = 'CONVERT',
>>>            labels = ['No', 'Yes'])
>>> plt.show()    ⟵ Displays the plot
```

Initiates a loop that iterates over each bar and annotates the height of each bar on top of it

Sets the rotation angle of the x-axis tick labels to 0 degrees, effectively keeping them horizontal

Adds a legend with custom labels; default placement is in the upper-right corner of the plot

As we move forward to visualize the results, it's worth noting that the color scheme for a Matplotlib grouped bar chart defaults to a predefined color cycle if not explicitly set. Although we had the option to customize the colors by adding the color parameter to the plot() method, we chose to keep things simple with the default settings. Figure 6.1 shows the grouped bar chart we've generated.

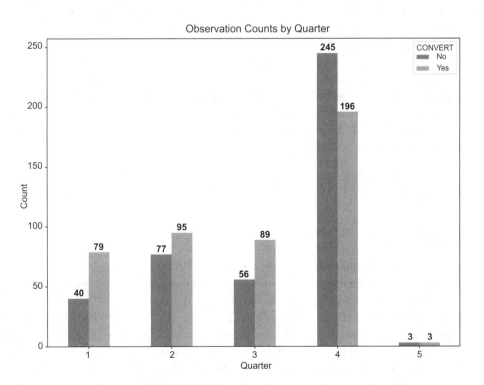

Figure 6.1 A grouped bar chart that displays the CONVERT class label counts by QUARTER. Teams were more successful than not in converting fourth-down attempts in the first three quarters, but less successful in the fourth quarter.

At least during the 2023 regular season and postseason, teams were more successful than not when attempting fourth-down conversions during the first three quarters, but less successful when doing so in the fourth quarter. This suggests that the quarter in which a play occurs might be an important feature for predicting the likelihood of a fourth-down conversion.

TO_GO

We might hypothesize that teams are more likely to convert a fourth-down attempt when only a few yards are needed and less likely to be successful when more yards are required. Let's quickly test this hypothesis by calling the `mean()` method to compute the TO_GO average by each CONVERT class label:

```
>>> mean_to_go_by_convert = nfl_pbp.groupby('CONVERT')['TO_GO'].mean()
>>> print(mean_to_go_by_convert)
CONVERT
0    5.947743
1    2.560606
Name: TO_GO, dtype: float64
```

Teams that successfully converted fourth-down attempts needed to gain, on average, 2.56 yards to keep possession and get another set of downs. When unsuccessful, teams needed almost 6 yards, on average, to convert. For those of you not terribly familiar with American football, which is sometimes described as a game of inches, that's a tremendous variance.

Because the mean can be influenced by outliers, it's important to also compute the median—that is, the middle value when the data is sorted from lowest to highest—grouped by the CONVERT class labels. Although the median is not completely unaffected by outliers and skewed data, it is less affected than the mean.

To do this, we simply swap out the `mean()` method from the previous snippet of code and replace it with the `median()` method:

```
>>> median_to_go_by_convert = nfl_pbp.groupby('CONVERT')['TO_GO'].median()
>>> print(median_to_go_by_convert)
CONVERT
0    4.0
1    1.0
Name: TO_GO, dtype: float64
```

The median, just like the mean, is a measure of central tendency. Teams that failed on their fourth-down conversion attempts needed a median of 4 yards, whereas teams that succeeded required a median of just 1 yard.

Let's plot the TO_GO distributions grouped by the CONVERT class labels with a Matplotlib paired histogram. A paired histogram—which we introduced in the previous chapter—is a type of visualization where two histograms are plotted on the same axes to compare the distributions of a single variable across two different groups. This allows for easy visual comparison of how the variable behaves within each group:

```
>>> convert_0_data = nfl_pbp[nfl_pbp['CONVERT'] == \
>>>                          0]['TO_GO']
```
◁— Filters the data frame to extract the values of TO_GO where CONVERT equals 0

6.2 Importing, wrangling, and exploring the data

```
>>> convert_1_data = nfl_pbp[nfl_pbp['CONVERT'] == \
>>>                  1]['TO_GO']
>>> plt.subplot()
>>> plt.hist(convert_0_data, alpha = 0.5,
...          label = 'CONVERT = No')
>>> plt.hist(convert_1_data, alpha = 0.5,
...          label = 'CONVERT = Yes')
>>> plt.title('Yards Needed for First Down by CONVERT')
>>> plt.xlabel('Yards Needed for First Down')
>>> plt.ylabel('Frequency')
>>> plt.legend()
>>> plt.show()
```

- Filters the data frame to extract the values of TO_GO where CONVERT equals 1
- Initializes the plot
- Generates the first histogram where CONVERT equals 0
- Generates the second histogram; alpha makes the plots half transparent
- Sets the title
- Sets the x-axis label
- Sets the y-axis label
- Adds a legend
- Displays the plot

The result is shown in figure 6.2. The distributions are similar in that they are both right-skewed. A right-skewed distribution is a probability distribution where the majority of the data points are concentrated on the left, with the tail extending to the right; it is also known as a positive-skewed distribution because the long tail extends into the positive, rather than the negative, direction.

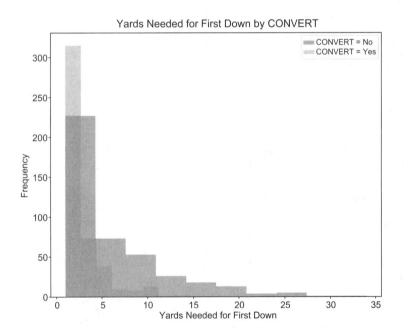

Figure 6.2 Paired histograms that display the distributions of TO_GO grouped by the CONVERT class labels. When teams succeeded on their fourth-down attempts, they usually needed fewer than 3 yards to convert, and definitely fewer than 5 yards. When teams failed to convert on fourth down, they often needed to gain more than 5 yards and sometimes up to 25 yards or more.

Yet the distributions are also different. When CONVERT equals 1, there is a concentration of higher frequencies around lower values, with a relatively short tail; alternatively, when CONVERT equals 0, the distribution is more spread and the tail is much longer. This distinction suggests that TO_GO, which represents the yards needed for a first down, plays a crucial role in determining the likelihood of a fourth-down conversion. The shorter distances correlate with higher conversion success, indicating that teams are more likely to succeed when the required yardage is minimal. In practical terms, this insight could have significant implications for coaching strategies and decision-making during games. Coaches might prioritize plays that minimize the yardage needed on fourth down or adjust their strategies based on the specific value, rather than relying solely on the game quarter or other factors. This understanding could lead to more informed and effective play-calling, potentially increasing a team's chances of success in critical fourth-down situations.

SCORE_DIFFERENTIAL

A quick reminder: we transformed SCORE_DIFFERENTIAL so that it consistently reflects the point margin from the standpoint of the team possessing the ball and therefore attempting the fourth-down conversion. Let's call the mean() and median() methods in succession to compute those measures grouped by the CONVERT class labels:

```
>>> mean_score_differential_by_convert = \
>>>     nfl_pbp.groupby('CONVERT')['SCORE_DIFFERENTIAL'].mean()
>>> print(mean_score_differential_by_convert)
CONVERT
0   -7.125891
1   -3.688312
Name: SCORE_DIFFERENTIAL, dtype: float64

>>> median_score_differential_by_convert = \
>>>     nfl_pbp.groupby('CONVERT')['SCORE_DIFFERENTIAL'].median()
>>> print(median_score_differential_by_convert)
CONVERT
0   -7.0
1   -4.0
Name: SCORE_DIFFERENTIAL, dtype: float64
```

To begin with, it seems that teams typically opt for a fourth-down conversion when they're trailing. Our next snippet of code returns the nfl_pbp counts where the variable SCORE_DIFFERENTIAL is negative (team in possession of the ball is trailing), positive (the same team is leading), and zero (the score is tied):

```
>>> score_differential_counts = (nfl_pbp['SCORE_DIFFERENTIAL'] \
>>>                 .agg({'negative': lambda x: (x < 0).sum(),
>>>                       'positive': lambda x: (x > 0).sum(),
>>>                       'zero': lambda x: (x == 0).sum()}))
>>> print(score_differential_counts)
negative    577
positive    212
zero         94
Name: SCORE_DIFFERENTIAL, dtype: int64
```

The code uses the agg() method along with lambda functions to apply specific conditions to SCORE_DIFFERENTIAL, thereby computing the number of instances remaining in the nfl_pbp data frame that are negative, positive, and zero. In this instance, agg() aggregates results from different conditions applied to SCORE_DIFFERENTIAL into one result set, and the lambda functions are used to define custom aggregation functions for specific conditions within the agg() method.

During the 2023 NFL regular season and postseason, approximately two-thirds (577 of 883) of fourth-down conversion attempts were made by teams trailing their opponent. These teams tended to be behind by a touchdown when failing to convert and by more than a field goal when successful, as indicated by our previous mean and median calculations.

Another plot of paired histograms should be even more insightful. This time, we're plotting the distribution of SCORE_DIFFERENTIAL by the two CONVERT class labels:

```
>>> convert_0_data = \
>>>     nfl_pbp[nfl_pbp['CONVERT'] == \
>>>         0]['SCORE_DIFFERENTIAL']
>>> convert_1_data = \
>>>     nfl_pbp[nfl_pbp['CONVERT'] == \
>>>         1]['SCORE_DIFFERENTIAL']
>>> plt.subplot()
>>> plt.hist(convert_0_data, alpha = 0.5,
>>>          label = 'CONVERT = No')
>>> plt.hist(convert_1_data, alpha = 0.5,
>>>          label = 'CONVERT = Yes')
>>> plt.title('Score Differential by CONVERT')
>>> plt.xlabel('Score Differential')
>>> plt.ylabel('Frequency')
>>> plt.legend()
>>> plt.show()
```

- Extracts the values of SCORE_DIFFERENTIAL where CONVERT equals 0
- Extracts the values of SCORE_DIFFERENTIAL where CONVERT equals 1
- Initializes the plot
- Generates the first histogram where CONVERT equals 0
- Generates the second histogram; alpha makes the plots half transparent
- Sets the title
- Sets the x-axis label
- Sets the y-axis label
- Adds a legend
- Displays the plot

Although the code is more or less the same—aside from swapping out variables—figure 6.3 shows that the results are not the same as before. The data is normally distributed

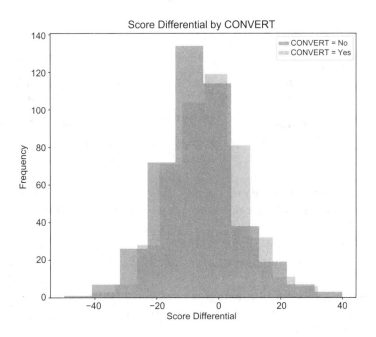

Figure 6.3 Paired histograms that display the distributions of SCORE_DIFFERENTIAL grouped by the CONVERT class labels. Regardless of the CONVERT class label, the distribution is normally distributed about the mean.

about the respective means—around −7 when CONVERT equals 0 and about −3 when CONVERT equals 1. However, there is notably less distinction between the distributions compared to what we observed with the TO_GO plot, which suggests that SCORE_DIFFERENTIAL is most likely less significant than TO_GO when it comes to predicting whether teams will convert on fourth down. It may or may not be more significant than QUARTER.

OFFENSIVE_TEAM_VENUE

OFFENSIVE_TEAM_VENUE indicates which team—Road or Home, mapped and converted to 0 and 1—possesses the ball. The following snippet of code creates a grouped bar chart to show the number of observations for fourth-down conversion attempts, categorized by whether the offensive team is playing at home or on the road and whether they succeeded or failed. This chart helps us compare the distribution of conversion attempts and their outcomes based on the venue:

```
>>> grouped_data = \
>>>     (nfl_pbp.groupby(['OFFENSIVE_TEAM_VENUE', 'CONVERT']) \
>>>         .size().unstack(fill_value = 0))
>>> grouped_data.plot(kind = 'bar')
>>> for p in plt.gca().patches:
>>>     plt.gca().annotate(str(p.get_height()),
>>>                        (p.get_x() + p.get_width() /
>>>                        2., p.get_height()),
>>>                        ha = 'center', va = 'bottom',
>>>                        fontweight = 'bold',
>>>                        color = 'black')
>>> plt.title('Observation Counts by \
>>>            Road vs. Home')
>>> plt.xlabel('Road or Home')
>>> plt.ylabel('Count')
>>> plt.xticks([0, 1], labels = ['Road Team', 'Home Team'],
>>>            rotation = 0)
>>> plt.xticklabels(['Road Team', 'Home Team'])
>>> plt.legend(title = 'CONVERT', labels = ['No', 'Yes'],
>>>            loc = 'upper right')
>>> plt.show()
```

- Groups the data by OFFENSIVE_TEAM_VENUE and CONVERT
- Creates a grouped bar chart
- Initiates a loop that iterates over each bar and annotates the height of each bar on top of it
- Sets the title
- Sets the x-axis label
- Sets the y-axis label
- Sets the position of the ticks on the x axis at positions 0 and 1 to match customization; rotates the angle of the x-axis tick labels to 0 degrees
- Sets the labels for the ticks on the x axis
- Adds a legend with custom labels; places the legend in the upper-right corner of the plot
- Displays the plot

Our second grouped bar chart (see figure 6.4) illustrates the distribution of fourth-down conversion attempts and their outcomes, thereby providing a clear comparison between road and home teams. Teams playing at home were successful in about 55% of their fourth-down conversion attempts, with 227 out of 408 being successful. In contrast, visiting teams had a success rate of less than 50%, converting just 233 out of 473 attempts. (Note that a pair of conversion attempts on a neutral field is not shown.) However, whether this distinction is significant enough to predict the outcome of fourth-down conversion attempts remains to be seen.

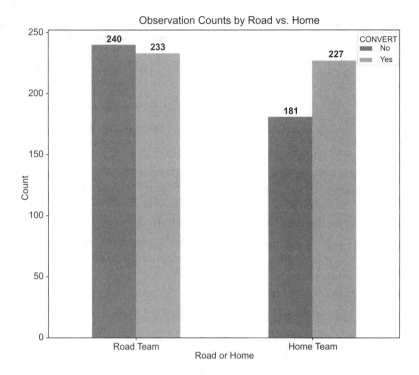

Figure 6.4   Counts of fourth-down conversion attempts categorized by the OFFENSIVE_TEAM_VENUE and CONVERT class labels. Teams playing at home were more successful than visiting teams in converting fourth-down attempts.

PLAY_TYPE

PLAY_TYPE is a categorical variable: a running play is represented by 0 and a passing play by 1. Because teams often pass when many yards are needed to convert a fourth down and frequently run when fewer yards are required, PLAY_TYPE could serve as an effective proxy for TO_GO, or at least an extension of it. Our next snippet of code creates a third, and final, grouped bar chart that plots the observation counts of running and passing plays by the CONVERT class labels. The code should be familiar by now:

```
>>> grouped_data = \                                            Groups the data by
>>>     (nfl_pbp.groupby(['PLAY_TYPE', 'CONVERT']) \            PLAY_TYPE and CONVERT
>>>      .size().unstack(fill_value = 0))
>>> ax = grouped_data.plot(kind = 'bar')                        Creates a grouped
>>> for p in plt.gca().patches:                                 bar chart
>>>     plt.gca().annotate(str(p.get_height()),
>>>                        (p.get_x() + p.get_width() /
>>>                        2., p.get_height()),                 Initiates a loop that
>>>                        ha = 'center', va = 'bottom',        iterates over each bar and
>>>                        fontweight = 'bold',                 annotates the height of
>>>                        color = 'black')                     each bar on top of it
>>> plt.title('Observation Counts by \
>>>            Run vs. Pass')                                   Sets the title
```

```
>>> plt.xlabel('Running or Passing Play')            ◁         Sets the
>>> plt.ylabel('Count')                  ◁   Sets the y-axis label   x-axis label
>>> plt.xticks([0, 1], labels = ['Run', 'Pass'],
               rotation = 0)             ◁         Sets the position of the ticks on the x
>>> ax.set_xticklabels(['Run', 'Pass'])  ◁         axis at positions 0 and 1 to match
>>> plt.legend(title = 'CONVERT',                  customization; rotates the angle of the
>>>            labels = ['No', 'Yes'])   ◁         x-axis tick labels to 0 degrees
>>> plt.show()        ◁
                                Adds a legend with   Sets the labels for the
          Displays the plot     custom labels        ticks on the x axis
```

Figure 6.5 shows the breakdown of running and passing plays from the 2023 NFL regular season and postseason categorized by the CONVERT class labels. Although teams passed the ball on fourth down much more frequently than they ran it (555 times to 328), running plays actually led to more fourth-down conversions than passing plays (233 conversions to 229). This doesn't necessarily suggest that teams should have called more running plays on fourth downs; rather, these results might reflect the number of yards needed for a conversion.

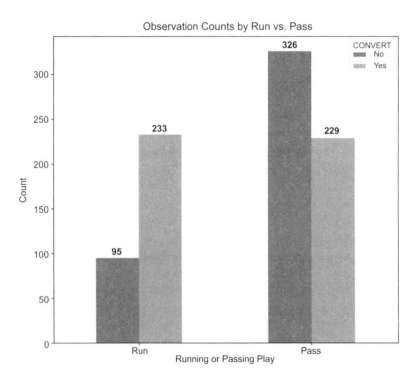

Figure 6.5 Counts of fourth-down conversion attempts categorized by the PLAY_TYPE and CONVERT class labels. Teams that ran the ball on fourth downs were much more successful in converting those attempts compared to teams that passed the ball instead. This doesn't necessarily mean that running is a better strategy than passing; rather, it might simply reflect the yards required for a conversion.

The next code snippet calculates the `TO_GO` mean and median by the `PLAY_TYPE` class labels:

```
>>> mean_to_go_by_play_type = \
>>>     nfl_pbp.groupby('PLAY_TYPE')['TO_GO'].mean()
>>> print(mean_to_go_by_play_type)
PLAY_TYPE
0    1.948171
1    5.491892
Name: TO_GO, dtype: float64

>>> median_to_go_by_play_type = \
>>>     nfl_pbp.groupby('PLAY_TYPE')['TO_GO'].median()
>>> print(median_to_go_by_play_type)
PLAY_TYPE
0    1.0
1    4.0
Name: TO_GO, dtype: float64
```

Regardless of the measure used, it's obvious that teams called a running or passing play based on the yards needed to convert a fourth down. However, it will be interesting to observe how `PLAY_TYPE` influences our decision tree, especially in relation to `TO_GO`. It's time to find out.

6.3 Fitting a decision tree

Decision trees are a popular and intuitive machine learning model used for both classification and regression tasks. They work by splitting the data into subsets based on the value of input features, creating a tree-like model of decisions. Each internal node represents a test on an attribute, each branch represents the outcome of the test, and each leaf node represents a class label or continuous value.

Decision trees are highly interpretable, as they closely mimic human decision-making processes, making it easy to understand how the model arrives at its conclusions. Additionally, they typically require minimal data preparation and can handle both numerical and categorical data equally well.

Let's look at a very simple and straightforward example of a decision tree for demonstration purposes (see figure 6.6). It illustrates the decision-making process for determining whether a home loan will be approved based on the applicant's age and income.

Starting at the root node, the decision tree first evaluates whether the applicant's age is 30 years or fewer. If the answer is yes, we move to the left side of the tree. Here, the tree examines the applicant's income at the first internal node, checking whether it is $50,000 or less. If the income is indeed $50,000 or less, the decision at the leaf node is "No," meaning the applicant is not approved for the loan. Conversely, if the applicant's income exceeds $50,000, the decision at the corresponding leaf node is "Yes," and the loan is approved.

Simple Decision Tree

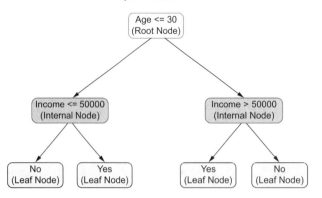

Figure 6.6 A decision tree demonstrating the home loan approval process based on the applicant's age and income. The tree is interpreted from top to bottom, starting at the root node and progressing to the leaf nodes. The left branch is followed when conditions are true, and the right branch is followed when conditions are false.

On the right side of the tree, where the applicant's age is greater than 30, the tree evaluates whether the applicant's income is more than $50,000. If the income exceeds $50,000, the decision at the left leaf node is "Yes," indicating that the loan is approved. However, if the income is $50,000 or less, the tree directs us to a "No" decision at the right leaf node, indicating that the loan will not be approved.

We will next fit a decision tree model to the nfl_pbp data set, aiming to predict the outcome of fourth-down conversion attempts based on various game features. Through this analysis, we seek to identify the most significant factors influencing the outcome of these attempts.

Decision trees are fit by following these steps:

1 Split the data into mutually exclusive subsets for training and testing.
2 Fit the model on the training subset.
3 Predict responses, or outcomes, on the testing subset.
4 Evaluate the model.
5 Plot the decision tree.

We will start by defining our feature (independent) variables and the target (dependent) variable, and then we will split the data into two parts. For now, we will concentrate on demonstrating how to fit a decision tree in Python; afterward, we will explain the mechanics and mathematical foundations.

6.3.1 Splitting the data

Our first snippet of code creates a new data frame called X by extracting the variables from nfl_pbp that we just analyzed. This is a common approach for defining the feature set to fit a decision tree:

```
>>> X = nfl_pbp[['QUARTER', 'TO_GO', 'OFFENSIVE_TEAM_VENUE',
>>>              'SCORE_DIFFERENTIAL', 'PLAY_TYPE']]
```

The numeric variable YARDS_GAINED would have been an appropriate target variable if we were set on solving a regression task, but it was imported solely to be combined with `TO_GO` to derive the binary target variable `CONVERT` to set up our classification problem.

Next we extract `CONVERT` from the `nfl_pbp` data frame and assign it to the variable y. This, too, is a common step in preparing data for machine learning, where y typically represents the target variable or the label that the model will predict:

```
>>> y = nfl_pbp['CONVERT']
```

In a decision tree model, it is crucial to split the data into training and test sets to evaluate the model's performance effectively. The training set is used to build and fit the model, allowing it to learn the patterns and relationships within the data. The test set, which the model has not seen before, is then used to assess how well the model generalizes to new, unseen data. This split helps in detecting overfitting and ensures that the model's predictions are robust and reliable. Here, we split the features (X) and target variable (y) into training and test sets by calling the `train_test_split()` method from scikit-learn (`sklearn`), a machine learning library. The `train_test_split()` method requires a minimum of three parameters: the selected features, the target variable, and the proportion of the data that should be assigned to the test set. We will train our decision tree on 70% of the data and then test it on the remaining 30%. Passing `random_state` as a fourth parameter to `train_test_split()` ensures that the split is reproducible. Every time our code runs, the data will be split in the same way, which is crucial for reproducibility in experiments:

```
>>> from sklearn.model_selection import train_test_split
>>> X_train, X_test, y_train, y_test = \
>>>     train_test_split(X, y, test_size = 0.3, random_state = 0)
```

The `shape` attribute returns the dimensions, or shape—that is, the number of rows and columns—of the data frame it is called on. This is a quick and easy way to confirm the 70/30 split of our data:

```
>>> print(X_train.shape)
(618, 5)
```

So, `X_train` contains 618 rows, which is equal to 70% of 883, and 5 columns. We should therefore expect `X_test` to contain 265 rows (derived by subtracting 618 from 883) and 5 columns, and we should expect `y_train` and `y_test` to contain 618 and 265 rows, respectively:

```
>>> print(X_test.shape)
(265, 5)

>>> print(y_train.shape)
(618,)

>>> print(y_test.shape)
(265,)
```

We've completed feature selection and data splitting; we're now ready to build our decision tree.

6.3.2 Fitting the model

Building a decision tree in Python is a two-step process. First, we create a decision tree classifier object using the `DecisionTreeClassifier()` method from `sklearn`:

```
>>> from sklearn.tree import DecisionTreeClassifier
>>> clf = DecisionTreeClassifier(criterion = 'gini', \
>>>                              max_depth = 3, random_state = 0)
```

The preceding code snippet naturally requires some explanation:

- `DecisionTreeClassifier()` initializes a decision tree classifier object named `clf`.
- In the context of decision trees, `criterion` refers to the function used to measure the quality of a split—`gini` is the default, but discretionary; `entropy` is also an option.
  - Gini impurity (`criterion = 'gini'`) measures how often a randomly chosen element from the set would be incorrectly labeled if it were randomly labeled according to the distribution of the labels in the set. It is by far the most common criterion method. Much more on Gini impurity later.
  - Entropy (`criterion = 'entropy'`) measures the level of impurity or disorder in a set of data. It is based on the concept of information gain and calculates the reduction in entropy after a data set is split.
  - Both methods are used to evaluate the quality of a split, but they may lead to different results in practice. Gini impurity tends to compute faster and is typically the preferred method; by contrast, entropy may be more sensitive to changes in class probabilities.
- `max_depth = 3` is a discretionary parameter that sets the maximum depth of the decision tree, which is to say we are choosing to prune the tree while building it, rather than performing these two tasks sequentially. Pruning is a technique used to prevent overfitting in decision trees by trimming parts of the tree that are not statistically significant or do not contribute significantly to its predictive accuracy. It involves removing branches of the tree that have little effect on its performance, thereby simplifying the model and improving its generalization to unseen data.
- `random_state = 0` is yet another discretionary parameter that sets the random seed to ensure reproducible results. When the same seed is used, the random splitting of data during construction remains consistent across multiple runs.

That was the first step. The second step involves training the classifier using the `fit()` method with the training data, `X_train` and `y_train`. In other words, `fit()` builds the decision tree by fitting it to the 70% training split we created earlier:

```
>>> clf = clf.fit(X_train, y_train)
```

Now that we've fit the model to the training subset, we'll next make predictions on the 30% test subset the model hasn't yet seen.

6.3.3 Predicting responses

To predict the CONVERT class labels, we utilize the trained decision tree classifier, `clf`, to make predictions on the test data set (`X_test`) and assign the predicted values to an object called `y_pred`:

```
>>> y_pred = clf.predict(X_test)
```

This is a NumPy array that includes 265 predictions, the size of the 30% test set, encoded to 0 and 1. These predictions can then be cross-referenced with the actual CONVERT class labels, also encoded as 0 or 1, to evaluate the predictive power of our decision tree. This just so happens to be our next task.

6.3.4 Evaluating the model

The `metrics.accuracy_score()` method is used to calculate the accuracy of a classification model. It requires two arguments: `y_test`, which contains the true labels of the test set, and `y_pred`, which contains the predicted labels of the test set. Our code multiplies the result by 100 to convert the accuracy to a percentage.

The `print()` method displays the result rounded up or down to the nearest whole number:

```
>>> from sklearn import metrics
>>> clf_accuracy = metrics.accuracy_score(y_test, y_pred) * 100
>>> print(f'Accuracy: {round(clf_accuracy, 0)}%')
Accuracy: 61.0%
```

The accuracy of our decision tree classifier on the test set is 61%. This means the model correctly predicted the outcome of 61% of the fourth-down conversion attempts in the test set. In other words, out of all the instances in the test set, the model's predictions matched the actual outcomes 61% of the time. Although this is better than random guessing, there is room for improvement. This result suggests that our model captures some patterns in the data, but it may not be fully capturing all the complexities or may need further tuning or more features to improve its predictive performance.

CONFUSION MATRIX

A confusion matrix, introduced in chapter 5, is a table used to evaluate the performance of a classification model. It provides a detailed breakdown of the model's performance compared to the actual values, allowing for a more granular analysis of the model's performance. The confusion matrix contains four key components for binary classification:

- *True positives (tp):* The number of correctly predicted positive observations (true and predicted labels equal 1)
- *True negatives (tn):* The number of correctly predicted negative observations (true and predicted labels equal 0)
- *False positives (fp):* The number of incorrectly predicted positive observations (true labels equal 0, predicted labels equal 1)

- *False negatives (fn):* The number of incorrectly predicted negative observations (true labels equal 1, predicted labels equal 0)

We have already calculated the accuracy rate of our decision tree. The confusion matrix will provide deeper insight into the model's performance by breaking down the results based on class labels. This will help us determine whether our model performs consistently across all classes or if there are disparities:

```
>>> from sklearn.metrics import confusion_matrix,
>>> conf_matrix = confusion_matrix(y_test, y_pred)
>>> print(conf_matrix)
[[71 67]
 [36 91]]
```

The final results are as follows:

- $tp = 91$
- $tn = 71$
- $fp = 67$
- $fn = 36$

Using Python as a calculator, we can apply these figures to a pair of arithmetic operations to compute the accuracy rate by class. The accuracy rate when the true label is 0 is

$$\text{True Label}_0 = \left(\frac{tn}{tn + fp}\right) 100$$

And when the true label is 1, the accuracy rate is

$$\text{True Label}_1 = \left(\frac{tp}{tp + fn}\right) 100$$

Thus,

```
>>> accuracy_rate_0 = 71 / (71 + 67) * 100
>>> print(f'Accuracy: {round(accuracy_rate_0, 0)}%')
Accuracy: 51.0%

>>> accuracy_rate_1 = 91 / (91 + 36) * 100
>>> print(f'Accuracy: {round(accuracy_rate_1, 0)}%')
Accuracy: 72.0 %
```

Our decision tree's performance was subpar when the true label was 0, with a 51% accuracy rate, which is no better than random guessing. However, it performed significantly better when the true label was 1, achieving a 72% accuracy rate. This disparity suggests that the model is better at predicting one class over the other—successful over unsuccessful fourth-down conversion attempts—possibly due to imbalanced data or differing patterns in the features for each class. An imbalanced data set occurs when one class label appears more frequently than the other, which can lead the model to favor the majority class and underperform on the minority class.

6.3.5 Plotting the decision tree

The following snippet of code generates a visual representation of the decision tree classifier, `clf`, using the `plot_tree()` method from the `sklearn.tree` module (see figure 6.7). It specifies the feature names and class names to be displayed in the tree plot. The `filled = True` parameter instructs Python to fill the decision tree nodes with colors to represent the majority class in each node; `rounded = True` rounds the edges of the nodes for aesthetic value; and `fontsize = 12` increases the font from the default setting to make the tree and its attributes more readable:

```
>>> from sklearn import tree
>>> plt.figure()
>>> tree.plot_tree(clf, feature_names = ['QUARTER',
>>>                                      'TO_GO',
>>>                                      'OFFENSIVE_TEAM_VENUE',
>>>                                      'SCORE_DIFFERENTIAL',
>>>                                      'PLAY_TYPE'],
>>>                class_names = ['0', '1'],
>>>                filled = True,
>>>                rounded = True,
>>>                fontsize = 12)
>>> plt.tight_layout()
>>> plt.show()
```

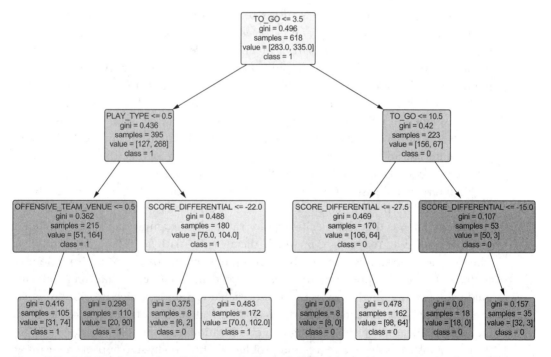

Figure 6.7 A plotted decision tree that represents the model's decision-making process, showing how features are used to split the data and make predictions. This tree was pruned during construction, so it contains fewer splits and even fewer (less significant) features than otherwise. Python automatically adds color shading to each node based on the predicted class label and purity of the split, thereby making the tree easier to interpret visually.

The tree has already been pruned, meaning it has fewer splits and utilizes fewer features than it otherwise would. You might notice that some splits, such as those on TO_GO, are made on non-integer values (e.g., TO_GO <= 3.5), even though TO_GO is an integer variable. This is a standard outcome when using decision trees in Python, as the algorithm doesn't automatically restrict splits to integer thresholds. Although it might look unusual, this approach does not affect the model's predictive accuracy and is commonly accepted in practice. For now, take a moment to observe the structure, but don't worry about interpreting the details just yet—this will be explained in great detail momentarily.

Decision trees, especially after pruning, are relatively easy to interpret because they visually represent the decision-making process through a series of straightforward splits based on feature values. However, despite their intuitive nature and resemblance to human decision-making, they require a thorough walkthrough to fully grasp their structure. The underlying mechanics and mathematical foundations of decision trees, including concepts like impurity and pruning criteria, are not straightforward and can be complex to understand without a solid background in machine learning.

6.3.6 *Interpreting and understanding decision trees*

The structure of a decision tree consists of several key components: the root node, internal nodes, and leaf nodes. The *root node* is the topmost node of the tree and represents the initial decision point from which all subsequent branches originate. *Internal nodes*, located between the root and the leaves, represent intermediate decision points that split based on specific feature values, leading to further branches. *Leaf nodes*, also known as *terminal nodes*, are the endpoints of the tree and represent the final class labels or predictions. In a plotted decision tree, the root node is easily identified as it is positioned at the top and has arrows pointing to the first set of internal nodes. Internal nodes have both incoming and outgoing arrows, whereas leaf nodes only have incoming arrows, indicating they do not split further.

To interpret a decision tree, start at the root node and follow the branches based on the conditions provided at each node. These conditions are typically in the form of "if-else" statements that test specific feature values. For example, at the root node, we see the condition TO_GO <= 3.5, which dictates the path to follow depending on whether the condition is true or false. Continue down the tree, moving from node to node, following the branches that match the conditions. Each internal node will guide you through further splits until you reach a leaf node, which provides the final prediction. The path taken from the root to a leaf represents a series of decisions based on the feature values, leading to a classification outcome (or a regression value if we were instead solving a regression problem). This step-by-step approach ensures a clear understanding of how the model makes its predictions, reflecting the logical flow of decision-making within the tree. In fact, decision trees are constructed in the same way they should be interpreted—beginning at the top with the root node.

ROOT NODE

The first step in constructing a decision tree, whether in Python, another software application, or manually, is to determine which feature to assign to the root node. This is achieved by identifying the decision or split that best separates the class labels, which is done by calculating the weighted average Gini impurity for each feature. Getting to this measure is relatively straightforward when working with categorical variables such as PLAY_TYPE but not so much when working with numeric variables like TO_GO. Understanding how to compute Gini impurities and the weighted average Gini impurity for both categorical and numeric variables is essential for determining which feature and which split should be assigned to the root node.

Gini impurity is a measure of the impurity or diversity of a single feature within a data set. Specifically, it evaluates how well, or not so well, a feature can split the data into different classes, aiming to minimize the impurity at each node in the decision tree. Gini impurity ranges from 0 (perfectly pure, where all elements are of a single class) to 0.5 (maximum impurity, where elements are equally distributed across classes):

It is calculated using the following equation:

$$\text{Gini impurity} = 1 - (\text{Probability of "Yes"})^2 - (\text{Probability of "No"})^2$$

At the decision nodes—that is, the root node and the internal nodes—Gini impurity should be calculated separately for each side of a condition, assuming an imbalance in row counts; these values are then combined to obtain the weighted average Gini impurity, which represents the total impurity for a single feature.

Let's use the categorical variable PLAY_TYPE as an example for demonstration purposes. We previously computed the counts of fourth-down conversion attempts categorized by the PLAY_TYPE and CONVERT class labels—but we ran that query against the entire nfl_pbp data set. Because our decision tree was fit on the X_train and y_train subsets from nfl_pbp, we need to join X_train and y_train into a single object by calling the pd.concat() method and then compute the counts for each PLAY_TYPE and CONVERT combination using groupby() and size():

```
>>> train_data = pd.concat([X_train, y_train], axis = 1)
>>> counts = train_data.groupby(['PLAY_TYPE', 'CONVERT']).size()
>>> print(counts)
PLAY_TYPE  CONVERT
0          0           64
           1          175
1          0          219
           1          160
dtype: int64
```

Before we plug these figures into the Gini impurity equation, it's useful to refresh our understanding from chapter 2 of how to calculate empirical probabilities, or probabilities derived from trials or real-world observations:

$$\text{Probability(Event)} = \frac{\text{number of successes observed}}{\text{number of observations made}}$$

It's also important to remember conditional probabilities from chapter 3, because awareness of specific circumstances can narrow the sample space, leading to more precise and relevant probabilities.

When the condition `PLAY_TYPE` <= 0.5 from our decision tree is true, it indicates that a running play (encoded as `0`) was called on fourth down. This resulted in 175 successful conversions and 64 failed attempts, leading to a loss of possession. Thus, our denominator equals the sum of 175 and 64, or 239. The numerator is therefore 175 for the probability of a successful conversion and 64 for the probability of a failed attempt. So, when `PLAY_TYPE` <= 0.5, the Gini impurity is

$$\text{Gini impurity(True)} = 1 - \left(\frac{175}{175 + 64}\right)^2 - \left(\frac{64}{175 + 64}\right)^2 = 0.3922$$

When the same condition is false, it means a passing play (encoded as `1`) was called on fourth down, which resulted in 160 successful and 219 unsuccessful conversion attempts. Our denominator is therefore the sum of 160 and 219, or 379. The numerator is 160 for the probability of a successful conversion and 219 for the probability of a failed attempt. Thus, when `PLAY_TYPE` is > 0.5, the Gini impurity is

$$\text{Gini impurity(False)} = 1 - \left(\frac{160}{160 + 219}\right)^2 - \left(\frac{219}{160 + 219}\right)^2 = 0.4879$$

The total Gini impurity, or the weighted average Gini impurity, is derived by multiplying the Gini impurities by the observation percentages—38.67% of the `train_data` observations are running plays and 61.33% are passing plays—and then summing these products, like so:

$$\text{Weighted Average Gini impurity} = 0.3922\,(0.3867) + 0.4879\,(0.6133) = 0.4509$$

Thus, the total Gini impurity for `PLAY_TYPE` equals 0.4509.

This must be greater than the Gini impurity for `TO_GO` because `TO_GO`, not `PLAY_TYPE`, is the feature assigned to the root node. We'll verify this assumption by explaining and demonstrating how the Gini impurity is derived for a numerical variable. It's a three-step process:

1. Sort the data in ascending order.
2. Calculate the averages between adjacent values.
3. Calculate the impurity values for each average. The split should occur where the Gini impurity is the lowest. For `TO_GO`, this point is at the average of 3 and 4.

Our next chunk of code splits `train_data` into two parts based on whether `TO_GO` is less than or equal to 3.5 or greater than 3.5. It then groups each subset by the `CONVERT` class labels and returns the row counts for each:

6.3 Fitting a decision tree

```
>>> to_go_less_than_3_5 = \
>>>     train_data[train_data['TO_GO'] <= 3.5]
>>> to_go_greater_than_3_5 = \
>>>     train_data[train_data['TO_GO'] > 3.5]
>>> counts_less_than_3_5 = (to_go_less_than_3_5 \
>>>                         .groupby('CONVERT').size())
>>> print('Counts for TO_GO <= 3.5:')
>>> print(counts_less_than_3_5)
>>> counts_greater_than_3_5 = (to_go_greater_than_3_5 \
>>>                            .groupby('CONVERT').size())
>>> print('Counts for TO_GO > 3.5:')
>>> print(counts_greater_than_3_5)
Counts for TO_GO <= 3.5:
CONVERT
0    127
1    268
dtype: int64
Counts for TO_GO > 3.5:
CONVERT
0    156
1     67
dtype: int64
```

- Creates one data frame where TO_GO is less than or equal to 3.5
- Creates another data frame where TO_GO is greater than 3.5
- Computes the counts from the first data frame by the CONVERT class labels
- Prints a header for the results
- Prints the results
- Computes the counts from the second data frame by the CONVERT class labels
- Prints a header for the results
- Prints the results

From these figures, we can compute the impurity values for both sides of the TO_GO <= 3.5 split:

$$\text{Gini impurity(True)} = 1 - \left(\frac{268}{268 + 127}\right)^2 - \left(\frac{127}{268 + 127}\right)^2 = 0.4363$$

$$\text{Gini impurity(False)} = 1 - \left(\frac{67}{67 + 156}\right)^2 - \left(\frac{156}{67 + 156}\right)^2 = 0.4204$$

If the data were equally divided across both sides of the TO_GO split, we could obtain the weighted average Gini impurity by simply adding 0.4603 and 0.3004 together. However, 63.92% of the data is on the left (true) side of the TO_GO <= 3.5 split, and the remaining 36.08% is on the right (false) side. Thus, we get the weighted impurity this way:

$$\text{Weighted Average Gini impurity} = 0.4363\,(0.6392) + 0.4204\,(0.3608) = 0.4305$$

Not only is this the lowest Gini impurity within TO_GO, but it is also the lowest impurity value across the feature set; as a result, TO_GO is assigned to the root node. Therefore, *it is the most significant variable for predicting the final class labels*. Now that we've explained how a feature is assigned to the root node, we will deconstruct the rest of the tree.

NODE ATTRIBUTES
One advantage of decision trees—we'll review the pros and cons of decision trees before shifting our focus to random forests—is their alignment between construction

and interpretation methodologies. Decision trees are constructed from the top down, beginning with the root node and then branching out into internal (or decision) nodes and leaf nodes. This structure mirrors the process of decision-making, where we start with overarching considerations (the root node) and gradually refine our choices based on specific criteria (internal nodes) until we arrive at a final decision (leaf nodes). Interpreting a decision tree involves understanding this hierarchical structure and the criteria used at each node to guide the decision-making process.

The information contained within every node of a decision tree—be it root, internal, or leaf—is typically referred to as the *node attributes* or occasionally as the *node properties* (see figure 6.8). Prioritizing the explanation of these attributes before adopting a broader perspective of our decision tree is crucial, as understanding the former undoubtedly enhances our comprehension of the latter.

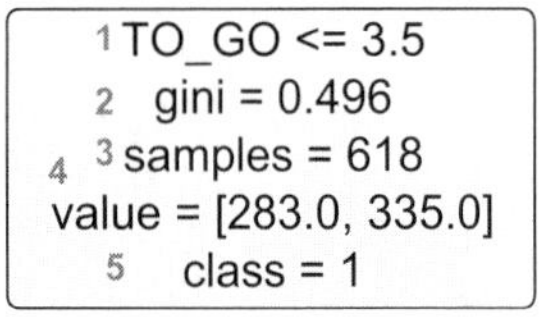

```
1 TO_GO <= 3.5
2 gini = 0.496
3 samples = 618
4 value = [283.0, 335.0]
5 class = 1
```

Figure 6.8 A close look at the root node attributes from the plotted decision tree. The root node and the internal nodes all contain these same attributes; leaf nodes have these attributes, too, minus the condition statement at the top.

Let's examine the note attributes in figure 6.8 line by line:

- *Line 1* shows the *condition statement*, often referred to as the *decision* or *split*. If the condition evaluates to true—for instance, if TO_GO is <= 3.5 or if PLAY_TYPE is <= 0.5—proceed to the left node; otherwise, proceed to the right node. Condition statements apply to the root node and internal nodes only.
- *Line 2* displays the *unweighted* Gini impurity. Another, potentially more practical approach to conceptualizing this measure is to consider it as representing the probability of incorrect classification if chosen randomly. Therefore, the closer the Gini impurity is to zero, the better the node is at classifying the data.
- *Line 3* shows the number of records from the training set that satisfy the condition of the node. The root node contains 618 observations, or samples—395 sent to the left of the tree and the other 223 sent to the right. The highest level of internal nodes—the nodes directly beneath the root node—also contains 618 samples when their individual samples are added together, and so forth. Decision trees don't drop any records. Pruning removes features and splits that don't provide significant differentiation, thereby simplifying the tree and making it easier to interpret and use; however, the records remain and, if necessary, are reallocated to other internal nodes.
- *Line 4* is an array that represents the distribution of samples among the target feature classes *at that node*. For example, at the root node, our training data includes 283 instances where CONVERT equals 0 and 335 instances where CONVERT equals 1. Similarly, when the data is further subset to 395 records based

on `PLAY_TYPE`, there are 127 instances where `CONVERT` equals 0 and 268 additional instances where `CONVERT` equals 1.
- *Line 5* shows the classification at that stage of the tree. For instance, if we were to stop the tree at the root node, we should classify `CONVERT` as a successful fourth-down conversion (encoded as 1), because at this level, there is a higher probability of converting on fourth down than not. Of course, the classification becomes more accurate as we move down the tree.

As we move forward to examine the remainder of our decision tree and demonstrate how to interpret it, it's important to emphasize one key point: pruning the tree has made this analysis far more manageable. Without pruning, the tree could have had three to four times as many nodes, making it much more complex; instead, it contains just two levels of internal nodes. Although this wasn't our primary objective, we prioritized simplicity and usability to avoid the risk of overfitting.

INTERNAL AND LEAF NODES

A decision tree is evaluated from the root node down to the leaf nodes, similar to how it is constructed. There are numerous permutations of "if-else" conditions along the way, thereby creating many unique paths from start to finish. Let's start by examining the two internal nodes directly beneath the root node (see figure 6.9).

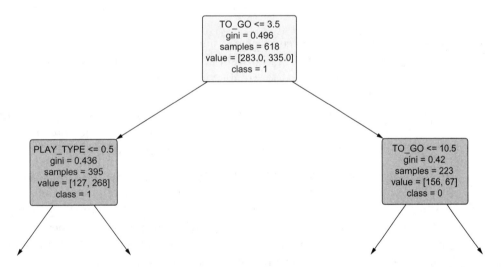

Figure 6.9 A close look at the very top of our decision tree: the root node and the first level of internal nodes. The root node has arrows pointing away from it, whereas internal nodes have arrows pointing toward and away from them.

When a condition is true, we always move to the left side of the tree; otherwise, we move to the right. Thus, when `TO_GO` is less than or equal to 3.5, we proceed to `PLAY_TYPE`; if `TO_GO` is greater than 3.5, we proceed instead to another `TO_GO` condition.

This particular split is especially meaningful because if the tree stopped at the first level of internal nodes, we would have opposite classifications for our target variable (and these internal nodes would instead be leaf nodes).

Before we proceed further down the tree, several points need to be addressed:

- The decision tree algorithm recursively splits the data at each node. After determining the root node, the data is then divided into subsets based on the best feature and threshold for that node.
- For each subset created by the root node split, the algorithm evaluates all possible features and thresholds to determine the best split. The split is the one that minimizes impurity (or, alternatively, information gain if we had selected entropy as our criterion instead of Gini) for that particular subset.
- Each split is optimized locally within the subset of data, which means different features or different thresholds of the same feature may be chosen for different branches.
- Numeric variables often have complex relationships with the target variable that can't be fully captured by a single split. Additional splits on the same numeric variable allow the tree to model these relationships more accurately.
- After the initial split at the root node, the resulting subsets might have different distributions and characteristics. A numeric variable that provided a useful split at the root might still be useful within these subsets, albeit with different thresholds.
- The hierarchical structure of decision trees means each node independently selects the best feature and threshold from the data available at that node. This allows the same numeric variable to be used multiple times with different conditions.
- During the construction of the tree, each node is evaluated independently. If a numeric variable has lower impurity at an unused threshold compared to other features and conditions, it will be selected again for further splits.

In short, the decision tree algorithm recursively splits data at each node by selecting the best remaining feature and threshold combination that minimizes impurity, optimizing each split locally within subsets. Numeric variables—which are split various ways depending on the number of unique values in the set—may be used multiple times with different thresholds to capture complex relationships with the target variable, as each node independently evaluates and selects the optimal feature and condition from top to bottom.

The left subtree is first divided by the categorical feature PLAY_TYPE, followed by subsequent splits at OFFENSIVE_TEAM_VENUE (categorical) and SCORE_DIFFERENTIAL (numeric). Because PLAY_TYPE is the topmost internal node, it is the most significant feature on this side of the tree. The left branch of the tree shows a strong propensity toward predicting a class label of 1, particularly when PLAY_TYPE assumes a value of 0. In instances where PLAY_TYPE equals 1, the predictive outcome is then determined by the split at SCORE_DIFFERENTIAL, which implies that OFFENSIVE_TEAM_VENUE holds relatively little significance: despite its role in reducing Gini impurity, it consistently predicts the majority class regardless of the condition (see figure 6.10).

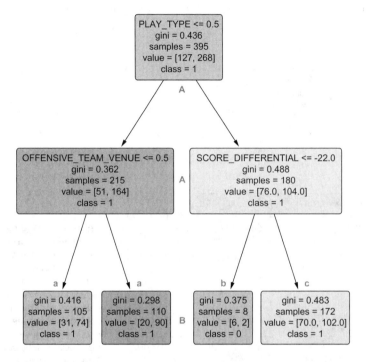

Figure 6.10 A closer look at the left subtree: two levels of internal nodes (A) and, at the bottom, four leaf nodes (B). When PLAY_TYPE is 0, thereby indicating a running play, the decision tree predicts a successful fourth-down conversion attempt (a); it doesn't matter if the team on offense is the road or home team. Alternatively, when PLAY_TYPE is 1, indicating a passing play, the decision tree evaluates SCORE_DIFFERENTIAL before making a prediction. If the team on offense is trailing by 22 points or more, the tree predicts a failed fourth-down conversion attempt (b); but if the team on offense is trailing by fewer than 22 points, the decision tree predicts a successful conversion (c).

The right subtree of the decision tree begins with the split on TO_GO <= 3.5 at the root. This split effectively divides the data, leading to a significant reduction in impurity. The subsequent split on TO_GO <= 10.5 at the top of the subtree further refines this separation, establishing a clear pathway for the classification process. SCORE_DIFFERENTIAL then plays a pivotal role, introducing additional conditions that further dissect the data into smaller, more homogenous subsets. Despite these multiple splits, the consistency in class predictions (class 0) throughout the leaf nodes indicates that the initial TO_GO split is highly effective in distinguishing the target class. The SCORE_DIFFERENTIAL conditions primarily serve to reduce the Gini impurity, enhancing the purity of the nodes without altering the overall class prediction. This consistent prediction pattern underscores the strong influence of the initial TO_GO split and highlights how subsequent conditions refine the data to confirm the class rather than change it (see figure 6.11). The right subtree therefore effectively uses both TO_GO and SCORE_DIFFERENTIAL to create a robust and consistent classification pathway down to the leaf nodes.

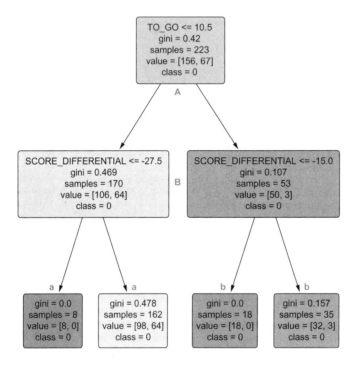

Figure 6.11 The right branch of the decision tree uses internal nodes TO_GO (A) and SCORE_DIFFERENTIAL (B) to establish a classification pathway, with the initial TO_GO split playing a crucial role in distinguishing the target class, followed by subsequent refinements that confirm the predicted class labels (a and b).

Although it was pruned, the decision tree algorithm strategically removed the feature QUARTER because it complicated the model more than it improved the model's predictive power. Incorporating additional features often boosts predictive accuracy, but sometimes the added complexity may not yield proportional benefits, particularly in decision trees where more features can lead to a proliferation of nodes and branches, potentially diminishing the clarity and usability of the outcomes.

On taking a broader perspective and considering the sequence of introduced features in the tree, with the understanding that feature significance diminishes from top to bottom, our decision tree strongly correlates with the preliminary analysis conducted prior to its construction. It was anticipated that TO_GO and PLAY_TYPE would hold the greatest predictive weight in determining the CONVERT class labels, a notion then validated by the structure of the tree. Before we transition from discussing a single decision tree to exploring a forest of trees, let's outline the advantages and disadvantages of decision trees as a machine learning approach compared to other models.

6.3.7 Advantages and disadvantages of decision trees

We have periodically referenced the pros and cons of decision trees, but let's take this opportunity to succinctly summarize their advantages and disadvantages. All model types come with inherent strengths and weaknesses, and decision trees are no exception. Understanding these points will help you determine whether decision trees are the best fit for your specific problem-solving needs.

Advantages:

- Decision trees are easy to understand and interpret. Their visual representation makes them accessible to non-experts, and they clearly show the decision-making process.
- Decision trees do not require normalization or scaling of data, making preprocessing simpler.
- They capture nonlinear relationships between features and the target variable without the need for complex transformations.
- Decision trees handle numeric and categorical data equally well.
- They provide insights into feature importance, indicating which features are most influential in predicting the target variable.
- They are relatively robust to outliers, as splits are based on the majority of the data.
- Decision trees can be used to solve both classification and regression problems.

Disadvantages:

- Decision trees are prone to overfitting, especially if left unpruned.
- Small changes in the data can result in a completely different tree structure, thereby making them unstable.
- They can be biased if one class is dominant. They may also perform poorly on imbalanced data sets without proper tuning.
- Large trees can become complex and therefore difficult to interpret, negating one of their advantages.
- Most decision trees create splits that are perpendicular to feature axes, which may not capture more complex relationships effectively.
- A single decision tree might lack the predictive power achievable through other methods.
- Decision trees use a greedy algorithm for splitting, meaning they make the best immediate decision at each step (splitting the data based on the most significant feature at that moment) without considering the overall effect on the entire tree.

Many of these disadvantages can be mitigated by fitting a random forest instead of a single decision tree.

6.4 Fitting a random forest

Random forest models are an ensemble learning technique that builds on the principles of decision trees to enhance predictive performance and robustness. Unlike a single decision tree, which can be prone to overfitting and instability, a random forest constructs multiple decision trees during training and merges their outputs to produce more accurate and stable predictions.

In a random forest, multiple decision trees are used to make a final prediction, each contributing to the overall decision. For example, consider two simple trees in the forest:

- Tree 1:
  - Root node: Age ≤ 30
  - Internal node (left): Income $\leq 50,000$
  - Leaf node (left): No (loan not approved)
  - Leaf node (right): Yes (loan approved)

- Tree 2:
  - Root node: Income $> 40,000$
  - Internal node (right): Age > 30
  - Leaf node (left): Yes (loan approved)
  - Leaf node (right): No (loan not approved)

Each tree independently classifies the data, and the final prediction is determined by the majority vote of all the trees in the random forest.

Each tree in the forest is trained on a different subset of the data, and features are randomly selected at each split, which helps to reduce variance and prevent overfitting. Although decision trees are easy to interpret and visualize, random forests, being aggregations of many trees, offer greater predictive power and resilience to noisy data at the expense of interpretability. This makes random forests a powerful tool for classification and regression tasks where accuracy and generalization are prioritized.

Random forests and decision trees are both fundamental tools in machine learning, but they differ significantly in methodology and performance. A decision tree operates by recursively partitioning the data based on the most significant features at each node, ultimately forming a tree-like structure of decisions. Although decision trees are easy to interpret and visualize, they are susceptible to overfitting, especially when they grow too deep. Overfitting occurs because the model captures noise and minor fluctuations in the training data, resulting in poor generalization to new, unseen data. Additionally, decision trees can be unstable, so small changes in the data can lead to a completely different tree structure.

In contrast, random forests mitigate these issues by employing an ensemble approach, combining the predictions of multiple decision trees to produce a more robust and accurate model. Each tree in a random forest is trained on a random subset of the data (with replacement, known as *bootstrap sampling*) and a random subset of features at each split. This randomness introduces diversity among the trees, thereby reducing the likelihood of overfitting. The final prediction is typically made by averaging the predictions (for regression) or taking a majority vote (for classification) from all the trees in the forest. Although this ensemble method enhances predictive performance and stability, it does so at the cost of interpretability. Unlike a single decision tree, which provides a clear decision path, the aggregated nature of random forests makes it more challenging to understand the individual decision-making process. However, the trade-off is often worthwhile in practice, as random forests generally offer superior accuracy and resilience to noisy data compared to individual decision trees.

This specific sampling technique—random subsets of data and features—is used to reduce correlation between individual trees. If every tree saw the same data and features, they would likely make similar mistakes. By introducing randomness, each tree learns different patterns, which increases the overall diversity of the forest and leads to better generalization when making predictions on unseen data.

Fitting a random forest in Python is very similar to fitting a decision tree, as both use straightforward commands from the scikit-learn library. However, there is a lot more happening behind the scenes with random forests, including the training of multiple trees on different data subsets and feature selections, to create a robust ensemble model.

6.4.1 Fitting the model

Typically, we start by importing a data set, identifying meaningful relationships between features and the target variable, and splitting our data frame into training and testing subsets. However, those steps are firmly in our rearview mirror. Because we are fitting a random forest to the data we've been working with all along, we can skip to model fitting, using the training subset previously derived from the `nfl_pbp` data frame.

Whereas the `DecisionTreeClassifier()` method initializes a decision tree classifier object, the `RandomForestClassifier()` method, also from Python's scikit-learn library, initializes a random forest classifier object named `rf`. The first of four parameters passed to `RandomForestClassifier()` is `n_estimators = 50`, which sets the number of trees in the random forest to `50`.

Although there are no strict rules dictating the number of trees to fit in a random forest—it all depends on factors such as the dimensionality of the data, computational resources available, and desired model performance—there are some general guidelines:

- Increasing the number of trees in the forest can improve the model's performance, up to a certain point. Adding more trees can help reduce overfitting and improve the generalization ability of the model.
- However, there are diminishing returns associated with adding more trees. After a certain point, the improvement in model performance achieved by adding additional trees becomes marginal, and the computational cost increases.
- The computational resources required to fit a large number of trees are not incidental; it is therefore essential to consider factors like processing power and memory when deciding on the number of trees to fit.

- Although there is no one-size-fits-all rule, a common heuristic is to start with a moderate number of trees (e.g., 50) and adjust based on performance results. In practice, the optimal number of trees may vary depending on the task and the data.

The remaining three parameters are identical to those we previously passed to the `DecisionTreeClassifier()` method:

- `criterion = 'gini'` specifies the criterion used to measure the quality of a split at each node. The Gini impurity criterion measures the probability of incorrectly classifying a randomly selected element if it were randomly labeled according to the distribution of samples in the node.
- `max_depth = 3` restricts the maximum depth of each decision tree in the forest to the root node, two levels of internal nodes, and the leaf nodes. Although pruning prevents overfitting and improves interpretability, it may also hinder the model's ability to capture complex patterns in the data, thereby sacrificing some of its complexity and expressiveness.
- `random_state = 0` sets the random seed to ensure reproducible results if and when the same seed is used in the future.

The `RandomForestClassifier` class from the `ensemble` module of the scikit-learn library must be imported first. Although the code structure resembles that of fitting a decision tree classifier, it originates from a separate module:

```
>>> from sklearn.ensemble import RandomForestClassifier
>>> rf = RandomForestClassifier(n_estimators = 50,
>>>                             criterion = 'gini',
>>>                             max_depth = 3,
>>>                             random_state = 0)
```

The `RandomForestClassifier()` method does the following:

- Initializes a random forest classifier object with 50 trees
- Limits the maximum depth of each tree to three levels
- Uses the Gini impurity criterion for splitting nodes
- Guarantees reproducibility, as long as the same seed is used in subsequent runs

Next a call is made to the `fit()` method, which trains the random forest classifier, `rf`, using the training data (`X_train`) and corresponding labels (`y_train`) previously cut from the `nfl_pbp` data frame. This step enables the model to learn patterns in the data, preparing it for making predictions on new data:

```
>>> rf.fit(X_train, y_train)
```

This is *the* critical step in the process of training a random forest classifier using the scikit-learn library. Here, `rf` represents an instance of the `RandomForestClassifier` class, which was just configured, of course, with parameters such as the number of trees, maximum depth, and impurity criterion. The `fit()` method is called on this instance, taking X_train and y_train as required arguments. X_train is a 2D array or data frame containing the training data's feature variables, and y_train is a 1D array or series containing the corresponding target labels. By invoking the fit() method, the classifier learns from the provided data, building multiple decision trees on different subsets of the data and features, and combining their predictions to form an ensemble model.

During the training process, each decision tree in the random forest is trained on a bootstrap sample (a random sample with replacement) of the training data. At each split in the tree, a random subset of features is considered to determine the best split, introducing randomness that helps reduce overfitting and improve generalization. This method ensures that the model captures diverse patterns and relationships within the data. Once the training is complete, the random forest model is equipped with the decision rules derived from the training data, ready to make predictions on new, unseen data.

6.4.2 Predicting responses

Predictions are then made on the test data (X_test) using the random forest classifier trained on X_train and y_train. The predicted class labels are stored in an object called y_pred:

```
<<< y_pred = rf.predict(X_test)
```

Each tree in the forest makes a series of predictions; the final predictions in a classification tree are determined by majority voting among the trees.

6.4.3 Evaluating the model

Because random forests consist of an ensemble of decision trees, they are evaluated using similar methods. The metrics_accuracy_score() method was previously called to calculate the accuracy rate of our decision tree; we will call it again to compute this for our random forest. Using similar methods to calculate standard metrics across various models, such as decision trees versus random forests or different random forest variants, simplifies the model selection process.

The metrics_accuracy_score() method compares the true labels from the test set to the predicted labels and computes an accuracy rate; that figure is then multiplied by 100 to convert that measure to a percentage. The print() method displays the result, which has been rounded to the nearest whole number:

```
>>> rf_accuracy = metrics.accuracy_score(y_test, y_pred) * 100
>>> print(f'Accuracy: {round(rf_accuracy, 0)}%')
Accuracy: 62.0%
```

The marginal increase in accuracy from 61% with a decision tree to 62% with a random forest on the same data set may seem underwhelming at first glance. However, this difference in performance reflects deeper insights into the nature of the data and the models themselves. Although the random forest's improvement is modest, it's crucial to recognize that its architecture inherently offers advantages over a single decision tree. Random forests operate by aggregating predictions from multiple decision trees, each trained on different subsets of the data with random feature selection. This ensemble approach typically results in a more robust and generalized model, capable of capturing complex patterns and reducing the risk of overfitting compared to a standalone decision tree.

Several factors could be at play in holding back the random forest's performance. First, the data may lack distinguishing features or exhibit high levels of noise, limiting the model's ability to discern meaningful patterns. Additionally, the hyperparameters of the random forest, such as the number of trees and maximum depth, may not have been optimized for this specific data set, potentially constraining its predictive power. Furthermore, the data set's characteristics, such as class imbalance or the presence of outliers, could pose challenges that affect model performance. However, even with these limitations, the random forest is likely to be more robust than a single decision tree, as it uses the collective wisdom of multiple trees, making it better equipped to handle variations in the data and more likely to generalize well to new, unseen instances.

CONFUSION MATRIX

The 62% accuracy rate of our model is an overall measure across both classes. By generating a confusion matrix, we can obtain more detailed insights—specifically, we can evaluate the model's performance for each CONVERT class label:

```
>>> conf_matrix = confusion_matrix(y_test, y_pred)
>>> print(conf_matrix)
[[68 70]
 [32 95]]
```

The confusion matrix displays the model's performance metrics. In the lower-right quadrant, we find the true positives, which represent instances where the model correctly predicted the positive class (95). True negatives, indicating correct predictions of the negative class, are located in the upper-right quadrant (70). Conversely, false positives, indicating incorrect predictions of the positive class, are in the upper-left quadrant (68), whereas false negatives, representing incorrect predictions of the negative class, reside in the lower-left quadrant (32). These figures can be plugged into a pair of arithmetic operations to get the accuracy rates per class. The accuracy rate when the true label is 0 is

$$\text{True Label}_0 = \left(\frac{tn}{tn + fp}\right) 100$$

where

- tn represents the true negatives.
- fp represents the false positives.

And the accuracy rate when the true label is 1 is

$$\text{True Label}_1 = \left(\frac{tp}{tp + fp}\right) 100$$

where

- *tp* represents the true positives.
- *fn* represents the false negatives.

Using Python again as a calculator, we get the accuracy rates for each class label:

```
>>> accuracy_rate_0 = 70 / (70 + 68) * 100
>>> print(f'Accuracy: {round(accuracy_rate_0, 0)}%')
Accuracy: 51.0%

>>> accuracy_rate_1 = 95 / (95 + 32) * 100
>>> pr print(f'Accuracy: {round(accuracy_rate_1, 0)}%')
Accuracy: 75.0%
```

The random forest performed similarly to the decision tree across classes: it struggled when the true label was 0 but performed quite well (better than the decision tree, in fact) when the true label was 1.

6.4.4 Feature importance

Understanding the importance of each feature in a random forest model is crucial for interpreting its predictions and gaining insights into the underlying data patterns. In a decision tree, we can easily discern the importance of features by plotting the stand-alone tree and observing the splits. However, in a random forest, which consists of multiple decision trees (50 in this case), plotting each individual tree is impractical. Instead, we need to take a different approach to evaluate feature importance across the entire forest. By analyzing feature importance, we can identify which features have the most significant effect on the model's decisions, enabling better understanding and transparency and potentially guiding further data preprocessing or feature engineering steps.

Feature importance in a random forest is typically measured by how much each feature contributes to reducing impurity—features that consistently lead to better splits across many trees are assigned higher importance scores. Feature importance can be visualized either by printing it in a table format or by plotting it as a simple bar chart using methods from the `matplotlib` library. We are doing the latter:

```
>>> importances = rf.feature_importances_
>>> features = X.columns
>>> indices = np.argsort(importances)[::-1]
```

- `importances = rf.feature_importances_` — Retrieves the importance scores of each feature used in the trained random forest model
- `features = X.columns` — Extracts the column names of the feature matrix X, representing the feature names used in the model
- `indices = np.argsort(importances)[::-1]` — Sorts the indices in the importances array in descending order, so the most important features are listed first

```
>>> sorted_features = features[indices]
>>> sorted_importances = importances[indices]
>>> plt.figure()
>>> plt.bar(sorted_features, sorted_importances)
>>> plt.xlabel('Feature')
>>> plt.ylabel('Feature Importance')
>>> plt.title('Feature Importance in \
              RandomForestClassifier')
>>> plt.tight_layout()
>>> plt.show()
```

In a feature importance plot generated from a `RandomForestClassifier`, the values represent the relative importance of each feature in predicting the target variable (see figure 6.12). A feature importance value of 0.6 for one feature indicates that this feature contributes significantly to the model's predictions, suggesting it has a strong

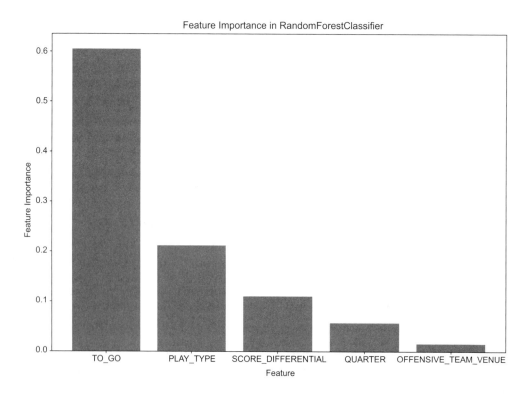

Figure 6.12 A feature importance plot generated from the `RandomForestClassifier`. It displays the relative importance of each feature to the final predicted class labels, where, if stacked, a single bar would equal 1. The features are sorted, from left to right, in descending order of relative importance, with `TO_GO` and `PLAY_TYPE` accounting for approximately 80% of the model's predictive power.

influence on the target variable. Conversely, a feature importance value of 0.1 for another feature implies that this feature has less effect on the predictions compared to the first feature, but it still contributes to the model's overall performance. Therefore, higher values indicate more important features, whereas lower values indicate less influential features.

These findings accurately reflect the analysis conducted prior to fitting our decision tree. It appears that the random forest, in contrast to the decision tree, was able to detect discrepancies in CONVERT class labels between quarters 1 through 3 versus quarter 4.

6.4.5 Extracting random trees

Although it's not practical to plot or display 50 trees, we can extract a small random sample (see figures 6.13 and 6.14). By presenting a subset of randomly extracted trees from the random forest ensemble, the diversity inherent in the model is revealed. Each of these individual trees is trained on distinct subsets of the data and features, providing insight into the varied decision-making processes that contribute to the overall predictive capability of the random forest. Visualizing these trees allows us to analyze differences in feature importance, node splitting criteria, and the overall structure of the ensemble, demonstrating the robustness and adaptability of the random forest algorithm:

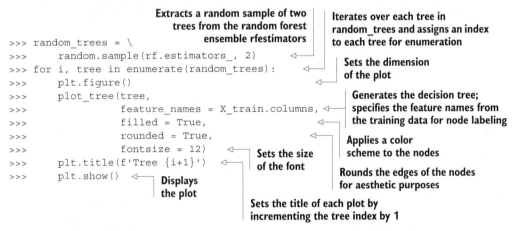

The second random tree (figure 6.14) has a very different structure from the first (figure 6.13). In contrast to decision trees, random forest trees lack a direct attribute displaying the classification at each node. Despite the challenge of identifying the randomly selected features for each tree, owing to potential pruning effects, it remains intriguing to observe the diversity among trees. Particularly notable are variations in sample sizes, as well as the assignment of features and splits to the root node. Although examining two trees offers nothing definitive in terms of the final class predictions, analyzing a pair of randomly extracted trees provides valuable insights into the ensemble's inner workings, shedding light on the model's robustness and the variability in feature importance and decision-making processes across different trees.

182   CHAPTER 6 *Fitting a decision tree and a random forest*

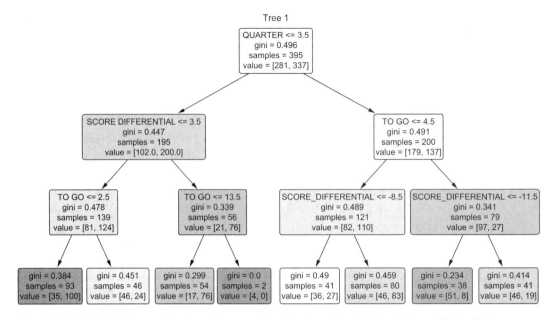

Figure 6.13 The first of two random trees from a random forest model containing 50 trees. Notice that QUARTER is at the root node; thus, based on this one random split of the data, QUARTER, which didn't factor into our decision tree model, is the most significant variable in this subset for predicting the final class labels.

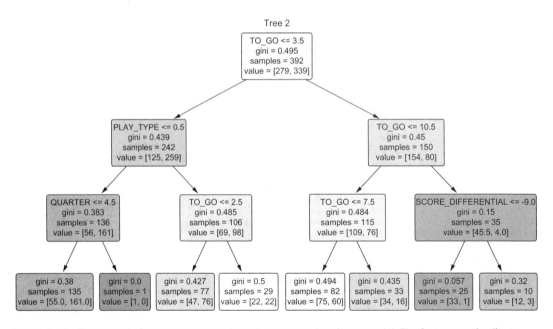

Figure 6.14 The second of two random trees from the same random forest model. The features and splits to construct one tree versus another can, and will, vary significantly.

In this chapter and the two that preceded it, we covered the foundations and applications of linear and logistic regressions, examined the intricacies of decision trees, and explored the ensemble learning technique of random forests. These models have provided us with a diverse set of tools to address a wide range of data types and predictive challenges. In the next chapter, we will advance to fitting time series models, focusing on their unique temporal dependencies and autocorrelations. This will involve techniques such as ARIMA and exponential smoothing, providing a comprehensive approach to forecasting and analyzing sequential data.

Summary

- A decision tree is a supervised machine learning model used for classification and regression tasks. It splits the data into subsets based on feature values, creating a tree structure with decision nodes and leaf nodes representing predictions. Decision trees are easy to interpret and visualize.
- Training a decision tree involves splitting the data based on features to minimize node impurities. It uses the training set for learning and the test set for evaluation, ensuring unbiased accuracy and generalization assessment.
- Evaluating a decision tree includes computing overall accuracy by comparing predicted and actual labels in the test set. A confusion matrix provides a detailed performance breakdown, showing true/false positives and negatives for each class, helping to identify areas for improvement.
- Building a decision tree involves recursive splitting based on significant features to maximize class separation, continuing until the subsets are pure or meet stopping criteria. Interpretation follows the path from root to leaves, ensuring consistent model construction and understanding.
- A random forest is a supervised model for classification and regression, consisting of multiple decision trees trained on different data and feature subsets. This ensemble method typically enhances accuracy and reduces overfitting by aggregating predictions from multiple trees, providing robust performance.
- Evaluating a random forest involves steps similar to a decision tree, including computing overall accuracy and using a confusion matrix for granular performance insights. The aggregated results from multiple trees offer a more robust evaluation and reliable performance across classes.
- Feature importance in random forests measures each feature's contribution to predictive power by assessing impurity reduction across all trees. This provides a comprehensive view of influential features, helping to identify and prioritize significant variables for accurate predictions.
- Although this chapter focuses on decision trees and random forests, other powerful tree-based methods like XGBoost and Gradient Boosting are also popular for tackling complex classification and regression problems. These models build on the strengths of decision trees, using advanced techniques to boost accuracy and handle challenging data patterns and offering further options for sophisticated analysis beyond what we covered here.

Fitting time series models

This chapter covers
- Time series components and analysis
- ARIMA models
- Exponential smoothing models
- Model evaluation and diagnostics
- Forecasting

Transitioning from traditional models like linear and logistic regression and decision trees and random forests to time series analysis represents a shift from working with unordered data sets to analyzing sequential, time-ordered data where temporal patterns, such as trends and seasonality, may play a significant role. In many statistical methods, we often work with independent and identically distributed data, where predictions are made based on historical data without considering the order of the data points. However, in time series analysis, the temporal order of observations is crucial, as each data point may depend on prior values.

This chapter will examine the fundamentals of time series analysis, providing a comprehensive overview of models like ARIMA (used for capturing patterns based on past values) and exponential smoothing (which forecasts future values by weighing recent observations more heavily). We will explore practical applications by forecasting closing stock prices of a public company and comparing competing models fit to the same data. Note, however, that stock prices are influenced by numerous unpredictable factors, such as public opinion, which can limit the accuracy of forecasts. By the end of this chapter, you will be equipped with foundational techniques and tools to perform reliable time series forecasting, thereby enabling you to make informed decisions based on temporal data.

7.1 Distinguishing forecasts from predictions

In time series analysis, we focus on making *forecasts* rather than *predictions*. Although these terms are often used interchangeably, they have distinct meanings in this context. Most machine learning models make predictions based on patterns in the input data, but they often do not account for time order unless specifically designed for time-dependent data. Forecasts, on the other hand, involve predicting future values based on past observations, accounting for the time-based structure of the data. This transition necessitates understanding the temporal dependencies and patterns that characterize time series data.

Working with time series or longitudinal data involves analyzing data points collected or recorded at specific time intervals (seconds, minutes, hours, days, months, etc.). This contrasts with cross-sectional data, where observations are collected at a single point in time. Time series data can be found in various fields, including finance (e.g., closing stock prices), economics (e.g., gross domestic product), healthcare (e.g., patient vital signs), and digital analytics (e.g., web traffic). Analyzing such data often aims to uncover trends, seasonal patterns, and cyclic behaviors that can provide insights and support forecasting.

The two most common methods for time series forecasting are ARIMA (autoregressive integrated moving average) and exponential smoothing. ARIMA models are powerful tools that combine autoregression (AR), differencing (I for *integration*), and moving averages (MAs) to model time series data. These models are particularly useful for capturing various temporal dependencies and trends within the data. On the other hand, exponential smoothing techniques, including simple, double, and Holt–Winters exponential smoothing, are used to smooth out the noise in the data and highlight underlying trends and seasonal patterns.

Both ARIMA and exponential smoothing methods offer valuable approaches to time series forecasting, each suited to different data characteristics. ARIMA models are powerful for capturing complex temporal dependencies and trends, especially in data with autocorrelations or nonstationarity. Exponential smoothing methods, on the other hand, are valued for their simplicity and effectiveness in highlighting short-term fluctuations and long-term trends in relatively stable data sets. By selecting the appropriate method, whether ARIMA for more intricate patterns or exponential smoothing for consistent trends, we can generate forecasts that better inform decision-making across various domains.

7.2 Importing and plotting the data

Forecasting stock prices is one of the most popular and challenging time series use cases due to its direct effect on financial markets and investment decisions. Stock prices are influenced by a multitude of factors, including economic indicators, company performance, mergers and acquisitions, market sentiment, geopolitical events, and even psychological factors such as investor behavior. The complex interplay of these variables makes predicting stock prices accurately a formidable task.

Several reasons contribute to the difficulty of accurately forecasting stock prices. First, stock prices exhibit nonstationary and volatile behavior, meaning they can vary significantly over time and are influenced by sudden shifts in market conditions or investor sentiment. These abrupt changes can make it challenging to capture long-term trends and forecast short-term movements. Second, financial markets are generally efficient and incorporate new information rapidly. Even small pieces of news or economic data can cause significant price movements, making it challenging for models to consistently outperform the market—although high-frequency trading may exploit brief inefficiencies. Third, the underlying dynamics driving stock prices are often nonlinear and may not adhere to simple linear relationships. Traditional statistical methods like ARIMA and exponential smoothing models may struggle to capture these complex patterns effectively.

Despite these challenges, similar methods and approaches in time series analysis apply across different domains. Techniques such as ARIMA and exponential smoothing are versatile tools used not only for stock price forecasting but also for predicting demand in retail, traffic patterns in transportation, energy consumption, and many other applications. The fundamental principles of identifying patterns, incorporating seasonality or trends, and handling noisy data remain consistent, underscoring the broad applicability of time series analysis techniques.

Although forecasting stock prices poses unique difficulties due to the intricate nature of financial markets and the rapid dissemination of information, the methodologies employed in time series analysis offer valuable insights and predictive capabilities across diverse fields beyond finance. This versatility highlights the robustness and utility of time series models in tackling forecasting challenges across various domains.

7.2.1 Fetching financial data

When it comes to retrieving historical market data directly in a Python script, establishing a connection to Yahoo Finance is no doubt the best way to go. The yfinance library is a powerful tool that streamlines the process. This library offers seamless access to a wide range of financial data, including historical stock prices, trading volumes, dividends, and more. By specifying the ticker symbol and date range, analysts and researchers can efficiently fetch and utilize data for various financial analyses and modeling tasks. Furthermore, yfinance integrates well with other Python libraries such as pandas, allowing for easy manipulation, visualization, and further analysis of the fetched data.

This makes it an invaluable resource for anyone involved in financial research, market analysis, or investment strategy development within the Python ecosystem.

Our first order of business is to import the yfinance library (assuming it has already been installed, of course). Importing it is no different than importing any other Python library:

```
>>> import yfinance as yf
```

We now have direct access to every method and attribute offered by the yfinance library, which is easily accessible via the yf alias.

Our next line of code is a straightforward assignment statement that initializes a variable called `ticker_symbol` with the ticker symbol AAPL. Because AAPL is a character string, it must be bounded by single or double quotation marks:

```
>>> ticker_symbol = 'AAPL'
```

In finance, a ticker symbol is a unique series of letters assigned to a security for trading purposes; it identifies a specific stock or security on a stock exchange or trading platform. For example, AAPL is the ticker symbol for Apple, Inc.

> **Ticker symbols**
>
> There are several efficient methods to retrieve ticker symbols. Financial websites—not just Yahoo Finance, but also Google Finance, for instance—allow you to search by company name to find the corresponding ticker symbol. Similarly, financial news websites like MarketWatch, Bloomberg, and CNBC provide search functions for this purpose. Stock exchange websites, including the NYSE and NASDAQ, offer search tools to locate ticker symbols for listed companies. Additionally, financial data platforms such as Morningstar, Reuters, and S&P Capital IQ include ticker symbol lookup features.

Assigning the ticker symbol to a variable is optional, but doing so significantly simplifies code maintenance. Rather than manually replacing every instance of a specific ticker symbol (like AAPL) throughout the code, defining it in one place allows you to change it more easily whenever needed.

To efficiently fetch historical stock data, we've created a function, `fetch_stock_data()`, that encapsulates the data-fetching steps. This approach makes the code more modular, reusable, and adaptable to different stocks, date ranges, and intervals. By using a function, you can quickly fetch data for any ticker symbol without duplicating code, which also reduces the chance of errors when changing parameters:

```
>>> def fetch_stock_data(ticker_symbol, start_date, end_date,
                         interval = '1d'):
        ticker_data = yf.Ticker(ticker_symbol)
>>> stock_data = ticker_data.history(start = start_date,
                                     end = end_date,
                                     interval = interval)
>>> return stock_data
```

This function works in two main steps: first, it initializes a `Ticker` object associated with the given ticker symbol, connecting Python to Yahoo Finance's data for that stock. Second, it calls the `history()` method on the `Ticker` object to fetch the stock's historical data. Passing the start and end dates (formatted in the ISO 8601 format YYYY-MM-DD) and specifying the desired interval allows for precise and accurate retrieval of historical data.

You can then use this function to fetch stock data for any ticker symbol and date range by providing the relevant parameters. Because the `interval` parameter defaults to `'1d'`, you don't need to specify it unless you want data at a different frequency, like hourly (`'1h'`) or weekly (`'1wk'`):

```
>>> stock_data = fetch_stock_data('AAPL', '2023-10-01', '2024-04-30')
```

This approach makes your code more flexible, allowing you to retrieve data for any stock symbol or time period simply by changing the function parameters. Additionally, specifying dates in ISO 8601 format ensures compatibility with the `history()` method and prevents interpretation errors. In this example, the `fetch_stock_data()` function streamlines the data-fetching process. Specifying the start and end dates in ISO 8601 format ensures compatibility, as it is the required date format for the code to run without throwing an error.

> **ISO 8601 date formats**
>
> ISO 8601 is an internationally recognized standard for representing dates and times in a clear and unambiguous manner. It specifies formats such as YYYY-MM-DD for dates, ensuring consistency across different countries and systems. In programming and data analysis, adhering to ISO 8601 ensures compatibility and simplifies date handling, as it reduces ambiguity about the order of year, month, and day components. This standard also includes formats for times, durations, and combined date-time representations, providing a comprehensive framework for precise date and time representation in various applications, from financial data analysis to software development and beyond.
>
> In Python, the `datetime` module facilitates working with ISO 8601-compliant dates and times, allowing for easy parsing. Embracing ISO 8601 promotes clarity and interoperability, which are essential for accurate data processing and communication across diverse platforms and regions.

We now have a pandas data frame called `stock_data` that contains seven months of Apple market information. Apart from the temporal aspect of the data, our primary interest lies in the daily closing price of the stock. Therefore, we subset `stock_data` to extract the `Close` variable and assign the resulting data to a new data frame named `close_prices`:

```
>>> close_prices = stock_data[['Close']]
```

This dropped the date index: financial data series are typically indexed by date, or timestamp, which means each observation corresponds to one interval of market activity. Our next line of code resets the `close_prices` index with a default numeric index starting from zero:

```
>>> close_prices = close_prices.reset_index(drop = True)
```

This was another discretionary operation, but replacing the timestamp with a numeric index, which squarely corresponds to trading days (days when financial markets are open), will simplify our upcoming time series charts. Using numerical labels on the *x* axis makes the charts cleaner and more straightforward, thereby avoiding the clutter of date timestamps. However, note that this approach depends on the specific market's open and close times, which may differ across exchanges.

7.2.2 Understanding the data

The `info()` method returns summary information about a pandas data frame, including row and column counts, non-null counts, and data types. It's a quick and easy way to get an additional understanding of a data frame before considering further analysis or preprocessing steps:

```
>>> print(close_prices.info())
<class 'pandas.core.frame.DataFrame'>
RangeIndex: 145 entries, 0 to 144
Data columns (total 1 columns):
 #   Column  Non-Null Count  Dtype
---  ------  --------------  -----
 0   Close   145 non-null    float64
dtypes: float64(1)
memory usage: 1.3 KB
None
```

As expected, the data retrieved from Yahoo Finance shows no null values, and the closing price of Apple's stock, representing the price at the end of each trading day, is consistently displayed as floating-point numbers. Stock prices are typically presented as floating-point numbers (floats) due to their inherent need for precision in representing fractional values, such as cents and smaller price increments. This format ensures that financial data retains accuracy and granularity, which is crucial for comprehensive analysis and decision-making in trading and investment contexts. By using floats, financial data sets can accommodate a wide range of price fluctuations while maintaining computational efficiency and compatibility across various financial platforms and systems.

The `head()` and `tail()` methods print the top and bottom of a data frame, defaulting to five rows each when no parameters are specified. Note that historical stock prices may change slightly over time due to adjustments for dividends, stock splits, or corrections by data providers; so, your results may differ, albeit slightly:

190 CHAPTER 7 *Fitting time series models*

```
>>> print(close_prices.head())
        Close
0   173.300247
1   171.953735
2   173.210495
3   174.457260
4   177.030579

print(close_prices.tail())
         Close
140  166.899994
141  169.020004
142  169.889999
143  169.300003
144  173.500000
```

Interestingly, the stock's closing price on April 30, 2024, remained nearly unchanged compared to October 1, 2023. However, as we are about to discover, there were substantial fluctuations in the price over these seven months.

7.2.3 Plotting the data

Plotting time series data, particularly daily stock prices, is essential for visualizing trends, patterns, and fluctuations in financial markets. These plots provide valuable insights into the performance of stocks over time, helping analysts and investors identify key price movements and make informed decisions. By plotting daily stock prices, we can observe how prices evolve throughout each trading day, capture trends such as upward or downward movements, and detect potential support and resistance levels. Visualizations of daily stock prices also facilitate the comparison of historical performance, enabling stakeholders to assess volatility, trading volumes, and overall market sentiment. These visual representations serve as foundational tools in technical analysis and quantitative research, offering a clear and intuitive way to interpret complex market dynamics.

The following snippet of `matplotlib` code generates a time series chart displaying the closing prices of Apple's stock from October 1, 2023, through April 30, 2024 (see figure 7.1):

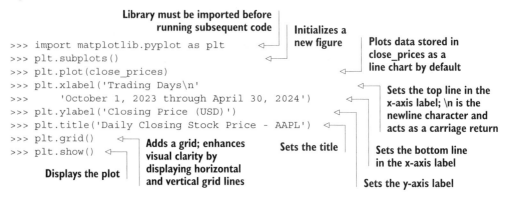

Although Apple's stock was priced at roughly $173 when the market closed on October 1, 2023, and again when the market closed on April 30, 2024, the price was highly volatile over these seven months, soaring to nearly $198 in December 2023 and plunging to $165 in April 2024. Such volatility is hardly unusual in financial markets, where stock prices frequently experience significant fluctuations due to various economic and company-specific factors. This inherent unpredictability makes it challenging to accurately forecast future stock prices when using such volatile prices as a baseline.

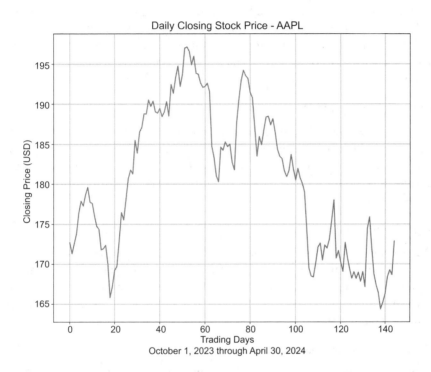

Figure 7.1 The daily closing price of Apple (AAPL) stock between October 1, 2023, and April 30, 2024. The more volatility in time series data, stock prices, and so on, the more challenging it is to fit an accurate forecast.

Nevertheless, we will fit an ARIMA model and then a series of exponential smoothing models to the first six months of data and then generate a forecast for the following month. This forecast will be compared to the actual stock prices to evaluate the accuracy and effectiveness of these time series models in predicting future price movements.

7.3   Fitting an ARIMA model

An ARIMA (autoregressive integrated moving average) model is a fundamental tool in time series analysis and forecasting, capable of capturing complex patterns and dynamics within sequential data. ARIMA models combine three key components—

autoregression (AR), integration (I), and moving averages (MAs)—to effectively model time-dependent data. Each component addresses different aspects of the time series, making ARIMA versatile for a wide range of applications in finance, economics, weather forecasting, and more. Next, we will define each component and briefly explain how they work together to make ARIMA a powerful forecasting tool.

7.3.1 Autoregression (AR) component

The AR part of ARIMA models the linear relationship between an observation and a specified number of its previous values, known as *lagged observations* or *autoregressive terms*. This component assesses how past values of the series influence its current value. For instance, in an $AR(1)$ model, the current value is regressed on its immediate past value. By incorporating these past observations, ARIMA can capture underlying trends and patterns in the data.

7.3.2 Integration (I) component

The I part signifies the differencing of the time series to make it stationary. Stationarity implies that the statistical properties of the series, such as mean and variance, do not change over time. Differencing involves subtracting the previous observation from the current observation, which removes trends or seasonal patterns that could affect the series' stability.

7.3.3 Moving average (MA) component

The MA component models the relationship between the current value of the series and random noise in the past. It captures short-term fluctuations that are not accounted for by the autoregression and differencing components. In an MA model, the current value is expressed as a linear combination of past error terms, helping to smooth out irregularities in the data.

7.3.4 Combining ARIMA components

Typically, the I component is addressed first in ARIMA modeling. This involves determining the order of differencing, d, required to make the time series stationary. Once the data has been differenced adequately, the subsequent steps involve identifying the AR and MA components, p and q, respectively. This sequential approach ensures that each component of the ARIMA model is appropriately specified to capture the underlying patterns and dynamics of the time series data. When fitting an ARIMA, the nonnegative integers assigned to p, d, and q are provided to the model to generate the forecast.

Before diving into finer details, it is prudent to introduce the concepts of stationarity and differencing. These concepts are foundational as they pave the way for understanding how to determine the appropriate degree of differencing, d, essential in preparing time series data for ARIMA modeling. Stationarity is crucial because it ensures that the statistical properties of the time series, such as mean and variance, remain consistent over time. Differencing, on the other hand, plays a key role in transforming nonstationary data into a stationary form by removing trends or seasonal patterns. Understanding these concepts sets a solid foundation for effectively applying ARIMA models in time series analysis and forecasting.

7.3.5 Stationarity

Stationarity is a fundamental concept in time series analysis, defining the behavior of a stochastic process where statistical properties remain constant over time. In simpler terms, a stationary time series is one whose mean, variance, and autocovariance (covariance between two time points) do not change over time. This stability allows for reliable forecasting and statistical inference.

STATISTICAL PROPERTIES

Stationarity in time series analysis entails specific properties that ensure the statistical characteristics of the data remain consistent over time, facilitating reliable modeling and forecasting.

First, a *constant mean* implies that the average value of the time series does not change across different time points. Mathematically, for any given time t, $E(Y_t)$, where E denotes the expected value or mean, remains the same. This property suggests that the central tendency of the data does not shift over time, providing a stable reference point for understanding the series' behavior.

Second, *constant variance* dictates that the variability or spread of the time series observations remains uniform across all time points. Formally, $Var(Y_t)$, representing the variance of Y_t, does not depend on t. This characteristic ensures that the magnitude of fluctuations around the mean remains consistent, indicating that the data points scatter evenly around the mean without systematic changes in dispersion over time.

Third, *constant autocovariance* involves the relationship between the series' values at different time points. Autocovariance measures the covariance between two time points, t and s, denoted as $Cov(Y_t, Y_s)$. Importantly, in a stationary time series, autocovariance only depends on the lag $|t - s|$, the absolute difference between t and s, not on the specific values of t and s themselves. This means the degree of dependence between observations remains consistent regardless of when the observations occur, reflecting a stable correlation structure over time.

Achieving stationarity typically involves identifying and addressing trends and seasonality within the data. *Trends* refer to long-term movements or patterns, whereas *seasonality* involves repeating patterns at regular intervals. Differencing is a common technique used to achieve stationarity by subtracting the previous observation from the current observation. This process removes trends or seasonal patterns, thereby stabilizing the mean and variance of the time series.

In summary, the properties of stationarity—constant mean, constant variance, and constant autocovariance—provide a foundational framework for understanding and analyzing time series data. These characteristics ensure that the statistical properties of the data remain consistent over time, facilitating accurate modeling, forecasting, and inference.

194   CHAPTER 7 *Fitting time series models*

Visualizing nonstationary and stationary data in a quadrant of plots provides a clear comparison of their distinct characteristics in time series analysis (see figure 7.2). Nonstationary data typically exhibits trends, seasonality, or changing variances over time, making patterns less predictable and statistical inference challenging without proper preprocessing. In contrast, stationary data remains stable with constant statistical properties such as mean and variance, enabling more reliable modeling and forecasting. This visual comparison helps in understanding the effect of stationarity on data analysis and highlights the importance of techniques like differencing to achieve stationarity before applying models such as ARIMA for accurate predictions.

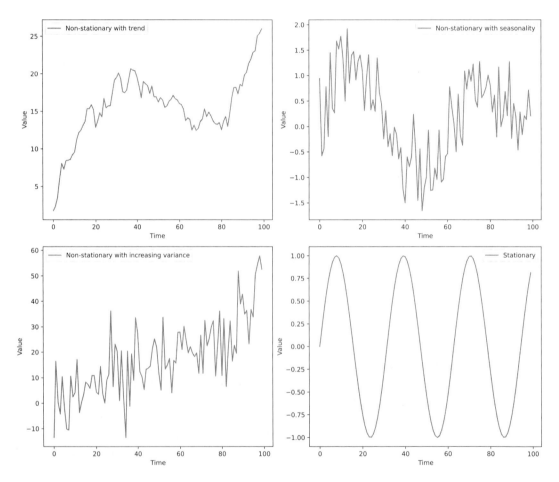

Figure 7.2 Four illustrative time series charts. Three of the subplots display nonstationary data; in contrast, the plot in the lower-right quadrant displays stationary time series data.

Three of the subplots display nonstationary data: one with an increasing trend, not unlike the closing price of Apple's stock during the last quarter of 2023; another with a seasonal pattern; and a third with increasing variance over time. The fourth subplot, in the lower-right quadrant, shows a stationary time series that oscillates around a constant mean.

7.3.6 Differencing

Differencing is a fundamental technique in time series analysis used to transform a nonstationary time series into a stationary one. Stationarity, characterized by constant statistical properties over time (such as mean, variance, and autocovariance), is crucial for many time series models like ARIMA, which assume stationary data for accurate forecasting and inference.

PURPOSE

The primary objective of differencing is to remove trends and seasonality present in the time series data. Trends represent long-term movements or shifts in the data, whereas seasonality refers to periodic fluctuations that occur at fixed intervals. Both trends and seasonality can introduce nonconstant mean and variance, making the data nonstationary and especially challenging from which to base accurate forecasts.

TYPES

There are two primary ways to differentiate nonstationary data: first-order differencing and seasonal differencing. First-order differencing involves subtracting each observation from its previous observation (or, subtracting the daily closing price of Apple stock from the previous day's closing price):

$$Y'_t = Y_t - Y_{t-1}$$

Here, once more, are the closing prices from the first five trading days of October 2023 (these were previously returned by calling the head() method):

[173.300247, 171.953735, 173.210495, 174.457260, 177.030579]

A first-order differenced series from five observations is derived by following these four steps:

1. Calculate the difference between the second and first closing prices:

    171.953735 − 173.300247 = −1.346512

2. Calculate the difference between the third and second closing prices:

    173.210495 − 171.953735 = 1.256760

3. Calculate the difference between the fourth and the third closing prices:

    174.457260 − 173.210495 = 1.246765

4. Calculate the difference between the fifth and fourth closing prices:

    177.030579 − 174.457260 = 2.573319

So, the first-order differenced series is

$$[-1.346512, 1.256760, 1.246765, 2.573319]$$

The record count inevitably drops by one because it's impossible, of course, to subtract from the first entry in a data series.

First-order differencing effectively transformed the time series by stabilizing its mean and other statistical properties, which are essential for accurate time series analysis. By subtracting each data point from its previous value, we removed the linear trend that was also present in the original data. The stabilized series is now (presumably) stationary, with constant variance and autocovariance, making it more suitable for modeling and forecasting purposes. This transformation ensures that the intrinsic dynamics of the data are captured more accurately, without the distorting effects of any trend.

However, first-order differencing does not always completely address nonstationarity, particularly when there are more complex trends. In such cases, second-order differencing is necessary, where the differencing process is applied twice:

$$Y_t'' = Y_t' - Y_{t-1}'$$

This additional step helps to further stabilize the series by removing any residual trends that first-order differencing could not entirely eliminate.

The second type of differencing, known as seasonal differencing, is particularly useful for time series data exhibiting regular, repeating patterns due to seasonal effects. This technique involves subtracting the value of a data point from the value at the same position in the previous season. For instance, in monthly data with yearly seasonality, the differencing period would be 12. Mathematically, if s represents the seasonal period, seasonal differencing is performed as follows:

$$Y_t' = Y_t - Y_{t-s}$$

Seasonal differencing helps to remove these repeating patterns, thereby stabilizing the mean and other statistical properties of the data, just like first-order differencing. By eliminating seasonal effects, the series becomes more stationary, making it suitable for accurate modeling and forecasting. This process is essential in domains like weather forecasting, where temperatures and precipitation patterns recur annually, or in tourism and hospitality, where travel and hotel bookings typically show seasonal peaks and troughs. A second order of seasonal differencing may sometimes be required if the first order of seasonal difference fails to stabilize the time series sufficiently.

The plot of Apple's daily closing stock price from October 1, 2023, to April 30, 2024, does not exhibit any clear seasonal patterns. Instead, the data shows significant volatility and general trends typical of stock price movements without any distinct periodicity. This lack of repeating cycles indicates that the series is nonseasonal. Given this characteristic, we will apply first-order differencing to the data, as necessary, to stabilize its statistical properties and remove any linear trends, rather than using seasonal differencing.

7.3.7 Stationarity and differencing applied

Of course, we are assuming Apple's daily closing stock price is nonstationary, based on our understanding of stationarity and our observations so far. However, rather than immediately applying first-order differencing, we will first demonstrate two methods to determine whether a time series is nonstationary.

For accurate forecasting of closing stock prices, it's crucial to partition the historical data into separate sets for training and testing. The initial six months of data will be used to train the forecasting model. Subsequently, the model's predictions for the next month will be plotted alongside the actual closing prices to assess its accuracy. So, instead of determining the stationarity (or nonstationarity) of the entire time series, we will assess it against just the training set.

The following line of code generates a Boolean mask (bln_msk) by evaluating the close_prices index. It selects all observations from our time series that satisfy the condition specified by the len() method, creating a distinct subset:

```
>>> bln_msk = (close_prices.index < len(close_prices) - 22)
```

This subset is assigned to a new data frame called train, which includes the closing prices from October 1, 2023, through March 31, 2024. The remaining 22 entries, corresponding to the trading days in April 2024, are assigned to another data frame called test:

```
>>> train = close_prices[bln_msk].copy()
>>> test = close_prices[~bln_msk].copy()
```

To reiterate, our ARIMA model will be fitted to the train subset, meaning all subsequent preprocessing steps should be, and will be, applied to this same subset.

VISUAL INSPECTION

Visual inspection is typically the first method used in time series analysis to evaluate whether a time series is stationary or, alternatively, shows trends and seasonality. Among various techniques, examining autocorrelation function (ACF) and partial autocorrelation function (PACF) plots provides valuable insights into the temporal dependencies and structure of the data.

The ACF quantifies the correlation between a time series and its lagged values (previous observations) at various time lags k. It helps analysts understand how past values influence current and future observations. Mathematically, the ACF at lag k, denoted as ρ_k, is defined as

$$\rho_k = \frac{\text{Cov}(X_t, X_{t-k})}{\sqrt{\text{Var}(X_t) \times \text{Var}(X_{t-k})}}$$

Here's a breakdown of the components:

- The *covariance* ($\text{Cov}(X_t X_{t-k})$) measures how two random variables (X_t and X_{t-k}) change together. Specifically, it quantifies the extent to which X_t and X_{t-k} deviate from their respective means together. The formula for covariance at lag k is given by

$$\text{Cov}(X_t, X_{t-k}) = \frac{1}{T} \sum_{t=1}^{T-k} (X_t - \mu)(X_{t+k} - \mu)$$

  where T is the total number of observations and μ is the mean of the time series.

- The *variance* ($\text{Var}(X_t)$) quantifies the variances of X_t and X_{t-k}, which measure the spread of the data points around their mean. Variance is defined as the average of the squared differences from the mean. The variance of the time series X_t is

$$\text{Var}(X_t) = \frac{1}{T} \sum_{t=1}^{T} (X_t - \mu)^2$$

To generate an ACF plot, autocovariances are computed for lags from 0 up to a maximum lag K, normalized by the square root of the variances, and plotted against lag k. The plot visually displays how each lag correlates with the current values in the time series, thereby providing a clear picture of the temporal dependencies within the data.

The PACF measures the direct relationship between observations separated by exactly k time units while adjusting for effects of the intervening lags. PACF at lag k, denoted as ϕkk, isolates the correlation between X_t and X_{t-k} by removing the influence of the intervening terms $X_{t-1}, X_{t-2}, \ldots, X_{t-k+1}$

Mathematically, PACF at lag k is computed with the following equation:

$$\phi kk = \frac{\text{Cov}(X_t, X_{t-k} | X_{t-1}, X_{t-2}, \ldots X_{t-k+1})}{\text{Var}(X_t) \times \text{Var}(X_{t-k} | X_{t-1}, X_{t-2}, \ldots X_{t-k+1})}$$

Here's a breakdown of the individual components:

- The *conditional covariance* ($\text{Cov}(X_t X_{t-k})) | (X_{t-1}, X_{t-2}, \ldots, X_{t-k+1})$) measures how X_t and X_{t-1} change together while accounting for the influence of the intermediate lags $X_{t-1}, X_{t-2}, \ldots, X_{t-k+1}$.
- The *conditional variance* ($\text{Var}(X_t) | \text{Var}(X_{t-1}, X_{t-2}, \ldots, X_{t-k+1})$) measures the spread of X_{t-k} values around their mean, conditioned on the intermediate lags $X_{t-1}, X_{t-2}, \ldots, X_{t-k+1}$

To generate a PACF plot, these partial autocorrelations ϕkk are computed for lags from 0 up to a chosen maximum lag K and plotted against lag k. This plot highlights the lags where significant direct relationships exist between the time series values, providing insight into stationarity and nonstationarity, as well as the appropriate number of autoregressive terms to include in a time series model.

ACF PLOT

The ACF is plotted by calling the `plot_acf()` method from the `statsmodels` library, with `train` as our time series data:

```
>>> from statsmodels.graphics.tsaplots import plot_acf, plot_pacf
>>> acf = plot_acf(train)
```

Python subsequently returns a Matplotlib figure (see figure 7.3).

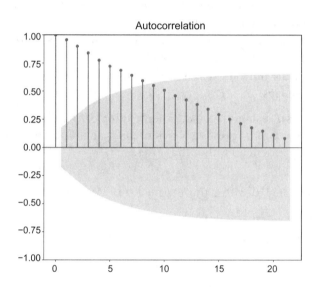

Figure 7.3 An ACF plot showing the correlation of a time series with its own past values (lags). The vertical lines represent the autocorrelation coefficients for different lags, with the shaded area indicating the confidence interval. Values outside this shaded region suggest significant autocorrelation, indicating a pattern in the data that could be used for time series forecasting. The gradual decline in the bars signifies the "memory" effect of the time series, where past values influence future observations.

The ACF plot displays the autocorrelation between the time series and its lagged values, providing insights into how past observations influence current and future values. (Autocorrelation measures how a time series relates to its own past values, whereas correlation typically measures the relationship between two distinct variables. Despite their differences in application, both autocorrelation and correlation are quantified in a similar manner and should be interpreted similarly.) On the horizontal axis (x axis), the plot shows different lags K, representing the number of time steps by which the series is shifted. The vertical axis (y axis) shows the correlation coefficients. These coefficients quantify the strength and direction of the linear relationship between the time series and its lagged versions.

Correlation coefficients always equal some number between −1 and +1:

- A coefficient of +1 indicates a perfect positive correlation: as the time series increases, the lagged values increase proportionally.
- A coefficient of −1 indicates a perfect negative relationship: as the time series increases, the lagged values decrease proportionally.

- A coefficient of 0 implies no linear relationship between the time series and its lagged values.

In an ACF plot, each bar represents the autocorrelation coefficient for a specific lag. The height and direction of the bar indicate the magnitude and sign of the correlation. The shaded area around the horizontal line at zero represents the confidence intervals, typically at a 95% confidence level. Correlations within this shaded area are not statistically significant, suggesting that observed correlations could be due to random noise rather than a genuine pattern in the data.

Interpreting an ACF plot involves assessing the decay of correlations over lags:

- Rapid decay in correlations suggests the time series may be stationary, with little dependence on past observations beyond a few lags.
- Persistent significant correlations across many lags indicate potential non-stationarity or the presence of long-term dependencies in the data.
- Peaks at regular intervals indicate seasonal patterns, with significant correlations repeating at those lags.

The ACF plot clearly indicates nonstationary data, characterized by significant correlations that persist over multiple lags, suggesting a lack of decay in autocorrelation and the presence of temporal dependencies within the series.

PACF PLOT

The PACF is plotted by making a call to the `plot_pacf()` method, also from the `statsmodels` library:

```
>>> pacf = plot_pacf(train)
```

Once more, Python returns a Matplotlib figure (see figure 7.4).

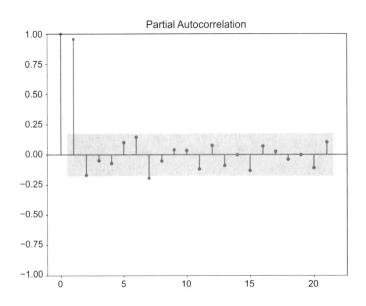

Figure 7.4 A PACF plot showing the correlation between a time series and its own past values (lags), controlling for the effects of earlier lags. The vertical lines represent the partial autocorrelation coefficients for each lag, with the shaded area indicating the confidence interval. Values outside this shaded region suggest significant partial autocorrelation, which can help identify the appropriate number of autoregressive terms in a time series model. The sharp drop after the first few lags indicates that only the first few lags have a significant direct effect on the current value of the series.

The PACF plot shows the direct relationship between a time series observation and its lagged values while accounting for the effects of intervening lags; it provides insights into how each lagged observation directly influences the current observation, adjusting for other lags in between. The x axis represents the number of time units, or lags, between the current observation and its lagged values. The y axis shows the partial autocorrelation coefficients, ranging from −1 to +1. These coefficients measure the strength and direction of the relationship between the current observation and its lagged values, after adjusting for the influence of intermediate lags.

Each bar in the PACF plot represents the partial autocorrelation coefficient for a specific lag. The height and direction of the bar indicate the magnitude and sign of the partial correlation. Similar to the ACF plot, the PACF plot typically includes a shaded region around the horizontal line at zero. This area represents the confidence intervals, typically at a 95% confidence level. Coefficients within this shaded area are statistically insignificant, indicating correlations that could arise due to random noise rather than meaningful patterns in the data.

High partial autocorrelation at lag 1 indicates a strong direct relationship between the current value and its immediate past value, which is common in both stationary and nonstationary series. The key is what happens at higher lags.

The fact that correlations from lag 2 onward fall within the shaded area implies these correlations are not statistically significant. This pattern suggests that the influence of past values diminishes quickly. The rapid decay in partial autocorrelation after lag 1, with subsequent lags showing insignificant correlations, typically suggests that the time series is stationary. In a stationary series, any dependence on past values tends to weaken rapidly.

In summary, whereas the ACF plot indicates nonstationarity in the time series, the PACF plot suggests the possibility of stationarity. To gain a definitive understanding, we will now pivot toward a more precise method by running a statistical test to determine whether the daily closing prices of Apple stock are stationary or nonstationary.

Augmented Dickey–Fuller test

The Augmented Dickey–Fuller (ADF) test is a widely used statistical test in time series analysis for determining whether a time series is stationary. The ADF test helps to identify a stochastic trend in the data that causes its statistical properties, such as mean and variance, to change over time, thereby indicating nonstationarity. One of the main advantages of the ADF test is its ability to handle complex time series with autocorrelation by including lagged terms. However, a limitation of the ADF test is its sensitivity to the chosen lag length, which can affect results, and its tendency to have lower power in detecting stationarity in short or noisy time series.

The null hypothesis of the ADF test is that the data is nonstationary. We will therefore require a p-value from the test below the typical 5% threshold to reject the null hypothesis and conclude the data is stationary. The test involves estimating the following regression model:

$$\Delta Y_t = \alpha + \beta t + \gamma Y_{t-1} + \sum_{i=1}^{p} \delta_i \Delta Y_{t-1} + \epsilon_t$$

where

- ΔY_t is the first difference of the time series Y_t
- α is a constant term (drift).
- β_t is a time trend.
- γY_{t-1} represents the lagged value of the time series.
- $\sum_{i=1}^{p} \sigma_i \Delta Y_{t-1}$ includes the lagged differences of the time series to account for higher-order autoregressive processes.
- ϵ_t is the error term.

The key parameter in this model is γ (gamma). If γ is significantly different from zero, it suggests the data does not have a stochastic trend, leading to a low p-value and therefore a rejection of the null hypothesis. Alternatively, if γ is not significantly different from zero, it suggests the data does, in fact, contain a stochastic trend; the ADF test will return a p-value above the 5% threshold, meaning we should fail to reject the null hypothesis. By running the ADF test, analysts can make a more precise determination of the stationarity of a time series, complementing visual inspections from ACF and PACF plots.

The following snippet of Python code runs an ADF test on the `train` data frame and outputs the associated p-value:

```
>>> from statsmodels.tsa.stattools import adfuller
>>> adf_test = adfuller(train)
>>> print('p-value:', adf_test[1])
p-value: 0.5761116196186049
```

Because the p-value of the test is above 5%, we should fail to reject the null hypothesis and conclude that the daily closing prices of Apple stock, at least between October 1, 2023, and March 31, 2024, is nonstationary. This, of course, means we need to difference the data before fitting our ARIMA model.

FIRST-ORDER DIFFERENCING

First-order differencing is a technique used in time series analysis to remove trends and make the data stationary by subtracting each observation from the previous one. This process helps stabilize the mean of a time series by eliminating changes in the level of the series.

In the next line of Python code, we use the `diff()` method to compute the difference between consecutive observations in the `train` data set, effectively applying first-order differencing. The `dropna()` method then removes any NaN values created by the differencing operation, resulting in a cleaned data series stored in a new object called `train_diff`:

```
>>> train_diff = train.diff().dropna()
```

7.3 Fitting an ARIMA model

Next, we plot the differenced data in a `matplotlib` time series chart (see figure 7.5):

```
>>> train_diff.plot()                                   ◁── Initializes a line plot
>>> plt.xlabel('Trading Days:\n'
>>>     'October 1, 2023 through March 31, 2024')       ◁── Sets the x-axis label
>>> plt.ylabel('Differences in Closing Prices')         ◁── Sets the y-axis label
>>> plt.title('1st Order Differencing')                 ◁── Sets the title. Note that the sequence of labels and titles does not affect the plot.
>>> plt.legend().set_visible(False)                     ◁── Disables the legend
>>> plt.show()                                          ◁── Displays the plot
```

After applying first-order differencing to the time series data, the resulting series exhibits characteristics indicative of stationarity. Specifically, the differenced data oscillates around a constant mean, which suggests that any underlying trend present in the original series has been effectively removed. This transformation stabilizes the mean of the series, making it more suitable for further time series analysis and modeling techniques that assume stationarity. The visual inspection of the differenced data plot confirms the absence of pronounced trends or varying levels, reinforcing the appearance of stationarity.

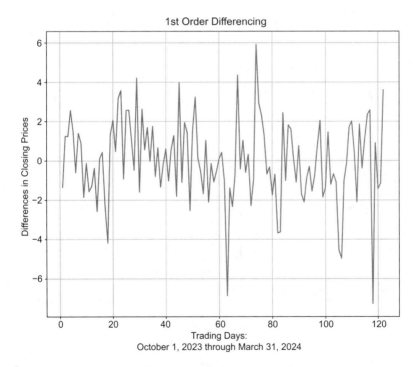

Figure 7.5 Time series data that was converted from nonstationary to stationary by first-order differencing

Although the time series now *appears* stationary, we should nevertheless create a new set of ACF and PACF plots and then conduct a second ADF test to confirm stationarity. The following snippet of `matplotlib` code creates ACF and PACF plots for the `train_diff` data frame and combines them with our previous ACF and PACF plots into a single figure:

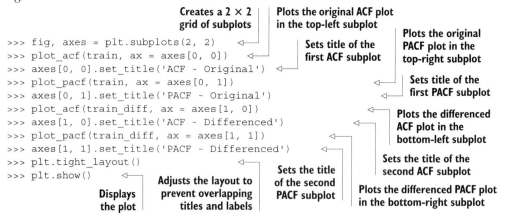

```
>>> fig, axes = plt.subplots(2, 2)
>>> plot_acf(train, ax = axes[0, 0])
>>> axes[0, 0].set_title('ACF - Original')
>>> plot_pacf(train, ax = axes[0, 1])
>>> axes[0, 1].set_title('PACF - Original')
>>> plot_acf(train_diff, ax = axes[1, 0])
>>> axes[1, 0].set_title('ACF - Differenced')
>>> plot_pacf(train_diff, ax = axes[1, 1])
>>> axes[1, 1].set_title('PACF - Differenced')
>>> plt.tight_layout()
>>> plt.show()
```

- Creates a 2 × 2 grid of subplots
- Plots the original ACF plot in the top-left subplot
- Sets title of the first ACF subplot
- Plots the original PACF plot in the top-right subplot
- Sets title of the first PACF subplot
- Plots the differenced ACF plot in the bottom-left subplot
- Sets the title of the second ACF subplot
- Sets the title of the second PACF subplot
- Plots the differenced PACF plot in the bottom-right subplot
- Adjusts the layout to prevent overlapping titles and labels
- Displays the plot

Figure 7.6 presents the autocorrelation and partial autocorrelation functions for both the original and differenced time series data. The top row displays the ACF (left) and

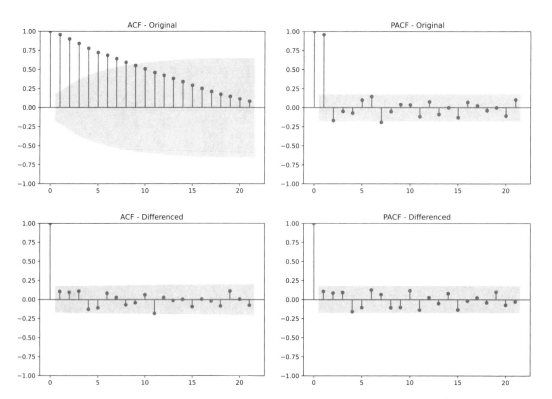

Figure 7.6 ACF and PACF plots for the original time series (top row) and first-order differenced time series (bottom row). The left column displays the ACF, showing how each observation is correlated with its previous values, whereas the right column presents the PACF, illustrating the direct effect of each lag. These plots are provided to compare the effect of first-order differencing on the time series' correlation structure.

PACF (right) for the original data, whereas the bottom row shows the ACF (left) and PACF (right) for the differenced data. The effects of first-order differencing are highlighted here, with both the original and differenced plots provided for easy comparison of how differencing affects the time series' autocorrelation structure.

After subjecting the data to first-order differencing, the resulting ACF and PACF plots reveal notable characteristics. Both plots exhibit a strong positive correlation at lag 0, which is expected due to the autocorrelation with itself. However, beyond lag 0, there are no statistically significant correlations observed in either plot. This lack of significant correlations suggests that the differenced data has effectively removed any systematic patterns or trends that were present in the original series. This transformation indicates that the differenced series may now be stationary, as evidenced by the absence of autocorrelation at lags other than 0.

Encouraging as these results are, let's verify the stationarity of the differenced time series through an ADF test to ensure reliability:

```
>>> adf_test_diff = adfuller(train_diff)
>>> print('p-value:', adf_test_diff[1])
p-value: 1.2486140415792743e-16
```

With a remarkably low p-value of 1.25×10^{-16} obtained from the ADF test, we confidently reject the null hypothesis of nonstationarity for the differenced time series. This strongly suggests that the differenced data is stationary, as there is substantial evidence against the presence of a stochastic trend.

ARIMA models, as a reminder, are structured into three components: autoregression (AR), integration (I), and moving average (MA). Each component corresponds to a parameter in the model notation ARIMA(p, d, q), where p represents the order of the AR component (AR(p)), d signifies the number of differencing operations needed to achieve stationarity (I(d)), and q denotes the order of the MA component (MA(q)). Having determined that d should be 1, reflecting the single differencing operation that rendered our initially nonstationary data stationary, our focus now shifts to identifying suitable values for p and q.

7.3.8 AR and MA components

Although we have established only one of the three necessary parameters for our ARIMA model, we have nevertheless completed roughly 90% of the groundwork. Determining the AR(p) and MA(q) components should be straightforward, as we have already identified the I(d) component to achieve stationarity in the time series data.

AUTOREGRESSION COMPONENT

The AR component in an ARIMA model captures the linear relationship between a time series and its own past values, reflecting the idea that future values of the series can be predicted using its own historical data. After creating ACF and PACF plots for the differenced time series data, we observe that there is a significant correlation only at lag 0 in both the ACF and PACF plots, whereas correlations at other lags are statistically insignificant.

In the ACF plot, a significant correlation at lag 0 indicates that each observation is highly correlated with its immediate predecessor, suggesting a strong dependence on the previous time point. This pattern is mirrored in the PACF plot, where a significant spike at lag 0 directly reflects this immediate correlation without additional significant spikes at subsequent lags.

Given this singular significant correlation at lag 0 in both plots, the appropriate choice for the AR component is likely AR(1). AR(1) implies that the current observation depends linearly on its immediate previous observation, aligning with the observed autocorrelation structure in the time series data. The lack of significant correlations at other lags reinforces the simplicity of the model, indicating that additional AR terms beyond AR(1) are unnecessary to explain the data's temporal dependencies.

Choosing AR(1) as the AR component ensures that the model captures the essential autocorrelation pattern without introducing unnecessary complexity. This decision is supported by both the theoretical underpinnings of ARIMA modeling and the empirical evidence provided by the ACF and PACF plots.

MOVING AVERAGE COMPONENT

The MA component models the relationship between the current observation and the residual errors from a moving average model applied to lagged observations. After generating ACF and PACF plots for the differenced time series data, we observe that there are no significant correlations at any lags in the ACF plot beyond lag 0. This lack of significant correlations indicates that there is no remaining autocorrelation in the differenced series after accounting for the AR component.

Similarly, in the PACF plot, there are no significant spikes beyond lag 0, reinforcing the absence of direct correlations between the current observation and its lagged values. This pattern suggests that the observed variations in the time series are well explained by the immediate past values rather than by longer-term trends captured by a moving average process.

Given the absence of significant correlations in both the ACF and PACF plots, the appropriate choice for the MA component is likely MA(0). MA(0) implies that there is no residual autocorrelation in the series beyond the immediate lagged values, aligning with the stationary nature of the differenced time series data. This simplicity in the model specification avoids unnecessary complexity and ensures that the model focuses on the most relevant dependencies in the data.

Choosing MA(0) as the MA component is supported by the empirical evidence from the ACF and PACF plots, which indicate no significant autocorrelation at any lags not previously accounted for. This determination allows us to confidently specify the ARIMA(p, d, q) model with an MA component of MA(0).

Although our analysis supports the choice of AR(1) and MA(0), alternative configurations, such as AR(2) and MA(1), might be appropriate in cases where the ACF and PACF plots show significant correlations at additional lags. An AR(2) model, for instance, would suggest that the current observation depends not only on the previous value but also on the value two time steps prior, capturing a deeper dependency. Similarly, an MA(1) model would imply that residual errors from one previous time step influence the current observation, potentially capturing more complex noise patterns in the data. In this case, however, the simpler AR(1) and MA(0) specifications are well-suited to our observed autocorrelation structure.

When deciding between applying another differencing operation versus increasing the AR order, the key is to determine whether the data still exhibits nonstationarity. If the ACF shows a slow decay or persistent correlations across many lags, this may indicate the need for additional differencing. In contrast, if the data appears stationary but shows significant spikes at specific lags in the PACF, it's generally more appropriate to increase the AR order rather than differencing further.

7.3.9 Fitting the model

The following snippets of code demonstrate how to fit an ARIMA model to time series data using the `statsmodels` library. Fitting an ARIMA model, particularly when setting the AR component to 1, at least somewhat resembles fitting a simple linear regression, as both involve estimating parameters to minimize prediction errors based on historical data.

The first snippet imports the `ARIMA` class from the `statsmodels.tsa.arima.model` module:

```
>>> from statsmodels.tsa.arima.model import ARIMA
```

The next snippet outlines the specifications for an ARIMA model fitted to the `train` subset of our original time series. The `order` parameter is a tuple that specifies the three key components of the model:

1. *Autoregressive order (*p*):* The first element in the `order` tuple is p, which is set to 1 in this instance. This parameter defines the number of lagged observations included in the model. By setting `p = 1`, we instruct the model to use one past value of the time series to predict the current value. This choice was based on our examination of the autocorrelation plots after the data was differenced and identifying significant versus insignificant lagged correlations, suggesting that one lag is sufficient to capture the dependencies in the data.

2. *Differencing Order (*d*):* The second element in the `order` tuple is d, which is also set to 1. This parameter represents the number of times the data needs to be differenced to achieve stationarity. Setting `d = 1` means we are applying first-order differencing—subtracting each observation from the previous one—to stabilize the mean and other statistical properties of the series.

3. *Moving average order (*q*):* The third element in the `order` tuple is q, set to 0 in this case. This parameter indicates the number of lagged forecast errors included in the model. By setting `q = 0`, we specify that the model does not need to include any past forecast errors to predict future values. This decision was made based on the analysis of autocorrelation plots, where no significant cor-

relations are observed at higher lags, thereby suggesting that past errors do not add predictive power.

The `train` and `order` parameters are passed to the `ARIMA` class to create an instance of that class called `model`:

```
>>> model = ARIMA(train, order = (1, 1, 0))
```

In short, the preceding line of code creates an ARIMA model tailored to the characteristics of the `train` data frame, where

- p = 1 indicates using one past observation.
- d = 1 applies first-order differencing to ensure stationarity.
- q = 0 excludes past forecast errors from the algorithm.

After configuring the model with the appropriate parameters and providing it with the preprocessed training data, the next step is to fit the model. This process entails estimating the model's parameters based on the provided data. When the `fit()` method is called, the model begins adjusting its internal coefficients to minimize the difference between observed values in the training data and those predicted by the model. The fitting process primarily relies on maximum likelihood estimation (MLE), a statistical method used to find the parameters that maximize the likelihood of observing the given data under the model assumptions. This approach ensures that the ARIMA model effectively captures the temporal dependencies present in the differenced time series (`train_diff`), which include AR, I, and MA components. By iteratively optimizing these parameters, the model enhances its capability to forecast future values based on historical patterns discerned from the training data:

```
>>> model_fit = model.fit()
```

Once the fitting process is complete, `model_fit` encapsulates the trained ARIMA model with optimized parameters. This fitted model is then ready to be utilized to make predictions on new data or for further analysis and diagnostics. Overall, `model.fit()` represents the pivotal stage where theoretical model specifications are aligned with empirical data.

Finally, the line `print(model_fit.summary())` outputs a summary table providing key statistical information—goodness of fit measures and parameter estimates, for instance—about the fitted model. The summary is crucial for evaluating the significance and effectiveness of the model in capturing the underlying patterns and dependencies of the time series data:

```
>>> print(model_fit.summary())
                          SARIMAX Results
==============================================================================
Dep. Variable:                  Close   No. Observations:                  123
Model:                 ARIMA(1, 1, 0)   Log Likelihood                -264.006
Date:                Thu, 20 Jun 2024   AIC                            532.013
Time:                        16:20:48   BIC                            537.621
Sample:                             0   HQIC                           534.291
```

```
                                       -123
Covariance Type:                       opg
==========================================================================
                 coef    std err         z      P>|z|      [0.025    0.975]
--------------------------------------------------------------------------
ar.L1          0.1084      0.091     1.196      0.232      -0.069     0.286
sigma2         4.4371      0.441    10.068      0.000       3.573     5.301
==========================================================================
Ljung-Box (L1) (Q):                    0.01   Jarque-Bera (JB):        12.14
Prob(Q):                               0.92   Prob(JB):                 0.00
Heteroskedasticity (H):                1.57   Skew:                    -0.36
Prob(H) (two-sided):                   0.15   Kurtosis:                 4.37
==========================================================================

Warnings:
[1] Covariance matrix calculated using the outer product
of gradients (complex-step).
```

This concludes the model fitting process. Next, we will demonstrate how to interpret these results and evaluate the overall fit of our ARIMA model. After that, we will forecast April 2024 closing prices and plot them alongside the actual closing prices.

7.3.10 Evaluating model fit

The summary results are broadly divided into four sections: general information (upper left), goodness of fit (upper right), parameters (middle), and residuals (bottom).

GENERAL INFORMATION

The general information section provides basic details about the model and the data used to train the model:

- `Dep. Variable`—The name of the variable containing the original time series data.
- `Model`—The order of the fitted model, or the nonnegative integers assigned to p, d, and q.
- `Sample`—The number of samples, or records, in the time series.
- `Covariance Type`—The method used to estimate the covariance matrix of the model's parameter estimates, which is crucial for assessing parameter uncertainty. In time series models, the `opg` method (short for outer product of gradients) is often used to calculate this matrix by approximating it based on the outer product of gradients from the likelihood function. This approach provides an efficient and consistent way to estimate parameter variances, which are essential for constructing confidence intervals and hypothesis tests on the model's parameters. Other covariance types may also be used depending on the model, each with different trade-offs in terms of computational efficiency and accuracy.

GOODNESS OF FIT

This section displays metrics that assess the model's overall fit to the data. They are typically used to compare and contrast competing models fit to the same data:

- `No. Observations`—Number of samples used to train the model.
- `Log Likelihood`—Measures how well the model's parameters explain the observed data, calculated based on the likelihood function. A higher log-likelihood value suggests that the model fits the data more closely, as it implies that the observed values are more probable under the model's parameters. Although this metric is useful for comparing models, it does not account for model complexity, which is where criteria like AIC, BIC, and HQIC come in.
- `AIC` (short for Akaike Information Criterion)—Balances model fit with simplicity by introducing a penalty for adding more parameters. It is calculated by taking twice the number of parameters in the model and subtracting this value from twice the log-likelihood. Lower AIC values indicate a better model, as they reflect both strong fit and parsimony. This criterion helps in selecting models that generalize well to new data, although it may lean toward more complex models in large data sets.
- `BIC` (short for Bayesian Information Criterion)—Like AIC, balances model fit and complexity, but applies a stronger penalty for the number of parameters, especially as sample size increases. It is calculated by taking the number of parameters, multiplying it by the natural logarithm of the sample size, and then subtracting this from twice the log-likelihood. Due to this stronger penalty for additional parameters, BIC tends to favor simpler models, making it particularly useful when avoiding overfitting, which is a priority. In model comparison, a lower BIC indicates a better model, as it suggests an optimal balance of fit and simplicity.
- `HQIC` (short for Hannan–Quinn Information Criterion)—Like AIC and BIC, evaluates the trade-off between model fit and complexity, with an emphasis on sample size. It is calculated by taking the number of parameters, multiplying it by twice the natural logarithm of the natural logarithm of the sample size, and then subtracting this from twice the log-likelihood. This penalty grows with sample size but at a slower rate than BIC, making HQIC particularly useful for smaller data sets, where it allows for a more balanced evaluation of model complexity. As with AIC and BIC, a lower HQIC value indicates a preferable model, reflecting an effective balance between fit and simplicity.

PARAMETERS

This section lists the estimated coefficients for the model's parameters:

- `ar.L1`—Represents the only parameter in an ARIMA(1, 1, 0) model. For an ARIMA model with $p = 1$ (one AR parameter), $d = 1$ (one order of differencing), and $q = 0$ (no MA parameters), the model equation is given as

$$X_t = \phi_1 X_{t-1} + \epsilon_t$$

where

- X_t is the value of the time series at time t.
- ϕ_1 is the coefficient of the AR parameter at lag 1.

- X_{t-1} is the value of the time series at the previous time step.
- ϵ_t is the error term at time t, assumed to be white noise.

- `coeff`—The estimated coefficient for the model's one parameter.
- `std err`—The standard error of the coefficient estimate, indicating the precision of the same. A lower standard error suggests that the estimate is more precise and likely to be closer to the true population value. In statistical terms, a standard error of 0.091 implies that the coefficient estimate could vary by approximately ±0.091 units around its approximate mean if the model were estimated repeatedly from different data samples.
- `z`—Represents the z-statistic for the coefficient, or the number of standard deviations by which the estimated coefficient differs from zero. In statistical terms, a z-statistic equal to 1.196 suggests that the coefficient is relatively close to zero and may not be statistically significant, as it does not exceed the conventional threshold of approximately 1.196 standard deviations (which corresponds to a 5% significance level).
- `P>|z|`—The p-value associated with the z-statistic, indicating the significance of the coefficient estimate. Because the p-value (0.232) is greater than the typical 5% threshold for significance, the coefficient may not have a material effect on the model's forecast.
- `[0.025 and 0.975]`—The 95% confidence interval for the coefficient estimate, showing the range within which the true coefficient value is likely to fall.
- `sigma2`—The estimated variance of the residual errors (white noise) in the model. More precisely, it represents the estimated variance of the residual errors left unexplained by the ARIMA model. It indicates how much the actual data points typically deviate from the predicted values. A higher `sigma2` implies larger fluctuations or errors in the predictions, whereas a lower `sigma2` suggests that the model fits the data more closely with smaller residual errors. Similar to measures of goodness of fit, `sigma2` is more appropriately used for comparative purposes rather than to assess an individual model in isolation.

RESIDUALS

This section provides statistics and diagnostic test results evaluating the residuals—that is, the differences between observed and predicted values—to identify issues like autocorrelation and heteroskedasticity. Rather than reviewing these from the summary table, visual diagnostic methods are typically used for thorough assessment (see chapter 4).

The following `matplotlib` code snippet produces two side-by-side plots that depict the distribution of residuals. As in regression analysis, the Residuals plot should reveal no noticeable trend or pattern, indicating randomness and unbiased errors. Meanwhile, the Density plot is expected to exhibit a bell-shaped curve, signifying a normal distribution centered around a mean of zero (see figure 7.7):

```
>>> residuals = model_fit.resid[1:]        ◁─┐  Extracts the residuals from the
>>> fig, ax = plt.subplots(1, 2)              │  fitted ARIMA model (model_fit)
>>> residuals.plot(title = \               ◁──┤
>>>                'Residuals', ax = ax[0])    │  Creates a single figure
>>> residuals.plot(title = \                   │  containing two plots arranged
>>>                'Density',                  │  in a 1 × 2 configuration
>>>                kind = 'kde',             ◁─┤
>>>                ax = ax[1])                 │  Sets the plot type and
>>> plt.tight_layout()                      ◁──┤  title of the first plot
>>> plt.show()                   ◁─┐           │
                                   │           │  Sets the plot
      Displays the plots           │           │  type and title of
      as a single figure           │           │  the second plot
                                                │
                                                │  Adjusts subplot parameters,
                                                │  as necessary, to prevent
                                                │  overlapping elements
```

Both plots exhibit the expected characteristics.

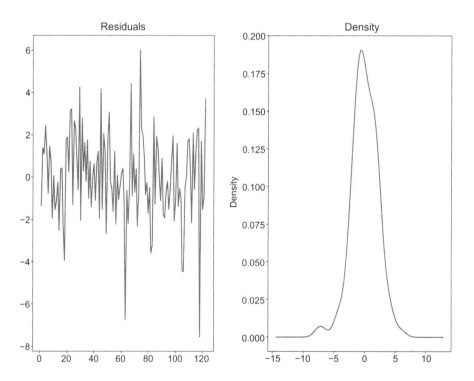

Figure 7.7 Left: The model residuals display no obvious pattern or trend. Right: The same residuals are normally distributed around a mean of zero.

When residuals show no obvious pattern or trend and are normally distributed, it suggests that the model adequately captures the underlying patterns in the data and that the assumptions of the model, such as constant variance and independence of errors, are likely met. Furthermore, examining the ACF and PACF plots of the residuals reveals that nearly every lag exhibits no statistically significant correlations, indicative of white noise. This reinforces confidence that our ARIMA model effectively captured the underlying data trends (see figure 7.8).

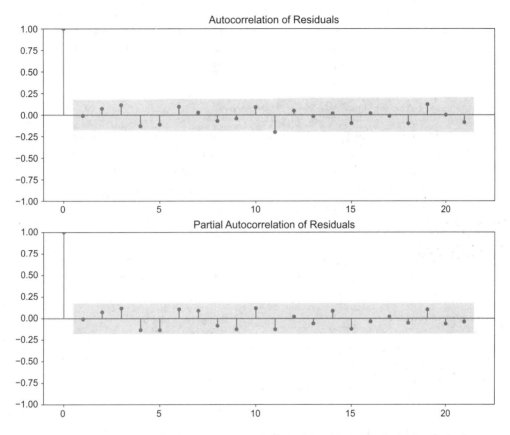

Figure 7.8   ACF plot (top) and PACF plot (bottom) of the model residuals. The lack of statistically significant correlations further suggests that the ARIMA model sufficiently captured trends in the time series.

Our evaluation of the ARIMA model provided mixed results: for instance, although the autoregressive parameter in the ARIMA(1, 1, 0) model has a p-value well above the standard 5% threshold for significance, the diagnostic tests on the model residuals were notably promising. Next, we will forecast the April 2024 closing prices using this model and visually compare the predicted values against the actual values to evaluate its predictive accuracy.

7.3.11 Forecasting

The next step in our analysis involves forecasting future values—April 2024 closing prices—from the data used to train our ARIMA model: closing prices from October 1,

2023, through March 31, 2024. This is achieved with the next line of code: `model_fit.forecast()` generates out-of-sample forecasts based on the length of the `test` data frame previously subset from the original time series. Specifically, it uses the estimated parameters of the ARIMA model to predict the values for the specified number of periods. This method is crucial for evaluating the model's predictive performance, as it provides a direct comparison between the forecasted values and the actual observed values in the `test` set. By assessing these predictions, we can better understand how well our model captures the underlying patterns in the data and its effectiveness in making future projections:

```
>>> forecast_test = model_fit.forecast(len(test))
```

After generating the forecast values, the next step is to incorporate these predictions into our `close_prices` data frame for comparison purposes. The next line of code appends a new variable to `close_prices` called `Forecast`. It populates `Forecast` with `NaN` for those trading days that correspond to the training period, and otherwise the forecasted closing prices forecasted by the model:

```
>>> close_prices['Forecast'] = [None] * len(train) + list(forecast_test)
```

When the data is plotted, we have a single time series from October 1, 2023 through March 31, 2024, and two time series for April 2024—the actual closing prices and the predicted closing prices:

```
>>> close_prices.plot()                    ◁─┤ Generates a plot of all variables in the close_prices data
>>> plt.xlabel('Trading Days:\n'
        'October 1, 2023 through April 30, 2024')   ◁─┤ Sets the x-axis label
>>> plt.ylabel('Differences in Closing Prices')     ◁─┤ Sets the y-axis label
>>> plt.title('Actual vs. \
        Forecasted Closing Price - AAPL')           ◁─┤ Sets the title
>>> plt.grid()                              ◁─┤ Adds a grid
>>> plt.show()                              ◁─┤ Displays the plot
```

Figure 7.9 shows the result. The ARIMA model forecasted a daily closing price of approximately 173.51 for April 2024. The actual daily closing price during the same month, which experienced considerable volatility, averaged around 169.43. This discrepancy indicates that although the ARIMA model provided a reasonable estimate, it overpredicted the average closing price, albeit by a small margin. This result underscores the importance of accounting for both forecast accuracy and the inherent volatility of stock price movements. This flat forecast is a result of the ARIMA model structure, which—after differencing—tends to predict future values as a continuation of the most recent trend, leading to a constant forecast when no strong momentum or seasonal pattern is present in the training data.

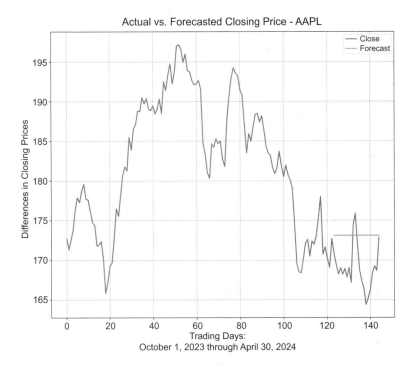

Figure 7.9 The actual closing prices of Apple stock from October 1, 2023, through April 30, 2024, plus the forecasted closing price of the stock throughout April 2024 generated from an ARIMA model.

As we've seen, the ARIMA model is a powerful tool for capturing various patterns in time series data, particularly when there are clear trends or seasonal components. However, although ARIMA is effective in certain scenarios, it might not always be the best fit for every type of time series, especially when the data exhibits smooth, gradual changes over time. This brings us to the next approach in our forecasting toolkit: exponential smoothing models. Unlike ARIMA, which focuses on autoregression and moving averages, exponential smoothing directly models the level, trend, and seasonality in the data, making it especially useful for time series that require a more responsive, adaptive approach to forecasting. Let's explore how exponential smoothing can be applied to our time series data.

7.4 Fitting exponential smoothing models

Exponential smoothing models are a class of forecasting techniques that apply weighting factors that decrease exponentially over time. Unlike ARIMA models, which focus on understanding the underlying data structure and stochastic nature of the time series, exponential smoothing models emphasize smoothing the data to make forecasts. They are particularly useful for time series where the most recent observations are more relevant for forecasting than older observations.

7.4.1 Model structure

Whereas ARIMA models rely heavily on the statistical properties of the data and typically require detailed analysis of autocorrelation and partial autocorrelation functions to identify the appropriate model parameters, exponential smoothing models—including simple, double, and Holt–Winters exponential smoothing—apply weighted averages of past observations with weights that decay exponentially. They do not explicitly model the underlying data structure but rather smooth the data to identify trends and seasonality.

7.4.2 Applicability

Although ARIMA models may be best suited for time series data that exhibits clear patterns over time, including trends and seasonality, and where the goal is to understand the data-generating process, exponential smoothing models are more effective for time series that are primarily concerned with making short-term forecasts where the most recent data points are (presumably) more indicative of future values. These models are less complex and often easier to implement.

7.4.3 Mathematical properties

Whereas ARIMA models incorporate differencing to make the time series stationary and use lagged values of the series and/or lagged forecast errors to train the model, exponential smoothing models use weighted averages of past observations, where weights decrease exponentially. For instance, the simple exponential smoothing model is

$$\hat{y}_{t+1} = \alpha y_t + (1 - \alpha)\hat{y}_t$$

where α is the smoothing parameter between 0 and 1, y_t is the actual observation at time t, and $\hat{y}_{t+1}$ is the forecast for the next period.

7.4.4 Types of exponential smoothing models

As previously mentioned, there are three types of exponential smoothing models:

- Simple exponential smoothing (SES) is most suitable for forecasting time series with no clear trend or seasonal pattern. It works best for time series that are stationary around a constant mean.
- Double exponential smoothing (DES) extends SES to data with trends. It incorporates a trend component to account for linearity in the time series.
- Holt–Winters exponential smoothing (H-W) extends DES to handle seasonality and therefore works well with data that contains trends and a seasonal component. It comes in two variations: additive (for constant seasonal variation) and multiplicative (for changing seasonal variation).

We will demonstrate how to fit each type of exponential smoothing model in Python. We will then compare the Holt–Winters model to the ARIMA model by evaluating the AIC and BIC measures of both models. Finally, we will generate a forecast using the Holt–Winters model and plot the forecasted closing prices against the actual closing prices.

7.4.5 Choosing between ARIMA and exponential smoothing

Exponential smoothing models provide a simpler and often more intuitive approach to time series forecasting compared to ARIMA models. Although ARIMA models excel at capturing the underlying data-generating process and are powerful for long-term forecasting, exponential smoothing models are advantageous for their simplicity and effectiveness in short-term forecasting, especially when the most recent observations are more predictive of future values. By fitting both ARIMA and Holt–Winters exponential smoothing models, we can compare their forecasts and determine which method better suits our specific forecasting needs.

7.4.6 SES and DES models

The following code snippet demonstrates how to fit an SES model to the training data using the `statsmodels` library. This type of model is particularly suited for time series data without trend or seasonal components, where more recent observations are given exponentially greater weights:

```
>>> from statsmodels.tsa.holtwinters import SimpleExpSmoothing
>>> ses_model = SimpleExpSmoothing(train).fit()
```

Here, the `SimpleExpSmoothing` class is imported from `statsmodels`, and an SES model is fitted to `train` using the `fit()` method. This operation results in an SES model that assigns exponentially decreasing weights to older observations, effectively smoothing the data for better forecasting. The fitted model can then be used to make predictions based on the most recent patterns in the data.

The next code snippet demonstrates how to fit a DES model using the `statsmodels` library. This model, often referred to as *Holt's linear trend model*, is particularly useful for time series data that exhibit a trend component:

```
>>> from statsmodels.tsa.holtwinters import ExponentialSmoothing
>>> des_model = ExponentialSmoothing(train, trend = 'add').fit()
```

The `ExponentialSmoothing` class is imported from `statsmodels`, and an instance of the DES model is created with the `train` data set. The `trend = 'add'` parameter indicates that an additive trend component should be included in the model. By then calling the `fit()` method, the model parameters are optimized to best capture any underlying trend in the data.

The key difference between the DES model and the SES model lies in the ability to handle trends. Although the SES model focuses solely on smoothing the data without considering any trend, the DES model incorporates an additive trend component. This makes the DES model more suitable for time series where the data exhibits a linear trend over time.

Both the SES and DES models assign exponentially decreasing weights to older observations, giving more importance to recent data points. However, the DES model takes it a step further by smoothing the trend component, which helps capture the data dynamics better.

The SES model is ideal for time series without trends or seasonal patterns, providing a straightforward method for smoothing. In contrast, the DES model is designed for time series data with a trend, making it more robust for such data sets. This enhancement allows the DES model to deliver more accurate forecasts for data with an underlying trend.

7.4.7 Holt–Winters model

H-W, also known as triple exponential smoothing, builds on the foundations of SES and DES by incorporating a seasonal component in addition to the level and trend components. Whereas SES focuses on smoothing data without trends and DES adds the capability to model linear trends, H–W takes it a step further by addressing seasonal variations. This makes it particularly effective for time series data that exhibits both trend and seasonal patterns, such as monthly sales data or daily stock prices with recurring cycles. By simultaneously modeling level, trend, and seasonality, H–W provides a comprehensive framework for more accurate and insightful forecasting.

MODEL FITTING

The following snippet of code utilizes the H–W method, advancing from DES by integrating seasonal patterns into the model. It employs the `ExponentialSmoothing` class from `statsmodels` to fit a Holt–Winters model to the training data set, incorporating both trend and seasonal components in the process. The `'add'` parameter for `trend` specifies an additive trend component, whereas `'add'` for `seasonal` indicates an additive seasonal component. With `seasonal_periods = 5`, the model assumes recurring seasonal cycles within the six-month training period, anticipating a pattern every five days:

```
>>> hw_model = ExponentialSmoothing(train,
>>>                                 trend = 'add',
>>>                                 seasonal = 'add',
>>>                                 seasonal_periods = 5).fit()
```

This enhancement over DES extends its capability to forecast data featuring regular seasonal fluctuations, offering a more comprehensive approach to time series forecasting.

MODEL EVALUATION AND COMPARISON

Rather than generating a detailed summary table akin to our ARIMA model approach, our focus now shifts to retrieving and printing just the AIC and BIC measures for our Holt–Winters model. This streamlined approach allows us to swiftly compare these goodness-of-fit metrics with those from our ARIMA model, aiding in the assessment of which model better fits the underlying patterns within the data:

```
>>> print(f"AIC: {hw_model.aic}")
AIC: 198.23435477953498

>>> print(f"BIC: {hw_model.bic}")
BIC: 223.54401397788672
```

On comparing the AIC and BIC values between our Holt–Winters and ARIMA models, it becomes evident that both metrics are notably lower for the Holt–Winters model. This outcome is indicative of the Holt–Winters model providing a better fit to the data than the ARIMA model. Lower AIC and BIC values suggest that the Holt–Winters model not only captures the underlying patterns and trends in the time series data more effectively but also demonstrates superior predictive performance. This model comparison perspective underscores the potential advantages of utilizing the Holt–Winters approach, particularly when dealing with time series data that exhibit seasonal variations and trends.

FORECASTING

A forecast of April 2024 closing prices is generated just as before, except that we swap out the pointer to our ARIMA model (`model_fit`) in favor of our Holt–Winters model (`hw_model`). The forecast is then plotted against the actual closing prices by repurposing the same snippet of `matplotlib` code (see figure 7.10).

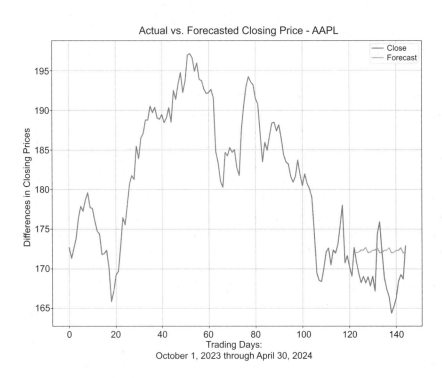

Figure 7.10 The actual closing prices of Apple stock from October 1, 2023, through April 30, 2024, plus the forecasted closing price of the stock throughout April 2024 generated from a Holt–Winters exponential smoothing model. The H–W forecast is slightly more accurate than the forecast from our ARIMA model.

The H–W model predicted a daily closing price ranging from about 172.39 to 173.06, with an average of approximately 172.66. In contrast, the ARIMA model forecasted a constant closing price of 173.51. This indicates that the Holt–Winters forecast is slightly more accurate than the ARIMA forecast. Although exponential smoothing models are generally easier to fit than ARIMA models, their predictive accuracy may vary. Therefore, organizations often adopt a strategy of fitting multiple time series models using different methods and combining their forecasts to derive a final prediction.

> **Disclaimer about time series models**
>
> Time series models offer powerful tools for analyzing data that changes over time, allowing us to forecast trends, seasonal patterns, and cyclic behaviors with a structured approach. They're particularly valuable in fields like finance, economics, and inventory management, where understanding future trends can drive critical decisions. For example, models such as ARIMA and exponential smoothing capture both short- and long-term dependencies, making them adaptable to various applications. Time series models can also handle temporal autocorrelation, helping to produce more accurate forecasts when the order of observations matters.
>
> However, time series models have limitations. They rely on historical patterns to predict future values, which may not always hold true, especially in volatile or unpredictable markets. Sudden changes or external shocks, like economic crises or regulatory changes, can reduce their accuracy. Additionally, time series models assume stationarity or stable statistical properties, which can require extensive data transformation. It's essential to validate and test these models carefully, especially when using them in high-stakes scenarios. Users should remember that forecasts are probabilistic, not certain, and should be complemented with other analytical methods for a balanced perspective.

Throughout this journey, we've explored a wide array of machine learning and time series models, each offering unique strengths for different types of data and predictive challenges. From the foundational techniques of linear and logistic regression, which allowed us to model relationships and probabilities, to the more complex decision trees and random forests, which excel at capturing nonlinear patterns and interactions, we've built a solid foundation in predictive modeling. We then ventured into time series analysis, applying ARIMA models to uncover trends and seasonality, and exponential smoothing to create responsive forecasts for dynamic data. These comprehensive analyses have equipped us with a versatile toolkit for tackling a wide range of predictive tasks. As we transition from model fitting to linear programming, and specifically to constrained optimization, we shift our focus to optimizing decision-making processes, using the powerful insights gained from our modeling efforts to drive effective resource allocation and strategic planning.

Summary

- A time series model is a statistical tool used to understand and predict the behavior of data points indexed by time. It analyzes patterns and trends within sequential data, aiming to capture dependencies and variations over time. Time series models typically account for seasonality, trends, and irregular fluctuations in data, making them essential for forecasting future values or understanding historical patterns.
- ARIMA (autoregressive integrated moving average) is a popular time series forecasting model that combines autoregressive (AR), differencing (I), and moving average (MA) components. ARIMA models are versatile for handling a wide range of time series data by capturing their temporal structure, seasonality, and trend. The AR component models the relationship between an observation and a lagged value, whereas the MA component models the dependency between an observation and a residual error from a moving average model. The differencing component handles nonstationary data by transforming it into a stationary series.
- Exponential smoothing models do not require as much preprocessing as ARIMA models because they primarily focus on smoothing past data to make forecasts. They do not involve complex parameter determination through differencing or identifying autoregressive and moving average components, as ARIMA models do. This simplicity in preprocessing makes exponential smoothing models easier and quicker to implement for forecasting time series data with less historical analysis and adjustment.
- Simple exponential smoothing is a forecasting technique that assigns exponentially decreasing weights to past observations. It is suitable for time series data without trends or seasonal patterns. SES is characterized by its reliance on a single smoothing factor, which controls the rate of decay of older observations. Despite its simplicity, SES can provide effective short-term forecasts by emphasizing recent data over historical values.
- Double exponential smoothing extends SES by incorporating a trend component into the forecasting process. In addition to the smoothing parameter for level smoothing, DES introduces a trend smoothing parameter. This model is suitable for time series data exhibiting a trend but no seasonal pattern. DES forecasts are influenced by both recent observations and the trend observed in previous periods, making it more robust than SES for data with a linear trend.
- Holt–Winters exponential smoothing extends double exponential smoothing by adding a seasonal component to handle time series data with seasonal variations. It therefore includes three smoothing parameters: level smoothing, trend smoothing, and seasonal smoothing. This model is effective for forecasting data with both trend and seasonal patterns, providing a flexible approach to capture and forecast seasonal variations in time series data.

Transforming data into decisions with linear programming

This chapter covers
- Linear programming
- Constrained optimization
- Objective functions
- Inequality and other constraints

In today's competitive business environment, managers and decision-makers are constantly challenged to make the most of limited resources. These resources can include time, money, labor, materials, and more. The goal is to maximize efficiency, profitability, or output, or, alternatively, to minimize costs, waste, or time. Achieving this requires careful planning and precise execution. One of the most effective tools for this purpose is linear programming.

Linear programming is a powerful mathematical approach to solving a specific type of constrained optimization problem, where both the objective and the constraints are represented by linear relationships. As a key tool in operations research and management science, linear programming has widespread applications across various industries. From optimizing supply chains to maximizing profits, linear programming helps decision-makers find efficient solutions to complex, resource-limited challenges.

In essence, linear programming involves defining an objective function, which is a formula that needs to be maximized or minimized, subject to a set of constraints. These constraints represent the limitations or requirements that must be satisfied. By converting a real-world problem into a mathematical model, linear programming allows us to explore different scenarios and identify the optimal solution.

One of the most popular applications of linear programming is in the field of logistics and transportation. Companies use it to determine the most efficient way to distribute products from multiple warehouses to various retail locations, minimizing transportation costs while ensuring timely delivery. Another significant application is in manufacturing, where linear programming helps in scheduling production runs, balancing workloads, and minimizing waste.

More broadly, constrained optimization, a field that includes linear programming, focuses on finding the best solution within a set of given constraints. Constrained optimization is widely used across fields such as economics, engineering, finance, and even sports. For example, investors use constrained optimization to construct portfolios that maximize returns while adhering to risk tolerance levels and regulatory constraints. In engineering, constrained optimization helps design systems and components that meet performance standards while minimizing costs.

8.1 Problem formulation

In previous chapters, we solved real-world problems using real data. In this chapter, although the data will be illustrative, the challenge remains genuine and significant. Every organization faces the annual task of prioritizing which capital projects to pursue from a backlog of dozens, given limited budgets and resources. We will demonstrate the application of linear programming and constrained optimization techniques to strategically select projects that maximize value within given constraints.

To bring this scenario to life, we'll consider a fictional organization named Advanced Analytics and Infrastructure Management (AAIM), which is the data solutions provider for a sales and distribution company. AAIM specializes in reporting, advanced analytics, and the management of analytic infrastructure. This organization follows the Agile methodology to prioritize, plan, and execute its projects, referred to as features in Agile terminology.

> **Agile**
> In Agile methodology, work is structured in a hierarchical manner to ensure manageability and clarity. At the top of the hierarchy are *epics*, which are large bodies of work encompassing multiple *features*. An epic represents a high-level goal or objective that can span multiple sprints or even entire releases. To make these goals more

(continued)

achievable, epics are broken down into features. Features represent significant functionalities or pieces of work derived from epics. They are more detailed and can typically be completed within a release or across several sprints.

Each feature is further broken down into *user stories*. User stories are short, simple descriptions of functionalities from the perspective of the user, defining specific requirements. They are small enough to be completed within a single sprint. Finally, user stories are decomposed into *tasks*, which are the smallest unit of work in Agile. Tasks represent specific actions or steps required to complete a user story and are typically assigned to individual team members. This structured approach ensures that large objectives (epics) are systematically divided into manageable parts (features), detailed requirements (user stories), and actionable steps (tasks) for efficient execution and tracking.

8.1.1 The scenario

Every year, AAIM faces the challenge of selecting the most valuable features to work on from a comprehensive backlog. This selection process is crucial because resources such as budget, time, and workforce are always limited. Prioritizing the right features not only ensures efficient use of these resources but also aligns with the strategic objectives of the organization.

AAIM has shortlisted 20 features to deliberate over, each falling under one of three strategic objectives, or epics:

1. Enhance Data Infrastructure
2. Improve Data Analytics
3. Advance Machine Learning and AI Capabilities

To make informed decisions, AAIM will utilize linear programming techniques to balance its limited resources with its strategic goals, ensuring that each epic receives appropriate attention and resources. This structured approach operates under the assumption that linear constraints accurately represent resource limitations and relationships. Although linear programming is effective for many resource allocation problems, it's worth noting that in some cases, nonlinear constrained optimization may be more appropriate for capturing complex, nonlinear interactions. By using linear programming, however, AAIM can maximize its impact and drive forward its key objectives effectively.

8.1.2 The challenge

AAIM must prioritize and select features from those shortlisted from its backlog, ensuring that the selection process adheres to the following constraints:

- *Budget constraints*—The estimated cost of selected features must not exceed a specific limit for the year and overall.

- *Resource constraints*—The features selected must align with the available workforce and time.
- *Strategic balance*—Each epic should have a balanced representation of features to ensure all strategic objectives are advanced.

By adhering to these constraints, AAIM can strategically plan its project portfolio.

8.1.3 The approach

To address this challenge, AAIM will use linear programming to formulate and solve the problem. The steps involved in this process include the following:

- *Defining the objective function*—The objective function will aim to maximize the priority score of selected features, which is a measure of value derived from each feature relative to the effort required.
- *Setting the constraints*—Constraints will be defined for budget limits, resource availability, and strategic balance. Specifically, each epic should have a minimum of three and a maximum of four features selected.
- *Formulating the linear programming model*—By translating the real-world scenario into a precise mathematical model, AAIM can systematically represent its resources, constraints, and objectives. This modeling step is essential, as it allows AAIM to explore various scenarios and identify the optimal feature selection within its limitations, setting the stage for strategic and efficient decision-making.

This approach will ensure that AAIM effectively prioritizes and selects the most valuable projects to pursue, thereby making the best use of its limited resources while equally advancing its strategic objectives.

PRIORITY SCORES

One of our first tasks will be to calculate priority scores for selected features. To illustrate how priority scores are derived, let's consider one of AAIM's features: the Automated Data Cleaning Pipeline. This feature involves developing an automated data cleaning pipeline to preprocess raw data, handle missing values, and correct data inconsistencies. The prioritization process evaluates both the value and effort associated with this feature, resulting in a priority score that helps determine its value relative to other features.

The value assessment is as follows (each criterion is scored on a scale of 1 to 5, with 5 being the highest score):

1. Customer impact: high (5 points)
   – Automates a significant portion of the data preparation process, saving time for data scientists and improving productivity
2. Revenue generation: medium (3 points)
   – Enables faster data processing, leading to quicker insights and faster time-to-market for data-driven products

3 Strategic alignment: high (5 points)
   – Aligns with the organization's goal to improve operational efficiency and data quality
4 Risk mitigation: medium (3 points)
   – Reduces the risk of human error in data preprocessing and ensures more consistent data quality

Total value points: 16

The effort assessment is as follows (again, each criterion is scored on a scale of 1 to 5, with 5 being the highest score):

1 Complexity: high (5 points)
   – Requires significant development effort and testing to ensure the pipeline handles various data formats and edge cases
2 Dependencies: medium (3 points)
   – Depends on the availability of raw data sources and integration with existing data processing tools
3 Technical Challenge: high (5 points)
   – Involves advanced data engineering techniques and potential use of machine learning models for data imputation

Total effort points: 13

To prioritize features, AAIM calculates the priority score as the ratio of total value points to total effort points:

$$\text{Priority Score} = \frac{\text{Total Value Points}}{\text{Total Effort Points}}$$

Therefore, the priority score for the automated data cleaning pipeline feature equals

$$\text{Priority Score(Automated Data Cleaning Pipeline)} = \frac{16}{13} = 1.23$$

Despite the complexities and other challenges, the value proposition of the automated data cleaning pipeline feature still surpasses the estimated level of effort. However, its overall ranking among the other 19 features shortlisted from the backlog remains to be determined, particularly as we factor constraints into the decision-making process.

> **Agile and linear optimization**
> Agile methodology and linear optimization techniques, such as linear programming and constrained optimization, complement each other effectively in project management. Although not every Agile team constructs optimization frameworks, and not every organization using optimization techniques practices Agile, the integration of

> these approaches can be highly beneficial. Agile employs quantitative methods to score features based on a combination of value and effort. These scores are crucial in prioritizing work and ensuring that the most impactful features are addressed first.
>
> In Agile, features are often evaluated using metrics like customer impact, revenue generation, strategic alignment, and risk mitigation. Each feature receives a value score and an effort score. The value score represents the potential benefit, whereas the effort score indicates the resources required for implementation. This quantitative evaluation aligns perfectly with the principles of linear optimization.
>
> The score derived from these Agile evaluations can serve as an objective function in a constrained optimization framework. By maximizing the priority score, which is the ratio of value to effort, organizations can ensure that their resources are allocated efficiently. Constraints such as budget limits, resource availability, and strategic balance across different epics can be incorporated into the optimization process.
>
> Thus, Agile's quantitative scoring system provides a structured basis for developing a linear optimization framework, ensuring that project prioritization is both strategic and data-driven. This integration allows for intelligent selection of features, maximizing value while adhering to resource constraints.

This straightforward value-versus-effort calculation—not uncommon in Agile teams—offers a clear and structured approach for the team to make informed decisions about feature prioritization; in fact, it provides an objective function to use within our constrained optimization framework. By focusing on initiatives that offer the highest value relative to the effort invested, AAIM ensures that resources are allocated efficiently and effectively, maximizing their overall effect.

8.1.4 Feature summaries

Tables 8.1–8.3—one for each epic—list the features shortlisted from the backlog. Each table includes the estimated cost for the first year, the total cost to complete, and the priority score. The features are not listed in any particular order.

Table 8.1   Features aligned with the Enhance Data Infrastructure epic

Feature name	First-year cost	Total cost	Priority score
Automated Data Cleaning Pipeline	$50,000	$80,000	1.23
Real-time Data Ingestion	$70,000	$120,000	1.29
Data Privacy and Compliance Tools	$80,000	$130,000	1.19
Real-time Data Monitoring and Alerts	$60,000	$100,000	1.38
Integration with External Data Sources	$50,000	$85,000	1.42
Feature Engineering Automation	$55,000	$90,000	1.45

Table 8.2 Features aligned with the Improve Data Analytics and Reporting epic

Feature name	First-year cost	Total cost	Priority score
Interactive Data Visualization Dashboard	$60,000	$100,000	1.67
Predictive Maintenance Model	$55,000	$90,000	1.13
Fraud Detection System	$80,000	$130,000	1.43
Automated Reporting Tool	$45,000	$70,000	1.56
Supply Chain Optimization Model	$75,000	$125,000	1.13
Anomaly Detection in Real-time Data	$60,000	$95,000	1.14

Table 8.3 Features aligned with the Advance Machine Learning and AI Capabilities epic

Feature name	First-year cost	Total cost	Priority score
Customer Segmentation Analysis	$40,000	$60,000	1.50
Personalized Marketing Recommendation Engine	$65,000	$110,000	1.46
Churn Prediction Model	$50,000	$85,000	1.64
Text Mining for Sentiment Analysis	$35,000	$55,000	1.63
Customer Lifetime Value Prediction	$50,000	$80,000	1.50
Time Series Forecasting	$55,000	$90,000	1.23
Recommendation System for Cross-selling	$65,000	$110,000	1.50
Automated ML Model Selection and Tuning	$70,000	$115,000	1.43

To summarize, AIMM will prioritize features to achieve strategic objectives efficiently. The selection process involves the following criteria:

- *Objective function*—The goal is to maximize the priority scores of the selected features, ensuring the highest value relative to the effort required without violating any constraints established beforehand.
- *Number of features*—AAIM will prioritize a minimum of 9 features and a maximum of 12 features.
- *Epic balance*—Each epic will receive a commitment of three or four features to ensure balanced progress across all strategic objectives.
- *Budget constraints*
  - *Yearly investment*—The total investment for the selected features will not exceed $700,000 over the next year.
  - *Total investment*—The combined cost of these features will not exceed $1.1 million over their complete lifecycle.

By adhering to these constraints and focusing on maximizing priority scores, AAIM will strategically allocate resources to ensure a balanced and high-impact advancement of its objectives. This approach uses linear programming and constrained optimization to achieve the most optimal results.

8.2 Developing the linear optimization framework

To effectively utilize linear programming for project prioritization, it's crucial to understand the core requirements of a linear programming problem. The key characteristic of linear programming is that all mathematical relationships involved in the problem must be linear. In other words, the objective function and all constraints should be expressed as linear equations or inequalities.

The core requirements are as follows:

1 *Linear relationships*—The function that we aim to maximize or minimize must be a linear combination of the decision variables. For example, if we are maximizing the priority score, the objective function should look like this:

$$\text{Maximize } Z = c_1 x_1 + c_2 x_2 + \ldots + c_n x_n$$

where Z is the objective function; $c_1, c_2, \ldots, c_n$ are coefficients representing the value of each feature, represented by the priority score, which is the ratio between the expected value and estimated effort; and $x_1, x_2, \ldots, x_n$ are binary decision variables indicating whether a feature is selected ($x_i = 1$) or not selected ($x_i = 0$).

The constraints must also be linear, meaning each constraint should form a linear equation or inequality. For instance,

$$a_1 x_1 + a_2 x_2 + \ldots + a_n x_n \leq b$$

where $a_1, a_2, \ldots, a_n$ are coefficients; $x_1, x_2, \ldots, x_n$ are decision variables; and b is a constant representing the limit, or constraint (e.g., maximum investment).

2 *Quantitative objective function*—The objective function is a quantitative measure that the linear programming model aims to optimize. This function could represent maximizing priority scores, minimizing costs, or balancing both aspects, depending on the specific goals of the organization.

3 *Constraints*—Constraints are the restrictions or limitations on the decision variables. These could include budget limits, resource availability, and strategic goals. Each constraint must be expressed in linear form.

Constraints ensure that the solution is feasible and practical within the given limits: for example, ensuring that the total investment does not exceed a specified budget:

$$\sum_{i=1}^{n} \text{cost}_i \times x_i \leq \text{Budget}$$

Strategic constraints might include balancing the number of features selected from each epic to ensure comprehensive progress across all strategic objectives.

4 *Alternatives*—The decision variables (x_1, x_2, ..., x_n) represent the alternatives or choices available. The linear programming model evaluates different combinations of these variables to identify the optimal set of features that maximizes the objective function while satisfying all constraints.

By adhering to these requirements, the linear optimization framework ensures that the selected features provide the highest possible value within the given constraints. This structured approach allows AAIM to strategically allocate resources, ensuring a balanced and effective advancement of its objectives.

8.2.1 Explanation of linear equations and inequalities

In the context of linear programming, linear equations and inequalities are fundamental components:

- *Linear equations*—Mathematical expressions in which each term is either a constant or the product of a constant and a single variable. The equation represents a straight line when graphed. For example,

$$3x_1 + 4x_2 = 12$$

This equation states that the sum of 3 times x_1 and 4 times x_2 equals 12. Both x_1 and x_2 are variables, and the coefficients (3 and 4) and the constant term (12) are all linear.

- *Linear inequalities*—These are similar to linear equations but involve inequality signs ($\leq$, $\geq$, $<$, $>$) instead of an equal sign. For instance,

$$5x_1 + 2x_2 \leq 20$$

This inequality means the sum of 5 times x_1 and 2 times x_2 must be less than or equal to 20. Linear equalities represent half-planes when graphed and define the feasible region in a linear programming problem.

In summary, both the objective function and the constraints in a linear programming problem must be expressed using these linear forms to ensure the problem remains solvable using linear programming techniques. This requirement is crucial because it ensures that the relationships between variables are proportional and additive, which is essential for finding the optimal solution.

8.2.2 Data definition

To tackle the challenge of project prioritization, we begin by establishing a robust data source that itemizes the alternatives. The provided data set includes detailed information about each feature, such as the epic it belongs to, the name, the cost for the first

8.2 Developing the linear optimization framework

year, the total cost, the value points, and the effort points. This structured data serves as the foundation for our linear optimization framework.

Next, we build out the linear optimization framework by defining the constraints and the objective function and solving the optimization problem. Here is the step-by-step sequence:

1. *Data definition*—We start by defining a list of `Feature` instances, where each instance represents a feature with associated attributes like epic, name, cost for the first year, total cost, value points, and effort points. (Alternatively, a spreadsheet imported as a pandas data frame would work just as well.)
2. *Objective function*—The objective function is designed to maximize the priority score of the selected features. This score is calculated as the ratio of value points to effort points, and we negate the values because the `linprog` method in `scipy.optimize` performs minimization by default.
3. *Constraints*—We establish several constraints to ensure the solution is practical and aligns with organizational goals:
   - *Budget constraints*—Total costs for the first year and overall must not exceed specified limits.
   - *Epic constraints*—Each epic should have at least three and at most four features selected. This ensures balanced progress across all strategic objectives.
4. *Decision variable bounds*—Each feature can either be selected (1) or not selected (0), so the decision variables are binary.
5. *Solving the linear programming problem*—Using the `linprog()` function, we solve the optimization problem to find the optimal set of features that maximizes the priority score while adhering to all constraints.
6. *Result evaluation*—We check whether the solution is successful. If it is, we extract and display the selected features, along with their costs and priority scores. This helps in understanding which features provide the greatest value relative to their effort and cost, ensuring efficient resource allocation.

Our first snippet of Python code uses a data class named `Feature` to define the attributes of each feature in a structured way. We then create an object called `features`, which contains multiple instances of `Feature`. Each instance represents a feature and includes detailed attributes, such as the `epic` it belongs to, the feature `name`, the first-year cost (`cost_1yr`), the total cost (`total_cost`), the value points (`value_points`), and the effort points (`effort_points`). Organized by their respective epics, these feature instances allow for clear categorization, making it easy to analyze and prioritize features based on strategic objectives.

This data class structure enhances readability and enables efficient data manipulation, supporting optimization and decision-making processes. Note that the subsequent code requires the `dataclass` decorator, which is imported from the `dataclasses` module, to define the `Feature` class. For brevity, only the first four and last four features are shown here. These instances correspond to tables 8.1–8.3, with the distinction that the code displays value and effort points separately, whereas the tables calculate a priority score based on these variables:

```
>>> from dataclasses import dataclass
>>> @dataclass
>>> class Feature:
>>>     epic: str
>>>     name: str
>>>     cost_1yr: int
>>>     total_cost: int
>>>     value_points: int
>>>     effort_points: int
>>> features = [
>>>     Feature('Enhance Data Infrastructure',
>>>         'Automated Data Cleaning Pipeline',
>>>             50000, 80000, 16, 13),
>>>     Feature('Enhance Data Infrastructure',
>>>             'Real-time Data Ingestion',
>>>             70000, 120000, 18, 14),
>>>     Feature('Enhance Data Infrastructure',
>>>             'Data Privacy and Compliance Tools',
>>>             80000, 130000, 19, 16),
>>>     Feature('Enhance Data Infrastructure',
>>>             'Real-time Data Monitoring and Alerts',
>>>             60000, 100000, 18, 13),
>>> # Other feature details not included
>>> # for space considerations

>>>     Feature('Advance Machine Learning and AI Capabilities',
>>>             'Customer Lifetime Value Prediction',
>>>             50000, 80000, 15, 10),
>>>     Feature('Advance Machine Learning and AI Capabilities',
>>>             'Time Series Forecasting',
>>>             55000, 90000, 16, 13),
>>>     Feature('Advance Machine Learning and AI Capabilities',
>>>             'Recommendation System for Cross-selling',
>>>             65000, 110000, 18, 12),
>>>     Feature('Advance Machine Learning and AI Capabilities',
>>>         'Automated ML Model Selection and Tuning',
>>>             70000, 115000, 20, 14)
>>> ]
```

Now that we have clearly defined our data source, we can proceed to the next step: demonstrating how to define the objective function. This crucial component will allow us to effectively prioritize and select features based on our established criteria, ensuring that we maximize value while adhering to our constraints.

8.2.3 Objective function

The following line of code sets up the objective function for our optimization problem. By iterating through each feature in the features list, it calculates a priority score as the ratio of value points to effort points for each feature. The negative sign is applied to each calculated priority score to transform the problem, allowing a minimization algorithm to effectively maximize this value-to-effort ratio. This transformation ensures that the optimization solver will prioritize features that offer the highest value relative to their effort:

```
>>> c = [-f.value_points / f.effort_points for f in features]
```

It produces what is known as a Python list comprehension. List comprehensions are a concise way to create lists in Python, offering a syntactically compact and readable method to build lists from existing lists or iterables. In this context, the list comprehension iterates over each feature in the `features` list. Each `Feature` instance represents a specific feature with various attributes such as `value_points` and `effort_points`.

The expression `f.value_points / f.effort_points` calculates the priority score for each feature `f`. This score is a ratio indicating the value derived per unit of effort, where a higher ratio suggests that the feature provides more value for the effort required.

The negative sign (-) before the expression is used because linear programming solvers like `linprog()` typically minimize the objective function by default. By negating the priority scores, we effectively transform the problem of maximizing priority scores into a minimization problem, which the solver can handle directly.

The result of the list comprehension is a list of these negated priority scores, which will be used as coefficients in the objective function for the linear programming solver. The `print()` method returns the derived priority scores, rounded to two digits right of the decimal point:

```
>>> print([round(val, 2) for val in c])
[-1.23, -1.29, -1.19, -1.38, -1.42, -1.45, -1.67, -1.13, -1.43, -1.56,
-1.13, -1.14, -1.5, -1.46, -1.64, -1.62, -1.5, -1.23, -1.5, -1.43]
```

Aside from the negation of the priority scores for each feature, these scores align perfectly with those in tables 8.1–8.3.

8.2.4 Constraints

Our next snippet of code defines the inequality constraints for a linear programming problem and returns the constraints as NumPy arrays: `cost_1yr` must be ≤ to 700000, and `total_cost` must be ≤ to 1100000. In other words, AIMM has just enough resources to invest up to $700,000 in the coming year and no more than $1.1 million in total for the selected features:

```
>>> import numpy as np
>>> A_ub = np.array([
>>>     [f.cost_1yr for f in features],
>>>     [f.total_cost for f in features]
>>> ])
>>> b_ub = np.array([700000, 1100000])
```

The variable `A_ub` is a matrix that represents the coefficients of the inequality constraints for the linear programming problem. In this case, it is constructed as a NumPy array, using list comprehensions that iterate over the `features` list. One list comprehension extracts the `cost_1yr` (cost in the first year) for each feature in the `features` list, thereby creating an array of the first-year costs of all features. This array becomes the first row of the `A_ub` matrix, representing the coefficients for the first inequality constraint related to the first-year budget.

Similarly, another list comprehension extracts the `total_cost` for each feature in the `features` list, creating an array of the total costs of all features. This list becomes the second row of the `A_ub` matrix, representing the coefficients for the second inequality constraint related to the total allowable budget.

A call to the `print()` method returns the `A_ub` matrix, now represented as a NumPy matrix:

```
>>> print(A_ub)
[[ 50000  70000  80000  60000  50000  55000  60000  55000  80000
   45000  75000  60000  40000  65000  50000  35000  50000  55000
   65000  70000]
 [ 80000 120000 130000 100000  85000  90000 100000  90000 130000
   70000 125000  95000  60000 110000  85000  55000  80000  90000
  110000 115000]]
```

End of the second row in the array. Figures represent the estimated total cost for each feature.

End of the first row in the array. Figures represent the estimated first-year cost for each feature.

The variable `b_ub` is a vector that represents the right-hand side values of the inequality constraints defined by `A_ub`. Each element in `b_ub` corresponds to a specific constraint:

- `7000000` represents the maximum allowable budget for the first year. The first inequality constraint ensures that the sum of the selected features' first-year costs does not exceed this amount.
- `1100000` represents the maximum allowable total budget for the entire project duration. The second inequality constraint ensures that the sum of the selected features' total costs does not exceed this amount.

Together, `A_ub` and `b_ub` define the set of linear inequality constraints for the optimization problem. These constraints ensure that the selected features do not exceed the specified budget limits, both for the first year and overall. When used in conjunction with the optimization solver, these constraints help in finding the optimal set of features that maximizes the objective function (priority scores) while adhering to the budgetary limits.

Beyond budgetary constraints, AAIM wants to pursue a mix of features that enable it to balance its investment across different epics or strategic objectives. This approach ensures that its resources are not only optimally utilized within financial limits but also strategically distributed to support diverse areas of development. By balancing investments across epics, AAIM can ensure comprehensive progress in enhancing data infrastructure, improving data analytics and reporting, and advancing machine learning and AI capabilities.

The following code snippet introduces additional constraints to achieve this balance. It iterates over each epic, creating constraints to ensure that at least three and no more than four features are selected from each epic. For each epic, two rows are constructed and appended to the `A_ub` matrix: one representing the lower bound (at least three features) and the other representing the upper bound (no more than four features). The corresponding values are added to the `b_ub` vector, completing the inequality constraints necessary for the linear programming model:

```
>>> epics = ['Enhance Data Infrastructure',
>>>          'Improve Data Analytics and Reporting',
>>>          'Advance Machine Learning and AI Capabilities']

>>> for epic in epics:
>>>     row_min = [-1 if f.epic == epic else 0 for f in features]
>>>     row_max = [1 if f.epic == epic else 0 for f in features]
>>>     A_ub = np.vstack([A_ub, row_min])
>>>     A_ub = np.vstack([A_ub, row_max])
>>>     b_ub = np.append(b_ub, -3)
>>>     b_ub = np.append(b_ub, 4)
```

The preceding code can best be explained by breaking it down into the following parts:

- `epics = ['Enhance Data Infrastructure',...` initializes a list to define the epics that will be iterated over to create the constraints.
- `for epic in epics` loops through each epic in the `epics` list to create and add constraints for that epic.
- `row_min...` creates a row for the `A_ub` matrix using a list comprehension. Each element in the row is `-1` if the feature belongs to the current epic or `0` otherwise. Negative coefficients are used to set up a "greater than or equal to" inequality for the minimum constraint.
- Similarly, `row_max...` creates another row for the `A_ub` matrix using a list comprehension. Each element is `1` if the feature belongs to the current epic or `0` if otherwise. The positive coefficients are used to set up a "less than or equal to" inequality for the maximum constraint `row_min`, which is appended to the `A_ub` matrix.
- `A_ub = np.vstack...` appends the `row_min` array to the `A_ub` matrix using the NumPy `vstack()` function, ensuring consistency with its array structure.
- `b_ub = np.append...` appends `-3` to the `b_ub` vector using the NumPy `append()` function. This enforces that the sum of selected features for the current epic is at least 3 (since the inequality `-sum ≥ -3` translates to `sum ≤ 3`).
- `A_ub = np.vstack...` appends the `row_max` array to the `A_ub` matrix, adding the coefficients for the "at most 4" constraint.

- `b_ub = np.append...` appends 4 to the `b_ub` vector, representing the right-hand side of the inequality. This enforces that the sum of selected features for the current epic is at most 4.

The last bit of code ensures that the selected features are balanced across the three epics by adding constraints to the linear programming model. Specifically, it guarantees that each epic has at least three and at most four features selected. This is done by constructing and appending rows to the `A_ub` matrix and corresponding values to the `b_ub` vector, which represent the inequality constraints for the optimization problem.

8.2.5 Decision variable bounds

Our next code snippet is an integral part of setting up a linear programming problem, specifically in defining the bounds for the decision variables. In linear programming, decision variables represent the choices to be made—in this case, whether to select a feature or not. This particular line of code utilizes a list comprehension to create a list of tuples, where each tuple represents the bounds for a corresponding decision variable. Because each decision variable must be either 0 or 1, this setup represents a binary integer programming problem—a specialized form of linear programming with discrete, yes-or-no choices:

```
>>> x_bounds = [(0, 1) for _ in features]
```

In the context of our problem, each feature can be either selected or not, which corresponds to a binary decision variable. The values for these decision variables can only be 0 or 1, where 0 indicates the feature is not selected and 1 indicates it is selected. The line of code iterates over the list of features, creating a tuple (0, 1) for each feature. This tuple is the bound for the decision variable associated with that feature.

By defining `x_bounds` in this manner, we ensure that the optimization solver respects these bounds when determining the optimal solution. Essentially, this constraint enforces that the solution comprises only binary decisions, aligning with the reality of project selection, where a feature can either be included or excluded.

This list of tuples, `x_bounds`, is then passed to the solver along with other parameters like the objective function and constraints. The solver uses this information to explore feasible solutions within the specified bounds and find the optimal set of features that maximize the priority scores while adhering to budgetary and strategic constraints.

8.2.6 Solving the linear programming problem

So far, we have laid the groundwork for solving a project prioritization problem using linear programming. We began by defining a data set of features, each belonging to specific epics and characterized by attributes such as cost, value points, and effort points. Using this data set, we constructed the objective function, aimed at maximizing the priority scores of the selected features. We also established budgetary constraints, ensuring that the total cost for the first year and the overall cost stay within specified limits.

Additionally, we introduced constraints to balance the number of selected features across different epics. This ensures that resources are evenly distributed across strategic objectives, with at least three and no more than four features chosen from each epic. We then defined the bounds for our decision variables, ensuring they are binary (0 or 1), representing whether a feature is selected or not.

The following code uses the `scipy` library to solve the linear programming problem:

```
>>> from scipy.optimize import linprog
>>> import numpy as np
>>> result = linprog(c, A_ub = A_ub, b_ub = b_ub,
>>>                  bounds = x_bounds, method = 'highs')
```

The first line imports the `linprog` method from the `optimize` module of the `scipy` library. The `linprog()` method is used to solve linear programming problems, enabling us to find the optimal solution that maximizes or minimizes a specified objective function while adhering to a set of linear constraints.

It achieves this by taking in the following parameters:

- `c` is the coefficient list for the objective function, which we previously defined to represent the negated priority scores of the features. By minimizing this objective function, we effectively maximize the priority scores.
- `A_ub` is the matrix representing the coefficients of the inequality constraints. Each row in `A_ub` corresponds to a constraint, and each column corresponds to a decision variable (feature). The entries in `A_ub` specify how each decision variable contributes to each constraint.
- `b_ub` is the vector containing the right-hand-side values for the inequality constraints. Each entry in `b_ub` corresponds to a constraint, defining the upper bound that the linear combination of decision variables (weighted by `A_ub`) must not exceed.
- `bounds` is a parameter specifying the bounds for each decision variable. In our case, we defined `x_bounds` as 0 or 1, thereby indicating that each decision variable must represent whether or not a feature is selected.
- `method` parameter determines the algorithm used to solve the linear programming problem. The `'highs'` method selects and applies the most appropriate algorithm, such as `'simplex'` or `'interior-point,'` depending on the problem's size and complexity.

The `result` variable stores the output from the `linprog()` method. This output includes three important attributes that can be returned by calling the `print()` method. The first, `result.success`, is a Boolean—that is, a data type that can have just one of two possible values, `True` or `False`—indicating whether or not the optimization was successful:

```
>>> print(result.success)
True
```

When `result.success` is printed and returns `False`, it indicates that the optimization problem could not be solved with the given constraints. This could be due to several reasons, such as the constraints being too restrictive, thereby making the problem infeasible, or the problem not having a bounded solution within the specified constraints.

The second attribute, `result.x`, is an array that contains the values of the decision variables that optimize the objective function. These values indicate which features are selected (with values of `1`) and which are not (with values of `0`) in the context of a binary decision problem. Essentially, `result.x` provides the optimal solution to the linear programming problem, showing how the resources should be allocated to maximize the priority scores while satisfying all the constraints:

```
>>> print(result.x)
[ 0. 1. 0. 1. 1. 1. 1. 0. 1. 1. 0. 1. 1. 0. 1. 1. 1. 0.
 -0. 0.]
```

So, for example, the first feature listed in our data source, Automated Data Cleaning Pipeline, should not be selected, but the second feature, Real-time Data Ingestion, should be.

Overall, the maximum of 12 features were selected, as determined by summing the values in the `result.x` array:

```
>>> print(sum(result.x))
12.0
```

The third attribute, `result.fun`, is the value of the objective function at the optimal solution. This value represents the maximum (or minimum) priority score achieved by the selected features, adjusted for the negation used in the setup. By evaluating `result.fun`, we can determine the effectiveness of our feature selection in terms of maximizing the priority score while adhering to all constraints. This provides a quantitative measure of the optimal solution's overall value.

Our next call to the `print()` method returns the sum of the priority scores from the selected features. This total is multiplied by `-1` to reverse the negation applied during setup and then rounded to include no more than two digits to the right of the decimal point:

```
>>> print(round(result.fun * -1, 2))
17.6
```

When the sum of the priority scores (17.6) is divided by the number of allowed features (12), we get an average priority score equal to 1.47.

By calling the `linprog()` method with our defined parameters, we solve the project prioritization problem, identifying the optimal set of features that maximize the priority scores while adhering to budgetary and strategic constraints. This approach ensures that AAIM can make informed, strategic decisions about resource allocation, ultimately driving efficient and balanced progress across its key objectives.

8.2.7 Result evaluation

Given the success of our linear optimization problem, we can confidently state that AAIM can invest in up to 12 features without exceeding its budgetary constraints for this year or next. This means AAIM can prioritize 12 of the features it shortlisted from the backlog. Although it is possible to manually derive these features by matching the `result.x` array with our features list, this approach is cumbersome and inefficient.

Fortunately, there is a more efficient method to obtain the full result set, which includes the list of selected features as well as the final budget numbers for both the current and following year. By using the attributes provided in the optimization result, we can easily extract and present this information. The selected features can be identified directly from the `result.x` array, where a value of `1` indicates selection. Additionally, the final budget numbers can be computed by summing the relevant cost attributes of the selected features. This method simplifies the process while ensuring accurate and complete reporting of the optimization outcomes.

Here's one example of how this can be achieved this programmatically:

```
>>> if result.success:                              # Checks whether the optimization problem is successfully solved
>>>     selected_features = [f for f, \             # Creates a list of features that were selected in the optimization solution
>>>         x in zip(features, result.x) \
>>>                         if x == 1]
>>>     print('Selected Features:')                 # Prints the header
>>>     for f in selected_features:                 # Initiates a loop to iterate over each selected feature
>>>         print(f'Epic: {f.epic}, '               # Prints the epic of the current feature in the loop
>>>             f'Feature: {f.name}, '              # Prints the feature name
>>>             f'Cost in 1 Year: ${f.cost_1yr}, '  # Prints the feature cost for the current year
>>>             f'Total Cost: ${f.total_cost}, '    # Prints the total feature cost
>>>             f'Priority Score: {f.value_points /
>>>                 f.effort_points:.2f}')          # Derives and prints the priority score
>>>     total_cost_1yr = \
>>>         sum(f.cost_1yr for f in selected_features)   # Calculates the total cost for the first year for all selected features
>>>     total_cost = \
>>>         sum(f.total_cost for f in selected_features) # Calculates the total overall cost for all selected features
>>>     print(f'\nTotal Cost in 1 Year: $' \
>>>         f'{total_cost_1yr}')                    # Prints the total cost for the first year
>>>     print(f'Total Cost: ${total_cost}')         # Prints the total overall cost
>>> else:
>>>     print('Optimization failed.')               # Prints "Optimization failed" if the optimization was not successful

Selected Features:
Epic: Enhance Data Infrastructure,
Feature: Real-time Data Ingestion,
Cost in 1 Year: $70000, Total Cost: $120000, Priority Score: 1.29

Epic: Enhance Data Infrastructure,
Feature: Real-time Data Monitoring and Alerts,
Cost in 1 Year: $60000, Total Cost: $100000, Priority Score: 1.38

Epic: Enhance Data Infrastructure,
Feature: Integration with External Data Sources,
```

```
Cost in 1 Year: $50000, Total Cost: $85000, Priority Score: 1.42

Epic: Enhance Data Infrastructure,
Feature: Feature Engineering Automation,
Cost in 1 Year: $55000, Total Cost: $90000, Priority Score: 1.45

Epic: Improve Data Analytics and Reporting,
Feature: Interactive Data Visualization Dashboard,
Cost in 1 Year: $60000, Total Cost: $100000, Priority Score: 1.67

Epic: Improve Data Analytics and Reporting,
Feature: Fraud Detection System,
Cost in 1 Year: $80000, Total Cost: $130000, Priority Score: 1.43

Epic: Improve Data Analytics and Reporting,
Feature: Automated Reporting Tool,
Cost in 1 Year: $45000, Total Cost: $70000, Priority Score: 1.56

Epic: Improve Data Analytics and Reporting,
Feature: Anomaly Detection in Real-time Data,
Cost in 1 Year: $60000, Total Cost: $95000, Priority Score: 1.14

Epic: Advance Machine Learning and AI Capabilities,
Feature: Customer Segmentation Analysis,
Cost in 1 Year: $40000, Total Cost: $60000, Priority Score: 1.50

Epic: Advance Machine Learning and AI Capabilities,
Feature: Churn Prediction Model,
Cost in 1 Year: $50000, Total Cost: $85000, Priority Score: 1.64

Epic: Advance Machine Learning and AI Capabilities,
Feature: Text Mining for Sentiment Analysis,
Cost in 1 Year: $35000, Total Cost: $55000, Priority Score: 1.62

Epic: Advance Machine Learning and AI Capabilities,
Feature: Customer Lifetime Value Prediction,
Cost in 1 Year: $50000, Total Cost: $80000, Priority Score: 1.50

Total Cost in 1 Year: $655000
Total Cost: $1070000
```

By using this approach, AAIM can quickly and conveniently obtain a comprehensive view of the selected features and their associated costs, ensuring that all strategic and budgetary goals are met. This method not only makes the process more efficient but also provides a clear and detailed summary of the optimization results.

One of the advantages of this framework is its flexibility in accommodating various "what-if" scenarios by simply adjusting the parameters. For example, we can explore the effect of changing the constraints to require a minimum of two and a maximum of three features per epic, or setting different budget limits, such as a $550,000 investment in the first year and a total of $850,000. This adaptability allows AAIM to quickly assess different strategic options and make informed decisions based on changing priorities or resource availability without necessitating a complete code rewrite.

In the next chapter, we will transition from linear programming to another powerful decision-making technique: Monte Carlo simulations. This approach allows us to model and analyze uncertainty and variability in complex systems, providing valuable insights for informed decision-making and effective risk management.

Summary

- Linear programming is a crucial technique for efficiently allocating limited resources, such as budget, time, and materials, to achieve the best possible outcomes. It ensures that resources are utilized in the most effective way to maximize benefits or minimize costs.
- A fundamental aspect of linear programming is that both the objective function and the constraints must be linear. This means all relationships in the model are proportional and additive, making the mathematical formulation simpler and solvable using efficient algorithms.
- The foundation of linear programming involves defining an objective function that needs to be either maximized or minimized. This function is subject to a set of linear constraints, which represent the real-world limitations and requirements, such as budget caps, resource availability, and minimum performance standards.
- One of the major strengths of linear programming is its flexibility. It allows for easy adjustments to the parameters and constraints, enabling the exploration of various "what-if" scenarios. This adaptability helps decision-makers understand the potential effects of different strategic choices and changes in resource availability.
- Linear programming can accommodate both binary decision variables, which represent yes/no decisions (e.g., whether to undertake a project or not), and continuous decision variables, which represent quantities that can take any value within a given range. This versatility makes it suitable for a wide range of optimization problems.
- By incorporating multiple constraints, linear programming helps ensure that decisions are balanced and strategically sound. It supports comprehensive decision-making by allowing for the consideration of various objectives and priorities, ensuring that all strategic goals are advanced in a harmonious manner.

Running Monte Carlo simulations

This chapter covers
- Monte Carlo simulations
- Mathematical foundations
- Applications to discrete random variables
- Applications to continuous random variables
- Generating and interpreting simulation results

Monte Carlo simulations are a powerful and versatile tool used to model and analyze complex systems and processes across many fields. They are named after the Monte Carlo Casino in Monaco, reflecting the reliance on random sampling methods, which are reminiscent of the inherent randomness in gambling. This connection stems from early applications of these methods in probabilistic studies during the mid-20th century. The basic idea behind Monte Carlo simulations is to use random sampling to generate a range of possible outcomes for a given problem. These outcomes can then be analyzed to understand the probability distribution and potential variability of the results. This approach is particularly useful when analytical solutions are impractical or impossible, such as in systems with high complexity, nonlinear relationships, or numerous interacting variables. Monte Carlo simulations provide a way to approximate solutions in these challenging scenarios.

Our goal is to equip you with the knowledge and practical skills to effectively run Monte Carlo simulations and understand their mathematical foundations. This chapter begins with simulations on discrete random variables, where outcomes are finite and distinct (e.g., the number of absentee employees). It then extends to continuous random variables, where outcomes can take on any value within a range (e.g., the closing prices of a public stock). Understanding the nuances between these two types of data is crucial for effectively applying Monte Carlo methods to real-world problems. By the end of this chapter, you will understand not only how to implement these simulations but also how to interpret their results to make informed decisions in the face of uncertainty. By combining theoretical explanations with hands-on examples, this chapter bridges the gap between abstract concepts and their practical applications. This dual approach ensures that you will gain both a foundational understanding and the practical skills necessary to confidently run Monte Carlo simulations.

9.1 Applications and benefits of Monte Carlo simulations

Monte Carlo simulations are versatile tools with widespread applications across various fields. In finance, they model portfolio performance under extreme market conditions by simulating asset price behaviors under diverse scenarios, helping assess risk and uncertainty. Engineers use Monte Carlo methods to predict the structural integrity of systems, such as bridges under varying loads, by modeling the effects of uncertain parameters. In project management, these simulations are invaluable for forecasting timelines and budgets, accounting for uncertainties in task durations and costs. Scientists employ Monte Carlo techniques to simulate complex physical processes, such as particle diffusion or molecular behavior in gases, offering insights into phenomena that cannot be directly observed.

One of the key strengths of Monte Carlo simulations is their ability to handle both discrete and continuous random variables (see chapter 2). Discrete random variables, such as the number of defective items in a batch, take on specific values. In contrast, continuous random variables, such as the time required to complete a task, can take on any value within a defined range. By incorporating randomness and variability into the modeling process, Monte Carlo simulations create realistic representations of real-world systems, capturing the inherent uncertainties that deterministic models can miss.

Compared to traditional deterministic models—which provide single-point estimates based on fixed inputs—Monte Carlo simulations generate a distribution of outcomes based on variability in those inputs. For example, rather than predicting that a project will take exactly 20 days, a Monte Carlo simulation might reveal a 70% chance of completion within 22 days and a 10% chance of exceeding 25 days. This probabilistic view gives stakeholders a clearer understanding of risks and tail events. Moreover, unlike closed-form analytical models, Monte Carlo can accommodate nonlinear relationships, irregular distributions, and interaction effects between variables—making it especially valuable in complex, real-world scenarios where exact solutions are either unavailable or unreliable.

Monte Carlo simulations are particularly useful when systems exhibit significant uncertainty or variability. Traditional deterministic models rely on fixed input values and provide single-point predictions, which fail to account for the full range of possible outcomes in complex systems. Monte Carlo simulations overcome this limitation by generating a wide range of scenarios based on random sampling. This allows for deeper insights into the probabilities of various outcomes and the factors driving these changes, making them an ideal tool for systems that evolve over time or respond to varying conditions.

The process of conducting a Monte Carlo simulation involves several essential steps. First, a mathematical model of the system is developed, incorporating the relevant variables and their relationships. Next, probability distributions for the uncertain variables are defined. These distributions describe the possible range of values each variable can take and the likelihood of each value. The simulation then samples values from these distributions to generate a large number of scenarios or trials, each representing a possible outcome based on the sampled inputs. Finally, the results of these trials are aggregated and analyzed to produce a probability distribution of outcomes, offering insights into the variability and uncertainty inherent in the system.

For example, when modeling stock prices, historical data is used to create a probability distribution for price changes. By simulating multiple scenarios, analysts can visualize the potential range of future prices and calculate key summary statistics, such as the mean, standard deviation, and price range. This provides a clearer understanding of the likely behavior of the stock over time, empowering investors to make data-driven decisions.

Monte Carlo simulations enable decision-makers to navigate uncertainty and make strategic choices with confidence. By understanding the likelihood of potential outcomes, stakeholders can tailor their actions to mitigate risks or capitalize on opportunities. For instance, if a simulation reveals a high probability of significant stock price fluctuations, investors may adopt a more cautious strategy. Conversely, if the simulation indicates stability, they might invest more aggressively. Ultimately, Monte Carlo simulations are robust analytical tools that help individuals and organizations address uncertainty in complex environments effectively.

9.2 *Step-by-step process*

Monte Carlo simulations involve a systematic approach to model and analyze uncertainty and variability in complex systems. This section breaks down the process into six essential steps, thereby offering a clear roadmap for implementing these simulations effectively:

1. *Establishing a probability distribution*—Define the probability distribution for each uncertain variable in the system. These distributions describe the possible values a variable can take and the likelihood of each value occurring. For example, a normal distribution might model daily stock returns, whereas a Poisson distribution might be used to offset employee absenteeism. Selecting the appropriate distribution—and specifying its parameters, such as mean and variance—is critical and often informed by historical data, domain knowledge, or assumptions about the behavior of the variable.

2. *Computing a cumulative probability distribution*—Transform the probability distribution into a cumulative distribution function (CDF). The CDF accumulates the probabilities of all values up to a given point, making it easier to map random numbers to outcomes. For instance, if a variable has probabilities of 0.2, 0.3, and 0.5 for three possible outcomes, its cumulative probabilities will be 0.2, 0.5, and 1.0. The CDF ensures every possible outcome corresponds to a specific range of cumulative probabilities.

3. *Establishing an interval of random numbers*—Using the cumulative probability distribution, assign intervals of random numbers to each possible outcome. These intervals match the cumulative probabilities, such that a random number generated within an interval corresponds to its associated outcome. For example, if a variable has a cumulative probability of 0.4 for its first outcome, the interval [0.00, 0.40] maps to that outcome. This mapping ensures the simulation aligns with the defined probabilities.

4. *Generating random numbers*—Generate a series of random numbers to simulate variability in the system. Each random number is assigned to one of the intervals established in the previous step, determining the corresponding outcome. Python's pandas library provides robust random number generators that support a variety of probability distributions. Setting a random seed ensures reproducibility of the simulation results.

5. *Simulating a series of trials*—Run the simulation by conducting multiple trials. In each trial, random values are sampled for all variables, representing one possible outcome of the system. The greater the number of trials, the more robust the simulation results, as they reduce the influence of anomalies or extreme values. For example, a simulation with 10,000 trials provides a more reliable approximation of the system's behavior than one with only 100 trials.

6. *Analyzing the results*—Aggregate and analyze the outcomes from all trials to generate insights. The results can be visualized using histograms, cumulative distribution plots, or scatterplots. Key summary statistics, such as the mean, standard deviation, and range, help describe the variability and central tendencies of the simulated outcomes. For instance, if simulating project completion times, the mean represents the expected duration, whereas the range shows the best- and worst-case scenarios. Analyzing these results allows decision-makers to evaluate risks and make informed choices.

We will begin by manually performing a small number of Monte Carlo simulations on discrete data. This hands-on approach will break down the fundamental concepts and steps, providing a solid foundation for understanding the methodology. Next, we will scale up the process to run hundreds of simulations on the same discrete data, demonstrating how increased iterations capture a more comprehensive range of outcomes and improve the reliability of results. Finally, we will apply Monte Carlo simulations to continuous data, showcasing their flexibility and applicability to a broader set of problems. This progression will not only highlight the versatility and power of Monte Carlo simulations but also equip you with the skills to apply them effectively across various scenarios.

9.3 Hands-on approach

To demonstrate the practical application of Monte Carlo simulations, we begin with a relatable example: optimizing staffing levels for a small call center. Staffing is a critical operational challenge: too few employees lead to service-level violations—such as excessive wait times or dropped calls—whereas overstaffing results in idle workers and wasted payroll expenses. The inherent variability in daily employee attendance and call volume makes deterministic models inadequate. Monte Carlo simulations, by incorporating randomness and exploring a range of scenarios, offer a robust solution for balancing competing risks.

In this example, we will focus on modeling the daily variability in staffing caused by employee absenteeism. Specifically, we will use discrete random variables, where the outcomes (e.g., the number of absent employees) take on countable, distinct values. This is a practical starting point, as working with discrete data simplifies the simulation process while laying the groundwork for more advanced applications with continuous data.

Our approach involves manually performing a small number of Monte Carlo simulations to illustrate the fundamental steps and concepts. By starting with a manageable number of trials, you can see how each simulation contributes to a larger picture of potential outcomes. This hands-on process ensures that you understand the relationship between random sampling, probability distributions, and the resulting insights. It also reinforces a key modeling principle: always verify how the process behaves with known inputs before automating, as even flawed or incomplete data can produce seemingly valid outputs. In this scenario, the call center manager aims to determine the optimal level of overstaffing needed to maintain service standards while minimizing idle time.

9.3.1 Establishing a probability distribution (step 1)

The first step in performing a Monte Carlo simulation is to define a probability distribution for the uncertain variable in question. For our call center example, the variable of interest is the number of absentee employees on a given day. Based on historical data, the manager observes that absenteeism closely follows a Poisson distribution (see chapter 3).

9.3 Hands-on approach

The Poisson distribution is particularly suited for modeling count-based data, like the number of absentees per day, where events occur independently and the average rate of occurrence, denoted as lambda (λ), remains constant. Here, the average absentee rate is set to two employees per day. Using this distribution, we can calculate the probabilities of observing zero, one, two, or more absentees, providing a realistic foundation for staffing decisions.

Our first snippet of Python code calculates these probabilities and organizes them into a pandas data frame for easy interpretation, where k represents the number of absentee employees and Probability (%) represents the respective probabilities:

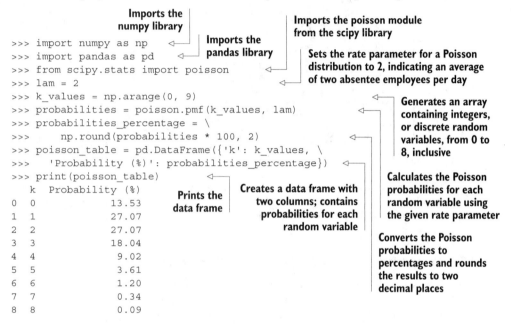

Of course, it's often helpful to display the same data in graphical format. The Matplotlib bar plot in figure 9.1 shows the percentage probabilities for each discrete random variable in the poisson_table data frame.

The displayed distribution represents the Poisson probabilities for the number of absentee employees (k) in a call center, based on a rate parameter (λ) of 2. According to the distribution, the likelihood of zero absentees is 13.53%, whereas the probabilities of having one or two absentees are each 27.07%. Beyond this point, the probabilities decrease steadily as the number of absentees increases. This right-skewed, or positively skewed, distribution emphasizes that smaller numbers of absentee employees are more likely, reflecting the expected daily average of two absentees. Such a pattern provides a realistic foundation for simulating and planning staffing needs in the face of variability.

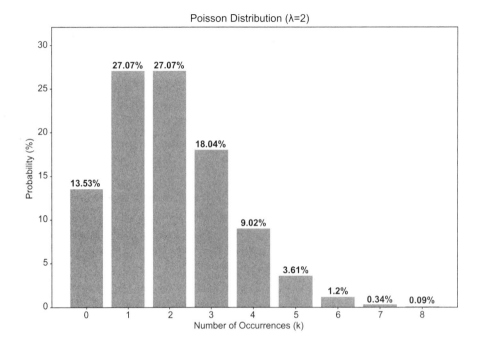

Figure 9.1 A Poisson distribution with a rate parameter (λ) of 2. At lower rate parameters, the distribution is right-skewed, indicating that smaller outcomes are more likely, whereas larger outcomes become increasingly rare.

9.3.2 *Computing a cumulative probability distribution (step 2)*

The second step in performing a Monte Carlo simulation involves computing a cumulative probability distribution. This distribution provides a cumulative view of the likelihood that the random variable will take a value less than or equal to a specific outcome. For instance, in the context of our call center example, the cumulative probability of having up to two absentee employees includes the probabilities for zero, one, and two absentees summed together. Or, put differently, the cumulative probability at a given point k is the sum of the probabilities of all outcomes from 0 to k.

Although individual probabilities are useful for understanding the likelihood of specific outcomes, cumulative probabilities allow us to map random numbers to outcomes efficiently, a critical step in generating random scenarios. By summing the probabilities for all outcomes up to a given value, we can establish intervals that align with the cumulative probabilities, thereby simplifying the simulation process.

To manually compute a cumulative probability distribution, we do the following:

1 Start with the individual probabilities for each outcome.
2 Add each probability to the total of all preceding probabilities to compute the cumulative probability for that outcome.
3 Repeat this process for all outcomes until the cumulative probability for the final value equals 1 (or 100%).

9.3 Hands-on approach

With respect to our Poisson example, where λ equals 2,

- The probability of zero absentee employees is 13.53%.
- The cumulative probability of having one or fewer absentee employees is the sum of 13.53% and 27.07%, or 40.60%.
- The cumulative probability of having two or fewer absentee employees is the sum of 40.60% and 27.07%, or 67.67%, and so on.

We can get the same results programmatically by making a call to the `poisson.cdf()` method. The following snippet of code calculates the cumulative probabilities for each value of `k` and stores the results in a column called `Cumulative Probability (%)` appended to the end of `poisson_table`:

```
>>> cumulative_probabilities = \
>>>     poisson.cdf(k_values, lam)
>>> cumulative_percentage = \
>>>     np.round(cumulative_probabilities * 100, 2)
>>> poisson_table = pd.DataFrame({'k': k_values, \
>>>             'Probability (%)': probabilities_percentage, \
>>>             'Cumulative Probability (%)': \
>>>             cumulative_percentage})
>>> print(poisson_table)
   k  Probability (%)  Cumulative Probability (%)
0  0            13.53                       13.53
1  1            27.07                       40.60
2  2            27.07                       67.67
3  3            18.04                       85.71
4  4             9.02                       94.73
5  5             3.61                       98.34
6  6             1.20                       99.55
7  7             0.34                       99.89
8  8             0.09                       99.98
```

- *Calculates the cumulative Poisson probabilities for each random variable*
- *Converts the probabilities to percentages and rounds the results to two decimal places*
- *Returns a data frame called poisson_table that now includes three, rather than two, columns*
- *Prints the data frame*

Cumulative probabilities are often best visualized using a bar line plot (see figure 9.2). The bars represent the Poisson probabilities for each discrete random variable, whereas the line with circular markers represents their cumulative probabilities. The bars correspond to the primary y axis on the left, whereas the line corresponds to the secondary y axis on the right. The cumulative probability curve starts at 0% for the smallest outcome (k = 0) and gradually approaches 100% as larger outcomes are included. For example, the cumulative probability at k = 3 is 85.71%, meaning there is an 85.71% chance of having three or fewer absentees on any given day.

The cumulative distribution provides the foundation for the next step in the simulation process: mapping random numbers to specific outcomes. By establishing cumulative intervals, we can efficiently assign random values to the corresponding outcomes, ensuring that the generated scenarios reflect the defined probabilities. This step enhances the realism and reliability of the Monte Carlo simulation by accurately representing the variability inherent in the system.

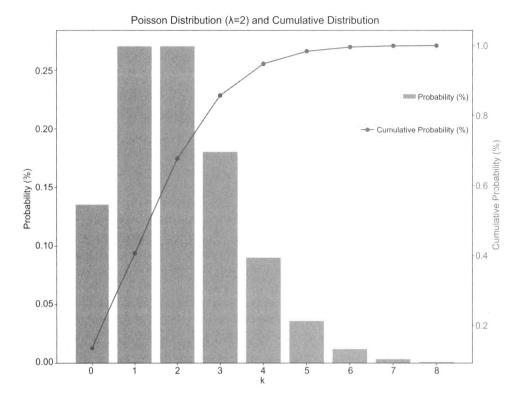

Figure 9.2 A Poisson distribution and its cumulative distribution, with the bars representing the Poisson probabilities and the line representing the cumulative probabilities. The bars correspond to the primary y axis on the left, whereas the line with circular markers corresponds to the secondary y axis on the right.

9.3.3 Establishing an interval of random numbers for each variable (step 3)

The third step in performing a Monte Carlo simulation is translating the probability distributions of discrete random variables into intervals of random numbers. These intervals provide a practical way to simulate outcomes by mapping random numbers to specific values based on their probabilities.

To achieve this, a list of random digits from 00 to 99 is generated to represent all possible outcomes in the simulation. Each discrete random variable (k) is then assigned a portion of these random digits proportional to its probability. For example, if a particular k value has a probability of 27%, it will be assigned approximately 27 random digits from the list.

The assignment process begins at the start of the list and proceeds sequentially. The number of random digits allocated to each k value is determined based on its probability percentage, ensuring that every k value receives at least one digit. These digits are grouped into ranges, which are then assigned to the corresponding k values.

If the range reaches the end of the list, it wraps back to the beginning to ensure all 100 digits are used effectively. This process provides a clear mechanism for generating outcomes that align with the probability distribution.

The following snippet of Python code performs this assignment programmatically:

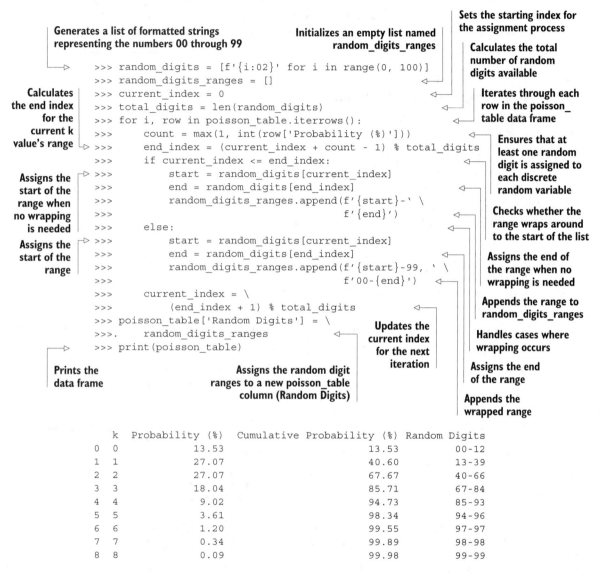

```
    k  Probability (%)  Cumulative Probability (%) Random Digits
0   0            13.53                       13.53         00-12
1   1            27.07                       40.60         13-39
2   2            27.07                       67.67         40-66
3   3            18.04                       85.71         67-84
4   4             9.02                       94.73         85-93
5   5             3.61                       98.34         94-96
6   6             1.20                       99.55         97-97
7   7             0.34                       99.89         98-98
8   8             0.09                       99.98         99-99
```

This method ensures that random sampling aligns closely with the defined probability distribution. For instance,

- The `k = 1` value, with a probability of 27.07%, is assigned a range of random digits from `13` to `39`. This range encompasses 27 digits, reflecting the higher likelihood of this outcome.

- Conversely, `k = 6`, with a probability of just 1.20%, is assigned a single digit, `97`, illustrating its lower probability.

By creating these intervals, we effectively bridge the gap between abstract probability distributions and the practical process of generating random outcomes. This structured approach forms the backbone of Monte Carlo simulations, ensuring that the generated scenarios accurately represent the underlying probabilities. As we move to the next step, these intervals will be used to simulate numerous scenarios, enhancing our understanding of potential outcomes and supporting data-driven decision-making.

9.3.4 Generating random numbers (step 4)

The fourth step in a Monte Carlo simulation involves generating random numbers, which serve as the foundation for simulating real-world scenarios. These random numbers will be mapped to the intervals established in the previous step to generate corresponding outcomes. Random numbers between 00 and 99 can be generated using various methods, ranging from traditional random digit tables to modern programming techniques.

In Python, random number generation is both flexible and efficient, offering tools to automate the process. Instead of relying on manual lookup tables, we can programmatically generate a sequence of random digits tailored to the requirements of our simulation. Additionally, setting a seed ensures reproducibility, allowing the same sequence of random numbers to be generated in future runs—a critical feature for testing and validation.

The following code demonstrates how to generate 100 random digits and randomly select 10 of them, formatted as two-digit strings:

```
>>> np.random.seed(1)
>>> random_digits = \
>>>     np.random.choice(100, 10, replace = False)
>>> formatted_digits = \
>>>     [f'{digit:02}' for digit in random_digits]
```

- `np.random.seed(1)` — Sets a random seed to ensure that the same random digits are generated across multiple runs, thereby enabling reproducibility
- `np.random.choice(100, 10, replace = False)` — Randomly selects 10 digits from the range 00 to 99 without replacement, ensuring that no digit is repeated in this selection
- `[f'{digit:02}' for digit in random_digits]` — Formats each digit as a two-digit string (e.g., 00, 24) to maintain consistency with earlier steps

If the simulation requires more iterations, such as 500 random numbers, we can modify the code to sample with replacement, ensuring sufficient variability, like so:

```
>>> random_digits = np.random.choice(100, 500, replace = True)
```

In this case, allowing replacement ensures that digits can be selected multiple times, a necessity for larger simulations that require independent random samples.

Generating random numbers programmatically eliminates manual effort and reduces the chance of human error. It also ensures that the random digits align with the intervals defined in step 3, allowing seamless integration into the simulation process. By using Python's random number generation tools, we can efficiently create inputs for any Monte Carlo simulation or similar analysis.

9.3.5 Simulating a series of trials (step 5)

The fifth step in performing a Monte Carlo simulation involves running a series of trials to generate a distribution of outcomes. Each trial maps a randomly selected digit to its corresponding `k` value, based on the intervals established earlier. This step demonstrates how randomness in the simulation leads to variability in outcomes, offering insights beyond those provided by deterministic models.

To illustrate, suppose one of the randomly selected digits is 73. Based on the mapping established in step 3, this digit falls into the range assigned to k = 3. Although the expected value based on the rate parameter (λ) is two absentee employees, this trial suggests the call center manager should prepare for three absentee employees instead. This single trial highlights how Monte Carlo simulations account for the randomness inherent in real-world scenarios and provide alternative staffing recommendations compared to deterministic models.

This is just one outcome from a single trial. In this example, we are running 10 simulations, each using one of the randomly selected digits from the previous step. Each digit is mapped to a corresponding k value, generating a distribution of possible outcomes. These outcomes provide the call center manager with a range of staffing scenarios, allowing them to better understand variability and make more informed decisions. By analyzing this range, the manager can balance the risk of understaffing with the cost implications of overstaffing.

The following line of code displays the list of formatted random digits generated earlier. These digits are used to simulate outcomes in the trials:

```
>>> print('Random Digits:', formatted_digits)
Random Digits: ['80', '84', '33', '81', '93', '17', '36', '82', '69', '65']
```

Table 9.1 shows how each random digit maps to its corresponding `k` value based on the Poisson distribution defined earlier. Each `k` value represents the number of additional associates required for the given trial. Summing these `k` values and calculating their mean provides an estimate of the average number of additional staff needed across all simulations.

Table 9.1 Random numbers aligned to k values

Random number	k value
80	3
84	3
33	1
81	3
93	4
17	1
36	1

Table 9.1 Random numbers aligned to k values *(continued)*

Random number	k value
82	3
69	3
65	2
Sum	24
Mean	2.4

The calculated mean (2.4) provides the call center manager with a realistic estimate of the average number of additional staff needed, accounting for variability in absenteeism. This approach goes beyond deterministic averages by considering a range of possible scenarios and their associated probabilities.

How should the call center manager use these results in making staffing decisions? By simulating multiple scenarios, the manager gains insights into the potential variability in staffing needs. For example,

- *Understaffing risks*—If the mean suggests 2.4 additional staff, the manager might choose to overstaff slightly to minimize service disruptions during peak absenteeism periods.
- *Cost optimization*—Conversely, if the simulations consistently indicate lower absenteeism, the manager might avoid unnecessary overstaffing, thereby reducing labor costs.

This process highlights how Monte Carlo simulations empower decision-makers to plan more effectively in uncertain environments, balancing risks and costs to achieve operational efficiency.

9.3.6 *Analyzing the results (step 6)*

Based on the results of the Monte Carlo simulations, the call center manager can determine an optimal staffing strategy by weighing cost efficiency against service levels:

- *Cost efficiency*—If the primary concern is managing payroll costs, the simulations suggest overstaffing by an average of two employees. This approach balances adequate staffing with minimizing unnecessary expenses.
- *Service levels*—Conversely, if the manager prioritizes maintaining high service levels and minimizing risks like service disruptions, customer complaints, or churn, overstaffing by three employees is more prudent. This recommendation provides a buffer to accommodate variability in staff attendance, ensuring operations remain smooth even on days with above-average absenteeism.

By relying on Monte Carlo simulation results instead of solely on the historical rate parameter (λ), the manager can make more informed and nuanced decisions that align with the organization's priorities.

EXPECTED VALUE CALCULATION

The results of the Monte Carlo simulation not only differ from the historical rate parameter ($\lambda = 2$) but also deviate slightly from the expected staffing needs, which can be calculated as the expected value:

$$\text{Expected Overstaff} = \sum (\text{Probability of } k) \times (k)$$

or

$$\begin{aligned}\text{Expected Overstaff} = &\ (0.1353)\,(0) + (0.2707)\,(1) + (0.2707)\,(2) \\ &+ (0.1804)\,(3) + (0.0902)\,(4) + (0.0361)\,(5) \\ &+ (0.0120)\,(6) + (0.0034)\,(7) + (0.0009)\,(8)\end{aligned}$$

This equals 1.9976. Interestingly, this value closely matches the rate parameter ($\lambda = 2$), suggesting a relationship between the two. However, Monte Carlo simulations capture variability and uncertainty, offering additional insights that deterministic calculations cannot provide.

It is essential to recognize the limitations of small-scale simulations. With only 10 simulations, the results may not fully represent the system's true variability. Anomalous outcomes can arise, skewing the conclusions. Larger numbers of simulations tend to normalize over successive trials, providing more consistent and reliable results. This principle underscores the importance of running sufficient simulations to capture the full range of potential scenarios.

To avoid drawing conclusions from potentially skewed data, the next section demonstrates how to automatically run 500 Monte Carlo simulations using the same data and random digit assignments. By using Python, we will efficiently generate a more extensive set of results, providing a clearer and more dependable understanding of staffing requirements.

9.4 Automating simulations on discrete data

Automating the process to run 500 Monte Carlo simulations on the same discrete data set allows us to follow the same fundamental steps demonstrated earlier but with significant scalability. These steps include defining the probability distribution, computing the cumulative distribution, establishing intervals for random variables, generating random numbers, simulating a series of trials, and analyzing the results. The primary advantage of automation is the ability to substantially increase the number of trials, providing more reliable and robust insights.

By increasing the number of trials from 10 to 500, we enhance the statistical power of our simulations. A larger sample size smooths out anomalies that might appear in smaller trials, yielding a clearer and more accurate representation of the underlying probability distribution. This greater precision allows us to better understand the variability and uncertainty within the system, enabling more informed and reliable decision-making.

The following code snippet demonstrates how to automate 500 Monte Carlo simulations. It ensures reproducibility by setting a seed for the random number generator, normalizes the probabilities to sum to exactly 1, and calculates the frequency and percentage of each outcome:

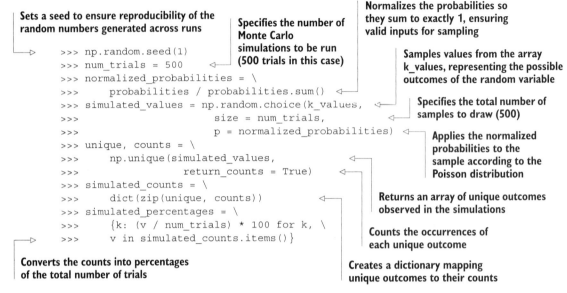

A few clarifications are in order:

- The process can easily scale to 1,000 or even 10,000 simulations by simply adjusting the num_trials parameter. However, increasing the number of trials beyond a certain point offers diminishing returns, as results stabilize when the sample size becomes sufficiently large.
- Ensuring that probabilities sum to exactly 1 is essential in Monte Carlo simulations. Initially, the probabilities for k > 8 were excluded due to their negligible values in a Poisson distribution with a rate parameter of 2. Normalizing the probabilities accounts for these omissions, providing an accurate foundation for simulations. For example, the probability of k = 0 increased slightly from 13.53% to 13.54%, and the probability of k = 3 increased from 18.04% to 18.05% after normalization.
- Despite running 500 simulations, no outcomes resulted in k = 8, consistent with the Poisson distribution's low probability for higher values when λ = 2. This highlights the robustness of the simulations in capturing more likely outcomes while demonstrating the rarity of extreme values.

The automated simulations provide a detailed distribution of results, which can be further analyzed to gain deeper insights. For example, plotting the outcomes of the 500 Monte Carlo simulations enables us to visually assess the distribution and identify patterns in the data. This analysis offers valuable input for decision-making, helping to address variability and uncertainty in real-world scenarios.

9.4.1 Plotting and analyzing the results

The resulting plot in figure 9.3 shows the outcomes of 500 Monte Carlo simulations for a Poisson distribution with a rate parameter (λ) of 2 (see figure 9.3). Each bar represents the percentage of trials that resulted in a specific k value, where k ranges from 0 to 7. The *y* axis represents the percentage of trials corresponding to each k value, and the *x* axis lists the k values. Labels atop each bar display the percentage values, making the frequencies clear and easy to interpret. This visualization highlights the relative likelihood of each outcome, aligning closely with the underlying theoretical distribution while reflecting the variability introduced by random sampling.

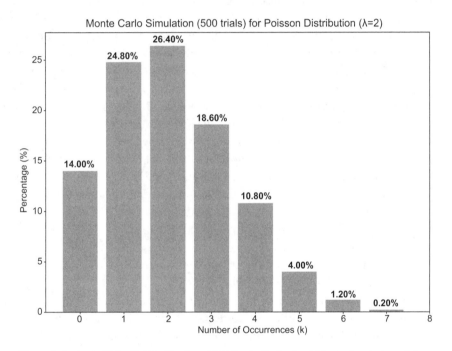

Figure 9.3 Probability distribution from 500 Monte Carlo simulations closely resembling a theoretical Poisson distribution with a rate parameter of 2. The labels atop the bars represent the percentage of trials that resulted in each unique random variable between 0 and 7. No trials result in a k value of 8, consistent with the low theoretical probability of such an outcome.

The results of the 500 simulations show a distribution of k values ranging from 0 to 7, with the percentage frequencies for each value clearly illustrated. When compared to a theoretical Poisson distribution with $\lambda = 2$, the simulated results align closely. As expected, slight variations occur due to the inherent randomness of the simulation, but these differences are minimal and well within acceptable bounds. Otherwise, none of our 500 simulations resulted in k = 8, reflecting the near-zero probability of this outcome in the Poisson distribution.

The call center manager now faces a decision: whether to rely solely on the rate parameter and assume an overstaffing need of two or to consider the Monte Carlo results. The simulation suggests that k = 3 or k = 4 may be slightly more likely than predicted by the theoretical Poisson distribution, potentially supporting a decision to overstaff by three instead of two. This choice would mitigate the risks of understaffing—such as service disruptions, delayed responses, and customer dissatisfaction—but at the cost of additional payroll expenditures.

Monte Carlo simulations offer several advantages that make them a robust alternative to purely theoretical approaches. These benefits include the following:

- *Realistic modeling of uncertainty*—Monte Carlo simulations incorporate randomness and variability directly into the modeling process. This allows for a more realistic representation of real-world scenarios, capturing the inherent uncertainty and fluctuations that may not be fully captured by theoretical distributions.
- *Flexibility and adaptability*—Monte Carlo simulations can be adapted to a wide range of problems and conditions. They can model complex systems with multiple variables and dependencies, providing insights into scenarios that are difficult or impossible to address using purely theoretical approaches.
- *Handling of non-normal distributions*—Many real-world phenomena do not follow standard distributions like the Poisson or normal distribution. Monte Carlo simulations can accommodate any distribution, whether it is normal, skewed, or entirely irregular, ensuring that the unique characteristics of the data are accurately represented.
- *Data-driven insights*—Although theoretical distributions are often based on historical observations, they can become outdated or fail to reflect recent changes. Monte Carlo simulations use current data and can be continually updated to provide the most relevant and timely insights.
- *Robustness to outliers*—Real-world data often contains outliers or anomalies that can skew theoretical models. Monte Carlo simulations, through repeated random sampling, can mitigate the effect of these outliers, leading to more reliable and robust conclusions.
- *Scenario analysis*—Monte Carlo simulations allow for the exploration of a wide range of potential outcomes by running numerous scenarios. This helps in understanding the full spectrum of possible results, identifying worst-case scenarios, and planning for contingencies.
- *Quantification of risk*—By simulating a large number of trials, Monte Carlo simulations provide a detailed probability distribution of outcomes. This quantification of risk helps in making more informed decisions by highlighting the likelihood and potential effects of different events.
- *Better decision support*—The ability to simulate various scenarios and analyze their outcomes provides decision-makers with a comprehensive view of potential risks and rewards. This leads to more informed and confident decision-making, as it is based on a broader range of data and scenarios.

This example demonstrates how Monte Carlo simulations complement theoretical distributions by providing a practical framework for decision-making under uncertainty. By simulating a wide range of possible scenarios, the call center manager can make informed choices that balance cost efficiency with service quality. These advantages highlight the versatility of Monte Carlo methods in handling both discrete and continuous data, as we will explore in the next section.

9.5 Automating simulations on continuous data

As we transition from working with illustrative discrete data to real continuous data, we will explore one of the most popular applications of Monte Carlo simulations: predicting future stock prices. Previously, we demonstrated how to fit time series models to forecast future closing prices. Now, we will use Monte Carlo methods to simulate a range of potential outcomes, providing a probability distribution of future prices.

Monte Carlo simulations provide a robust approach to predicting stock prices by incorporating the inherent uncertainty and variability of financial markets. Instead of relying solely on historical trends and deterministic models, Monte Carlo methods use random sampling to generate a range of possible future outcomes. This approach provides a deeper understanding of potential price movements and helps assess the risk and uncertainty associated with various investment strategies.

We will demonstrate how to apply Monte Carlo simulations to forecast future closing prices of a stock. By using real historical stock data, defining the necessary parameters, and running numerous simulations, we will generate a probability distribution of future prices. This process highlights the flexibility and power of Monte Carlo methods in handling real-world continuous data, particularly in quantifying risk and uncertainty. Through this demonstration, we will gain a comprehensive view of potential outcomes, enhancing our ability to make informed and strategic investment decisions.

9.5.1 Predicting stock prices with Monte Carlo simulations

When working with continuous data, such as predicting closing stock prices using Monte Carlo simulations, the process involves several distinct steps compared to working with discrete data. Following is a step-by-step breakdown of how Monte Carlo simulations work for continuous data and how we derive closing prices *per day* for each trial:

1 *Analyzing historical data*—First we gather historical stock price data. This data helps us understand the past behavior of the stock and estimate key statistical parameters, such as the mean return and standard deviation. Previously, when working with discrete data, we used historical outcomes to establish a probability distribution. Here, historical stock prices serve as the foundation for determining future price movements.

2 *Calculating log returns*—We then calculate the daily log returns of the stock. Log returns are preferred because they allow for easier compounding over multiple periods and offer a better statistical representation of price movements. The daily log return is calculated as

$$\text{Log Return} = \ln\left(\frac{P_t}{P_{t-1}}\right)$$

where P_t is the closing price on day t and P_{t-1} is the closing price on the previous day. In contrast to the discrete data approach, where we computed a probability distribution for each random variable, this step focuses on quantifying the daily percentage changes in stock prices.

3 *Computing statistical parameters*—Using the calculated log returns, we determine the mean (μ) and standard deviation (σ) of the daily returns. These statistical parameters model the randomness of future price movements. Previously, when working with discrete data, we used the probability distribution to create proportional intervals of random numbers. Here, μ and σ serve as inputs for generating future random returns.

4 *Generating random daily returns*—For each simulation, instead of generating random numbers and assigning them to intervals as we did for discrete data, we generate random daily returns directly from a normal distribution. This distribution is used because historical log returns usually approximate a normal distribution, and it is characterized by the mean and standard deviation calculated from the historical log returns. This step effectively simulates the randomness of stock price movements, capturing their variability.

5 *Simulating prices*—Starting from the last known closing price, we calculate future prices using the randomly generated daily returns to simulate future prices. The closing price for each day is calculated using the following formula:

$$P_{t+1} = P_t \times e^r$$

where e is the base of the natural logarithm, equal to approximately 2.72, and r is the randomly generated log return for that day. This process reflects the compounding nature of stock price returns over time. In contrast to the discrete data approach, where trials were based on random number intervals, this step generates a continuous path for stock prices.

6 *Simulating multiple trials*—We repeat these steps for a large number of trials (e.g., 500 simulations). Each trial represents one potential future trajectory of the stock price over the specified time horizon. By running numerous simulations, we create a robust data set representing a wide range of possible outcomes.

7 *Analyzing the results*—Finally, after completing all the simulations, we analyze the resulting distribution of simulated closing prices. This analysis provides insights into the range of possible future prices, their probabilities, and associated risks. Such analysis aids in making more informed financial decisions by quantifying potential variability and uncertainty in stock price movements.

By automating the process, we can efficiently perform a large number of Monte Carlo simulations, providing more reliable and robust results. This approach allows us to model the inherent randomness of stock price movements, offering valuable insights for financial forecasting and risk management. Monte Carlo simulations are a powerful tool for understanding the range of possible future outcomes and making strategic investment decisions based on data-driven insights.

9.5.2 Analyzing historical data (step 1)

In this first step, we prepare the historical stock data needed for our Monte Carlo simulations. Following a approach similar to that in chapter 7, where we worked with Apple stock data, we will now focus on General Motors (GM), the automaker behind brands such as Chevrolet, Cadillac, GMC, and Buick. This involves retrieving historical stock prices and processing them for use in our simulation. Specifically, we will gather daily closing prices for two periods: July 1, 2023, to December 31, 2023, and January 1, 2024, to January 31, 2024. The data from the latter half of 2023 will serve as the basis for our simulations, and the data from January 2024 will allow us to evaluate the accuracy of our forecasts.

Here's the Python code used to fetch and process the data:

```
>>> import yfinance as yf
>>> ticker_symbol = 'GM'
>>> ticker_data = yf.Ticker(ticker_symbol)
>>> stock_data_23 = ticker_data.history(start = '2023-07-01',
>>>                                     end = '2023-12-31',
>>>                                     interval = '1d')
>>> stock_data_24 = ticker_data.history(start = '2024-01-01',
>>>                                     end = '2024-01-31',
>>>                                     interval = '1d')
>>> close_prices_23 = stock_data_23[['Close']]
>>> close_prices_24 = stock_data_24[['Close']]
>>> close_prices_23 = \
>>>     close_prices_23.reset_index(drop = True)
>>> close_prices_24 = \
>>>     close_prices_24.reset_index(drop = True)
```

- Imports the yfinance library, used for fetching financial market data from Yahoo Finance
- Sets the variable ticker_symbol to the string 'GM', for General Motors
- Creates a Ticker object to interact with Yahoo Finance's API for the GM stock
- Retrieves historical daily stock data using dates in the ISO 8601 format
- Retrieves historical daily stock data; same stock, different start and end dates
- Subsets stock_data_23 to include just the Close column and creates a new data frame
- Subsets stock_data_24 to include just the Close column and creates a new data frame
- Resets the index; same method, different data frame
- Resets the index by removing the original and replacing it with a default integer index

We use the `describe()` method to generate key descriptive statistics for both periods. This provides a clear picture of the stock's behavior before running simulations:

```
>>> stats_23 = close_prices_23.describe()
>>> print(stats_23)
            Close
count  126.000000
mean    32.932516
std      3.654504
min     26.425901
```

```
25%      30.057603
50%      32.831583
75%      35.848412
max      40.051197

>>> stats_24 = close_prices_24.describe()
>>> print(stats_24)
            Close
count   20.000000
mean    35.455665
std      0.809152
min     34.387157
25%     35.021101
50%     35.192638
75%     35.804214
max     37.937252
```

The statistical summary for the second half of 2023 (July–December) shows an average closing price of approximately $32.93, with a standard deviation of $3.65, indicating moderate variability. Prices ranged from $26.43 to $40.05. In contrast, the summary for January 2024 reveals a higher average price of $35.46 but a much lower standard deviation of $0.81, indicating greater price stability. The January prices ranged from $34.39 to $37.94.

The historical data from 2023 serves as the foundation for generating random paths of future prices, allowing us to simulate potential price movements. The January 2024 data, on the other hand, acts as a benchmark for evaluating the accuracy of our simulations. The differences in variability between the two periods underscore the importance of incorporating realistic volatility into the Monte Carlo process to account for market dynamics effectively. By establishing this solid data foundation, we are prepared to move forward with the simulation steps, using historical insights to predict and evaluate future stock price behavior.

9.5.3 Calculating log returns (step 2)

The second step in our Monte Carlo simulation involves calculating the daily log returns from the closing prices in the `close_prices_23` data frame. Log returns are preferred in financial modeling because they offer a better statistical representation of relative price changes and are easily compounded over multiple periods.

To compute log returns, we calculate the natural logarithm of the ratio of each day's closing price to the previous day's closing price. This operation therefore captures the proportional change in price while accounting for compounding effects. The computed log returns are then stored in a new column called `Log Return`:

```
>>> close_prices_23['Log Return'] = \
>>>     np.log(close_prices_23['Close'] /
>>>         close_prices_23['Close'].shift(1))
>>> log_returns = close_prices_23['Log Return'].dropna()
```

Additional explanation of this code snippet is in order:

- The shift(1) method offsets the Close column by one row, aligning each day's closing price with the previous day's closing price for the ratio calculation.
- The np.log() function computes the natural logarithm of these ratios to derive the log returns.
- The dropna() method removes the missing value generated for the first row (as no prior closing price exists), ensuring a clean series of log returns.

The variable log_returns is then passed to a snippet of Matplotlib and seaborn code to create a density plot of the log returns for GM stock between July and December 2023 (see figure 9.4). This plot provides a visual representation of daily price changes during this period.

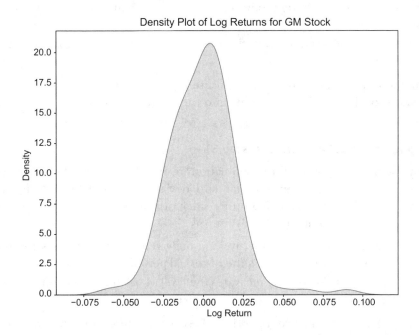

Figure 9.4 Density plot of the log returns for GM stock between July and December 2023. The distribution is approximately normal, centered around a mean close to zero, with most log returns clustered near zero but with some larger positive and negative values in the tails.

The density plot highlights the distribution of daily log returns. Key observations include the following:

- *Normality*—The log returns are approximately normally distributed, with most values clustered near zero. This suggests that daily price changes are small on average, with no extreme skewness in the data.

- *Tails*—The presence of longer tails indicates that although most daily changes are modest, there are occasional larger positive or negative returns. These tails represent days of higher market volatility.
- *Mean and standard deviation*—The plot's central tendency and spread provide the mean and standard deviation of the log returns, which are essential inputs for simulating future price movements.

This analysis of historical log returns serves as a foundational step in the Monte Carlo process. The distribution of log returns, which closely approximates a normal distribution, allows us to make the key assumption that future log returns will follow a similar pattern. This enables us to do the following:

- Generate realistic random samples based on the calculated mean and standard deviation.
- Incorporate the inherent randomness and variability observed in historical stock prices.
- Create simulations that reflect potential real-world scenarios with greater accuracy.

By using these statistical properties, we ensure that our Monte Carlo simulations are robust and provide meaningful insights into the range of possible future stock price movements.

9.5.4 Computing statistical parameters (step 3)

The third step in our Monte Carlo simulation involves calculating the key statistical parameters—that is, the mean and standard deviation—of the log returns. These parameters are critical for modeling future stock price movements as they define the central tendency and variability of daily returns:

- The mean (μ) represents the average daily return and indicates the overall trend of the stock price during the historical period.
- The standard deviation (σ) measures the level of volatility, reflecting the extent to which daily returns deviate from the mean.

The following code calculates and prints these parameters from the `log_returns` data:

```
>>> mu = log_returns.mean()
>>> print(mu)
-0.000605520424324896

>>> sigma = log_returns.std()
>>> print(sigma)
0.020045660849343817
```

We can conclude the following:
- The mean log return is approximately –0.00061, suggesting a slight downward trend in GM's stock price over the analyzed period.

- The standard deviation of 0.02005 indicates a moderate level of daily price fluctuations. This value reflects the stock's historical volatility, a critical factor in forecasting future movements.

These statistical parameters are essential inputs for generating random daily returns in the simulation process. By incorporating the calculated `mu` and `sigma`, we ensure that

- The simulated returns realistically reflect the historical behavior of the stock.
- The randomness in price movements accounts for both the trend (mean) and volatility (standard deviation) observed in the data.

Incorporating these parameters into our Monte Carlo model allows us to generate a wide range of potential outcomes, capturing the inherent uncertainty and variability of stock price movements. This step lays the foundation for creating accurate and reliable forecasts, enabling better decision-making in financial planning and risk assessment.

9.5.5 Generating random daily returns (step 4)

The fourth step in the Monte Carlo process involves defining the parameters for the simulation: the number of simulations to run and the forecast horizon. These parameters are crucial for ensuring the robustness and relevance of the predictions.

The following code snippet sets these two parameters:

```
>>> num_simulations = 500
>>> num_days = 20
```

Let's elaborate:

- *Number of simulations* (`num_simulations`)—Set to 500 to provide a comprehensive range of possible outcomes. Running a high number of simulations ensures that the model accounts for variability and provides robust predictions, reducing the effect of anomalies or outliers on the results. However, running significantly more simulations may lead to diminishing returns, as the results stabilize beyond a certain threshold, offering little additional insight.
- *Number of days* (`num_days`)—Set to 20, representing the actual number of trading days in January 2024. This corresponds to the record count in the `close_prices_24` data frame, aligning the simulation period with the actual stock price data for comparison.

Choosing an appropriate number of simulations and forecast days is vital:

- A higher number of simulations increases the reliability of the results by capturing a wider range of potential outcomes. However, it is essential to balance this with computational efficiency and recognize that beyond a certain point, additional simulations may yield diminishing returns as the results stabilize.
- Setting the forecast horizon to match real-world periods (such as a month of trading days) ensures that the predictions are relevant and actionable for decision-making.

With these parameters defined, we are ready to simulate 500 potential stock price trajectories over the 20 trading days in January 2024, providing a detailed and realistic forecast for future stock price movements.

9.5.6 Simulating prices (step 5)

The fifth step in the Monte Carlo process involves generating simulated stock prices using the parameters defined in the previous steps: the mean (`mu`), standard deviation (`sigma`), number of simulations (`num_simulations`), and forecast horizon (`num_days`). This step creates a distribution of potential future stock prices by incorporating the randomness and variability observed in historical log returns.

The following code snippet performs the simulation:

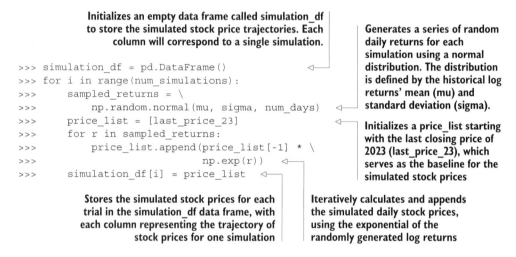

Let's explain further:

- For each simulation, a sequence of daily returns is randomly sampled from a normal distribution defined by the historical mean and standard deviation of log returns. This models the inherent randomness and variability in stock price movements.
- Starting from the last observed price in 2023, the sampled daily returns are compounded iteratively to calculate the stock price for each subsequent day. This compounding process reflects the geometric nature of stock price movements.
- Each simulated trajectory is stored in the data frame, with rows representing days and columns representing individual simulations. The result is a comprehensive view of 500 potential future stock price paths over the forecast period.

The resulting `simulation_df` data frame contains 500 columns, each representing a unique simulation of stock prices over 20 trading days in January 2024. This data frame serves as the foundation for visualizing and analyzing the distribution of potential future prices, enabling a deeper understanding of the range of outcomes and associated probabilities.

9.5.7 Simulating multiple trials (step 6)

The plot in figure 9.5 displays the results of our 500 Monte Carlo simulations for GM's closing stock price over the 20 trading days in January 2024. Each line represents the trajectory of stock prices for a single simulation trial, providing a visual summary of the range of possible outcomes.

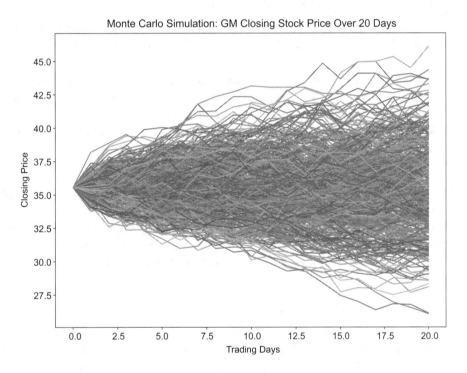

Figure 9.5 500 Monte Carlo simulations of GM's closing stock price for January 2024. Each line corresponds to a single simulation, depicting potential stock price trajectories based on the historical mean and volatility of log returns.

This visualization highlights the variability and uncertainty inherent in stock price movements. Key observations include the following:

- *Clustered trajectories*—Although some simulations show significant increases or decreases in stock price, the majority of trajectories remain clustered around the average trend. This clustering provides an indication of the most probable price range.

- *Divergent scenarios*—The presence of both extreme upward and downward movements in some trials reflects the stochastic nature of financial markets, where unexpected events can lead to substantial deviations.
- *Uncertainty across time*—The increasing spread of trajectories over the 20-day forecast horizon demonstrates how uncertainty accumulates as predictions extend further into the future, which highlights a critical limitation of long-term forecasts, as their utility diminishes due to compounding uncertainty, making them less reliable for precise decision-making. Caution is advised when relying on such forecasts for long-term planning, as they are better suited for understanding general trends rather than exact outcomes.

This plot provides several actionable insights:

- *Risk assessment*—The variability in trajectories can help investors assess the level of risk associated with the stock, identifying both the potential upside and downside.
- *Decision support*—By understanding the range of possible outcomes, decision-makers can plan for best-case and worst-case scenarios, tailoring investment strategies to align with their risk tolerance and objectives.
- *Market behavior*—The clustering of trajectories around the mean provides a visual approximation of the expected price behavior, useful for benchmarking expectations.

Monte Carlo simulations, as shown here, provide a robust framework for exploring potential future price paths and their associated probabilities. This enables a deeper understanding of market dynamics and empowers investors and analysts to make informed financial decisions. In the next section, we will delve further into the analysis of these simulated results, calculating key summary statistics to quantify the range and likelihood of outcomes.

9.5.8 Analyzing the results (step 7)

To analyze the outcomes of our 500 Monte Carlo simulations, we start by comparing the ending prices of the trials to the starting price. This analysis provides a broad view of the potential direction of stock prices and the likelihood of specific outcomes. Specifically, we count the number of simulations where the ending price is greater than or less than the starting price.

The following snippet of code performs this analysis by identifying the starting price and comparing it to the ending prices across all simulations:

```
>>> start_price = simulation_df.iloc[0, 0]
>>> ending_prices = simulation_df.iloc[-1, :]
>>> num_greater = \
>>>     (ending_prices > start_price).sum()
>>> num_less = \
```

Extracts the starting price from the first row and first column of the simulation_df data frame

Counts the number of simulations where the ending price is greater than the starting price

Extracts the ending prices from the last row of simulation_df

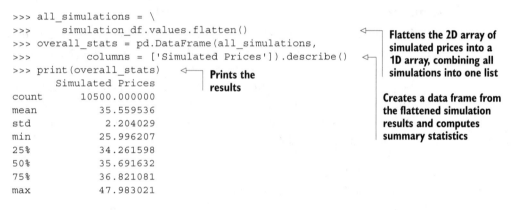

The results show that 219 simulations (43.8%) resulted in a higher ending price than the starting price, and 281 simulations (56.2%) ended lower. This suggests a slightly higher likelihood of the stock price decreasing over the simulated period. These probabilities provide insights into potential trends and highlight the uncertainty inherent in financial markets.

To gain a deeper understanding of the distribution of simulated stock prices, we calculate summary statistics across all simulations. Flattening the data frame allows us to analyze all simulated prices as a single data set:

The descriptive statistics reveal the following:

- *Mean*—Simulated prices average $35.56, closely matching the actual mean price of $35.46 observed in January 2024, which suggests that the simulations effectively capture the central tendency of stock prices.
- *Standard deviation*—Simulated prices have a standard deviation of $2.20, significantly higher than the actual value of $0.81, reflecting the simulations' broader exploration of potential variability in stock prices.
- *Range*—Simulated prices range from $25.99 to $47.98, compared to the observed range of $34.39 to $37.94, indicating the inclusion of extreme scenarios in the simulations.

The Monte Carlo simulations successfully approximate the mean and median of the actual January 2024 prices, reflecting the method's ability to capture central tendencies. However, the higher variability in the simulations highlights the method's purpose: to explore a wide range of potential outcomes, including extreme scenarios, rather than to match observed data precisely.

This variability underscores a pair of key insights:

- *Risk assessment*—The broader range of simulated prices helps investors prepare for worst-case and best-case scenarios, providing a comprehensive view of potential risks and rewards.
- *Decision-making support*—The simulations' clustering around the mean and median aligns with expected trends, offering confidence in planning strategies while acknowledging potential volatility.

Monte Carlo simulations remain a valuable tool for modeling uncertainty and assessing variability in complex systems. Although they may not precisely replicate observed outcomes, their ability to account for randomness and generate a spectrum of scenarios makes them indispensable for risk management and strategic planning. In the next chapter, we will build on this foundation by exploring decision trees to derive expected values and assess alternatives, further enhancing our capacity for data-driven decision-making.

Summary

- Monte Carlo simulations provide a powerful tool for modeling and analyzing complex systems with inherent uncertainty, offering insights into the range of possible outcomes and their probabilities. This chapter demonstrated how to apply Monte Carlo simulations to both discrete and continuous data, highlighting the differences in approach and the specific steps involved in each case.
- For discrete data, such as employee absenteeism, simulations relied on historical frequencies and discrete probability distributions to generate potential scenarios. For continuous data, such as stock price movements, the process involved calculating key statistical parameters like the mean and standard deviation to model the variability of outcomes.
- The simulations illustrated the importance of capturing inherent randomness and variability. Discrete simulations provided clarity in scenarios with distinct outcomes, whereas continuous simulations accounted for the fluidity of real-world processes. The chapter also emphasized the role of visual tools, such as density plots and trajectory graphs, in interpreting simulation results and understanding the implications of variability.
- Running a large number of simulations was highlighted as essential for achieving robust results, smoothing out anomalies, and providing reliable insights. By generating a range of potential future outcomes, Monte Carlo simulations empower decision-makers to assess risks, plan for contingencies, and optimize strategies in uncertain environments.
- The hands-on approach demonstrated in this chapter underscored the versatility of Monte Carlo methods in addressing both discrete and continuous uncertainties. Looking ahead, the next chapter builds on these methods, exploring decision trees to derive expected values and assess alternatives, further enhancing our capacity for data-driven decision-making.

Building and plotting a decision tree

This chapter covers
- Decision-making with and without probabilities
- Maximax and Maximin methods
- Minimax Regret method
- Expected Value method
- Decision trees

Decision-making is a critical process in both personal and professional contexts, where the stakes can be incredibly high—whether it's managing large sums of money, making career-defining choices, or navigating situations where people's lives are at risk. In such scenarios, an analytical and systematic approach to decision-making is not just beneficial but essential. Throughout this chapter, we will explore various decision-making methods, with a particular focus on building and plotting decision trees. Unlike the decision trees used in machine learning (see chapter 6), which are designed to classify data, these trees serve as a graphical representation of the decision-making process, outlining possible choices, chance events, associated probabilities, and potential payoffs. This approach helps to systematically determine the best course of action by applying the Expected Value method, which uses probabilities to weigh potential outcomes and make informed decisions.

Before diving into the Expected Value method, we will first explore decision-making approaches that do not rely on probabilities. These methods are crucial when probabilities for different outcomes are unknown or cannot be accurately estimated. We will discuss the Maximax, Maximin, and Minimax Regret methods, each suited to different decision-making styles and levels of risk tolerance. The *Maximax method*, favored by risk-takers, selects the option with the highest possible payoff by assuming the best-case scenario will occur. The *Maximin method*, designed for risk-averse decision-makers, chooses the option with the best worst-case scenario, thereby ensuring protection against unfavorable conditions. The *Minimax Regret method* minimizes the worst-case regret by choosing the option where the maximum possible difference between its outcome and the best possible outcome in each scenario is smallest.

When probabilities are known or can be estimated, the Expected Value (EV) method becomes a powerful tool for decision-making. By calculating the weighted average of all possible outcomes, the EV method balances risk and reward, offering a rational approach to choosing among alternatives. Decision trees, as a graphical extension of the EV method, allow for a more comprehensive analysis by visually mapping out decisions, chance events, probabilities, and payoffs. This visual representation simplifies the comparison of different scenarios, making it easier to identify the most advantageous course of action.

Recognizing that good decisions are not necessarily those with the best outcomes but those that are well-informed and systematically analyzed is key to effective decision-making. Even the most carefully considered decisions can lead to unfavorable outcomes due to inherent uncertainties. This principle is reflected in fields like reinforcement learning, where optimal strategies are derived from evaluating expected rewards over time. Therefore, understanding and applying the appropriate decision-making methods is essential in navigating complex and uncertain environments.

This chapter will begin by demonstrating decision-making methods that do not consider probabilities, providing foundational tools for uncertain situations. We will then transition to the EV method, showing how it can be visualized and enhanced using decision trees. By the end of this chapter, you will be equipped with a range of decision-making techniques and the ability to effectively use decision trees to analyze and resolve real-world problems with confidence.

10.1 *Decision-making without probabilities*

In decision-making, there are scenarios where the probabilities of different outcomes are unknown or cannot be reliably estimated. This introduces a level of uncertainty that requires different approaches to make informed choices. When probabilities are not available, decision-makers rely on various methods to evaluate potential actions and their associated payoffs. These methods, such as the Maximax, Maximin, and Minimax Regret, provide structured ways to assess options based on the best, worst, or regret-minimizing outcomes. In the following sections, we will explore these decision-making methods with illustrative data, explaining each in detail and demonstrating their application through Python code snippets.

10.1.1 Maximax method

The *Maximax method*, also known as the *optimistic approach*, is one decision-making strategy used in situations where the decision-maker has no control over the states of nature and there are no known or estimated probabilities for these states. This method assumes that the most favorable outcome will occur and focuses on identifying the decision alternative that offers the highest possible payoff. Payoff tables are typically used in this approach (and others), listing the various decision alternatives and the corresponding payoffs under different states of nature. These payoffs can represent profits, costs, or any other relevant measure of value.

For example, consider a pending decision between multiple investment opportunities. The states of nature might include different market conditions—strong or weak—over the next 12 months. The payoffs in the table would show the expected profits under each of these conditions. The Maximax method involves scanning the payoff table to find the maximum payoff for each decision alternative and then selecting the alternative with the highest of these maximum payoffs. This approach appeals to those with a highly optimistic outlook, as it assumes the best possible scenario will materialize.

To effectively apply the Maximax method, or any decision-making strategy, a systematic approach is essential. This process involves several key steps:

1. *List the possible alternatives.* Begin by identifying all possible decision alternatives available. These are the different courses of action that the decision-maker can choose from. Exactly *one* of these alternatives should be selected.
2. *Identify the possible states of nature that can occur.* These are the external conditions or scenarios that can affect the outcomes of the decision but are beyond the control of the decision-maker.
3. *List the payoffs for each combination of decision alternative and state of nature.* Payoffs can be measured in various terms, such as profits, costs, or utility, depending on the context of the decision.
4. *Select a decision-making method that suits the context and goals of the decision, and then decide.* For instance, using the Maximax method involves identifying the highest possible payoff for each alternative and selecting the alternative with the maximum of these values.

By following these steps, you can construct a payoff table, apply a decision-making methodology, and arrive at a well-informed final decision.

LIST THE POSSIBLE ALTERNATIVES

Imagine you have $1 million to invest. Your first step is to identify the investment alternatives under consideration. This involves simply listing the options available to you. They are as follows:

- Invest all $1 million in the stock market.
- Invest all $1 million toward a minority share in a professional soccer club.
- Divide the $1 million into two halves: put $500,000 into the stock market and the other $500,000 toward a small ownership stake in a professional soccer club.
- Deposit all $1 million in a savings account that pays 3.5% annually.

Accordingly, we create a vector called investment_alternatives that contains these four options:

```
>>> investment_alternatives = [
>>>     "Stock Market",
>>>     "Professional Soccer Club",
>>>     "Stock Market / Soccer Club (50/50)",
>>>     "Savings Account"
>>> ]
```

In a bit, investment_alternatives will be joined with a pair of other vectors to create a data frame that will double as a payoff table.

IDENTIFY THE POSSIBLE STATES OF NATURE

The second step is to determine the potential states of nature that, although beyond your control, can significantly affect the outcomes of your investment alternatives. These states of nature represent various scenarios or conditions under which the investments might perform differently. For instance, market conditions can dramatically influence the performance of any investment strategy within a year's time. Identifying these states of nature is crucial as it allows you to assess the potential risks and returns associated with each investment alternative under different scenarios. By considering these possibilities, you can better understand the range of outcomes and make more informed decisions.

For this example, we will consider two states of nature: a strong economy versus a weak economy. To represent these states, we initialize two vectors accordingly:

```
>>> strong_economy = []
>>> weak_economy = []
```

Next, we will add the payoff amounts to these vectors and combine them with investment_alternatives to create a data frame, thereby forming a comprehensive payoff table.

LIST THE PAYOFFS FOR EACH ALTERNATIVE AND STATE OF NATURE COMBINATION

In the third step, we list the payoffs for each combination of investment alternatives and states of nature. This involves determining the potential outcomes or returns for each alternative under both the strong and weak economic scenarios. Payoffs are typically represented as monetary values, such as profits or losses. By assigning specific payoff amounts to each alternative based on the assumed economic conditions, we can construct a detailed payoff table. This table serves as the foundation for applying various decision-making methods and ultimately guides us in selecting the best investment strategy.

10.1 Decision-making without probabilities

With that in mind, let's now add the payoff amounts to the `strong_economy` and `weak_economy` vectors:

```
strong_economy = ([100000, 60000, 80000, 35000])
weak_economy = ([-120000, -20000, -70000, 35000])
```

These are dollar amounts that represent the estimated one-year profit or loss for each investment alternative under different economic conditions. For example, a $1 million investment in the stock market will yield a $100,000 profit in a strong economy, but the same investment will result in a $120,000 loss in a weak economy.

This will become much clearer by creating a payoff table. We can do this by combining the three vectors into a pandas data frame, which will provide a structured and easily readable format for analyzing the estimated one-year profits or losses for each investment alternative under different economic conditions:

```
>>> import pandas as pd
>>> payoff_table = pd.DataFrame({
>>>     'Investment Alternatives': investment_alternatives,
>>>     'Strong Economy': strong_economy,
>>>     'Weak Economy': weak_economy
>>> })
>>> print(payoff_table)
          Investment Alternatives  Strong Economy  Weak Economy
0                    Stock Market          100000       -120000
1         Professional Soccer Club           60000        -20000
2   Stock Market / Soccer Club (50/50)       80000        -70000
3                 Savings Account           35000         35000
```

A *payoff table*, sometimes referred to as a *decision table*, is a structured way to display the possible outcomes of various decision alternatives under different states of nature. Each row represents a different investment alternative, whereas each column represents the potential economic conditions, such as a strong or weak economy. The values within the table indicate the estimated one-year profit or loss associated with each combination of investment alternative and economic state. This table supports various decision-making approaches, including the Maximax method, by providing a clear visual representation of the potential payoffs for each scenario. By analyzing this table, decision-makers can systematically evaluate and compare the outcomes to make more informed and strategic investment decisions.

SELECT A DECISION-MAKING METHOD, AND MAKE A DECISION

The Maximax method involves a straightforward two-step process for decision-making. First, you identify the highest payoff for each investment alternative and store these values in a new column within the payoff table. This step highlights the most optimistic outcomes for each alternative, reflecting the decision-maker's focus on the best possible scenario. Second, you find the highest value in this new column. The investment alternative corresponding to this highest payoff is the one selected under the Maximax method. This approach is suited for decision-makers who prioritize the potential for maximum gains, even if it involves higher risks.

To achieve this programmatically, we begin by creating a deep copy of the payoff_table data frame and assigning it to a new data frame called maximax. This step ensures that any changes made to maximax don't affect the original payoff_table:

```
>>> maximax = payoff_table.copy()
```

Then we add a new column called Maximax that takes the highest payoff from each row or investment alternative. The max() method computes the maximum value across each row within the Strong Economy and Weak Economy columns and assigns those values to the new column:

```
>>> maximax['Maximax'] = \
>>>     payoff_table[['Strong Economy', 'Weak Economy']].max(axis = 1)
>>> print(maximax)
           Investment Alternatives  Strong Economy  Weak Economy  Maximax
0                      Stock Market          100000       -120000   100000
1            Professional Soccer Club           60000        -20000    60000
2  Stock Market / Soccer Club (50/50)           80000        -70000    80000
3                   Savings Account           35000         35000    35000
```

That completes the first step. The second step involves finding the highest payoff contained in the Maximax column. This is done by applying the max() method to the Maximax column:

```
>>> highest_payoff = maximax['Maximax'].max()
>>> print("Highest Payoff:", highest_payoff)
>>> Highest Payoff: 100000
```

The highest payoff, a $100,000 profit in a strong economy, is associated with the stock market investment alternative. The Maximax method follows a straightforward, optimistic approach, selecting the option with the highest potential gain without considering risk. As a result, it does not account for potential losses—an alternative with a high payoff but also a significant downside may still be chosen under this method. Therefore, according to this method, you should invest all $1 million in the stock market. However, if you were more risk-averse, you might apply a different decision-making approach, such as the Maximin method, which prioritizes minimizing potential losses.

10.1.2 Maximin method

The *Maximin method*, often referred to as the *pessimistic* or *conservative approach*, is a decision-making strategy used in situations where the decision-maker seeks to minimize potential losses. Unlike the Maximax method, which focuses on maximizing potential gains, the Maximin method is about selecting the alternative with the best of the worst-case scenarios. In this approach, the decision-maker identifies the minimum payoff for each investment alternative across all possible states of nature. These minimum payoffs represent the worst possible outcomes for each decision. The decision-maker then chooses the alternative with the highest minimum payoff, ensuring that even in the most unfavorable conditions, the outcome will be as favorable as possible compared to other alternatives. This method is particularly useful when there is a high level of uncertainty and risk aversion, as it prioritizes minimizing losses over maximizing gains.

To replicate this process programmatically, we will do the following:

1 Create a deep copy of the `payoff_table` data frame, and assign it to a new data frame called `maximin`.
2 Compute the *minimum* values from each row, and store the results in a new column called `Maximin`.
3 Find the *maximum* value in `Maximin` to determine the best investment strategy.

The code is similar to previous snippets:

```
>>> maximin = payoff_table.copy()          ◁── Creates a deep copy of payoff_table and assigns it to maximin
>>> maximin['Maximin'] = \                  ◁── Creates a new column to store the minimum value from each row or investment alternative
>>>     payoff_table[['Strong Economy',
>>>                   'Weak Economy']].min(axis = 1)
>>> print(maximin)                          ◁── Prints the maximin data frame
         Investment Alternatives  Strong Economy  Weak Economy  Maximin
0                   Stock Market          100000       -120000  -120000
1        Professional Soccer Club           60000        -20000   -20000
2  Stock Market / Soccer Club (50/50)       80000        -70000   -70000
3                Savings Account           35000         35000    35000

>>> highest_payoff = maximin['Maximin'].max()   ◁── Scans the Maximin column in the maximin data frame and extracts the maximum value
>>> print("Highest Payoff:", highest_payoff)    ◁── Prints the results
Highest Payoff: 35000
```

If you were to take the Maximin approach, you would choose to invest your $1 million in a savings account that pays 3.5% annually. This method prioritizes the safest, most conservative option by focusing on the minimum possible payoff for each investment alternative. By selecting the option with the highest minimum payoff, the Maximin approach ensures that you will be guaranteed a $35,000 profit after one year, regardless of the state of the economy. This approach emphasizes security and risk aversion, making it an attractive choice for those who prefer to minimize potential losses. However, because it focuses solely on worst-case outcomes, the Maximin method may overlook higher-reward opportunities and is generally not well-suited for optimizing long-term growth.

10.1.3 Minimax Regret method

The *Minimax Regret method* is a decision-making approach that focuses on minimizing the potential regret associated with a decision, rather than maximizing profit or minimizing loss. *Regret*, in this context, is defined as the difference between the payoff of the best possible action and the payoff of the chosen action, given a particular state of nature. The Minimax Regret method involves several steps:

278 CHAPTER 10 *Building and plotting a decision tree*

1 *Construct a regret table by calculating the regret values for each decision alternative under each possible state of nature.* We do this by finding the highest payoff for each state of nature and then subtracting the payoff of each alternative from this maximum value. The resulting regret values indicate the potential missed opportunities or losses associated with not choosing the optimal action for each state.

2 *For each decision alternative, identify the maximum regret.* This represents the worst-case scenario for each option.

3 *Select the decision alternative with the smallest maximum regret.* This approach is particularly useful in situations where decision-makers want to avoid the feeling of regret associated with making suboptimal choices, thereby minimizing the potential negative effects of their decisions. The Minimax Regret method provides a balance between risk and reward, helping to mitigate potential losses while still considering the upside potential of different alternatives.

Thus, the Minimax Regret method is inherently more encompassing than either the Maximax or Maximin approach. To implement this in Python, we will do the following:

1 Create a deep copy of `payoff_table`, and assign it to a new data frame called `regret`.
2 Calculate the maximum values for each state of nature.
3 Create a pair of new columns, `Strong` and `Weak`, that each store the derived opportunity loss associated with every investment alternative and state of nature combination.
4 Create a new column, `Maximum`, that stores the maximum regret for each investment alternative.
5 Take the minimum regret from `Maximum`, and choose the investment alternative associated with that value.

Here's the snippet of code:

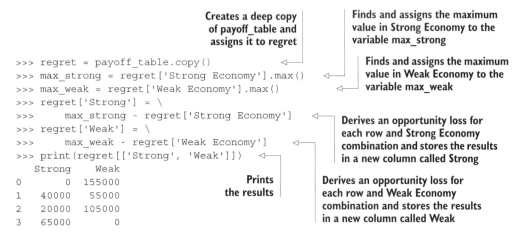

```
>>> regret['Maximum'] = \
>>>     regret[['Strong', 'Weak']].max(axis = 1)
>>> print(regret[['Strong', 'Weak', 'Maximum']])
   Strong   Weak  Maximum
0       0 155000   155000
1   40000  55000    55000
2   20000 105000   105000
3   65000      0    65000

>>> min_max_regret = regret['Maximum'].min()
>>> print(min_max_regret)
55000
```

- Creates a new column in regret by taking the maximum value from each row across the Strong and Weak columns
- Prints the results
- Finds the minimum value in the Maximum column from regret and assigns it to min_max_regret
- Prints the best minimum opportunity loss, or the alternative with the least regret

The results of the Minimax Regret analysis indicate that your best investment alternative is the one associated with the minimum value in the Maximum column. By minimizing the potential regret, the chosen alternative ensures the fewest missed opportunities. In this case, the best investment alternative, according to the Minimax Regret method, is to invest your $1 million in a professional soccer club.

In summary, decision-making methods such as Maximax, Maximin, and Minimax Regret provide different strategies for selecting the best investment alternative without applying probabilities to the various states of nature. The Maximax method focuses on maximizing the potential payoff by choosing the most optimistic scenario, whereas the Maximin method aims to maximize the minimum payoff, ensuring the best outcome in the worst-case scenario. The Minimax Regret method, on the other hand, minimizes potential regret by considering the missed opportunities. Each of these methods offers a unique perspective on decision-making under uncertainty. However, these approaches do not take into account the likelihood of different states of nature occurring. To incorporate probabilities and make more informed decisions, we turn to the EV method, which provides a more comprehensive analysis by weighing the payoffs against their probabilities.

10.1.4 Expected Value method

The EV method is a widely used decision-making technique in uncertain environments where the probabilities of different outcomes are known or can be estimated. It is particularly valuable in fields like finance, economics, and operations research, where decisions often involve various possible scenarios with associated probabilities. The essence of the EV method is to calculate the average outcome by weighting each possible outcome by its probability and summing these values. This approach helps decision-makers choose the option that offers the best expected return or the least expected loss, making it a fundamental tool for rational decision-making under uncertainty.

It differs from other decision-making strategies like Maximax, Maximin, and Minimax Regret in its approach to uncertainty and risk. Unlike these methods, which focus on either the best, worst, or regretful outcome, the EV method calculates the average outcome by weighting each possible scenario by its probability. This allows for a more balanced and rational decision-making process by considering the entire range of potential outcomes and their likelihoods, rather than focusing on extremes.

The EV method typically culminates in the construction of a decision tree, which is a graphical representation of the decision-making process. A decision tree consists of nodes representing decisions or chance events and branches representing the possible outcomes of these decisions or events. The tree starts with a decision node, followed by chance nodes that branch out into various possible outcomes, each associated with a probability and a payoff. By calculating the expected value at each decision node, decision-makers can systematically evaluate and compare different strategies, ultimately selecting the one with the highest expected value. This structured approach not only simplifies complex decision-making processes but also provides a clear visual aid for understanding and communicating the rationale behind each decision, making it an invaluable tool in various fields requiring strategic planning and risk management.

To illustrate, let's revisit the `payoff_table` data frame and consider the expected value of a $1 million investment in the stock market, assuming the probability of a strong economy is 0.75 and the probability of a weak economy is 0.25. It is important to note that the probabilities across all states of nature must sum to exactly 1.

The expected value is derived from the following formula:

$$EV(\text{stocks}) = \left(P_{\text{strong}} \times \text{Payoff}_{\text{strong}}\right) + \left(P_{\text{weak}} \times \text{Payoff}_{\text{weak}}\right)$$

where P_{strong} and P_{weak} are the probabilities of a strong and weak economy, respectively, and $\text{Payoff}_{\text{strong}}$ and $\text{Payoff}_{\text{weak}}$ are the corresponding payoffs.

Assuming the payoff for investing in the stock market is $100,000 in a strong economy and −$120,000 in a weak economy, we can plug in the values:

$$EV(\text{stocks}) = (0.75 \times 100{,}000) + (0.25 \times -120{,}000)$$

or

$$EV(\text{stocks}) = 75{,}000 + (-30{,}000)$$

or

$$EV(\text{stocks}) = 45{,}000$$

Thus, the expected value of investing in the stock market, given the specified probabilities and payoffs, is $45,000. This positive expected value indicates that, on average, investing in the stock market under these conditions would result in a significant gain.

To achieve the same result programmatically and cascade the same calculation to the remaining investment alternatives, we do the following:

10.1 Decision-making without probabilities

1. Assign probabilities to represent the likelihood of a strong versus weak economy. Because the probabilities across all states of nature (two in this case) must sum to exactly 1, we add a validation step so that if the probabilities do not sum to 1, Python returns an error message.
2. Write an arithmetic operation that calculates the expected value for each investment alternative and stores the results in a new column appended to the `payoff_table` data frame called EV.
3. Extract the maximum expected value from the EV column and make an investment decision based on that value.

Here's the snippet of Python code:

```
>>> strong_econ = 0.75              # Assigns a 75% probability of a strong economy
>>> weak_econ = 0.25                # Assigns a 25% probability of a weak economy
>>> if strong_econ + weak_econ != 1:
>>>     raise ValueError('The probabilities ' \
>>>                      must sum to 1.')
                                    # Throws an error if the probabilities of strong_econ and weak_econ do not sum to 1

>>> payoff_table['EV'] = \
>>>    (payoff_table['Strong Economy'] * strong_econ) + \
>>>    (payoff_table['Weak Economy'] * weak_econ)
                                    # Calculates the expected value for each investment alternative and stores the results in a payoff_table column called EV
>>> print(payoff_table)
              Investment Alternatives  Strong Economy  Weak Economy       EV
0                         Stock Market          100000       -120000  45000.0
1              Professional Soccer Club           60000        -20000  40000.0
2  Stock Market / Soccer Club (50/50)           80000        -70000  42500.0
3                      Savings Account           35000         35000  35000.0
                                    # Prints the revised payoff_table data frame

>>> max_ev = payoff_table['EV'].max()        # Extracts the maximum expected value from the EV column
>>> print("Maximum Expected Value:", max_ev) # Prints the highest expected value
Maximum Expected Value: 45000.0
```

The results are very close when we examine the expected value across each investment alternative. Even a small adjustment to the `strong_econ` and `weak_econ` estimates could tip the scales from one investment decision to another. Nevertheless, based on the calculated expected values, you should invest your $1 million in the stock market.

The EV method provides a systematic approach to decision-making under uncertainty by calculating the weighted average of possible outcomes based on their probabilities. As demonstrated, the expected values for different investment alternatives help identify the most favorable option: in this case, the stock market, with an expected value of $45,000. This quantitative evaluation aids in making informed choices by considering the likelihood of various scenarios. To further enhance our decision-making process, we can show these (or other) alternatives and their associated probabilities through a decision tree. A decision tree graphically represents decisions, possible events, and their outcomes, allowing for a clearer understanding of the potential paths and payoffs. Let's proceed to build and plot a decision tree to illustrate this process.

10.2 Decision trees

A decision tree is a graphical representation of the decision-making process, outlining the various paths one can take, the possible outcomes, and the associated probabilities and payoffs. Unlike a payoff table, which presents this information in a tabular format, a decision tree provides a more intuitive and visual approach, making it easier to grasp complex scenarios and their potential effects. It's important to note that these decision trees differ significantly from the decision tree model fit in chapter 6, which was used for data classification. Here, the focus is on mapping out decision processes rather than predicting outcomes based on data.

In a decision tree, there are two main types of nodes: decision nodes and chance nodes. *Decision nodes* signify points where a choice must be made. From these nodes, branches extend to chance nodes, which represent uncertain events with different possible outcomes. Each branch from a *chance node* carries a probability, indicating the likelihood of that particular outcome. The end points of these branches display the *payoffs*, which are the results of the decisions and chance events.

Using the investment alternatives EV solution as an example, a decision tree would start with a decision node representing the choice among the different investment options. From this node, branches would lead to chance nodes representing the economic conditions (strong or weak economy). Each chance node would then branch out to show the payoffs associated with each investment under different economic conditions, weighted by their respective probabilities.

Decision trees can be oriented either horizontally or vertically. When drawn horizontally, they extend from left to right, and when vertical, from top to bottom. However, the interpretation of decision trees works in the opposite direction: horizontally oriented trees are read from right to left, and vertically oriented trees from bottom to top. This reverse interpretation ensures that all probabilities and payoffs are considered cumulatively from the outcomes back to the initial decision.

The visual nature of decision trees makes them superior to payoff tables in many cases, as they allow for a clearer understanding of the sequence of events and the cumulative effect of decisions and chance occurrences. This comprehensive view aids in making more informed and strategically sound decisions.

The first step in constructing a decision tree is to create the schema. A decision tree *schema* is a structured blueprint that outlines the various decision points, chance events, their probabilities, and associated payoffs. It provides a clear framework to follow when building the tree, ensuring that all potential outcomes are accounted for systematically.

Once the schema is established, the tree can be plotted based on this detailed outline. We will demonstrate how to create the schema manually, showing the step-by-step process of defining decision nodes, chance nodes, probabilities, and payoffs. Additionally, we will show how to create the schema programmatically using methods from

Python's `anytree` library, which simplifies the creation and manipulation of tree structures. Finally, we will use Matplotlib to plot the decision tree, providing a visual representation that enhances understanding and aids in the decision-making process.

By following these steps, we can construct a clear and comprehensive decision tree that effectively communicates the decision-making process and helps identify the most favorable outcomes. To better demonstrate this, we will be working with new illustrative data and a new scenario involving a Major League Baseball player in free agency.

10.2.1 Creating the schema

A Major League Baseball player is currently in free agency, a period when he is free to negotiate and sign with any team after his previous contract has ended. He is considering two contract offers: one from the New York Yankees and another from the Los Angeles Dodgers. His primary goal is to sign with the team that will provide the most financial benefit over the lifetime of the contract, which is the same length for both offers.

The Yankees' offer is straightforward, guaranteeing the player $120 million after deducting agent fees, with no performance-based incentives. In contrast, the Dodgers' offer is more complex, potentially paying up to $150 million if specific performance thresholds (such as hits, home runs, etc.) are met. However, if these thresholds are not met, the player could earn as "little" as $90 million. The player understands that his ability to meet these performance targets depends heavily on his health. Regardless of his health, there are probabilities associated with meeting all, some, or none of the performance targets. Given these considerations, the player must carefully evaluate the potential financial outcomes of each contract offer to make the best decision for his career and financial well-being.

STEPS AND BEST PRACTICES

Creating a decision tree schema is the first step in constructing a decision tree. The schema acts as a blueprint, detailing the various decision points, chance events, probabilities, and payoffs. This structured approach ensures that all possible outcomes and their probabilities are systematically considered. Here are the steps and best practices to create a decision tree schema:

1. *Identify the primary decision points.* These are typically the major choices to be made. In our example, the decision points would be the player's choice between signing with the Yankees or the Dodgers.
2. *Identify and list any relevant variables that affect the decision.* For instance, agent fees need to be deducted from the total pay.
3. *Label each node as either a decision node or a chance node.* Decision nodes are points where a choice must be made. Chance nodes represent uncertain events with different possible outcomes.
4. *Outline the outcomes.* For each decision node, outline the possible outcomes or actions; for each chance node, list the possible events that could occur and their respective probabilities.

5 *Assign a probability to each chance event.* Ensure that the probabilities for all events stemming from a single chance node sum to 1.
6 *Determine and specify the payoffs associated with each possible outcome.* Payoffs are the results of the decisions and chance events.
7 *Structure the schema using indents or tabs to represent different levels of decisions and events.* This hierarchical structure helps show the flow from decision points to chance events and their respective outcomes.

By following these steps and using indents or tabs to structure the information hierarchically, we can create a comprehensive decision tree schema that clearly outlines all possible decisions, chance events, probabilities, and payoffs. This schema will then serve as a guide for constructing and visualizing the actual decision tree.

CREATING THE SCHEMA MANUALLY

The first step in building a decision tree is creating the schema, which serves as a structured blueprint for the decision-making process. This involves defining the decision tree's name, listing relevant variables, and identifying the main decision node. The decision tree's name encapsulates the overall decision context, such as Contract Options for a player considering different team offers. Variables such as agent fees are key factors that influence the decision. The decision node is the starting point of the tree, representing the primary choice to be made, such as whether to sign with the Yankees or the Dodgers. This foundational setup ensures that the decision tree is organized and ready for detailed branching into outcomes and probabilities.

At this stage, we are not using Python to create the schema; instead, we are constructing it manually. This manual process helps in understanding the structure and components of the decision tree before automating it programmatically:

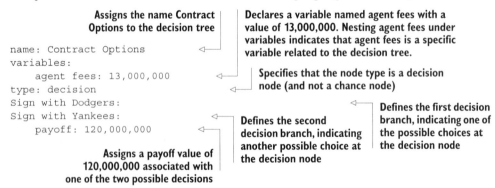

So far, we have created a comprehensive schema for our decision tree. The decision tree is named `Contract Options`. We have defined a variable, `agent fees`, which will be subtracted from the expected value of the decision to sign with the Dodgers. At the root of our decision tree, we have a decision node with two primary choices: `Sign with Dodgers` and `Sign with Yankees`. The Yankees' offer includes a guaranteed payoff of $120,000,000, including the subtraction of agent fees. In contrast, the Dodgers'

contract heavily relies on performance incentives, causing the total contract payout to vary based on different states of nature.

We then take the first step in building out the schema for the `Sign with Dodgers` part of the decision tree by applying the `agent fees` variable and creating a chance node. A chance node represents an uncertain event with various possible outcomes, each associated with a probability. This step sets up the foundation for detailing the probabilities and outcomes related to the player's health and performance incentives.

Additions to the schema are highlighted in **bold**:

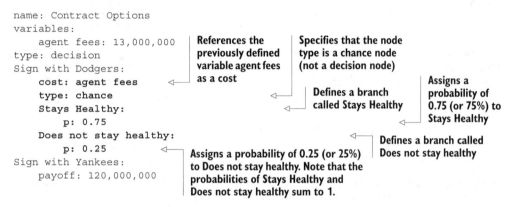

The expected value of the `Sign with Dodgers` decision will be affected by the variable `agent fees` and whether the player can maintain his health over the lifetime of the contract. The schema, therefore, now includes agent fees, which are a fixed cost, and introduces a chance node with probabilities for `Stays Healthy` at 0.75 and `Does not stay healthy` at 0.25. Probabilities from each chance node must sum to exactly 1. These probabilities will play a crucial role in determining the overall expected value of the Dodgers' offer.

We complete the schema by creating additional chance nodes and defining the probabilities and payoffs for each potential outcome. This includes detailing the likelihood and financial results for various performance incentives based on the player's health status.

Once again, changes to the schema are highlighted in **bold**:

```
name: Contract Options
variables:
    agent fees: 13,000,000
type: decision
Sign with Dodgers:
    cost: agent fees
    type: chance
    Stays Healthy:
        p: 0.75
        type: chance
        No Performance Incentives:
            p: 0.10
            payoff: 90,000,000
```

286 CHAPTER 10 *Building and plotting a decision tree*

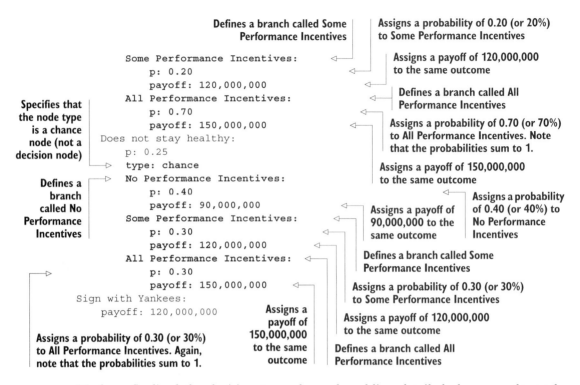

We have finalized the decision tree schema by adding detailed chance nodes and defining the probabilities and payoffs for each potential outcome. For the `Sign with Dodgers` decision, we have introduced a chance node to account for the player's health status. If the player stays healthy (p: 0.75), there are further chance nodes detailing the likelihood of meeting performance incentives: `No Performance Incentives` (p: 0.10) with a payoff of $90,000,000, `Some Performance Incentives` (p: 0.20) with a payoff of $120,000,000, and `All Performance Incentives` (p: 0.70) with a payoff of $150,000,000. These probabilities are illustrative but loosely informed by historical player performance trends and general expectations based on age and durability.

Similarly, if the player does not stay healthy (p: 0.25), there are also chance nodes with probabilities and payoffs: `No Performance Incentives` (p: 0.40) with a payoff of $90,000,000, `Some Performance Incentives` (p: 0.30) with a payoff of $120,000,000, and `All Performance Incentives` (p: 0.30) with a payoff of $150,000,000. The decision to sign with the Yankees offers a straightforward guaranteed payoff of $120,000,000. This comprehensive schema will serve as the blueprint for constructing the decision tree, ensuring that all possible outcomes, their probabilities, and associated payoffs are systematically represented.

CREATING THE SCHEMA PROGRAMMATICALLY

Now that we have detailed the final schema manually, we will transition to demonstrating how to build the same schema using methods from Python's `anytree` library. This programmatic approach will streamline the process and ensure accuracy in representing the decision tree structure. We will use this schema as the source for our

Matplotlib decision tree, illustrating how to show the decision-making process effectively using standard Python libraries and methods.

Even though we are about to create, or re-create, the schema programmatically, the steps remain just the same as before. Thus, we begin by naming the decision tree, defining any variables that will affect the expected value calculations, and establishing the decision node:

```
>>> from anytree import Node
>>> root = Node('Contract Options')
>>> agent_fees = 13000000
>>> dodgers = Node('Sign with Dodgers',
>>>                parent = root)
>>> yankees = Node('Sign with Yankees\n'
>>>                'Expected Payoff: $120,000,000',
>>>                parent = root,
>>>                payoff = 120000000)
```

- Imports the Node class from the anytree library
- Creates the root, or decision, node with the name Contract Options
- Assigns the value 13000000 to the variable agent_fees, which represents a fixed cost or fee
- Creates a child node labeled Sign with Dodgers under the root node
- Creates a child node labeled Sign with Yankees under the root node with an expected value equal to $120,000,000

With just a few lines of Python code, we have established the foundation for our decision tree schema.

Next, we establish a chance node to account for the player's health status, which significantly affects the expected value calculations. The code creates two child nodes under the Sign with Dodgers decision node: Stays Healthy with a probability of 0.75, and Does not stay healthy with a probability of 0.25. These chance nodes represent the potential health outcomes and their associated probabilities, providing a detailed view of the decision tree's branching based on the player's health:

```
>>> stays_healthy = Node('Stays Healthy\np=0.75',
>>>                      parent = dodgers)
>>> does_not_stay_healthy = Node('Does not stay healthy\np=0.25',
>>>                              parent = dodgers)
```

- Creates the first of two chance nodes under the Sign with Dodgers node
- Creates the second of two chance nodes under the Sign with Dodgers node

In this part of the decision tree schema, we introduce chance nodes to account for the player's health status. These nodes, labeled Stays Healthy with a 0.75 probability and Does not stay healthy with a 0.25 probability, are specified as branches under the Sign with Dodgers decision node. This structure models the uncertainties related to the player's health over the contract period.

Even though we're building the schema and not constructing the tree, Python distinguishes between chance nodes and decision nodes through their context and labeling within the schema. Decision nodes, such as Sign with Dodgers and Sign with Yankees, represent choices or actions. In contrast, chance nodes represent probabilistic events and include probabilities, like Stays Healthy with a 75% chance. The hierarchical arrangement and clear labeling of each node within the schema help clarify their roles and outcomes, ensuring the decision tree accurately reflects the complexities of real-world decision-making scenarios when it's eventually constructed.

The next step in building out the schema involves defining the subtrees under the `Stays Healthy` and `Does not stay healthy` chance nodes. A *subtree* is a smaller section of the decision tree that branches out from a specific node, representing a subset of possible outcomes and decisions:

```
>>> no_incentives = Node('None\np=0.10\npayoff=90M',
>>>                      parent = stays_healthy,
>>>                      payoff = 90000000)
>>> some_incentives = Node('Some\np=0.20\npayoff=120M',
>>>                        parent = stays_healthy,
>>>                        payoff = 120000000)
>>> all_incentives = Node('All\np=0.70\npayoff=150M',
>>>                       parent = stays_healthy,
>>>                       payoff = 150000000)
>>> no_incentives_dodgers = Node('None\np=0.40\npayoff=90M',
>>>                              parent = does_not_stay_healthy,
>>>                              payoff = 90000000)
>>> some_incentives_dodgers = Node('Some\np=0.30\npayoff=120M',
>>>                                parent = does_not_stay_healthy,
>>>                                payoff = 120000000)
>>> all_incentives_dodgers = Node('All\np=0.30\npayoff=150M',
>>>                               parent = does_not_stay_healthy,
>>>                               payoff = 150000000)
```

Creates the first of three child nodes under the Stays Healthy chance node, with an associated probability of 0.10 and a payoff of $90 million

Creates the second of three child nodes under the Stays Healthy chance node, with an associated probability of 0.20 and a payoff of $120 million

Creates the third of three child nodes under the Stays Healthy chance node, with an associated probability of 0.70 and a payoff of $150 million

Creates the first of three child nodes under the Does not stay healthy chance node, with an associated probability of 0.40 and a payoff of $90 million

Creates the second of three child nodes under the Does not stay healthy chance node, with an associated probability of 0.30 and a payoff of $120 million

Creates the third of three child nodes under the Does not stay healthy chance node, with an associated probability of 0.30 and a payoff of $150 million

The code defines the subtrees for the `Stays Healthy` and `Does not stay healthy` chance nodes, detailing the various performance incentive outcomes and their associated probabilities and payoffs. For both health scenarios, the performance thresholds—`No Performance Incentives`, `Some Performance Incentives`, and `All Performance Incentives`—have consistent payoffs of `90000000`, `120000000`, and `150000000`, respectively. However, the probabilities of these outcomes differ based on the player's health status. If the player stays healthy, there is a higher probability of meeting all performance incentives (70%) compared to when the player does not stay healthy (30%). Conversely, the likelihood of not meeting any performance incentives is higher if the player does not stay healthy (40%) than if he remains healthy (10%). This structure captures the effect of the player's health on the expected value of the Dodgers' contract.

The next step in building out the schema programmatically involves calculating the expected payoffs for the various scenarios and updating the nodes with these values. This process begins by defining variables for the expected payoffs when the player stays healthy and when he does not. More precisely, the code derives `stays_healthy_payoff` by weighting the payoffs of no, some, and all performance incentives by their respective probabilities. Similarly, `does_not_stay_healthy_payoff` is derived using the probabilities for the same performance thresholds under the scenario where the player does not stay healthy. Finally, these calculated expected payoffs are appended to the corresponding node labels, enhancing the decision tree with quantitative insights that clearly indicate the financial outcomes of each scenario. This comprehensive calculation step ensures that all potential outcomes are accurately represented and quantified in the decision tree:

```
>>> stays_healthy_payoff = (0.10 * 90000000 +
>>>                         0.20 * 120000000 +
>>>                         0.70 * 150000000)
>>> does_not_stay_healthy_payoff = (0.40 * 90000000 +
>>>                                 0.30 * 120000000 +
>>>                                 0.30 * 150000000)

>>> dodgers_expected_payoff = (0.75 * stays_healthy_payoff +
>>>                            0.25 * does_not_stay_healthy_payoff -
>>>                            agent_fees)

>>> dodgers.name += (f'\nExpected Payoff: \
>>>         f"${dodgers_expected_payoff:,.0f}')

>>> stays_healthy.name += (f'\nExpected Payoff: '
>>>         f'${stays_healthy_payoff:,.0f}')
>>> does_not_stay_healthy.name += (f'\nExpected Payoff: '
>>>         f'${does_not_stay_healthy_payoff:,.0f}')
```

- Calculates the expected value of the Stays Healthy chance node by plugging probabilities and payoffs into the expected value formula
- Calculates the expected value of the Does not stay healthy chance node by again plugging probabilities and payoffs into the expected value formula
- Calculates the expected value of the Dodgers' contract by using the expected value formula, combining the weighted payoffs of the chance nodes, and subtracting the agent fees
- Appends the expected value to the Stays Healthy chance node
- Appends the expected value of the Dodgers' contract to the label of the dodgers decision node
- Appends the expected value to the Does not stay healthy chance node

The last snippet of code calculates the expected values for each chance node in the decision tree based on the defined schema. It first determines the expected payoffs for the `Stays Healthy` and `Does not stay healthy` nodes by weighting each potential outcome by its probability. Then, it calculates the overall expected payoff for signing with the Dodgers by combining these values and subtracting the agent fees. The results are, of course, not immediately applied to a visual representation; rather, they are stored in memory, thereby preparing the updated information to be included in the decision tree when it is finally constructed and displayed.

10.2.2 Plotting the tree

The following snippet of Matplotlib code generates a visualization of the decision tree we have designed programmatically. The `plot_tree()` function takes the root node of the tree as an input and generates a horizontal diagram that visually represents the decision-making process.

The `add_edges()` method within `plot_tree()` recursively traverses the tree, positioning each node at specific coordinates to ensure that the nodes are correctly spaced horizontally and vertically. It starts from the root node and moves through each layer of the tree, adjusting the positions of child nodes relative to their parent nodes. This ensures that the tree structure is maintained and visually clear.

After determining the positions of all nodes, the function then uses `plt.text()` to place labels on each node. It distinguishes between different types of nodes by their content, using different background colors for decision nodes and chance nodes. Decision nodes are highlighted in green, and chance nodes are highlighted in orange. This color-coding helps to visually differentiate the various elements of the tree.

Finally, the function sets a title for the plot, removes the axis for a cleaner look, and displays the completed decision tree using `plt.show()`. This visualization step transforms the stored node information into a clear, interpretable diagram that highlights the decision paths and expected outcomes:

```
>>> import matplotlib.pyplot as plt              ◁─ Imports the matplotlib library
>>> def plot_tree(root):
>>>     def add_edges(node, pos = {}, x = 0, y = 0,
>>>                   layer = 1, dy = 3.0):        ◁─ Stores the position of the root, or decision, node
>>>         pos[node] = (x, y)
>>>         neighbors = node.children
>>>         if neighbors:                          ◁─ Adjusts horizontal spacing to keep adjacent nodes from overlapping
>>>             next_x = x + 2.
>>>             next_layer = layer + 1
>>>             for i, neighbor in enumerate(neighbors):   ◁─ Adjusts vertical spacing for the same reason
>>>                 next_y = y + dy * (i - \
>>>                          (len(neighbors) - 1) / 2)
>>>                 pos = add_edges(neighbor, pos = pos,
>>>                                 x = next_x, y = next_y,   ◁─ Recursively adds child nodes
>>>                                 layer = next_layer,
>>>                                 dy = dy / 1.5)
>>>                 plt.plot([x, next_x],                      ◁─ Creates a visual connection (line) between a parent node and its child nodes
>>>                          [y, next_y], 'k-')
>>>         return pos
>>>
>>>     pos = add_edges(root, dy = 12.0)            ◁─ Starts the process of assigning positions to each node in the tree, beginning with the root node
>>>     for node, (x, y) in pos.items():
>>>         if node.is_leaf:
>>>             plt.text(x, y, node.name,            ◁─ Adds labels or names to the leaf nodes (nodes with no children)
>>>                      va = 'center')
>>>         else:
>>>             if ('Contract Options' in node.name
>>>                 or 'Yankees' in node.name):
>>>                 plt.text(x, y, node.name,
>>>                          va = 'center',            ◁─ Applies visual formatting to the decision node to distinguish it from chance nodes
>>>                          bbox = dict(facecolor = 'green',
>>>                          edgecolor = 'black',
>>>                          boxstyle = \
>>>                          'round, pad = 0.5'))
```

```
>>>            else:
>>>                plt.text(x, y, node.name, va = 'center',
>>>                         bbox = dict(facecolor = 'orange',
>>>                                     edgecolor = 'black',
>>>                                     boxstyle = \
>>>                                     'round, pad = 0.5'))
```
Applies visual formatting to the chance nodes to distinguish them from the decision node

```
>>> plt.title('Decision Tree: Contract Options\n\n')
>>> plt.axis('off')
>>> plt.show()
```
Displays the plot

Removes axis lines and labels for a cleaner, more focused visualization of the decision tree

```
>>> plot_tree(root)
```
Creates the visual representation of the decision tree as defined by the plot_tree(root) function

Figure 10.1 shows the decision tree visualizing the contract options for a Major League Baseball player considering offers from the New York Yankees and the Los Angeles Dodgers. The tree outlines the possible outcomes and expected payoffs based on performance incentives and the player's health.

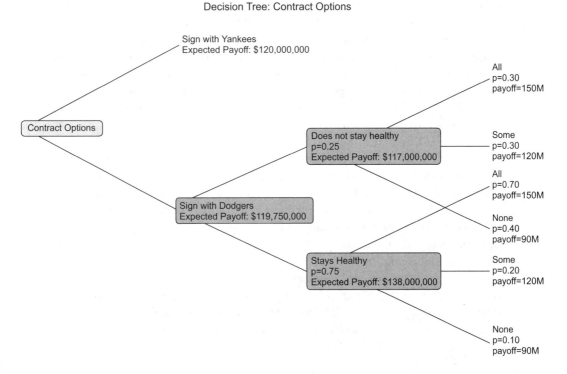

Figure 10.1 A decision tree that illustrates two very different contract offers. The tree outlines the expected payoffs based on different states of nature, allowing the player to accept the contract with the highest expected value.

Some best practices are evident in the diagram, such as using distinct colors to differentiate the decision nodes from chance nodes. Additionally, the use of clear, descriptive labels for each node, including probabilities and expected payoffs, enhances the interpretability of the tree. Ensuring that decision nodes and chance nodes have different shapes or sizes can further improve clarity; for example, chance nodes could be larger or differently shaped than decision nodes.

The tree should be evaluated or interpreted from right to left, despite being constructed from left to right. This reverse interpretation ensures that all probabilities and payoffs are considered cumulatively. Starting from the rightmost nodes, we see the outcomes based on performance incentives for the `Stays Healthy` and `Does not stay healthy` scenarios. Each of these chance nodes has associated probabilities and payoffs, which are combined to determine the expected value for each health scenario.

For instance, the `Stays Healthy` node has an expected payoff calculated from its branches: 10% for $90 million, 20% for $120 million, and 70% for $150 million, resulting in an expected payoff of $138 million. Similarly, the `Does not stay healthy` node has an expected payoff calculated from its branches: 40% for $90 million, 30% for $120 million, and 30% for $150 million, resulting in an expected payoff of $117 million. These expected values are then used to calculate the overall expected payoff for signing with the Dodgers, factoring in the probabilities of staying healthy (75%) and not staying healthy (25%), and subtracting agent fees.

Interpreting the tree, we compare the overall expected payoffs of the decision nodes. The `Sign with Yankees` node has a guaranteed expected payoff of $120 million, whereas the `Sign with Dodgers` node has an overall expected payoff of approximately $119.75 million. Given these calculations, the best decision for the player is to sign with the Yankees, as it offers the highest expected value. This structured approach allows for a clear, data-driven decision-making process, highlighting the most financially beneficial option based on the probabilities and outcomes provided.

In this chapter, we learned how to design and build a decision tree based on the Expected Value method, which combines payoffs and probabilities to make informed decisions. We explored the process of creating a decision tree schema, calculating expected values, and visually representing decision paths and outcomes. Additionally, we discussed other decision-making methods that do not rely on probabilities, such as the Maximax, Maximin, and Minimax Regret methods, highlighting different approaches to evaluating choices and managing uncertainty.

In the next chapter, we will explore mathematical systems that model transitions between different states over time, where each transition depends only on the current state and not on the previous history. These models are useful for predicting future states and understanding dynamic processes in various fields.

Summary

- The Maximax method is an optimistic decision-making approach that focuses on maximizing the maximum possible payoff. Decision-makers using this method choose the option with the highest potential reward, reflecting a high tolerance for risk and a preference for best-case scenarios.

- The Maximin method is a conservative decision-making approach that aims to maximize the minimum payoff. It involves selecting the option with the best worst-case scenario, making it suitable for risk-averse decision-makers who prioritize minimizing potential losses.
- The Minimax Regret method aims to minimize the maximum regret, which is the difference between the actual payoff and the best possible payoff that could have been achieved with perfect foresight. Decision-makers using this method focus on reducing the potential for regret by selecting the option that offers the least unfavorable outcome compared to the best possible alternative.
- The Expected Value method is a decision-making approach that calculates the average outcome by weighting each possible scenario by its probability. Decision-makers use this method to choose the option with the highest expected return or lowest expected loss, providing a balanced and rational evaluation of all potential outcomes and their likelihoods.
- Decision trees are graphical representations of decision-making processes that outline various choices, chance events, probabilities, and payoffs. They provide a clear, visual method for evaluating complex decision scenarios, including sequential decisions, by incorporating probabilities and calculating expected values at each stage.
- Creating the schema for a decision tree involves defining the decision nodes, chance nodes, probabilities, and payoffs. This structured blueprint ensures all possible outcomes are systematically considered, laying the groundwork for constructing the decision tree.
- Constructing the decision tree involves translating the schema into a visual format, typically using nodes and branches to represent decisions and chance events. This step allows for easy interpretation and analysis of the decision-making process, helping to show the potential paths and outcomes clearly.
- Real-world applications of these decision-making methods extend beyond theoretical exercises. Businesses use them to evaluate investment strategies, optimize resource allocation, assess project risks, and make strategic planning decisions in uncertain environments. By applying these frameworks, decision-makers can systematically analyze complex scenarios and improve the quality of their choices.

Predicting future states with Markov analysis

11

This chapter covers

- States, state probabilities, and transition matrices
- Vector of state probabilities
- Equilibrium conditions
- Absorbing states
- Matrix operations in Markov chains

Markov analysis is a mathematical technique used to predict future states of a system—such as a market, a machine, or a population—based on its current state and the probabilities of transitioning from one state to another. It is applicable specifically to systems that exhibit the Markov property, meaning future states depend only on the present state and not on the sequence of past events. This memoryless characteristic makes Markov analysis particularly useful for modeling dynamic processes where past influences can be effectively summarized by the present state.

The technique originated from the work of Andrey Markov, a Russian mathematician, in the early 20th century and has since been widely applied in various fields, including market share predictions and delinquency forecasting.

In market share analysis, businesses use Markov techniques to predict how market shares for different competitors will evolve over time based on current market conditions and consumer behavior patterns. For example, a company can estimate the likelihood of a customer switching from its brand to a competitor's brand within a given time period. Similarly, in forecasting delinquencies, financial institutions use Markov analysis to predict the probability that a borrower will move from one delinquency bucket to another, such as from being current on payments to being 30 days late, and then to 60 days late, and so on.

11.1 Understanding the mechanics of Markov analysis

Markov analysis works by defining a finite number of possible states and calculating the probability of transitioning from one state to another. These probabilities are organized in a transition probability matrix, which serves as the foundation for predicting future states. The analysis assumes that the probability of changing states remains constant over time, meaning the transition probabilities do not vary. Additionally, it is assumed that the size and makeup of the system do not change over time.

The key assumption behind all Markov analyses is that the future state of a system depends only on its current state and not on the sequence of events that preceded it. This property, known as the *Markov property*, allows for the prediction of any future state using the current state and the transition probability matrix. This matrix, a square matrix in which each element represents the probability of moving from one state to another, is central to Markov analysis.

Equilibrium conditions in Markov analysis refer to a state where the probabilities of being in each state remain constant over time. This occurs when the system has reached a *steady state*, meaning the distribution of states does not change as further transitions occur. Understanding equilibrium conditions is crucial for long-term predictions and stability analysis.

Absorbing states are special types of states in a Markov process: once entered, the system remains in that state permanently. These states are essential for analyzing processes that have terminal conditions, such as loan defaults and customer churn.

Throughout this chapter, we will demonstrate how to perform mathematical operations with matrices to conduct Markov analysis. This includes constructing and manipulating the transition probability matrix, calculating state probabilities, and determining equilibrium conditions. We will also explore how to identify and analyze absorbing states, providing a comprehensive understanding of how Markov analysis can be used to predict future states and inform decision-making in various practical applications. By the end of this chapter, you will have a solid understanding of the principles and techniques of Markov analysis, and you will be equipped with the skills to apply this powerful tool to a range of predictive modeling scenarios.

11.2 States and state probabilities

A *state* in Markov analysis represents a distinct condition or status that a process or system can be in at any given point in time. Identifying all possible states is the first step for understanding and predicting the behavior of the system. Each state provides a snapshot of the system's current condition, enabling analysts to model transitions and future states.

States are used to identify all possible conditions of a process or system. These conditions can be binary, representing two possible states. For instance, consider the engine of a classic automobile, which can either be running or not running. These two states encompass all possible conditions of the engine at any given moment.

States can also be more complex and involve multiple categories. For example, in the context of market share among four cellular carriers, the states could represent the percentage of the market held by each carrier. Here, the system's conditions are represented by the various market shares of the four carriers, providing a more detailed understanding of the market dynamics.

In Markov analysis, it is essential that the set of states be collectively exhaustive and mutually exclusive. *Collectively exhaustive* means all possible conditions of the system are represented within the set of states. No condition is left out. For instance, in the classic automobile example, the states "running" and "not running" cover all possible conditions of the engine. In the market share example, the states representing the market shares of all four cellular carriers must sum up to 100%, ensuring that all possible market conditions are included.

Mutually exclusive means no two states can occur simultaneously. Each state is distinct and non-overlapping. An automobile engine cannot be both running and not running at the same time. Similarly, in the market share example, a specific percentage of the market cannot be simultaneously attributed to two different carriers. Each percentage point of market share belongs to one and only one carrier.

By defining states that are both collectively exhaustive and mutually exclusive, analysts can accurately model the system and predict its future behavior. This clear delineation of states ensures a comprehensive and precise analysis, which is fundamental to the effectiveness of Markov analysis in predicting future states.

The second step is to determine the probabilities across states. These probabilities are stored in what is called a *vector of state probabilities*:

$$\pi(i) = \text{vector of state probabilities for period } i$$
$$= (\pi_1, \pi_2, \pi_3, \ldots, \pi_n)$$

where

- n equals the number of states.
- $\pi_1, \pi_2, \pi_3, \ldots, \pi_n$ equals the probability of being in state 1, state 2,…, state n.

11.2 States and state probabilities

With respect to the classic automobile engine, which can be in only one of two states for any given period—running or not running—it's relatively straightforward to mathematically represent the vector of state probabilities:

$$\pi(0) = (1, 0)$$

where

- $\pi(0)$ equals the vector of states for the automobile engine in period 0. A period can represent any unit of time, such as a day, a week, a quarter, or a year. However, it is essential that historical and future periods are measured consistently. Periods typically start at 0, so that period 1 represents the first period following the initial transition.
- π_1 equal to 1 represents the probability of being in the first state, which, in this case, means the probability of the automobile engine being in running condition.
- π_2 equal to 0 represents the probability of being in the second state, which means the probability of the automobile engine not running.

This indicates that the probability of the automobile engine being in running condition (state 1) is 1, whereas the probability of it not being in running condition (state 2) is 0 for the first period. However, in most cases, we need to consider systems with multiple items or components.

11.2.1 Understanding the vector of state probabilities for multistate systems

Consider the market share distribution among four (fictional) US cellular carriers: Horizon, TeleConnect, AmeriCon, and USAMobile. Collectively, these carriers own 100% of the US market, and their market shares can be represented as state probabilities:

- Horizon has a 40% share of the US market. In market share analysis, the share of the market is equivalent to probability. So, state 1 is assigned to Horizon with a probability of 0.40.
- TeleConnect owns 35% of the market, which is assigned as state 2 with a probability of 0.35.
- AmeriCon owns 20% of the market, making it state 3 with a probability of 0.20.
- USAMobile owns 5% of the market, designated as state 4 with a probability of 0.05.

These market shares represent the probabilities of consumers having wireless subscriptions to one of these carriers in period 0 (before any transitions have occurred). Each state probability signifies the likelihood of a randomly selected consumer being a customer of a particular carrier at this point in time.

Understanding the vector of state probabilities in a multistate system is crucial for predicting how these probabilities might change over time. By analyzing the transition probabilities between these states, we can forecast shifts in market share and make informed decisions based on anticipated trends. This method is applicable not only to market share analysis but also to various other fields where the system can be modeled as transitioning between different states.

These probabilities can therefore be stored in a vector of state probabilities, such as

$$\pi(i) = (0.40, 0.35, 0.20, 0.05)$$

where

- $\pi(i)$ equals a vector of state probabilities for the four cellular carriers for period 0.
- π_1 is the probability that a consumer has a subscription to Horizon (state 1), which is equal to 40%.
- π_2 is the probability that a consumer has a subscription to TeleConnect (state 2), which is equal to 35%.
- π_3 is the probability that a consumer has a subscription to AmeriCon (state 3), which is equal to 20%.
- π_4 is the probability that a consumer has a subscription to USAMobile (state 4), which is equal to 5%.

The probabilities sum to 1, and the respective market shares add to 100%.

Churn is a significant factor in the wireless industry, where subscriptions are typically on a month-to-month basis. This flexibility allows consumers to switch carriers frequently, especially as carriers continually introduce new and attractive contract offers. Consumers have the option to terminate their subscription with one carrier and take their existing phone number to a different carrier, making the market highly dynamic and competitive.

Based on a study of recent historical figures, we observe the following transition probabilities for the four US cellular carriers (Horizon, TeleConnect, AmeriCon, and USAMobile). These figures illustrate how likely customers are to stay with their current carrier or switch to a competitor in the next period, which is the following quarter:

- Horizon
  - 85% of customers will stay with Horizon.
  - 6% will switch to TeleConnect.
  - 7% will switch to AmeriCon.
  - 2% will switch to USAMobile.
- TeleConnect
  - 80% of customers will stay with TeleConnect.
  - 8% will switch to Horizon.
  - 10% will switch to AmeriCon.
  - 2% will switch to USAMobile.

11.2 States and state probabilities

- AmeriCon
  - 75% of customers will stay with AmeriCon.
  - 10% will switch to Horizon.
  - 10% will switch to TeleConnect.
  - 5% will switch to USAMobile.
- USAMobile
  - 70% of customers will stay with USAMobile.
  - 12% will switch to Horizon.
  - 10% will switch to TeleConnect.
  - 8% will switch to AmeriCon.

These transition probabilities reflect the competitive nature of the wireless market, where each carrier must continuously strive to retain its customers while attracting those from its competitors. Understanding these probabilities is crucial for predicting market dynamics and making strategic decisions in the wireless industry.

It is important to note that the transition probabilities for each carrier from period 0 to period 1 sum to 100%. This means every customer is accounted for, ensuring that the model reflects the entire customer base without any loss or gain in total numbers. This comprehensive accounting allows for accurate predictions and analyses of market share dynamics.

For example, 85% of Horizon's customers are expected to remain with Horizon, whereas the remaining 15% will switch to other carriers (6% to TeleConnect, 7% to AmeriCon, and 2% to USAMobile). Similarly, the transition probabilities for TeleConnect, AmeriCon, and USAMobile customers also sum to 100%, fully accounting for all possible movements between carriers.

This complete accounting is essential for understanding and predicting market behaviors, as it ensures that all potential customer movements are included in the analysis. It provides a clear and accurate picture of how market shares are likely to evolve over time, based on current trends and consumer behaviors.

The churn dynamics result in quarter-over-quarter market share gains for AmeriCon and USAMobile at the expense of Horizon and TeleConnect:

- Horizon's share of the US market drops from 40% to 39.4%.
- TeleConnect's market share drops by more than two percentage points, from 35% to 32.9%.
- AmeriCon now owns 21.7% of the US market, versus just 20% from the previous period.
- USAMobile's share of the market increases from 5% to 6%.

Let's go step by step to demonstrate how the market share for one of these carriers, Horizon, changed between periods 0 and 1:

1 Horizon, which initially held 40% of the US cellular market, retains 85% of its customers. Consequently, Horizon's share of the market decreases to 34%,

which is the product of 0.40 × 0.85 when the decimal result is converted to a percentage.

2. Horizon acquired a small percentage of customers from each of the other carriers, including 8% from TeleConnect. Given that TeleConnect held 35% of the US market, this translates to 0.35 × 0.08 = 0.028, or 2.8% of additional market share.
3. Horizon also attracted 10% of AmeriCon's 20% market share, which translates to 0.20 × 0.10 = 0.02, or an additional 2% market share.
4. Horizon acquired 12% of USAMobile's 5% share of the market, which translates to 0.05 × 0.12 = .06, or 0.6% of new market share.

Horizon's new share of the US cellular market is derived by adding these four products together: 34% + 2.8% + 2% + 0.6% = 39.4%.

We could repeat these steps for the remaining three carriers, and as long as the system remains intact—without mergers, acquisitions, new entrants into the marketplace, and with constant probabilities for changing states—we could predict the market share distribution two quarters or even two years into the future. However, there are more efficient ways of applying Markov analysis to make these predictions.

11.2.2 *Matrix of transition probabilities*

The *matrix of transition probabilities* is a square matrix used in Markov analysis to describe the probabilities of transitioning from one state to another within a system over a specified period. Each element in the matrix represents the probability of moving from a specific initial state to a specific subsequent state. More precisely, it is a matrix of *conditional* probabilities, as the future state depends on the current state, so that

$$P_{ij} = \text{conditional probability of being in future state } j \text{ given current state } i$$

The matrix of transition probabilities is a fundamental component in Markov analysis, representing the likelihood of transitioning between states in a given system over a specified period. The matrix is denoted as P and is structured as a square matrix, where each element P_{ij} indicates the probability of moving from state i to state j. For illustrative purposes, consider the following matrix of transition probabilities:

$$P = \begin{bmatrix} P_{11} & P_{12} & P_{13} & P_{1n} \\ P_{21} & P_{22} & P_{23} & P_{2n} \\ P_{31} & P_{32} & P_{33} & P_{3n} \\ P_{41} & P_{42} & P_{43} & P_{4n} \end{bmatrix}$$

For example, P_{13} represents the probability of transitioning from a current state of 1 to a future state of 3; or take P_{42}, which represents the probability of transitioning from state 4 to state 2.

Returning to the four US cellular providers, we established period-to-period probabilities for either staying with the current carrier or switching to a different carrier.

11.2 States and state probabilities

These probabilities are then incorporated into the following matrix of transition probabilities:

$$P = \begin{bmatrix} 0.85 & 0.06 & 0.07 & 0.02 \\ 0.08 & 0.80 & 0.10 & 0.02 \\ 0.10 & 0.10 & 0.75 & 0.05 \\ 0.12 & 0.10 & 0.08 & 0.70 \end{bmatrix}$$

The system under analysis is the US wireless market, where the states are defined as the four carriers that collectively hold 100% of the market share. In this system, Horizon represents state 1, TeleConnect is state 2, AmeriCon is state 3, and USAMobile is state 4. Thus, P_{13} represents the probability of transitioning from Horizon to AmeriCon, and P_{42} represents the probability of transitioning from USAMobile to TeleConnect. Overall, the entire matrix can be interpreted as follows:

- Row 1:
  - $P_{11} = 0.85$ = probability of being in state 1 given state 1 from the prior period
  - $P_{12} = 0.06$ = probability of being in state 2 given state 1 from the prior period
  - $P_{13} = 0.07$ = probability of being in state 3 given state 1 from the prior period
  - $P_{14} = 0.02$ = probability of being in state 4 given state 1 from the prior period
- Row 2:
  - $P_{21} = 0.08$ = probability of being in state 1 given state 2 from the prior period
  - $P_{22} = 0.80$ = probability of being in state 2 given state 2 from the prior period
  - $P_{23} = 0.10$ = probability of being in state 3 given state 2 from the prior period
  - $P_{24} = 0.02$ = probability of being in state 4 given state 2 from the prior period
- Row 3:
  - $P_{31} = 0.10$ = probability of being in state 1 given state 3 from the prior period
  - $P_{32} = 0.10$ = probability of being in state 2 given state 3 from the prior period
  - $P_{33} = 0.75$ = probability of being in state 3 given state 3 from the prior period
  - $P_{34} = 0.05$ = probability of being in state 4 given state 3 from the prior period
- Row 4:
  - $P_{41} = 0.12$ = probability of being in state 1 given state 4 from the prior period
  - $P_{42} = 0.10$ = probability of being in state 2 given state 4 from the prior period
  - $P_{43} = 0.08$ = probability of being in state 3 given state 4 from the prior period
  - $P_{44} = 0.70$ = probability of being in state 4 given state 4 from the prior period

The vector of state probabilities—that is, the respective market share for each carrier at period 0—combined with the matrix of transition probabilities allows us to predict future state probabilities. This allows us to model and forecast how market shares will evolve over subsequent periods based on the established probabilities of customers either staying with their current carrier or switching to a different one.

PREDICTING PERIOD 1 GIVEN PERIOD 0

The purpose of Markov analysis is to predict the future states of a system based on its current state and the probabilities of transitioning between states. In the context of the US cellular market, we can predict the distribution of market shares for the next period, such as period 1 or the start of the next quarter, given the market share at period 0. This prediction is achieved by multiplying the vector of state probabilities by the matrix of transition probabilities, which is mathematically expressed as follows:

$$\pi(1) = \pi(0)P$$

Thus, we can predict the respective market shares for Horizon, TeleConnect, AmeriCon, and USAMobile with the following matrix multiplication calculations:

$$= (0.40, 0.35, 0.20, 0.05) \begin{bmatrix} 0.85 & 0.06 & 0.07 & 0.02 \\ 0.08 & 0.80 & 0.10 & 0.02 \\ 0.10 & 0.10 & 0.75 & 0.05 \\ 0.12 & 0.10 & 0.08 & 0.70 \end{bmatrix}$$

$$= [(0.40)(0.85) + (0.35)(0.08) + (0.20)(0.10) + (0.05)(0.12),$$
$$(0.40)(0.06) + (0.35)(0.80) + (0.20)(0.10) + (0.05)(0.10),$$
$$(0.40)(0.07) + (0.35)(0.10) + (0.20)(0.75) + (0.05)(0.08),$$
$$(0.40)(0.02) + (0.35)(0.02) + (0.20)(0.05) + (0.05)(0.70)]$$
$$= (0.394, 0.329, 0.217, 0.06)$$

Matrix multiplication involves taking the dot product of each element in the initial vector with the corresponding row in the transition matrix. A *dot product* is an algebraic operation that takes two equal-length sequences of numbers and returns a single number, calculated as the sum of the products of corresponding elements. For example, to calculate the probability of being in the first state (Horizon) in the next period, we multiply each element in the initial vector by the corresponding element in the first column of the matrix and sum the results. The same process is repeated for the other states. This operation gives us a new vector that represents the predicted market shares for Horizon, TeleConnect, AmeriCon, and USAMobile in the next period.

PREDICTING PERIOD 2 GIVEN PERIOD 1

We have a new vector of state probabilities, but the matrix of transition probabilities remains the same. In fact, this matrix must remain constant for us to predict future states using Markov analysis. Given the new market shares, we can predict what the market share distribution will be in the next period by again multiplying the (new) vector of state probabilities by the matrix of transition probabilities. This iterative process allows us to forecast market dynamics over multiple periods accurately.

To predict period 2 from period 1, the following equation is used:

$$\pi(2) = \pi(1)P$$

11.2 States and state probabilities

This equation shows how we use the state probabilities from period 1 to project the market shares for period 2:

$$= (0.394, 0.329, 0.217, 0.06) \begin{bmatrix} 0.85 & 0.06 & 0.07 & 0.02 \\ 0.08 & 0.80 & 0.10 & 0.02 \\ 0.10 & 0.10 & 0.75 & 0.05 \\ 0.12 & 0.10 & 0.08 & 0.70 \end{bmatrix}$$

$$= [(0.394)(0.85) + (0.329)(0.08) + (0.217)(0.10) + (0.06)(0.12),$$
$$(0.394)(0.06) + (0.329)(0.80) + (0.217)(0.10) + (0.06)(0.10),$$
$$(0.394)(0.07) + (0.329)(0.10) + (0.217)(0.75) + (0.06)(0.08),$$
$$(0.394)(0.02) + (0.329)(0.02) + (0.217)(0.05) + (0.06)(0.70)]$$
$$= (0.39012, 0.31454, 0.22803, 0.06731)$$

We again observe a decline in market share for Horizon and TeleConnect, whereas AmeriCon and USAMobile experience increases. The magnitude of these losses and gains, however, is not as pronounced between periods 1 and 2 as it was between periods 0 and 1. This suggests that the market dynamics are stabilizing, with the initial significant shifts in market share giving way to more moderate changes in subsequent periods.

PREDICTING PERIOD 2 GIVEN PERIOD 0

Bypassing the need to predict period 1, it is possible to directly predict period 2 from period 0 using this equation:

$$\pi(2) = \pi(0)P^2$$

This method involves multiplying the original vector of state probabilities by the square of the transition probability matrix. The mathematical approach starts with squaring the transition probability matrix. This squared matrix encapsulates the probabilities of transitioning between states over two periods. Next, the initial vector of state probabilities is multiplied by P^2 to derive the state probabilities for period 2.

Multiplying a 4 × 4 matrix by itself is straightforward but messy and prone to errors when performed manually. To find each element in the resulting matrix, we take the dot product of the ith row of the first matrix with the jth column of the second matrix, like so:

- First row, first column:
  - $= (0.85)(0.85) + (0.06)(0.08) + (0.07)(0.10) + (0.02)(0.12)$
  - $= 0.7225 + 0.0048 + 0.0070 + 0.0024$
  - $= 0.7367$
- First row, second column:
  - $= (0.85)(0.06) + (0.06)(0.80) + (0.07)(0.10) + (0.02)(0.10)$
  - $= 0.0510 + 0.0480 + 0.0070 + 0.0020$
  - $= 0.1080$

- First row, third column:
  - $= (0.85)(0.07) + (0.06)(0.10) + (0.07)(0.75) + (0.02)(0.08)$
  - $= 0.0595 + 0.0060 + 0.0525 + 0.0016$
  - $= 0.1196$
- First row, fourth column:
  - $= (0.12)(0.02) + (0.10)(0.02) + (0.08)(0.05) + (0.70)(0.70)$
  - $= 0.0024 + 0.0020 + 0.0040 + 0.4900$
  - $= 0.4984$

Each of these 16 derived elements represents the probability of transitioning from one state to another over two periods and is placed in the corresponding position in the new matrix. Specifically, each element P_{ij}^2 is calculated as the sum of the products of the transition probabilities from state i to all intermediary states and from those intermediary states to state j. The placement of these elements follows a structured approach, moving from left to right within each row and from top to bottom through the rows. This ensures that the calculated probabilities are correctly aligned with their respective state transitions. The resulting matrix of transition probabilities at period 2, denoted as P^2, effectively captures the compounded effect of two transitions:

$$P = \begin{bmatrix} 0.7367 & 0.1080 & 0.1196 & 0.0357 \\ 0.1444 & 0.6568 & 0.1622 & 0.0366 \\ 0.1740 & 0.1660 & 0.5835 & 0.0765 \\ 0.2020 & 0.1652 & 0.1344 & 0.4984 \end{bmatrix}$$

We get the period 2 market share distribution by then multiplying P^2 by the original vector of state probabilities:

$$= (0.40, 0.35, 0.20, 0.05) \begin{bmatrix} 0.7367 & 0.1080 & 0.1196 & 0.0357 \\ 0.1444 & 0.6568 & 0.1622 & 0.0366 \\ 0.1740 & 0.1660 & 0.5835 & 0.0765 \\ 0.2020 & 0.1652 & 0.1344 & 0.4984 \end{bmatrix}$$

$= [(0.40)(0.7367) + (0.35)(0.1444) + (0.20)(0.1740) + (0.05)(0.2020),$
$(0.40)(0.1080) + (0.35)(0.6568) + (0.20)(0.1660) + (0.05)(0.1652),$
$0.40)(0.1196) + (0.35)(0.1622) + (0.20)(0.5835) + (0.05)(0.1344),$
$(0.40)(0.0357) + (0.35)(0.0366) + (0.20)(0.0765) + (0.05)(0.4984)$
$= (0.39012, 0.31454, 0.22803, 0.06731)]$

We have now demonstrated how to predict period 2 directly from period 0 using Markov analysis. By squaring the matrix of transition probabilities and then multiplying this new matrix by the original vector of state probabilities, we can effectively forecast future state distributions without needing to calculate intermediate periods. This method highlights the power and efficiency of Markov analysis in modeling complex systems and predicting their behavior over time. By using these techniques, we gain valuable insights into the dynamics of the system and can make more informed decisions based on these projections.

Having illustrated the manual process of predicting future states using Markov analysis, we next demonstrate how to make similar predictions programmatically. By utilizing Python and specifically the NumPy library to perform matrix mathematical operations automatically, we can efficiently apply Markov analysis to model and forecast state probabilities, further enhancing our ability to analyze complex systems with greater precision and speed.

MAKING FUTURE STATE PREDICTIONS PROGRAMMATICALLY

We now transition from the manual calculations of Markov analysis to a programmatic approach using Python. By utilizing the power of Python and the NumPy library, we can automate matrix mathematical operations to efficiently predict future state probabilities. This approach not only saves time but also ensures accuracy when dealing with complex systems and large data sets.

To illustrate this process, we will use the same US cellular market share data we worked with manually. By using Python and NumPy, we can seamlessly perform Markov analysis to predict changes in market share distribution over multiple periods.

We begin by defining the initial market shares for period 0 and the transition probability matrix. We then use the NumPy `dot()` method to calculate the market shares for period 1 by multiplying the initial state probabilities by the transition matrix. Next, we compute the market shares for period 2 in two ways: first by using the market shares from period 1, and second by directly multiplying the initial state probabilities by the squared transition matrix. This automated approach demonstrates the efficiency and precision of using Python for Markov analysis, allowing us to quickly and accurately predict future state probabilities.

First, we import the `numpy` library. Then we create a pair of `numpy` arrays: the vector of state probabilities representing the initial market shares for period 0, and the matrix of transition probabilities, which details the probabilities of transitioning from one state to another:

```
>>> import numpy as np

>>> pi_0 = np.array([0.40, 0.35, 0.20, 0.05])

>>> P = np.array([
>>>     [0.85, 0.06, 0.07, 0.02],
>>>     [0.08, 0.80, 0.10, 0.02],
>>>     [0.10, 0.10, 0.75, 0.05],
>>>     [0.12, 0.10, 0.08, 0.70]
>>> ])
```

The array assigned to `pi_0` is a list of initial market share values for the four states: Horizon, TeleConnect, AmeriCon, and USAMobile, respectively. The market shares are equivalent to probabilities, and the values in the array must always sum to exactly 1.

The array assigned to `P` is the transition probability matrix, which represents the probabilities of transitioning from one state to another. Each element P_{ij} indicates the probability of moving from state i to state j.

Our next snippet of code calculates the market shares for period 1 by performing a dot product between the vector of state probabilities (`pi_0`) and the transition probability matrix (`P`) and then prints the results:

```
>>> pi_1 = np.dot(pi_0, P)
>>> print('Market shares for period 1:')
>>> print(pi_1)
Market shares for period 1:
[0.394 0.329 0.217 0.06 ]
```

The `np.dot()` method takes the vector of state probabilities and the matrix of transition probabilities and computes the dot product between them. The result is a new vector, `pi_1`, which represents the market shares for period 1.

Now that we have calculated the market share distribution for period 1, we can proceed to predict the distribution for period 2. By making another call to the `np.dot()` method, we pass the newly obtained state probabilities from period 1 (`pi_1`) along with the transition probability matrix (`P`) to forecast the market shares for the next period:

```
>>> pi_2_from_1 = np.dot(pi_1, P)
>>> print('Market shares for period 2 given period 1:')
>>> print(pi_2_from_1)
Market shares for period 2 given period 1:
[0.39012 0.31454 0.22803 0.06731]
```

Finally, we predict the market shares for period 2 directly from period 0. This is done by first squaring the matrix of transition probabilities and then using the `np.dot()` method to multiply the squared matrix with the original vector of state probabilities. This approach allows us to bypass the intermediate step of calculating period 1 market shares:

```
>>> P2 = np.dot(P, P)
>>> print(P2)
[[0.7367 0.108  0.1196 0.0357]
 [0.1444 0.6568 0.1622 0.0366]
 [0.174  0.166  0.5835 0.0765]
 [0.202  0.1652 0.1344 0.4984]]

>>> pi_2_direct = np.dot(pi_0, P2)
>>> print('Market shares for period 2 given period 0:')
>>> print(pi_2_direct)
Market shares for period 2 given period 0:
[0.39012 0.31454 0.22803 0.06731]
```

The `np.dot()` method performs a dot product between two parameters. To obtain the square of the transition probability matrix `P` (resulting in `P2`), we pass `P` twice to `np.dot()`. Then we pass `P2` and the original vector of state probabilities (`pi_0`) to `np.dot()` to calculate the market shares for period 2 directly from period 0, thereby bypassing period 1. Clearly, applying Markov analysis programmatically to predict future states is significantly easier and more efficient than manually performing matrix mathematical operations.

Regardless of the method used, we observe that the rate of change in market share distribution diminished between periods 1 and 2 compared to the change from period 0 to period 1. This suggests that instead of USAMobile or AmeriCon becoming the market leader in the future, a state of equilibrium is eventually established, where subsequent changes in future states are so small as to be immaterial. Next, we will explore this phenomenon further.

11.3 Equilibrium conditions

Based on recent historical data, a classic automobile engine has a 90% probability of being in running condition during the current week if it was in the same condition the previous week, which means there is a 10% probability of the engine not running in the current week if it had been running the week prior. Conversely, if the engine was not running the previous week, there is a 20% probability that it will self-correct during the current week and therefore an 80% probability it will remain in that state for another week. Let state 1 represent the engine running and state 2 represent the engine not running. The probabilities of these two states must sum to exactly 1, as they are mutually exclusive and collectively exhaustive. These probabilities reflect the engine's behavior over time and are essential for constructing an accurate matrix of transition probabilities:

$$P = \begin{bmatrix} 0.90 & 0.10 \\ 0.20 & 0.80 \end{bmatrix}$$

where

- Row 1:
  - $P_{11} = 0.90$ = probability of being in state 1 given state 1 from the prior period
  - $P_{12} = 0.10$ = probability of being in state 2 given state 1 from the prior period
- Row 2:
  - $P_{21} = 0.20$ = probability of being in state 1 given state 2 from the prior period
  - $P_{22} = 0.80$ = probability of being in state 2 given state 2 from the prior period

To mathematically derive the probability of the engine being in state 1 over the next week, we multiply the vector of state probabilities by the matrix of transition probabilities:

$$\pi(1) = \pi(0)P$$
$$= (1, 0) \begin{bmatrix} 0.90 & 0.10 \\ 0.20 & 0.80 \end{bmatrix}$$
$$= [(1)(0.90) + (0)(0.20), (1)(0.10) + (0)(0.80)]$$
$$= (0.90, 0.10)$$

To predict states 1 and 2 for the week following, we multiply the new vector of state probabilities by the matrix of transition probabilities, which must remain constant:

$$\pi(2) = \pi(1)P$$
$$= (0.90, 0.10) \begin{bmatrix} 0.90 & 0.10 \\ 0.20 & 0.80 \end{bmatrix}$$
$$= [(0.90)(0.90) + (0.10)(0.20), (0.90)(0.10) + (0.10)(0.80)]$$
$$= (0.83, 0.17)$$

This means in two weeks' time (or two periods from now) there is an 83% probability of the engine running and a 17% probability of it not running. This does not necessarily mean that in six weeks or so the engine will be permanently out of commission. Systems typically stabilize and eventually settle into a steady state of mutually exclusive and collectively exhaustive probabilities.

This steady-state condition, also known as the *equilibrium distribution*, is a fundamental concept in Markov chains. A *Markov chain* is a stochastic process in which the probability of transitioning to a future state depends solely on the present state, not on the sequence of past states. In the case of the automobile engine, as the transition process repeats over time, the probabilities of being in each state will converge to a long-run equilibrium. This equilibrium, or steady-state distribution, represents the expected proportion of time the system will spend in each state over an extended period, providing valuable insights into the long-term behavior of the system.

11.3.1 Predicting equilibrium conditions programmatically

Mathematically, equilibrium conditions, sometimes referred to as *steady-state probabilities*, are achieved when the vector of state probabilities remains constant over time. This occurs because the transition probability matrix is already fixed, ensuring that the probabilities of transitioning from one state to another do not change. In a discrete-time Markov chain, this steady-state distribution describes the long-term proportion of time the system will spend in each state, regardless of its initial condition.

Using Python, we can iteratively compute these equilibrium conditions by repeatedly applying the transition probability matrix to the initial vector of state probabilities over multiple periods until the state probabilities stabilize. Unlike methods that rely on random sampling to approximate distributions, this approach directly

11.3 Equilibrium conditions

computes the steady-state probabilities using matrix operations. This allows us to efficiently analyze long-term system behavior and determine the steady-state distribution in a structured, deterministic manner.

The following snippet of Python code predicts the state probabilities over the next 20 periods, starting with an initial state vector and a transition probability matrix. This process involves repeatedly applying the transition matrix to the state vector and storing the results, ultimately allowing us to observe how the probabilities converge to their equilibrium values:

```
>>> pi_0 = np.array([1, 0])           # Creates an array that represents the
                                      # original vector of state probabilities
>>> P = np.array([
...     [0.90, 0.10],
...     [0.20, 0.80]                  # Creates an array that represents the
... ])                                # matrix of transition probabilities

>>> n_periods = 20                    # Sets the number of periods to predict
                                      # Initializes a list with the
                                      # vector of state probabilities
>>> state_probabilities = [pi_0]      # and stores it for each period

>>> for _ in range(n_periods):
...     pi_next = np.dot(state_probabilities[-1], P)
...     state_probabilities.append(pi_next)
                                      # Creates a loop over the specified
                                      # number of periods, calculates a dot
>>> for i, pi in enumerate(state_probabilities):   # product between the most recent
...     print(f'Period {i} = {pi}')                # state probabilities and the transition
                                                   # matrix, and then appends the results
Period 0 = [1 0]                                   # to the state_probabilities list
Period 1 = [0.9 0.1]
Period 2 = [0.83 0.17]
Period 3 = [0.781 0.219]              # Iterates over the same list
Period 4 = [0.7467 0.2533]            # and prints the state
Period 5 = [0.72269 0.27731]          # probabilities for each period
Period 6 = [0.705883 0.294117]
Period 7 = [0.6941181 0.3058819]
Period 8 = [0.68588267 0.31411733]
Period 9 = [0.68011787 0.31988213]
Period 10 = [0.67608251 0.32391749]
Period 11 = [0.67325776 0.32674224]
Period 12 = [0.67128043 0.32871957]
Period 13 = [0.6698963 0.3301037]
Period 14 = [0.66892741 0.33107259]
Period 15 = [0.66824919 0.33175081]
Period 16 = [0.66777443 0.33222557]
Period 17 = [0.6674421 0.3325579]
Period 18 = [0.66720947 0.33279053]
Period 19 = [0.66704663 0.33295337]
Period 20 = [0.66693264 0.33306736]
```

The results demonstrate how the probabilities of the engine being in a running condition (state 1) and not running (state 2) evolve over 20 periods. Starting with the engine fully in a running condition at period 0, the probabilities gradually shift until equilibrium conditions are achieved around period 10. At this point, the engine consistently has about a two-thirds probability of being in a running condition, or approximately 66.7%. This steady state continues with minimal fluctuations beyond period 10, indicating that the system has stabilized. This example highlights the effectiveness of Markov analysis in predicting long-term behavior and achieving equilibrium conditions within a system.

Perhaps even more fascinating is the observation that small adjustments in the matrix of transition probabilities can lead to significant changes in the steady-state probabilities. This sensitivity underscores the importance of accurately determining the transition probabilities, as even minor variations can dramatically alter the long-term behavior of the system.

To demonstrate this phenomenon, let's replace our original matrix of transition probabilities with the following matrix:

$$P = \begin{bmatrix} 0.80 & 0.20 \\ 0.10 & 0.90 \end{bmatrix}$$

This new matrix of transition probabilities shows a slight decrease in the probability of remaining in the same state and therefore an equal increase in the probability of transitioning to the other state compared to the original matrix.

We then run the same snippet of code, but with the new matrix of transition probabilities in lieu of the original matrix. Here are the results:

```
Period 0  = [1 0]
Period 1  = [0.8 0.2]
Period 2  = [0.66 0.34]
Period 3  = [0.562 0.438]
Period 4  = [0.4934 0.5066]
Period 5  = [0.44538 0.55462]
Period 6  = [0.411766 0.588234]
Period 7  = [0.3882362 0.6117638]
Period 8  = [0.37176534 0.62823466]
Period 9  = [0.36023574 0.63976426]
Period 10 = [0.35216502 0.64783498]
Period 11 = [0.34651551 0.65348449]
Period 12 = [0.34256086 0.65743914]
Period 13 = [0.3397926 0.6602074]
Period 14 = [0.33785482 0.66214518]
Period 15 = [0.33649837 0.66350163]
Period 16 = [0.33554886 0.66445114]
Period 17 = [0.3348842 0.6651158]
Period 18 = [0.33441894 0.66558106]
Period 19 = [0.33409326 0.66590674]
Period 20 = [0.33386528 0.66613472]
```

Comparing these results to the original results, we clearly see that small changes in the transition probabilities can lead to significant shifts in the steady-state probabilities.

With the new transition matrix, the steady-state probabilities drastically change, resulting in the engine having a higher likelihood of not running (approximately 67%) rather than running (approximately 33%) in the long term. This demonstrates the sensitivity of Markov analysis to the transition probabilities and highlights the importance of accurately estimating these probabilities to effectively predict the system's behavior. These observations on the sensitivity of transition probabilities naturally lead us to the concept of absorbing states and how their presence can further affect our analysis and predictions.

11.4 Absorbing states

In our previous analysis, we assumed that it is possible to transition from any state to any other state. However, this is not always the case. In some systems, certain states may act as end states: once such a state is entered, the system cannot transition to any other state. These are *absorbing states,* defined as states that, once reached, cannot be left. In other words, the probability of transitioning from an absorbing state to any other state is zero, and the probability of remaining in the absorbing state is one. Understanding absorbing states is crucial as they fundamentally alter the dynamics of a system and the way we predict future states.

Harmony Finance is a fictional bank that specializes in providing revolving credit to qualified customers. It issues credit cards to customers who meet specific eligibility criteria, allowing them to borrow money up to a set limit and repay it over time with interest. Most of Harmony Finance's customers manage their credit responsibly and pay off their balances in full every month. However, some customers become delinquent, meaning they miss their payment deadlines. Among these delinquent customers, a portion eventually have their accounts charged off, indicating that the bank considers the debt unlikely to be collected. Thus, an account can be (and must be) in only one of the following states in any given month:

- *State 1* (π_1)—The account is current, meaning there is no outstanding balance.
- *State 2* (π_2)—The account is charged off.
- *State 3* (π_3)—The account is in what's called early-stage delinquency, where two or three payments are due: the current payment plus one or two delinquent payments.
- *State 4* (π_4)—The account is in late-stage delinquency, where four to seven payments are due: the current payment plus three or more delinquent payments.

The first two states are absorbing states because it is impossible to transition from either of these states to any other state between consecutive months (or periods). Thus, the probability of an account being current this month and remaining in the same state next month is 100%, making the probability of it being in any other state zero. Similarly, if the account is charged off this month, it will remain in the charged-off state next month.

Based on trend analysis, Harmony Finance estimates that 80% of the accounts in early stage will become current by the next month, 10% will remain in early stage, and the remaining 10% will transition to late stage. It is impossible for an account to transition directly from early stage to charged-off status.

The analysis further estimates that 30% of the accounts now in late-stage delinquency will become current by the next month. Another 30% of these late-stage accounts are expected to transition back to early stage, and 30% will remain in late stage. Additionally, 10% of the late-stage accounts are projected to charge off.

Given the properties of absorbing states and the probabilities of transitioning between states, where possible, we can construct the following matrix of transition probabilities:

$$P = \begin{bmatrix} 1 & 0 & 0 & 0 \\ 0 & 1 & 0 & 0 \\ 0.80 & 0 & 0.10 & 0.10 \\ 0.30 & 0.10 & 0.30 & 0.30 \end{bmatrix}$$

where

- Row 1:
  - $P_{11} = 1$ = probability of being in state 1 given state 1 from the prior period
  - $P_{12} = 0$ = probability of being in state 2 given state 1 from the prior period
  - $P_{13} = 0$ = probability of being in state 3 given state 1 from the prior period
  - $P_{14} = 0$ = probability of being in state 4 given state 1 from the prior period
- Row 2:
  - $P_{21} = 0$ = probability of being in state 1 given state 2 from the prior period
  - $P_{22} = 1$ = probability of being in state 2 given state 2 from the prior period
  - $P_{23} = 0$ = probability of being in state 3 given state 2 from the prior period
  - $P_{24} = 0$ = probability of being in state 4 given state 2 from the prior period
- Row 3:
  - $P_{31} = 0.80$ = probability of being in state 1 given state 3 from the prior period
  - $P_{32} = 0$ = probability of being in state 2 given state 3 from the prior period
  - $P_{33} = 0.10$ = probability of being in state 3 given state 3 from the prior period
  - $P_{34} = 0.10$ = probability of being in state 4 given state 3 from the prior period
- Row 4:
  - $P_{41} = 0.30$ = probability of being in state 1 given state 4 from the prior period
  - $P_{42} = 0.10$ = probability of being in state 2 given state 4 from the prior period
  - $P_{43} = 0.30$ = probability of being in state 3 given state 4 from the prior period
  - $P_{44} = 0.30$ = probability of being in state 4 given state 4 from the prior period

This matrix of transition probabilities can be multiplied by a vector of state probabilities to predict the percentage of accounts across the four possible states for any given period.

Eventually, the system will achieve a steady state where all accounts settle into one of two absorbing states: either current or charged off. It is critical for Harmony Finance to project the breakdown between these two absorbing states to effectively manage risk, allocate resources, and strategize for future financial stability. Such analysis requires the use of what is called a *fundamental matrix*.

11.4.1 Obtaining the fundamental matrix

Obtaining the fundamental matrix is a three-step process, and the mathematical complexity increases with each subsequent step. First, we partition the matrix of transition probabilities by extracting each quadrant of probabilities into its own matrix, like so:

$$I = \begin{bmatrix} 1 & 0 \\ 0 & 1 \end{bmatrix}$$

$$0 = \begin{bmatrix} 0 & 0 \\ 0 & 0 \end{bmatrix}$$

$$A = \begin{bmatrix} 0.80 & 0 \\ 0.30 & 0.10 \end{bmatrix}$$

$$B = \begin{bmatrix} 0.10 & 0.10 \\ 0.30 & 0.30 \end{bmatrix}$$

where

- I = an identify matrix with diagonal 1s and 0s.
- 0 = a matrix with just 0s.

The fundamental matrix (F) is obtained by taking the inverse of the difference between matrix B and matrix I; it is expressed by the following mathematical equation:

$$F = (I - B)^{-1}$$

We are therefore subtracting matrix B from matrix I as the second step. The superscript -1 indicates that we then take the inverse of the difference to obtain F so that

$$F = (I - B)^{-1}$$

or

$$F = \left(\begin{bmatrix} 1 & 0 \\ 0 & 1 \end{bmatrix} - \begin{bmatrix} 0.10 & 0.10 \\ 0.30 & 0.30 \end{bmatrix} \right)^{-1}$$

Subtracting matrix B from matrix I returns the following:

$$F = \begin{bmatrix} 0.90 & -0.10 \\ -0.30 & 0.70 \end{bmatrix}^{-1}$$

This is derived by subtracting each corresponding element of matrix B from matrix I:

$$I - B = \begin{bmatrix} 1 - 0.10 & 0 - 0.10 \\ 0 - 0.30 & 1 - 0.30 \end{bmatrix}$$

The third and final step is to get the inverse of this matrix. Fortunately, computing the inverse of a 2×2 matrix is relatively straightforward. However, the complexity increases exponentially as the number of rows and columns grows.

Generalizing the difference between matrix B and matrix I results in the following matrix:

$$\begin{bmatrix} a & b \\ c & d \end{bmatrix}$$

The inverse of this equals

$$\begin{bmatrix} a & b \\ c & d \end{bmatrix}^{-1}$$

or

$$\begin{bmatrix} d/r & -b/r \\ -c/r & a/r \end{bmatrix}$$

where $r = ad - bc$. Thus, we get r by subtracting the product of -0.10 and -0.30 from the product of 0.90 and 0.70. Therefore, $r = 0.63 - 0.03 = 0.60$.

The resulting matrix is derived by plugging in 0.60 for r and performing simple division:

$$F = \begin{bmatrix} 0.90 & -0.10 \\ -0.30 & 0.70 \end{bmatrix}^{-1}$$

or

$$F = \begin{bmatrix} 0.70/0.60 & -(-0.10)/0.60 \\ -(-0.30)/0.60 & 0.90/0.60 \end{bmatrix}$$

or

$$F = \begin{bmatrix} 1.167 & 0.167 \\ 0.500 & 1.500 \end{bmatrix}$$

From the fundamental matrix, Harmony Finance can accurately project the percentage of accounts that will ultimately settle into a current state and the percentage that will absorb into a charged-off state. This analysis allows Harmony Finance to forecast the long-term behavior of its accounts and make informed decisions based on the predicted distribution of account statuses.

11.4.2 Predicting absorbing states

The first step in making predictions is to multiply the fundamental matrix by matrix A:

$$FA = \begin{bmatrix} 1.167 & 0.167 \\ 0.500 & 1.500 \end{bmatrix} \times \begin{bmatrix} 0.80 & 0 \\ 0.30 & 0.10 \end{bmatrix}$$

or

$$FA = \begin{bmatrix} 0.9837 & 0.0167 \\ 0.8500 & 0.1500 \end{bmatrix}$$

This is derived by following matrix multiplication rules, so that

$$FA = \begin{bmatrix} (1.167)(0.80) + (0.167)(0.30) & (1.167)(0) + (0.167)(0.10) \\ (0.500)(0.80) + (1.500)(0.30) & (0.500)(0) + (1.500)(0.10) \end{bmatrix}$$

where

- $FA_{11} = (1.167)(0.80) + (0.167)(0.30) = 0.9336 + 0.0501 = 0.9837$
- $FA_{12} = (1.167)(0) + (0.167)(0.10) = 0 + 0.0167 = 0.0167$
- $FA_{13} = (0.500)(0.80) + (1.500)(0.30) = 0.400 + 0.450 = 0.8500$
- $FA_{14} = (0.500)(0) + (1.500)(0.10) = 0 + 0.150 = 0.1500$

Due to rounding errors, the elements in the top row of the matrix sum to 1.004 instead of 1. To correct this, we apply a manual adjustment by subtracting 0.004 from 0.9837, resulting in the following matrix:

$$FA = \begin{bmatrix} 0.9833 & 0.0167 \\ 0.8500 & 0.1500 \end{bmatrix}$$

Matrix FA indicates the probability of an account in one of the two non-absorbing states transitioning to one of the two absorbing states. More precisely, the figures in the top row indicate the probability of an account in early-stage delinquency transitioning to current (98.3%) or charging off (approximately 1.7%); the figures in the bottom row indicate the probability of a late-stage account transitioning to current (85%) versus charging off (15%), which underscores the criticality of Harmony

Finance collecting on accounts in early stage before they advance into late-stage delinquency.

11.4.3 Predicting absorbing states programmatically

Predicting absorbing states manually is a straightforward process, but it involves multiple steps that can be prone to human error. Despite its simplicity, the manual method requires careful attention to detail, which increases the risk of inaccuracies. Fortunately, we can achieve the same results more efficiently and accurately by using Python and specifically NumPy. With just a few lines of code, we can automate the calculations, thereby minimizing errors and saving time.

Most of the code should be familiar to you by now:

```
>>> P = np.array([
>>>     [1, 0, 0, 0],
>>>     [0, 1, 0, 0],
>>>     [0.80, 0, 0.10, 0.10],
>>>     [0.30, 0.10, 0.30, 0.30]
>>> ])
```
Creates an array that represents the matrix of transition probabilities

```
>>> I = np.array([
>>>     [1, 0],
>>>     [0, 1]
>>> ])
```
Creates an array that is the first submatrix of the transition probabilities matrix

```
>>> A = np.array([
>>>     [0.80, 0],
>>>     [0.30, 0.10]
>>> ])
```
Creates an array that is the second submatrix of the transition probabilities matrix

```
>>> B = np.array([
>>>     [0.10, 0.10],
>>>     [0.30, 0.30]
>>> ])
```
Creates an array that is the third submatrix of the transition probabilities matrix

```
>>> I_minus_B = I - B
>>> F = np.linalg.inv(I_minus_B)
```
Performs element-wise subtraction of matrix B from matrix I
Calculates the inverse of the matrix I_minus_B and assigns it to the variable F

```
>>> FA = np.dot(F, A)

>>> print('The final matrix FA is:')
>>> print(FA)

The final matrix FA is:
[[0.98333333 0.01666667]
 [0.85       0.15      ]]
```
Performs matrix multiplication between the fundamental matrix F and the matrix A, and assigns the resulting matrix to FA
Prints a descriptive message followed by the contents of the matrix FA

The preceding code defines the matrix of transition probabilities P; partitions it into three submatrices denoted I, A, and B; computes the fundamental matrix $F = (I - B)^{-1}$; and then multiplies F by A to get the final matrix FA. The resulting matrix FA is then printed, representing the probabilities of transitioning from non-absorbing states to absorbing states.

Markov analysis provides a powerful framework for predicting future states of a system based on current conditions and transition probabilities. By understanding and applying Markov techniques, we can model complex systems, forecast outcomes, and make informed decisions in various fields such as finance, market analysis, and operations. The ability to predict equilibrium conditions and identify absorbing states further enhances our strategic planning and resource allocation. Mastering these techniques equips us with essential tools to navigate uncertainty and optimize performance in dynamic environments. In the next chapter, we will demonstrate how to examine and test naturally occurring number sequences, which is crucial for identifying patterns and anomalies in data.

Summary

- Markov analysis is a statistical method used to predict the future states of a system based on its current state and the probabilities of transitioning from one state to another. It relies on the assumption that the future state depends only on the present state and not on the sequence of events that preceded it.
- The vector of state probabilities represents the probabilities of a system being in each possible state at a given period. It is used to describe the distribution of states in the system and is essential for predicting future states using Markov analysis.
- The matrix of transition probabilities is a square matrix where each element represents the probability of transitioning from one state to another in a given period. This matrix is fundamental in Markov analysis for determining the likelihood of moving between states and predicting future state distributions.
- To predict future states in Markov analysis, the vector of state probabilities and the transition probability matrix are used together through the mathematical operation known as the dot product. The vector of state probabilities represents the current distribution of the system across various states. By taking the dot product of this vector with the transition probability matrix, which contains the probabilities of moving from one state to another, we can calculate the vector of state probabilities for the next period. Repeatedly applying the dot product operation allows us to forecast the system's state distribution over multiple future periods, effectively predicting how the system will evolve over time.
- In Markov analysis, equilibrium conditions refer to a state where the system's probabilities stabilize and no longer change significantly over time. At equilibrium, the vector of state probabilities remains constant from one period to the next, indicating that the system has reached a steady state where the transitions between states balance out.
- Absorbing states are states that, once entered, cannot be left. When a system reaches an absorbing state, it remains in that state permanently. These states have a transition probability of 1 for remaining in the same state and 0 for transitioning to any other state.

- Markov analysis has diverse real-world applications across industries. It is used in finance for credit risk modeling and stock market analysis, healthcare for patient progression modeling, operations management for equipment maintenance and reliability analysis, and cybersecurity for detecting anomalous network behavior and predicting potential security threats. By applying Markov analysis to these domains, businesses and researchers can make data-driven decisions and optimize long-term outcomes.

Examining and testing naturally occurring number sequences

This chapter covers
- Benford's law and naturally occurring number sequences
- Chi-square goodness of fit test
- Mean absolute deviation
- The distortion factor and the z-statistic
- Mantissa statistics

Numeric data sets that follow a Benford distribution exhibit a much higher frequency of smaller leading digits than larger leading digits. The phenomenon is mostly prevalent in numeric data that spans several orders of magnitude and is therefore best represented on a logarithmic, rather than linear, scale.

Fraudsters often make the mistake of transmuting leading 1s and 2s to 8s and 9s on invoices, expenses, tax returns, and the like to maximize gains against their risks, on the assumption that, regardless of the data set, 8s and 9s are just as probable as 1s and 2s or that, when randomness prevails, larger digits should sometimes be expected to actually occur more frequently than smaller digits. In fact, Benford's law is most often used in fraud detection; serious deviations from a Benford distribution may be an indication of fraudulent activity and therefore the reason for further investigation. But there are other applications as well: data integrity, economic data analysis, scientific research, digital forensics, and population studies, just to name a few, which is to say state that Benford's law is a valuable tool for uncovering potential anomalies in numeric data sets across several domains.

Not unlike regression analysis and other techniques, Benford's law provides a powerful method for detecting patterns in data that might not be immediately obvious. It offers a data-driven approach to decision-making by identifying irregularities that standard statistical methods may overlook. By integrating probability-based methods and statistical validation, Benford's law complements the other quantitative techniques explored in this book, reinforcing the broader theme of using mathematical principles to analyze and interpret real-world data.

After getting you thoroughly grounded in all things Benford's law, we'll discuss where it best applies and where it absolutely does not; we'll draw a perfect Benford distribution and then compare it to uniform and random distributions that are commonly observed in data sets to which Benford's law does not apply; we'll then evaluate Benford's law on a trio of real-world data sets that should follow a Benford, or logarithmic, distribution; and finally, we'll run a series of statistical tests against one of our three data sets to measure how well, or not so well, the data conforms to a Benford distribution. Numeric data sets that should conform to Benford's law but don't *might* be an indication of fraudulent or other suspicious activity. By the end of this chapter, you should have a solid theoretical and practical understanding of Benford's law; you will know a Benford distribution by sight and have the ability to readily compare and contrast it against other probability distributions; and you will learn how to apply several statistical tests against numeric data to precisely determine whether numeric data truly obeys Benford's law. Let's get started with a methodical explanation of Benford's law and a brief discussion of where Benford's law is most prevalent.

12.1 Benford's law explained

According to Benford's law, which is sometimes referred to as the *first-digit law*, many sets of numeric data do not inherently follow a uniform or random distribution, as we might expect. (A uniform distribution is a probability distribution in which all outcomes are equally likely; a random distribution, on the other hand, is a probability distribution where the outcomes are not deterministic.) Instead, says Benford's law, smaller leading digits (1, 2, 3) occur much more frequently than larger leading digits (7, 8, 9). In data sets that follow Benford's law, the numeral 1 is the leading digit in approximately 30% of the observations, and the numeral 9 is the leading digit in fewer than 5% of the observations. (Zeros are never leading digits, so they are excluded from Benford's law; and in any event, zeros don't naturally fit into a logarithmic distribution, which is the very essence of Benford's law.)

12.1 Benford's law explained

In addition to being known as the first-digit law, Benford's law is sometimes referred to as the *Newcomb–Benford law*. That's because a mathematician named Simon Newcomb first discovered the phenomenon in 1881. Frank Benford, a physicist, shed light on it in 1938.

A set of numeric data is said to follow Benford's law when the leading digit, usually denoted as *d*, occurs with a probability in accordance with the following equation:

$$P(d) = \log 10(d+1) - \log 10(d) = \log 10\left(\frac{d+1}{d}\right) = \log 10\left(1 + \frac{1}{d}\right)$$

Let's do the math by substituting the digits 1 through 9 for *d* and then plot the distribution in a Matplotlib bar line chart. But first, we import the pandas library and create a data frame called df1; for the moment, df1 contains just a single variable, d, which is merely a list of integers between 1 (inclusive) and 10 (exclusive). The pd.DataFrame() method creates the data frame, d is the name of the lone variable, and the list() method generates a list of integers from 1 through 9 (inclusive):

```
>>> import pandas as pd
>>> df1 = pd.DataFrame({'d': list(range(1, 10))})
>>> print(df1)
   d
0  1
1  2
2  3
3  4
4  5
5  6
6  7
7  8
8  9
```

Next we call the assign() method to create a derived variable called benford, which equals the base-10 logarithm of 1 plus the quotient between 1 and the original df1 variable d, rounded to three decimal places. We're replicating the Benford probability equation with a line of Python code and plugging in the digits 1 through 9 in place of *d*. This sort of mathematical operation first requires that we import the NumPy library. The assign() method creates the new variable called benford and assigns it to the df1 data frame. The round() method rounds each result to three decimal places (although it could be any whole number we choose to pass):

```
>>> import numpy as np
>>> df1 = df1.assign(benford = round(np.log10(1 + (1 / df1.d)), 3))
>>> print(df1)
   d  benford
0  1    0.301
1  2    0.176
2  3    0.125
3  4    0.097
```

```
4   5    0.079
5   6    0.067
6   7    0.058
7   8    0.051
8   9    0.046
```

Now we have a data source for our bar line chart. Note that we must first import the `matplotlib` library before executing any of the code that follows:

```
>>> import matplotlib.pyplot as plt          ◁─ Imports the matplotlib library
>>> plt.bar(df1['d'], df1['benford'], color = 'dodgerblue',
>>>         edgecolor = 'dodgerblue')
>>> plt.plot(df1['d'], df1['benford'],
>>>          'r-o', linewidth = 1.5)
>>> for i, benford_value in enumerate(df1['benford']):
>>>     plt.text(i + 1, benford_value, f'{benford_value * 100:.2f}%',
>>>              ha = 'center', va = 'bottom',
>>>              fontweight = 'bold',
>>>              color = 'black')
>>> plt.title('Perfect Benford distribution',
>>>           fontweight = 'bold')    ◁─ Sets the title
>>> plt.xlabel('First Digit')                ◁─ Sets the x-axis label
>>> plt.ylabel('Distribution Percentage')                ◁─ Sets the y-axis label
>>> plt.xticks(range(1, 9))
>>> plt.gca().yaxis.set_major_formatter(
>>>     plt.FuncFormatter(lambda x, _: f'{x * 100:.0f}%')
>>> )
>>> plt.show()        ◁─ Displays the plot
```

- Creates a bar chart with a custom color scheme and assigns the x-axis and y-axis variables
- Draws a red solid line 15 times the default width over the bars, with circular markers
- Iterates over the benford values in df1, placing a bold black text label atop each bar that shows the value as a percentage with two decimal places
- Sets the range of the x-axis tick marks from 1 to 9
- Formats the y-axis labels as percentages (e.g., 30%)

Figure 12.1 shows what a perfect Benford distribution looks like. It may go without saying, but the probabilities should sum to exactly 1. We can verify this by passing the `df1` variable `benford` to the `sum()` method, like so:

```
>>> print(sum(df1.benford))
1.0
```

Furthermore, the values in the `benford` variable are proportional to the space between d and $d + 1$ on a logarithmic scale. Just as the numerals 1 and 2 and 2 and 3, for instance, are equally spaced on a linear scale, the numerals 10 and 100 and 100 and 1,000 are equally spaced on a logarithmic scale. Whereas linear scales have equal intervals and a constant difference between values, logarithmic scales have unequal intervals due to a constant ratio or multiplication factor between values. This property is important to understand because it highlights the usefulness of logarithmic scales in representing data that spans several orders of magnitude. In many real-world scenarios, data can sometimes vary widely in magnitude; thus, using a logarithmic scale allows for a more compact representation that better captures and shows this variation. And because Benford's law applies only to data distributed across several orders of magnitude, a logarithmic scale must prevail.

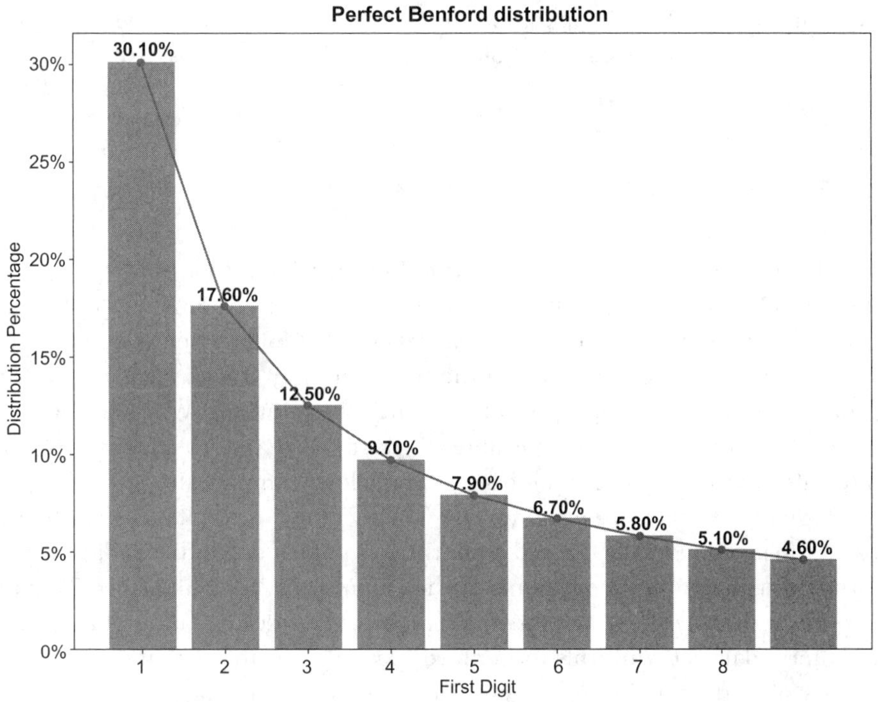

Perfect Benford distribution

Figure 12.1 A numeric data series perfectly follows a Benford distribution when the leading digits, plotted along the x axis, each have a likelihood of occurrence equal to the probability plotted along the y axis. So, for instance, the numeral 1 should be the leading, or first, digit in approximately 30% of the observations, and the numeral 9 should be the leading digit in fewer than 5% of the observations.

Consider once more that the probability of a leading digit d. $P(d)$ is expressed by the following formula:

$$P(d) = \log 10 \left(1 + \frac{1}{d}\right)$$

And let's further consider a pair of leading digits, 1 and 9, which means

$$P(1) = \log 10 \left(1 + \frac{1}{1}\right) = \log 10(2)$$

and

$$P(9) = \log 10 \left(1 + \frac{1}{9}\right) = \log 10(1.11)$$

Thus, the probability of the numeral 1 being the leading digit equals 0.301, whereas the probability of the numeral 9 being the leading digit equals 0.046. Here's how to perform these arithmetic operations in Python. The `np.log()` method calculates the base-10 logarithm of whatever whole or fractional number is passed to it:

```
>>> print(round(np.log10(2), 3))
0.301

>>> print(round(np.log10(1.1111111), 3))
0.046
```

We already know these results, of course. But there's another point to be made here: these results (0.301 and 0.046, respectively) represent not only the probabilities of 1 and 9 being leading digits in a numeric data set that follows Benford's law but also the space, or interval, from 1 and 9 to the next values on a logarithmic scale. Thus, the probabilities are exactly proportional to the interval width. We can infer, then, that the probabilities of leading digits under Benford's law are directly proportional to the intervals between successive powers of 10 on a logarithmic scale.

Perhaps even more interesting, and equally noncoincidental, is that the fractional part of logarithmic data, derived from the raw data and not the leading digits, is uniformly distributed between 0 and 1 when Benford's law is in effect. This property, known as the *uniform distribution of mantissas*, provides an additional way to assess whether a data set conforms to Benford's law. Rather than relying solely on the frequency of leading digits, we can evaluate how closely the mantissa values align with a uniform distribution, offering a statistical check on the data's adherence to a logarithmic pattern. Although measures like the mean and variance of the mantissa values can offer insights, it is their overall distribution that serves as a key indicator of Benford conformity. This approach allows for a more refined test of whether a data set truly follows Benford's law, beyond just comparing leading-digit frequencies. We'll explore this later when we examine the mantissa statistics.

12.2 Naturally occurring number sequences

It's frequently stated that Benford's law applies only to naturally occurring number sequences, which is somewhat nebulous. More precisely, Benford's law most accurately applies to numeric data when the following four conditions are met:

1. The data is distributed across multiple orders of magnitude. An *order of magnitude* is a measure of the scale, or size, of a value, most often expressed as a power of 10. So, for instance, when a value is 1 order of magnitude greater than another value from the same data series, it is approximately 10 times greater.
2. The data does not have any preestablished minimum or maximum. Although every finite data set technically has a minimum and a maximum, Benford's law is more likely to apply when these boundaries are not arbitrarily imposed. If the limits are naturally occurring rather than artificially constrained—such as physical measurement limits or policy-imposed caps—the data is more likely to exhibit Benford-like behavior.

3 The data does not consist of numerals used as identifiers. This includes Social Security numbers, bank account numbers, invoice numbers, telephone numbers, and employee numbers, just to name a few. These values are typically assigned systematically or sequentially rather than being the result of natural random processes. Because they do not arise from organic distributions or naturally varying magnitudes, they do not exhibit the logarithmic patterns required for Benford's law to apply.

4 The data has a mean that is greater—sometimes significantly greater—than the median. This means the data is right-skewed, or positively skewed; when plotted, most of the data is therefore on the left with a long thin tail extending to the right. This type of distribution often exhibits high kurtosis, indicating that the data has more extreme values or outliers than a normal distribution, further reinforcing the applicability of Benford's law.

Thus, Benford's law applies, for instance, to street addresses, lengths of rivers and other waterways, population counts, baseball statistics, sales figures, utility bills, electronic file sizes, and stock prices. It doesn't apply, just to give a few additional examples, to calendar dates, zip codes, or IQ scores.

12.3 Uniform and random distributions

Our purpose here is to plot uniform and random distributions for comparison purposes against a perfect Benford distribution. We sometimes assume, perhaps naively, that numeric data follows one of these two distributions when, in fact, Benford's law actually prevails if certain conditions are held to be true. We'll demonstrate how to generate uniform and random distributions by calling a pair of NumPy functions, create a pair of Matplotlib bar charts, and then print both plots as a single figure.

Comparing a Benford distribution to uniform and random distributions helps highlight the distinctive patterns and characteristics between each distribution type. More specifically, it highlights how the frequency of leading digits varies across data sets that obey Benford's law (where smaller digits are more frequent than larger digits) versus uniform distributions (where all digits occur with roughly equal probability) and random distributions (where digits occur with equal probability but without any specific pattern).

12.3.1 Uniform distribution

We need a data frame with two vectors. Our data frame, `df2`, first contains a variable called `row_number`, which is a list of integers between 1 (inclusive) and 1,001 (exclusive):

```
>>> df2 = pd.DataFrame({'row_number': list(range(1, 1001))})
```

Then we make a call to the `assign()` method to create a second `df2` vector, `uniform_distribution`. The `np.random.randint()` method generates 1,000 random integers between 1 (inclusive) and 10 (exclusive) and stores the results in uniform_distribution:

```
>>> df2 = df2.assign(uniform_distribution =
>>>                  np.random.randint(1, 10, size = 1000))
```

The head() and tail() methods return the first three and last three df2 observations:

```
>>> print(df2.head(n = 3))
   row_number  uniform_distribution
0           1                     4
1           2                     6
2           3                     5
>>> print(df2.tail(n = 3))
     row_number  uniform_distribution
997         998                     6
998         999                     1
999        1000                     1
```

You won't get these same results. That's because np.random.randint() returns an array of *random* integers. Although every value assigned to uniform_distribution will always equal some integer between 1 (inclusive) and 10 (exclusive), results will vary with every run; otherwise, it wouldn't be random.

Next we group df2 by the values in uniform_distribution, count the number of occurrences for each unique value, assign the results to a variable called count, and create a new data frame called results1. The groupby() method groups df2 by the unique values in the variable uniform_distribution; size() counts the number of occurrences for each unique value; and reset_index() stores the outputs from size() in a new column, or variable, called count. After all that, we get a new data frame called results1 that contains nine rows and a pair of columns called uniform_distribution and count:

```
>>> results1 = df2.groupby('uniform_distribution') \
>>>     .size() \
>>>     .reset_index(name = 'count')
>>> print(results1)
   uniform_distribution  count
0                     1    109
1                     2    116
2                     3    110
3                     4    110
4                     5    101
5                     6    112
6                     7    130
7                     8    104
8                     9    108
```

We'll temporarily hold these results in reserve until we've also generated a random distribution.

12.3.2 Random distribution

Once more we'll create a data frame, df3 this time, comprising two vectors. We'll recycle the row_number variable from the df2 data frame and assign it as the first df3 variable: df2[['row_number']] takes row_number from df2, and the copy() method makes a deep copy of it. By making a deep copy, we can make future modifications to df3 as necessary without affecting df2:

```
>>> df3 = df2[['row_number']].copy()
```

Next we'll create a second variable, random_distribution, and assign it to df3. The assign() method assigns random_distribution to df3, np.arrange() generates an array of integers between 1 (inclusive) and 10 (exclusive), and np.random_choice() randomly selects 1,000 values from this array, with replacement:

```
>>> df3 = df3.assign(random_distribution =
>>>             np.random.choice(np.arange(1, 10), size = 1000))
```

Sequential calls to the head() and tail() methods return the first three and last three df3 observations. Your results will differ:

```
>>> print(df3.head(n = 3))
   row_number  random_distribution
0           1                    3
1           2                    5
2           3                    1
>>> print(df3.tail(n = 3))
     row_number  random_distribution
997         998                    3
998         999                    3
999        1000                    7
```

Finally, we group df3 by the unique values in random_distribution, count the number of occurrences for each, store the results in a variable called count, and assign the results to a new data frame called results2. This is essentially the same snippet of code we first used to create results1; we've just swapped out parameters:

```
>>> results2 = (df3.groupby('random_distribution') \
>>>             .size() \
>>>             .reset_index(name = 'count'))
>>> print(results2)
   random_distribution  count
0                    1    105
1                    2    136
2                    3    118
3                    4    118
4                    5    111
5                    6    105
6                    7    106
7                    8     94
8                    9    107
```

Next, we'll pass `results1` and `results2` into separate snippets of Matplotlib code and create a pair of bar charts combined into a single figure.

12.3.3 Plotted distributions

We start by creating a single figure with two subplots, the first (`ax1`) on top of the second (`ax2`). So, our figure will have dimensions equal to two rows and one column:

```
>>> fig, (ax1, ax2) = plt.subplots(nrows = 2, ncols = 1)
```

Here are the snippets of code for our two Matplotlib bar charts. Most of this should be familiar by now:

Iterates over the count values in results1, placing a bold black text label atop each bar showing each value at the corresponding position on the x axis

Creates the first bar chart with a custom color scheme, and assigns the x-axis and y-axis variables

```
>>> ax1.bar(results1['uniform_distribution'], results1['count'],
>>>         color = 'steelblue',
>>>         edgecolor = 'steelblue')
>>> for i, n in enumerate(results1['count']):
>>>     ax1.text(results1['uniform_distribution'][i], n, str(n),
>>>             ha = 'center', va = 'bottom',
>>>             fontweight = 'bold',
>>>             color = 'black')
>>> ax1.set_title('Uniform distribution\nn = 1,000',
>>>.              fontweight = 'bold')
>>> ax1.set_xlabel('First Digit')
>>> ax1.set_ylabel('Count')
>>> ax1.set_xticks(range(1, 10))
>>> ax2.bar(results2['random_distribution'], results2['count'],
>>>         color = 'steelblue',
>>>         edgecolor = 'steelblue')
>>> for i, n in enumerate(results2['count']):
>>>     ax2.text(results2['random_distribution'][i], n, str(n),
>>>             ha = 'center', va = 'bottom',
>>>             fontweight = 'bold',
>>>             color = 'black')
>>> ax2.set_title('Random distribution\nn = 1,000',
>>>               fontweight = 'bold')
>>> ax2.set_xlabel('First Digit')
>>> ax2.set_ylabel('Count')
>>> ax2.set_xticks(range(1, 10))
>>> plt.tight_layout()
>>> plt.show()
```

Sets the title. Also, \n represents the newline character and therefore triggers a carriage return.

Sets the y-axis label

Sets the x-axis label

Sets the range of the x-axis tick marks from 1 to 9

Creates the second bar chart with a custom color scheme, and assigns the x-axis and y-axis variables

Iterates over the count values in results1, placing a bold black text label atop each bar showing each value at the corresponding position on the x axis

Sets the title

Sets the x-axis label

Sets the y-axis label

Sets the range of the x-axis tick marks from 1 to 9

Creates separation between the plots to prevent overlapping titles and labels

Displays both plots as a single figure

Finally, figure 12.2 shows the results. When a numeric data series is uniformly distributed, or supposed to be, each unique value has an equal probability of occurrence. With 9 unique values and 1,000 records, we might expect `np.random.randint()` to return 111 occurrences for each value, which, of course, it failed to do. But probabilities don't always translate to results, especially at lower record counts. Flipping a coin 10 times might return heads 8 times and tails just 2 times. That's not because the coin isn't fair; it's because we can sometimes get anomalous or less-than-perfect results when the record counts are low or the number of events is low. Had we instead passed, let's say, 10,000 records to the `np.random.randint()` method instead of just 1,000, no doubt these figures would have converged toward a perfect uniform distribution. But the larger point to be made is that a uniform distribution is very different from a Benford distribution. Even a distribution that is less than perfectly flat would not resemble a Benford distribution that is right-skewed or positively skewed.

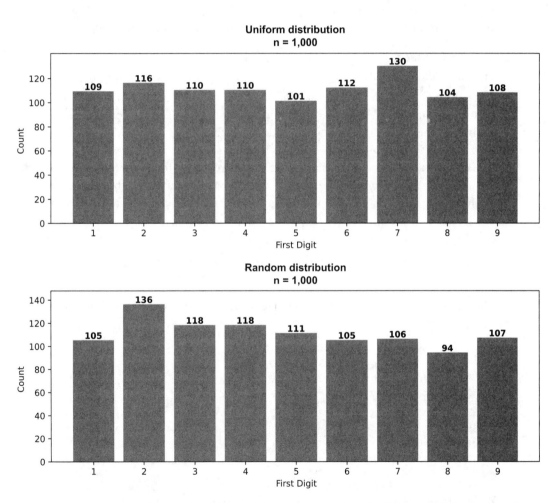

Figure 12.2 A uniform distribution of 1,000 records on top and a random distribution of 1,000 records on the bottom. Many numeric data sets take on one of these two probability distributions. In a Benford distribution, 1s, 2s, and 3s represent more than 60% of the occurrences, but in both these distributions, those digits represent barely 30% of the occurrences.

The same can be said for a random distribution. A Benford distribution, of course, has an obvious pattern; any random distribution, on the other hand, even with 1,000 records or much fewer, will almost always appear indiscriminate, which suggests the impossibility of mistaking a Benford distribution for any uniform or random probability distribution. Let's now examine three real-world data sets that should obey Benford's law to see how well they actually conform to a logarithmic distribution.

12.4 Examples

Our plan is to import three data sets, compute and plot the distribution of leading digits, and compare these distributions to a perfect Benford, or logarithmic, distribution. These three examples will dispel any lingering doubts that smaller leading digits are far more prevalent in some numeric data sets than larger leading digits.

12.4.1 Street addresses

The first of the three data sets we'll examine is a list of street addresses from East Baton Rouge Parish in Louisiana. The data was downloaded from the Baton Rouge website. According to Benford's law, approximately 30% of the street addresses should begin with the numeral 1, and fewer than 5% of the same addresses should begin with the numeral 9. Let's put that hypothesis to the test.

To import the data, saved as a .csv file in our working directory, we pass the full filename, bounded by opening and closing quotation marks, to the `pd.read_csv()` method. The `usecols = [0]` parameter instructs `pd.read_csv()` to import only the first column of the file. From this short snippet of code, we get a data frame called `street_addresses`:

```
>>> street_addresses = pd.read_csv('street_address_listing.csv',
>>>              usecols = [0])
```

Then we call the `info()` method to get a concise summary of the `street_addresses` data frame:

```
>>> print(street_addresses.info())
<class 'pandas.core.frame.DataFrame'>
RangeIndex: 194836 entries, 0 to 194835
Data columns (total 1 columns):
 #   Column      Non-Null Count   Dtype
---  ------      --------------   -----
 0   ADDRESS_NO  194836 non-null  object
dtypes: object(1)
memory usage: 1.5+ MB
None
```

We subsequently learn the following about our data:

- The number of rows, or entries, equals 194,836. The `info()` method excludes the header from the row count, so `street_addresses` contains 194,836 address numbers.

12.4 Examples

- There are no null values to be concerned with; we know this because the number of non-null values matches the row count.
- The one column we imported is ADDRESS_NO. Although the data contains other variables—street names, zip codes, and district numbers, just to name a few—our analysis requires address numbers only.

But to evaluate whether East Baton Rouge Parish street addresses conform to a Benford distribution, we need a data frame that groups the data by leading digits between 1 and 9 and contains the percentage of occurrences for each group relative to the total record count—in other words, a data frame much like df1, which means we need to perform a short series of data wrangling operations. We begin by adding a new variable to the street_addresses data frame called first_digit; it's created by calling the apply() method, which converts the values in ADDRESS_NO to strings, extracts the first character [0], and then stores it in our new variable. Consequently, street_addresses has a second variable, first_digit, in which each value represents the first, or leading, digit in the corresponding address number:

```
>>> street_addresses['first_digit'] = (street_addresses['ADDRESS_NO'] \
                                       .apply(lambda x: str(x)[0]))
```

A subsequent call to the head() method returns the first 10 records for our review:

```
>>> print(street_addresses.head(10))
    ADDRESS_NO first_digit
0   7353 STE B 282        7
1   9007 STE 9            9
2   5830 STE A6           5
3   4520 STE 103          4
4   8334 STE D            8
5   4250 UNIT 14          4
6         8316            8
7   1707 STE E            1
8        14261            1
9         8926            8
```

Next we apply the set() method to the first_digit variable. set() returns a set of unique values found in first_digit called unique_values:

```
>>> unique_values = set(street_addresses.first_digit)
>>> print(unique_values)
{'9', 'B', '8', 'T', '5', '3', '6', '1', '7', '4', '2', 'A'}
```

We have an issue that requires our immediate attention: street_addresses contains some number of records—we don't know how many—in which first_digit equals A, B, or T and therefore is not a numeral between 1 and 9. The following snippet of code subsets street_addresses in those records where first_digit equals a numeral between 1 and 9. In other words, it discards any and all records where first_digit equals a value other than a numeral between 1 and 9:

```
>>> street_addresses = street_addresses[street_addresses['first_digit'] \
>>>     .isin(['1', '2', '3', '4', '5', '6', '7', '8', '9'])]
```

Then we pass `first_digit` to the `astype()` method to convert it to an integer. Our next snippet of code requires `first_digit` to be either an integer (`int`) or a float (contains a fractional component); otherwise, it will throw an error and won't run. This is our final data wrangling operation:

```
>>> street_addresses['first_digit'] = (street_addresses['first_digit'] \
>>>                                    .astype(int))
```

Now that we have a variable of leading digits that's been cleansed and converted, we can perform our analysis. We import the `benford` library and then make a call to the `bf.first_digits()` method, which requires a minimum of two parameters:

- `street_addresses.first_digit` instructs `bf.first_digits()` to access the variable `first_digit` from the `street_addresses` data frame.
- `digs = 1` tells `bf.first_digits()` to evaluate just the leading digit (it doesn't matter that the values in `first.digit` are just one byte).

Here's the code:

```
>>> import benford as bf
>>> bf_street_addresses = bf.first_digits(street_addresses.first_digit,
>>>                                        digs = 1)
```

This returns two objects:

- A 9 × 4 data frame called `bf_street_addresses` with the following columns:
  - `First_1_Dig`, which contains the numerals 1 through 9.
  - `Counts`, which equals the number of occurrences grouped by leading digit.
  - `Found`, which equals the percentage of each group relative to the total record count, rounded to six decimal places.
  - `Expected`, which is similar to the `df1` variable `benford`, but rounded to six decimal places. It therefore represents a perfect Benford distribution.
- A preconfigured bar line chart that compares the observed distribution of leading digits to a perfect Benford distribution. The plot is displayed automatically. It contains the following elements:
  - An *x* axis called `Digits` that points to `First_1_Dig`
  - A *y* axis called `Distribution (%)` that points to `Found` and `Expected`
  - Bars that represent the observed distribution (`Found`)
  - A solid line that represents a perfect Benford distribution (`Expected`)
  - A title called `Expected vs. Found Distributions`
  - A legend in the upper-right corner

We intend to print the data frame later (and assign a derived variable to it for testing purposes), but figure 12.3 shows the plot in the meantime. Although it is not a perfect Benford distribution—the real world is rarely perfect—leading digits in street addresses from East Baton Rouge Parish nonetheless assume an obvious Benford distribution, where smaller leading digits are significantly more prevalent than larger leading digits. This pattern aligns with Benford's law because street addresses—unlike ZIP codes or assigned identifiers—arise from organic, right-skewed numeric growth and span multiple orders of magnitude. Although 1s are actually more numerous than we might expect, 1s plus 2s plus 3s equal 60.4% of the total record count, compared to a perfect Benford distribution where those same digits represent 60.2% of all observations. Let's now examine world population figures.

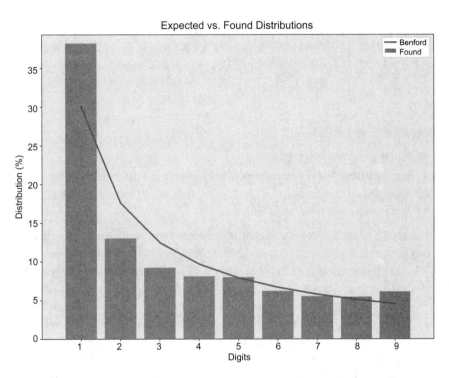

Figure 12.3 The distribution of leading digits in street addresses from East Baton Rouge Parish in Louisiana. The distribution closely resembles a perfect Benford distribution, where smaller leading digits are much more prevalent than larger leading digits. In fact, 1s, 2s, and 3s are the leading digits in 60.4% of the street addresses; in a perfect Benford distribution, those digits represent 60.2% of the observations.

12.4.2 *World population figures*

Our second of three data sets to examine is a .csv file downloaded from Kaggle that contains 2020 population counts for 235 countries and territories. We begin by calling the pd.read_csv() method to import a file that we since saved in our working directory, called population_by_country_2020.csv. Once again, we instruct pd.read_csv() to only read the data we absolutely require for our analysis; so, we pass a second parameter to the pd.read_csv() method, usecols = [1], which tells pd.read_csv()

to only import the second column from the left. As a result, we get a data frame called `populations`, which contains the per-country and per-territory population counts.

Next we call the `info()` method, which prints a concise summary of the `populations` data frame:

```
>>> populations = pd.read_csv(population_by_country_2020.csv',
>>>               usecols = [1])
>>> print(populations.info())
<class 'pandas.core.frame.DataFrame'>
RangeIndex: 235 entries, 0 to 234
Data columns (total 1 column):
 #   Column      Non-Null Count   Dtype
---  ------      --------------   -----
 0   Population  235 non-null     int64
dtypes: int64(1)
memory usage: 2.0 KB
None
```

This returns, most significantly,

- The number of rows, or entries
- An itemized list of columns from left to right, or starting from 0 (just `Population`)
- The number of non-null values

As before, we need a second variable of leading digits, converted to type integer, that we can plot and analyze.

We start by creating that variable, called `first_digit`, which now equals the leading digit from the original variable `Population`. The `apply()` method converts the values in `Population` to strings, extracts the first character [0], and stores it in `first_digit`. As a result, the `populations` data frame contains a second variable, `first_digit`, in which each value represents the first, or leading, digit in the corresponding population count.

A subsequent call to the `head()` method returns the first 10 records for our review:

```
>>> populations['first_digit'] = (populations['Population'] \
>>>                               .apply(lambda x: str(x)[0]))
>>> print(populations.head(10))
   Population  first_digit
0  1440297825            1
1  1382345085            1
2   331341050            3
3   274021604            2
4   221612785            2
5   212821986            2
6   206984347            2
7   164972348            1
8   145945524            1
9   129166028            1
```

Now we convert `first_digit` to an integer:

```
>>> populations['first_digit'] = populations['first_digit'].astype(int)
```

And then we pass `first_digit` to the `bf.first_digits()` method to get a data frame called `bf_populations` and another bar line chart that displays the observed versus expected distributions of leading digits:

```
>>> bf_populations = bf.first_digits(populations.first_digit, digs = 1)
```

Figure 12.4 shows the plot. Again, we get a distribution that is undoubtedly consistent with Benford's law. The smallest leading digits (1s, 2s, and 3s) represent 58.3% of the record count, and the largest leading digits (7s, 8s, and 9s) represent 14.1% of all records. By comparison, these same figures are 60.2% and 14.5% in a perfect Benford distribution. Pretty close.

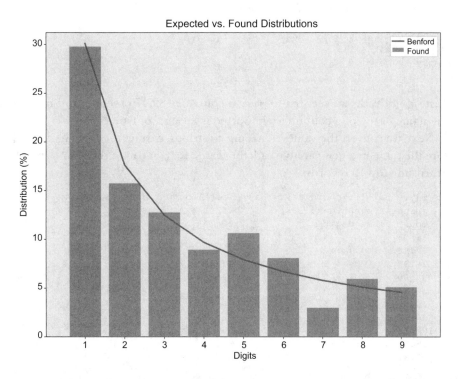

Figure 12.4 The distribution of leading digits in world population counts from 2020. Once more, we see a distribution in accordance with Benford's law. In this case, 1s, 2s, and 3s constitute 58.3% of the record count (versus a perfect Benford distribution of 60.2%), whereas 7s, 8s, and 9s represent 14.1% of all records (compared to 14.5% from a perfect Benford distribution).

Our third and final data set contains 2010 payment figures from a utility company operating on the West Coast of the United States. We'll travel a familiar path to get from the raw data to a summarized data frame for plotting and analysis.

12.4.3 Payment amounts

Our third and last data set to examine is corporate_payments.csv, also stored in our working directory. The data was acquired by attaching it to an R script and writing it to a .csv file. We make a call to the pandas `pd.read_csv()` method to import just the data contained in the fourth column and assign it to a data frame called `payments`; we then immediately call the `info()` method to get basic summary information returned. This snippet of code and most of the others that follow are similar to what you've previously been exposed to:

```
>>> payments = pd.read_csv('corporate_payments.csv',
>>>              usecols = [3])
>>> print(payments.info())
<class 'pandas.core.frame.DataFrame'>
RangeIndex: 189470 entries, 0 to 189469
Data columns (total 1 columns):
 #   Column       Non-Null Count   Dtype
---  ------       --------------   -----
 0   Amount       189470 non-null  float64
dtypes: float64(1)
memory usage: 1.4 MB
None
```

Most significantly, we see that `payments` contains 189,470 records and no null values. The name of the one column we imported is `Amount`, of type `float`.

Next, we convert the values in `Amount` to strings, extract the first character [0], and store the same in a new variable called `first_digit`. A call to the `head()` method then returns the top 10 records:

```
>>> payments['first_digit'] = payments['Amount'].apply(lambda x: str(x)[0])
>>> print(payments.head(10))
   Amount  first_digit
0   36.08            3
1   77.80            7
2   34.97            3
3   59.00            5
4   59.56            5
5   50.38            5
6   26.57            2
7  102.17            1
8   25.19            2
9   37.31            3
```

It's not uncommon for payments (or invoice amounts) to equal a negative number or 0, due to credits, adjustments, refunds or returns, free services, write-offs—whatever. Where `Amount` equals a negative number, we extracted the minus (-) operator rather than the leading digit; where `Amount` equals 0, we extracted a leading digit that shouldn't factor into our analysis. We therefore subset the `payments` data frame where `first_digit` is greater than or equal to 1 and less than or equal to 9:

```
>>> payments = payments[(payments.first_digit >= '1') &
                        (payments.first_digit <= '9')]
```

Then we convert the values in `first_digit` to integers:

```
>>> payments['first_digit'] = payments['first_digit'].astype(int)
```

And finally, we pass `first_digit` to the `bf.first_digits()` method, which returns a data frame called `bf_payments` as well as the bar line chart shown in figure 12.5.

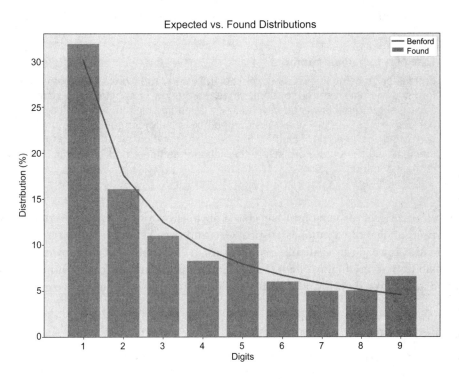

Figure 12.5 The distribution of leading digits in 2010 payment amounts from a utility company on the US West Coast. Again, we see a distribution that obviously obeys Benford's law. The smallest leading digits (1s, 2s, and 3s) represent exactly 59% of the total record count, and the largest leading digits (7s, 8s, and 9s) represent just 16.6% of the records. Once more, in a perfect Benford distribution, these figures are 60.2% and 14.5%, respectively.

We've demonstrated that street addresses, world population figures, and now payment amounts—three data sets that should follow Benford's law—do, in fact, follow Benford's law, at least on visual inspection. Computing the distribution of leading digits, plotting it, and estimating their likeness to a perfect Benford distribution is a great start. But there are statistical methods by which to get exact measurements; we'll demonstrate those next.

12.5 *Validating Benford's law*

Numeric data that, on visual inspection, assumes a Benford distribution may still contain enough anomalies to raise suspicion. We may, or may not, detect these by drawing bar line charts and comparing real-world distributions to a perfect Benford distribution, which is why it's important to also run statistical tests and compare the results to expected thresholds.

Our plan is to pass the populations data frame to several statistical and arithmetic functions to determine how well that data really conforms to an expected Benford distribution. Furthermore, we intend to pop the hood on these same operations to provide quantitative insights into what the numbers mean and how they're derived.

> **Law of anomalous numbers**
>
> In addition to being known as the first-digit law and the Newcomb–Benford law, Benford's law is also referred to, sometimes, as the law of anomalous numbers. That's because Benford's law goes beyond just the leading digit in naturally occurring number sequences; the law of anomalous numbers therefore generalizes the phenomenon when the analysis includes, for instance, the first two digits and not just the leading digit. Of course, our scope throughout has been the leading digit only, which is most common.

Although visual inspection of bar charts obviously provides initial insights and visualizations of data distribution, statistical tests and the like offer a more rigorous and systematic approach to evaluating conformity to Benford's law, thereby enhancing the reliability and credibility of conclusions and establishing a strong footing for decision and action. We'll perform four tests in all, beginning with a chi-square goodness of fit test.

12.5.1 Chi-square test

Our first test, a chi-square goodness of fit test, requires a single data wrangling operation as a prerequisite. We need to create a derived variable and assign it to the bf_populations data frame we generated earlier. So, we call the assign() method to create a new variable called Expected_Counts, which is derived by multiplying the values in the Expected column by the sum of the values in the Counts column. A subsequent call to the print() function returns the new and improved bf_populations data frame. Although this data set encompasses an entire population rather than a sample, the chi-square test still relies on having a sufficient record count to yield meaningful statistical conclusions:

```
>>> bf_populations = \
>>>     bf_populations.assign(Expected_Counts = \
>>>                    bf_populations.Expected * \
>>>                    sum(bf_populations.Counts))
>>> print(bf_populations)
            Counts     Found  Expected  Expected_Counts
First_1_Dig
1               70  0.297872  0.301030        70.742049
2               37  0.157447  0.176091        41.381446
3               30  0.127660  0.124939        29.360603
```

```
4          21    0.089362  0.096910     22.773853
5          25    0.106383  0.079181     18.607593
6          19    0.080851  0.066947     15.732496
7           7    0.029787  0.057992     13.628108
8          14    0.059574  0.051153     12.020843
9          12    0.051064  0.045757     10.753010
```

Thus, `Expected_Counts` represents the number of occurrences for each leading digit if world populations actually followed a perfect Benford distribution.

With that sorted out, we next import the `stats` module from the `scipy` library, which contains several methods for scientific and technical computing, and then make a call to the `stats.chisquare()` method. A chi-square test is a statistical test used to determine whether there is a significant association between categorical variables; it compares the observed distribution against the expected distribution and then evaluates if any variances are statistically significant. Our null hypothesis is that the data conforms to a Benford distribution. If our chi-square test returns a p-value less than 5%, we'll reject the null hypothesis and conclude the data either best conforms to some other probability distribution or, perhaps, contains more than a few suspicious anomalies. Alternatively, if our chi-square test returns a p-value greater than 5%, we'll fail to reject the null hypothesis and conclude the data does, in fact, obey Benford's law:

```
>>> import scipy.stats as stats
>>> x2 = stats.chisquare(bf_populations.Counts,
...                      bf_populations.Expected_Counts)
>>> print(x2)
Power_divergenceResult(statistic=7.192526063677557,
    pvalue=0.5160103482305225)
```

The test statistic equals 7.193, and the p-value equals 51%. Let's examine these results and demonstrate how they're derived, one by one.

CHI-SQUARE STATISTIC

The chi-square statistic is derived by applying the following equation to each leading digit and then summing the results:

$$x^2 = \sum \text{all cells} \frac{(O_i - E_i)^2}{E_i}$$

For every leading digit, we're squaring the difference between observed (O_i) and expected (E_i) counts and dividing that by the expected count (E_i); then we add the quotients, or the chi-square statistic for each leading digit, to get the chi-square statistic for the test. In other words, we're squaring the differences between `Counts` and `Expected_Counts` and dividing those differences by `Expected_Counts`. The best way of further demonstrating this is to arrange the figures in the form of a table and review the results: see table 12.1.

Table 12.1 Chi-square statistics for leading digits in world population counts

Leading digit	Observed (O_i)	Expected (E_i)	$\|O_i - E_i\|$	$(O_i - E_i)^2$	$(O_i - E_i)^2 / E_i$
1	70	70.742	0.742	0.551	0.008
2	37	41.381	4.381	19.193	0.464
3	30	29.361	0.639	0.408	0.014
4	21	22.774	1.774	3.147	0.138
5	25	18.608	6.392	41.858	2.196
6	19	15.732	3.268	10.680	0.679
7	7	13.628	6.628	43.930	3.224
8	14	12.021	1.979	3.916	0.326
9	12	10.753	1.247	1.555	0.145
	235	235			7.192

When computing the chi-square statistic by hand, we get 7.192, which essentially matches what our test returned (7.193). The variances in leading digits 5 and 7 are mostly accountable for the final test statistic.

Going from left to right, we have the following columns:

- *Leading digit* equals 1 through 9, or contains every unique leading digit in the variable `First_1_Dig` from the `bf_populations` data frame.
- *Observed* (O_i) equals the actual, or observed, count for every leading digit. Sums to 235, which of course ties back to the number of countries and territories in population_by_country_2020.csv.
- *Expected* (E_i) equals the expected count for every leading digit in accordance with a perfect Benford distribution. For instance, when the leading digit equals 2, we get the expected count by multiplying 235 times 0.176.
- $|O_i - E_i|$ equals the absolute difference between observed and expected counts.
- $(O_i - E_i)^2$ equals the square of the difference between observed and expected counts.
- $(O_i - E_i)^2 / E_i$ equals the square of the difference between observed and expected counts divided by the expected count. This is therefore the chi-square statistic per leading digit. We get the chi-square statistic for the test by summing the per-digit statistics.

The chi-square statistic is calculated as 7.192, closely matching the result obtained from the `stats.chisquare()` method.

DEGREES OF FREEDOM

The degrees of freedom (df) refer to the number of values in the final calculation of a statistical test that are free to vary. From a chi-square goodness of fit test, the df are derived by applying the following equation, where r equals the number of rows and c equals the number of columns, or categories, in a contingency table:

$$df = (r - 1)(c - 1)$$

Because the row count equals 9 and the number of categories equals 2, the df therefore equal $(9 - 1)(2 - 1)$, or 8. The `stats.chisquare()` method doesn't return this figure; however, it's important to derive it, if only to help us understand how we get the p-value, which of course determines whether the results are statistically significant.

P-VALUE

By cross-referencing the chi-square statistic (7.193) and the df (8) on a chi-square probabilities table, we can get an *estimated* p-value. Figure 12.6 shows a snippet from a chi-square probabilities table. To get an estimated p-value for our chi-square test, find the df on the far left and then locate the two consecutive critical values from the same row that bound the chi-square statistic. The p-value is between the two numbers from the same columns in the header. Thus, the p-value is equal to or greater than 0.10 and less than or equal to 0.90. Thankfully, the `stats.chisquare()` method returns an *exact* p-value with much less effort.

df	0.995	0.99	0.975	0.95	0.90	0.10	0.05	0.025	0.01	0.005
1	---	---	0.001	0.004	0.016	2.706	3.841	5.024	6.635	7.879
2	0.010	0.020	0.051	0.103	0.211	4.605	5.991	7.378	9.210	10.597
3	0.072	0.115	0.216	0.352	0.584	6.251	7.815	9.348	11.345	12.838
4	0.207	0.297	0.484	0.711	1.064	7.779	9.488	11.143	13.277	14.860
5	0.412	0.554	0.831	1.145	1.610	9.236	11.070	12.833	15.086	16.750
6	0.676	0.872	1.237	1.635	2.204	10.645	12.592	14.449	16.812	18.548
7	0.989	1.239	1.690	2.167	2.833	12.017	14.067	16.013	18.475	20.278
8	1.344	1.646	2.180	2.733	3.490	13.362	15.507	17.535	20.090	21.955
9	1.735	2.088	2.700	3.325	4.168	14.684	16.919	19.023	21.666	23.589
10	2.156	2.558	3.247	3.940	4.865	15.987	18.307	20.483	23.209	25.188

Figure 12.6 A snippet from a typical chi-square probabilities table from which we can get an estimated p-value by cross-referencing the degrees of freedom and the chi-square statistic. The degrees of freedom equal 8; the chi-square statistic equals 7.1925, which is between 3.490 and 13.362; the p-value therefore equals some number between 0.10 and 0.90. Although that's a substantial range, it falls entirely above the 5% threshold. Thus, without running any code, we can determine that the results are not statistically significant, and therefore we can, and should, fail to reject the null hypothesis.

Because the p-value is above the 5% significance threshold, we fail to reject the null hypothesis that the data conforms to a Benford distribution. Therefore, we conclude that the leading digits in world population counts do, in fact, obey Benford's law.

12.5.2 Mean absolute deviation

Whereas a chi-square goodness of fit test considers the size of the data as well as the variances between observed and expected counts, a mean absolute deviation (MAD) test ignores the number of rows in the data and merely takes into account the absolute differences between actual and expected proportions. It is expressed by the following equation:

$$\text{MAD} = \frac{\sum |P_i - PO_i|}{K}$$

Where P_i is the observed proportion, PO_i is the expected proportion in accordance with a perfect Benford distribution, and K is the number of leading digits.

In Python, we get the mean absolute deviation by passing `first_digit` from the `populations` data frame to the `bf.mad()` method. Because we're testing just the first, or leading, digit, rather than two or more digits, we also pass `test = 1` to `bf.mad`. And because we're not working with fractional numbers, we additionally pass `decimals = 0`:

```
>>> MAD = bf.mad(populations.first_digit, test = 1, decimals = 0)
>>> print(MAD)
0.012790028799782804
```

The mean absolute deviation is the sum of the per-digit absolute deviations divided by the number of digits (see table 12.2).

Table 12.2 Absolute deviations and the mean absolute deviation for leading digits in world population counts

Leading digit	Observed (P_i)	Expected (PO_i)	|P_i • PO_i| / K
1	0.298	0.301	0.003
2	0.157	0.176	0.019
3	0.128	0.125	0.003
4	0.089	0.097	0.008
5	0.106	0.079	0.027
6	0.081	0.067	0.014
7	0.030	0.058	0.028
8	0.060	0.051	0.009
9	0.051	0.046	0.005
	1.000	1.000	0.013

The data can be itemized like so:

- *Leading digit* equals 1 through 9, or contains every unique leading digit in the variable `First_1_Dig` from the `bf_populations` data frame.
- *Observed* (P_i) equals the actual, or observed, proportion for every leading digit. Sums to 1.
- *Expected* (PO_i) equals the expected proportion for every leading digit in accordance with a perfect Benford distribution. Sums to 1.

- $|P_i - PO_i| / K$ for the leading digits equals the absolute deviation between the observed and expected proportions. The bottom figure (0.013) is the mean absolute deviation, which is derived by summing the absolute deviations and dividing the total by the number of leading digits.

Mean absolute deviations equal to or very close to 0.000 suggest close conformity to Benford's law; on the other end, mean absolute deviations greater than 0.015 imply nonconformity. When the mean absolute deviation equals 0.013, as it does here, our best conclusion is that the data "marginally conforms" to an expected Benford distribution.

12.5.3 Distortion factor and z-statistic

The distortion factor (DF) is a statistic that represents the percentage of deviation between the actual mean of leading digits that presumably follow Benford's law and the expected mean of the same. It's a meaningful metric by itself, but when the distortion factor is then divided by the `first_digit` standard deviation, we get the z-statistic, which tells us whether we should reject or fail to reject a null hypothesis.

We get the distortion factor by plugging the actual mean (AM) and expected mean (EM) of the leading digits into the following equation:

$$DF = \frac{100(AM - EM)}{EM}$$

We can easily get the actual mean by passing `first_digit` to the `mean()` method:

```
>>> AM = populations['first_digit'].mean()
>>> print(AM)
3.5148936170212766
```

Getting the expected mean requires more effort. A perfect Benford distribution is, of course, constant, but the mean varies due to inconsistencies in data sizes. One way of computing an *approximate* mean of a perfect Benford distribution with 235 observations is to do the following:

1. Multiply each leading digit by the expected count: 1 × 70.742, 2 × 41.381, and so forth.
2. Add the nine products.
3. Divide the sum by 235.

We'll use Python as a calculator to get an approximate expected mean and again to compute the distortion factor:

```
>>> EM = ((1 * 70.742) + (2 * 41.381) + (3 * 29.361) +
...      (4 * 22.774) + (5 * 18.608) + (6 * 15.732) +
...      (7 * 13.628) + (8 * 12.021) + (9 * 10.753)) / 235
>>> print(EM)
>>> 3.4402382978723405
```

Now that we have the actual mean (3.515) and an approximate expected mean (3.440), we can compute the distortion factor:

```
>>> DF = (100 * (AM - EM)) / EM
>>> print(DF)
2.1700624400091013
```

So, the amount of deviation between the actual and expected means equals 2.17%. The closer the distortion factor is to 0%, the better the data conforms to a Benford distribution.

Let's now get the standard deviation of `first_digit` by making a call to the `np.std()` method. Standard deviation is a measure of the dispersion or variability of numeric data from its mean, thereby indicating how much those values deviate from the average:

```
>>> SD = np.std(populations['first_digit'])
>>> print(SD)
2.4760107519964065
```

Now that we have the distortion factor (2.17) and the `first_digit` standard deviation (2.48), we can compute the z-statistic; and from the z-statistic, we can make another conclusion about whether leading digits from 2020 world population counts conform well enough to an expected Benford distribution. We get the z-statistic by dividing the distortion factor by the standard deviation.

$$z\text{-statistic} = \frac{DF}{\text{Standard Deviation}}$$

Again, using Python as a calculator,

```
>>> z = DF / SD
>>> print(Z)
0.8764349824649916
```

Once more, our null hypothesis is that the data conforms to a Benford distribution. Calculated z-statistics between the critical values −1.96 and 1.96 are insignificant at the 5% threshold; thus, we should again fail to reject the null hypothesis that leading digits in world population counts obey Benford's law.

12.5.4 Mantissa statistics

The logarithm of any number is split into two parts: the numeral to the left of the decimal point is the *characteristic*, or integer, and the fractional part to the right of the decimal point is the *mantissa*. Take the number 287,437, for instance, which was the population of Barbados back in 2020, at least according to our data set; when we compute the logarithm of 287,437, we get 5.458543. The characteristic is 5, and the mantissa is 0.458543.

For our purposes, the key mantissa statistics are the mean, variance, excess kurtosis, and skewness. If the leading digits obey Benford's law, the mantissas should assume a uniform distribution, which can be established by computing the aforementioned statistics:

- The *mean*, often referred to as the *average*, is a measure of central tendency in a numeric data series. It represents the sum of all values divided by the number of records.
- The *variance* measures the amount of dispersion, or variability, in numeric data by quantifying the average squared deviation of each data point from the population mean.
- *Excess kurtosis* measures the tails, or the numeric data points farthest from the mean. It quantifies the "sharpness" or "flatness" of the tail, left or right, compared to a normal, or Gaussian, distribution. When it's equal to 0, the data has the same tail behavior as a normal distribution; when it's positive, the data contains more outliers than a typical normal distribution; and when it's negative, the data instead contains fewer outliers than a normal distribution.
- *Skewness* measures the asymmetry in the distribution of numeric data. When data is perfectly symmetrical, the skewness is 0; when right-skewed, the skewness is positive; and when left-skewed, the skewness is negative.

When data perfectly obeys Benford's law, the mantissas have the following properties:

$$\text{Mean(Mantissa)} = 0.50$$
$$\text{Variance(Mantissa)} = 0.08$$
$$\text{Excess Kurtosis(Mantissa)} = -1.20$$
$$\text{Skewness(Mantissa)} = 0$$

Before we compute these same statistics against the observed data, and then of course compare actual versus theoretical results, we first need to create a pair of derived variables and assign both to the populations data frame.

Our first variable is log, which equals the base-10 logarithm of the original variable Population. With respect to Barbados, for instance, Population equals 287437 and log equals 5.458543:

```
>>> populations['log'] = np.log10(populations['Population'])
```

Our second variable is mantissa, which equals the mantissa extracted from the variable log. This is derived by subtracting the characteristic, or integer, from log and assigning the difference to mantissa. To again use Barbados as an example, where log equals 5.458543, mantissa equals 0.458543:

```
>>> populations['mantissa'] = \
        populations['log'] - populations['log'].astype(int)
```

A call to the head() method displays the top 10 records for our review:

```
>>> print(populations.head(10))
   Population  first_digit       log  mantissa
0  1440297825            1  9.158452  0.158452
1  1382345085            1  9.140616  0.140616
```

```
2    331341050        3    8.520275    0.520275
3    274021604        2    8.437785    0.437785
4    221612785        2    8.345595    0.345595
5    212821986        2    8.328016    0.328016
6    206984347        2    8.315938    0.315938
7    164972348        1    8.217411    0.217411
8    145945524        1    8.164191    0.164191
9    129166028        1    8.111148    0.111148
```

Now that we have a variable in `populations` that contains the mantissas, we can proceed with calculating the four mantissa statistics.

To get the mean, we pass `mantissa` to the `mean()` method:

```
>>> print(populations['mantissa'].mean())
0.5087762832181758
```

To get the variance, we pass `mantissa` to the `var()` method:

```
>>> print(populations['mantissa'].var())
0.08797164279797032
```

To get the excess kurtosis, we call the `kurtosis()` method from `scipy` and pass a second parameter, `fisher = True`, in addition to the variable name (otherwise, the `kurtosis()` method would return the kurtosis instead of the excess kurtosis):

```
>>> from scipy.stats import kurtosis
>>> print(kurtosis(populations['mantissa'], fisher = True))
-1.177858418956045
```

And to get the skewness, we pass `mantissa` to the `skew()` method, also from `scipy`:

```
>>> from scipy.stats import skew
>>> print(skew(populations['mantissa']))
-0.1128415794074036
```

All of these statistics align very well with those from a perfect Benford distribution.

Finally, we previously mentioned that the mantissas should follow a uniform distribution if the leading digits, in fact, obey Benford's law. Let's complete our analysis by testing this hypothesis; we'll sort and rank the mantissas and then display the results in a Matplotlib plot alongside a perfect uniform distribution.

To sort the variable `mantissa` in ascending order, we make a call to the `sort_values()` method. This will be our *y*-axis variable:

```
>>> populations = populations.sort_values(by = 'mantissa')
```

And to get our *x*-axis variable, we next create a new variable, `rank`, that contains the numerals `1` through `236` (exclusive):

```
>>> populations['rank'] = list(range(1, 236))
```

The `head()` and `tail()` methods return the first three and last three records for our review:

```
>>> print(populations.head(3))
    Population  first_digit       log  mantissa  rank
90    10110233            1  7.004761  0.004761     1
89    10154978            1  7.006679  0.006679     2
88    10191409            1  7.008234  0.008234     3
>>> print(populations.tail(3))
     Population  first_digit       log  mantissa  rank
159      990447            9  5.995831  0.995831   233
92      9910892            9  6.996113  0.996113   234
91      9931333            9  6.997008  0.997008   235
```

The following snippet of Matplotlib code should be familiar by now, with one likely exception: plt.plot([0, 1], [0, 1])... draws a red dashed line that represents a perfect uniform distribution starting where *x* and *y* both equal 0 and ending where *x* and *y* equal 1. It is therefore a perfect diagonal line that represents a perfect Benford distribution:

```
>>> plt.plot(populations['rank'], populations['mantissa'],
>>>          color = 'slateblue', linewidth = 1.5)
>>> plt.plot([0, 1], [0, 1], transform = ax.transAxes,
>>>          color = 'red', linestyle = '--')
>>> plt.title('Rank Order of Mantissas', fontweight = 'bold')
>>> plt.xlabel('Rank')
>>> plt.ylabel('Mantissa')
>>> plt.show()
```

Figure 12.7 shows the plot. The sorted mantissas (represented by the solid line) do, in fact, follow a uniform distribution quite well.

By mixing the theoretical with the practical and by combining data wrangling and data visualization techniques, we discovered that real-world numeric data spanning multiple orders of magnitude follows a Benford, or logarithmic, distribution, and not

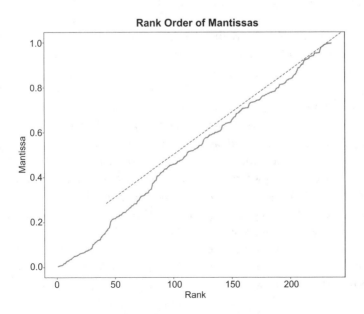

Figure 12.7 The dashed line represents a perfect uniform distribution of mantissas that we would expect to observe when leading digits perfectly obey Benford's law. The solid line represents the mantissas, sorted in ascending order, from the populations data frame. The observed mantissas assume a "close-enough" uniform distribution that further suggests world population counts obey Benford's law.

a uniform or random distribution, as many might expect. Furthermore, by subjecting one of our data sets to a battery of statistical tests, we learned how to go above and beyond visual inspection and to apply a series of rigorous and more precise methods to assess and definitively conclude adherence to Benford's law. These learnings empower us to apply similar and equally rigorous methods to other numeric data to test observed distributions against an expected Benford distribution. In the next chapter, we'll demonstrate how to plan, monitor, and control projects.

Summary

- Benford's law, also known as the first-digit law, states that many sets of numeric data follow a logarithmic distribution by which smaller leading digits are more prevalent than larger leading digits.
- Data sets that should obey Benford's law but instead take on a very different distribution might have been manipulated due to fraudulent or other suspicious activity. Significant deviations from Benford's law are just the smoke, not the fire, however. Further investigation might absolutely be warranted when significant deviations from a Benford distribution are observed; at the same time, we should refrain from drawing major conclusions from nothing other than a Benford analysis.
- Understanding Benford's law is especially important in an era where financial fraud, tax evasion, and other forms of data manipulation are increasingly sophisticated. By identifying anomalies in numerical data, analysts and investigators can uncover irregularities that may warrant deeper scrutiny, making Benford's law a valuable tool for fraud detection and forensic accounting.
- Data sets to which Benford's law best applies are those that are distributed across multiple orders of magnitude and don't have preestablished minimum and maximum values; these same sets of data are right-skewed, or positively skewed, by which the mean is greater than the median. Data sets that obey Benford's law are frequently referred to as naturally occurring number sequences.
- We imported three real-world data sets that, going in, were assumed to follow a Benford distribution. By extracting the leading digits from those data sets and plotting the frequency of occurrences for each, we subsequently discovered, at least from visual inspection, that they each obey Benford's law,
- Data comprising numerals used as identifiers may be the best example of numeric data that doesn't qualify as a naturally occurring number sequence. Scores—test scores and IQ scores, for instance—are another good example.
- Don't rely on visual inspection alone when performing a Benford analysis, and by the same token, don't reject or fail to reject a null hypothesis from just one statistical test when options are available. We tested world population data four times and determined from each analysis that 2020 world population figures, based on our rigorous statistical testing, align quite well with the characteristics of a Benford distribution.

13

Managing projects

This chapter covers

- Work breakdown structure (WBS), or hierarchical composition of project tasks
- The program evaluation review technique (PERT), or project scheduling using time estimates
- The critical path method (CPM), a technique to identify the longest sequence of dependent project tasks
- Calculating the probability of on-time completion
- Project crashing, or accelerating project timelines

Project management is a critical yet often undervalued skill set in the business world. Although single-level contributors are typically selected for projects based on their specific hard skills, project managers are frequently chosen not for their proven management capabilities but rather for the absence of these technical skills. This paradoxical approach undermines the effectiveness of project management, as it overlooks the specialized skills truly necessary for leading projects successfully. Effective project management requires the use of several quantitative techniques, from estimating activity times to finding the project's critical path, calculating the probability of on-time completion, and implementing strategies to accelerate project timelines. *Without a solid understanding and application of statistics and quantitative methods, projects cannot be managed intelligently or effectively.*

Projects are typically defined by three core components: scope, schedule, and budget. It's not uncommon to emphasize any two of these components in planning and especially during execution. Nevertheless, they are intricately interconnected, and any imbalance among them can jeopardize the success of a project. Although our focus here is on building and managing a well-constructed project plan buttressed by the use of quantitative techniques, be aware that cost overruns and even compromises in scope are often direct results of project delays. Therefore, a well-managed schedule is not only necessary to ensure on-time completion but also pivotal in maintaining the project's scope and budget.

Projects often fail from the outset due to inadequate planning, which sets the stage for further derailment during execution due to poor management. Effective project management is not just about strong leadership and clear communication; it also demands hard skills. Poor planning frequently leads to unrealistic timelines, unaccounted-for activities, and unforeseen challenges, while also setting incorrect expectations with stakeholders, often resulting in a cycle of over-promising and under-delivering. These initial shortcomings are then exacerbated by ineffective project management, culminating in missed deadlines and eventually cost overruns and compromised project goals. Successful project management demands a comprehensive skill set that encompasses not only leadership and communication but also a robust understanding of quantitative methods to accurately forecast timelines, allocate resources, and mitigate risks.

The use of advanced project management techniques and other quantitative methods is essential for developing a project plan with reasonable time estimates, accounting for uncertainty, distinguishing between critical and noncritical tasks, applying statistical measures to calculate the probability of on-time completion, and implementing strategies to compress the project schedule without reducing scope. By mastering these techniques, you will acquire the essential skills and other tools needed to manage projects large and small with efficiency and efficacy.

One of the prioritized projects from chapter 8 will serve as our test bed: we will demonstrate how to apply best-in-class project management techniques and other quantitative methods, manually and programmatically, to plan and manage the project toward on-time completion. We will begin by creating a work breakdown structure, an essential step in organizing and planning a project. It's important to understand that a work breakdown structure (WBS) is not the same as a project plan; rather, it serves as a detailed framework that forms the basis for developing the project plan.

13.1 Creating a work breakdown structure

Back in chapter 8, we applied a linear programming technique called constrained optimization to prioritize a subset of capital projects from a backlog based on their value-to-effort ratio within given constraints. One of the projects that made the cut was building an automated reporting tool.

13.1 Creating a work breakdown structure

As the first step toward planning and managing the implementation of this project, we will build out a WBS. The WBS is a tabular or visual decomposition of a project into its component activities that records all the dependencies among these activities. The WBS is the first step toward developing a comprehensive project plan, providing a detailed blueprint that guides the entire project management process. By organizing tasks in a clear and manageable structure, the WBS lays the groundwork for subsequent project planning and management while ensuring that all project activities are accounted for from the outset.

The WBS is therefore not the project plan, but rather the foundation for developing the plan with further details. It lays out activities and the dependencies, if any, required to start those activities. A detailed project plan will include not only the data from the WBS but also estimated activity times and other attributes that, when analyzed, allow us to identify those tasks that collectively make up the project's critical path. All of this will be added after we first demonstrate how to generate a WBS.

An *activity*, commonly referred to as a *task* or *subtask*, is a distinct component of work that must be finished in full for the project to be 100% complete. Throughout the project planning process, metrics and other attributes are incrementally assigned to each activity, including but not limited to dependencies.

A *dependency*, meanwhile, refers to a relationship between activities where, typically, at least one activity cannot begin until one or more preceding activities have been completed. Dependencies ensure that tasks are executed in a logical sequence, preventing scheduling conflicts and maintaining the project's workflow. Properly identifying and managing these dependencies is essential for accurate project planning and timely completion.

Here is a breakdown of the project activities along with their dependencies. If you prefer to skip the details, you can proceed directly to table 13.1:

- A: Define Project Objectives and Scope
  - Description: Establish the overall goals and boundaries of the project.
  - Dependencies: None
- B: Assemble Project Team
  - Description: Form the team that will work on the project.
  - Dependencies: A
- C: Gather Requirements from Stakeholders
  - Description: Collect and document the requirements from all stakeholders.
  - Dependencies: A, B
- D: Data Collection and Integration
  - Description: Collect and integrate data from various sources.
  - Dependencies: C
- E: Data Cleaning and Preprocessing
  - Description: Clean and preprocess the collected data for analysis.
  - Dependencies: D

- **F: Design Report Templates**
  - Description: Create templates for the reports to be generated.
  - Dependencies: C
- **G: Develop Data Processing Pipelines**
  - Description: Develop pipelines to process the data.
  - Dependencies: E
- **H: Implement Report Generation Logic**
  - Description: Implement the logic needed to generate reports from the data.
  - Dependencies: F
- **I: Develop User Interface for Report Access**
  - Description: Create the user interface for accessing the reports.
  - Dependencies: F
- **J: Integrate Data Pipelines with Report Generation**
  - Description: Integrate the data processing pipelines with the report generation system.
  - Dependencies: G, H
- **K: Conduct User Testing and Feedback**
  - Description: Test the system with users and gather feedback.
  - Dependencies: I, J
- **L: Finalize and Deploy Automated Reporting Tool**
  - Description: Finalize the tool based on feedback and deploy it.
  - Dependencies: K

Although the layout and sequence of these tasks may suggest a waterfall methodology, where tasks are completed in a linear, sequential manner, it's important to note that these tasks can be adapted to fit an Agile framework as well. In an Agile approach, tasks can be broken down into smaller, iterative cycles, known as *sprints*, allowing for continuous feedback and adjustments throughout the project. Agile methodology emphasizes flexibility, collaboration, and customer feedback, which can be incorporated into the development of the automated reporting tool. Regardless of the chosen methodology, a WBS is essential and must clearly outline all dependencies to ensure smooth project execution. These activities and their dependencies are summarized in table 13.1.

Table 13.1 WBS for completing the automated reporting tool project. It includes an outline of the key activities required, along with brief descriptions and their respective dependencies. Each activity is identified by a unique code and details the necessary steps and preceding tasks needed for successful project completion.

Activity	Description	Dependencies
A	Define Project Objectives and Scope	None
B	Assemble Project Team	A
C	Gather Requirements from Stakeholders	A, B

Table 13.1 WBS for completing the automated reporting tool project. It includes an outline of the key activities required, along with brief descriptions and their respective dependencies. Each activity is identified by a unique code and details the necessary steps and preceding tasks needed for successful project completion. *(continued)*

Activity	Description	Dependencies
D	Data Collection and Integration	C
E	Data Cleaning and Preprocessing	D
F	Design Report Templates	C
G	Develop Data Processing Pipelines	E
H	Implement Report Gathering Logic	F
I	Develop User Interface for Report Access	F
J	Integrate Data Pipelines with Report Generation	G, H
K	Conduct User Testing and Feedback	I, J
L	Finalize and Deploy Automated Reporting Tool	K

The WBS provides a comprehensive outline of the tasks required to deliver an automated reporting tool. Each activity is identified by a unique code, accompanied by a brief description and its respective dependencies. This structured approach is essential for effective project management, ensuring that all tasks are accounted for and executed in the correct sequence.

The WBS is constructed by listing all the necessary activities and specifying the dependencies for each task. For instance, the project begins with defining the project objectives and scope (Activity A), which sets the foundation for assembling the project team (Activity B). Following this, gathering requirements from stakeholders (Activity C) depends on the completion of both defining the project scope and assembling the team. This methodical approach ensures that all prerequisite tasks are completed before initiating subsequent activities, thereby minimizing potential delays and other issues.

We can draw several key insights from the table. The sequential flow of the project is evident, starting with the initial planning and team assembly, moving through data collection and processing, and culminating in user testing and deployment. The Dependencies column highlights the interconnections between tasks, illustrating the importance of coordinating various project elements. For example, tasks like gathering requirements and designing report templates are foundational and affect several subsequent activities.

Additionally, the WBS emphasizes the critical phases of integration and testing. Tasks such as integrating data pipelines with report generation (Activity J) and implementing report generation logic (Activity H) are pivotal, relying on earlier stages of data processing and report design. The final stages of the project involve conducting user testing and gathering feedback (Activity K), followed by the finalization and deployment of the automated reporting tool (Activity L). This ensures that the tool meets user requirements and is ready for operational use.

In summary, the WBS serves as a detailed roadmap for the project, ensuring that each task is executed in the correct order and dependencies are managed effectively. This approach not only aids in planning and scheduling but also helps in monitoring the project's progress, ultimately contributing to the successful completion of the project.

But although the WBS provides a comprehensive roadmap of the tasks and their dependencies, it leaves an essential question unanswered: how long will the project take? This is a critical aspect of project planning that the WBS alone does not address. To gain a clearer understanding of the project timeline, the next step is to estimate the completion time for each task. Adding these time estimates will allow us to create a more detailed project plan, predict the overall project duration, and identify the critical path tasks that dictate the project's completion time.

13.2 Estimating activity times with PERT

Analogous estimating is a technique used in project management to estimate the duration of project tasks based on the duration of similar tasks from previous projects. This method uses historical data and expert judgment to provide a quick and relatively accurate estimate of activity times, particularly when detailed information is not available. Analogous estimating works best when similar tasks have been previously performed on similar projects and the actual activity times have been recorded. However, in the absence of such data, we turn to a quantitative technique like the program evaluation and review technique (PERT) to estimate activity times more precisely.

PERT is a statistical tool used in project management to estimate the duration of project activities. It involves calculating a weighted average of three different activity time estimates to derive an expected activity time. These estimates are as follows:

- *Optimistic time* (a)—The shortest time in which the task can be completed, assuming everything proceeds better than expected
- *Pessimistic time* (b)—The longest time the task might take, assuming everything goes wrong
- *Most likely time* (m)—The best estimate of the time required to complete the task, assuming everything proceeds as normal

The accuracy of PERT estimates depends heavily on the quality of the inputs. It is crucial that the assigned resources or subject matter experts provide their own estimates for completing their tasks. These estimates should be thoughtful and based on their expertise and experience. Ensuring that the input data is reliable will significantly enhance the reliability of the PERT outputs, leading to more effective project planning and management.

These estimates are inserted into the following formula to get the expected activity time (t):

$$t = \frac{a + 4m + b}{6}$$

So, if the first task in the automated reporting tool project is optimistically estimated to take 2 weeks, pessimistically estimated to take up to 4 weeks, and most likely to be completed in 3 weeks, the expected time for that activity is

$$t_{(A)} = \frac{2 + (4)(3) + 4}{6}$$

or

$$t_{(A)} = 3$$

Only the expected activity time should be assigned to each task; the optimistic, pessimistic, and most likely estimates are merely inputs to calculate t. Thus, an expected activity time of 3 weeks should be assigned to Activity A.

PERT assumes that estimates in activity times follow a beta distribution. The *beta distribution* is a continuous probability distribution commonly used to model the uncertainty in various fields, including project management. It is characterized by two shape parameters that determine the skewness and spread of the distribution, allowing it to accurately represent the variability in activity durations. This distribution is particularly useful in PERT because it accommodates the optimistic, most likely, and pessimistic time estimates, providing a more comprehensive and realistic estimation framework. Like all probability distributions, the beta probability distribution can best be understood when visualized: see figure 13.1.

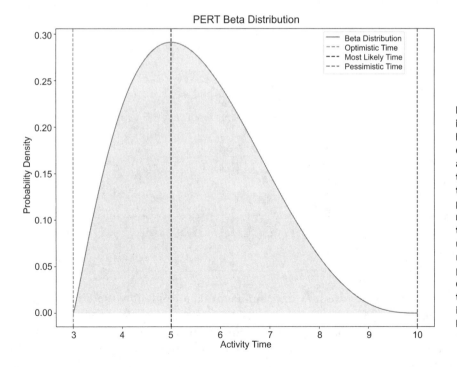

Figure 13.1 An illustration of the beta probability distribution assumed by PERT that displays the optimistic, pessimistic, and most likely activity times. The area under the curve represents the probability of different completion times, with the peak indicating the most likely duration.

Understanding the plot of the beta distribution helps illustrate how it captures the range and likelihood of different activity durations. It provides a clear line of sight into the probability of completing any task within the estimated times. This insight is crucial for project managers to make informed decisions, manage risks effectively, and ensure a realistic approach to scheduling and resource allocation.

The individual time estimates for every activity in the automated reporting tool WBS are provided in table 13.2. Several key points should be emphasized. First, the sum of the expected activity times does not represent the number of weeks it should take to complete the project. This is because some activities can be performed simultaneously by different resources, meaning the overall project timeline will likely be shorter than the sum of the individual expected times. Additionally, it is important to note that the most likely times and the expected times may not always align perfectly due to inherent variability in the estimates. This variance is significant as it influences the calculation of the probability of completing the project on time. Although planning primarily revolves around the expected times, understanding the variance is essential for accurately forecasting project completion and managing potential delays.

Table 13.2 Time estimates (in weeks) for automated reporting tool activities. Based on these estimates, the expected time to complete every activity sums to 39 weeks. However, because a subset of these activities can be performed in parallel, this does not represent the estimated project duration.

Activity	Optimistic, a	Most likely, m	Pessimistic, b	Expected time, t
A	2	3	4	3
B	1	2	3	2
C	2	3	4	3
D	3	5	7	5
E	2	3	4	3
F	2	4	6	4
G	2	4	6	4
H	2	3	4	3
I	2	3	4	3
J	2	4	6	4
K	2	3	4	3
L	1	2	3	2
				39

Despite these complexities, we now have sufficient data to identify the critical path. The *critical path* is crucial because it represents the longest sequence of tasks that must be completed on time for the project to be finished by the expected end date. Any delay in the tasks on the critical path will directly affect the overall project timeline, making it essential to monitor these activities closely. Identifying the critical path allows project managers to allocate resources efficiently and prioritize tasks to ensure that the project remains on track.

13.3 Finding the critical path

Finding the critical path is a vital step in project management, often achieved through the critical path method (CPM). The critical path represents the longest sequence of dependent tasks that determines the shortest possible duration to complete the project. Any delay in tasks on this path will directly delay the overall project timeline. Conversely, tasks not on the critical path may have some flexibility and can be delayed without affecting the project's end date. If there's a need to reduce the overall project timeline, it must be addressed by optimizing one or more tasks on the critical path. Understanding and managing the critical path ensures that project managers can effectively prioritize resources and mitigate potential delays.

To find the critical path, we first need to determine several key metrics based on the dependencies from the WBS and the expected activity times we just derived. These metrics are crucial for calculating the critical path and ensuring that the project is completed on time:

- *Earliest start time (ES)*—The earliest point in time when a task can begin, considering the completion of all preceding tasks
- *Earliest finish time (EF)*—The earliest point in time when a task can be completed, calculated by adding the expected activity time to the earliest start time
- *Latest start time (LS)*—The latest point in time a task can begin without delaying the project's overall completion
- *Latest finish time (LF)*—The latest point in time a task can be completed without delaying the project's overall completion

With tasks, dependencies, and expected activity times now clearly defined, we have established a comprehensive project plan. To identify the critical path, we will perform forward and backward passes through this plan, applying the dependencies and expected activity times to determine the earliest and latest start and finish times for each task. This process will ultimately reveal the critical path, highlighting the sequence of tasks that directly affect the project's overall timeline.

13.3.1 Earliest times

The earliest times in project scheduling are crucial for determining when activities can start and finish to ensure the project stays on track. The earliest finish time for any activity is calculated by adding the expected activity time to the earliest start time. For most activities, the earliest start time is the same as the earliest finish time of any immediate predecessors. However, if an activity depends on the completion of more than one prior activity, its earliest start time is determined by the latest of the earliest finish times of those preceding activities. This ensures that all necessary prerequisite activities are completed before a dependent activity begins.

The forward pass in project scheduling is the process of determining the earliest possible start and finish times for each activity within a project. This approach ensures that tasks are scheduled as soon as possible, which is essential for identifying the critical path and overall project timeline. In the automated reporting tool project plan, the forward pass begins at time zero. Activity A, which has no immediate predecessors, therefore has an earliest start time of 0 weeks. Given its expected duration of 3 weeks, the earliest finish time for Activity A is the sum of the earliest start time and its activity duration, resulting in 3 weeks.

Activity B can begin as soon as Activity A is completed. Therefore, the earliest start time for Activity B is the same as the earliest finish time of Activity A, which is 3 weeks. Considering that Activity B has an expected activity time of 2 weeks, its earliest finish time is calculated to be 5 weeks from the project start date. This process continues for all subsequent activities, ensuring that each task begins as soon as its predecessors are completed, thereby optimizing the project schedule. Through the forward pass, we can effectively map out the timeline of the project, ensuring that each activity is allocated the earliest possible start and finish times, which is critical for timely project completion.

The network diagram in figure 13.2 provides a visual representation of the automated reporting tool project plan. Each activity is labeled with its unique identifier. Lines and arrows between activities indicate dependencies, signifying that one or more activities must be completed before subsequent activities can begin. The sequence of digits beneath each activity represents the earliest start time, expected activity time, and earliest finish time, respectively.

This analysis indicates a project duration of 29 weeks, which is determined by the longest path in the network. However, to accurately identify the critical path and ensure timely project completion, a backward pass through the network is necessary to determine the latest start and finish times for each activity. Only when we have both the earliest and latest times can we then identify the project's critical path.

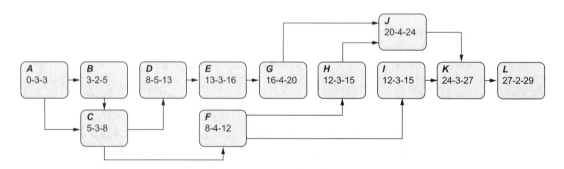

Figure 13.2 A visual representation of the automated reporting tool project plan, where each activity is represented by its unique identifier. Lines and arrows between activities represent dependencies. The sequence of digits immediately beneath each activity represents, in order, the activity's earliest start time, expected duration, and earliest finish time. The earliest times are derived by using a forward pass through the network. Based on this analysis, the project timeline is 29 weeks, which is the length of the longest path in the network.

13.3.2 Latest times

Determining the latest times for project activities is essential for understanding the flexibility within the project schedule. The latest finish time for any activity is the latest time it can be completed without delaying the overall project. This is calculated through a backward pass, starting from the project's finish and moving backward through the network. Similarly, the latest start time for an activity is the latest time it can begin without delaying the project, calculated by subtracting the activity duration from the latest finish time.

With respect to our project plan for the automated reporting tool, the process begins by setting the latest finish time for the final activity, which in this case is 29 weeks. For the final activity, Activity L, the latest finish time is 29 weeks, and the latest start time is calculated by subtracting the expected activity time (2 weeks) from the latest finish time, resulting in 27 weeks. This means Activity L must start by week 27 to finish by week 29.

Next, we move to the preceding activity, Activity K. The latest finish time for Activity K is set to the latest start time of Activity L, which is 27 weeks. The latest start time for Activity K is then calculated by subtracting its expected duration (3 weeks) from its latest finish time, resulting in 24 weeks. Therefore, Activity K must start by week 24 and finish by week 27 without delaying the project.

The backward pass continues through the network similarly for all activities. For tasks with multiple succeeding activities, the latest finish time is the minimum of the latest start times of all immediate successors. By calculating the latest start and finish times for each activity, we can determine the amount of slack time available. Activities with zero slack time are on the critical path, meaning any delay in these activities will directly affect the project's completion date. The network diagram version of the automated reporting tool project plan is updated to include a second three-digit sequence for each activity that represents the latest start time, the expected duration, and the latest finish time (see figure 13.3).

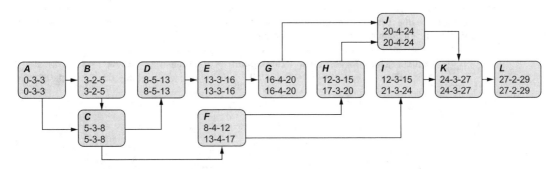

Figure 13.3 A second visual representation of the automated reporting tool project plan. The new three-digit sequence for each activity represents, in order, the latest start time, the expected duration, and the latest finish time. A quick and easy way of distinguishing critical tasks from noncritical tasks is to compare the three-digit sequences: critical tasks have similar three-digit sequences, whereas noncritical tasks do not.

Now that the earliest and latest start and finish times for each activity in the project plan are defined, calculating the slack time—that is, the amount of time that an activity can be delayed without causing a delay to subsequent activities or the overall project completion date—becomes a matter of simple arithmetic. This will allow us to determine the flexibility we have with scheduling each task without affecting the overall project timeline.

13.3.3 Slack

Slack is the amount of time an activity can be delayed without causing a delay to subsequent activities or the project's overall timeline. It is calculated as the difference between the latest and earliest start times or, alternatively, as the difference between the latest and earliest finish times (either method will return the same result). Activities with no slack are on the critical path, whereas those with some slack are not. In other words, activities with no difference between their earliest and latest start or finish times have zero slack and are therefore classified as critical path activities, meaning any delay in these will directly affect the project's schedule. On the other hand, activities that have a discrepancy between their earliest and latest times have some slack, thereby consigning them to a noncritical path. This slack allows these tasks to be delayed—up to a certain extent—without affecting the overall project timeline.

The results, both direct and derived, from the critical path method are presented in table 13.3. The earliest start and finish times were determined through a forward pass analysis of the project network, whereas the latest start and finish times were obtained via a backward pass analysis. Slack time for each activity was calculated by taking the difference between the latest and earliest start times (but could have been derived by instead taking the difference between the latest and earliest finish times). Activities with zero slack are classified as critical path tasks, meaning any delay in these activities will directly affect the project's overall timeline. Conversely, tasks with any amount of slack are not on the critical path.

Table 13.3 CPM results for the automated reporting tool project. Activities in any project have slack or no slack, which is derived by subtracting the earliest start from the latest start or, alternatively, by subtracting the earliest finish from the latest finish (it doesn't matter). Activities with no slack are on the critical path, whereas activities with slack are not.

Activity	Earliest start (ES)	Earliest finish (EF)	Latest start (LS)	Latest finish (LF)	Slack (LS – ES)	Critical path?
A	0	3	0	3	0	Yes
B	3	5	3	5	0	Yes
C	5	8	5	8	0	Yes
D	8	13	8	13	0	Yes
E	13	16	13	16	0	Yes
F	8	12	13	17	5	No

Table 13.3 CPM results for the automated reporting tool project. Activities in any project have slack or no slack, which is derived by subtracting the earliest start from the latest start or, alternatively, by subtracting the earliest finish from the latest finish (it doesn't matter). Activities with no slack are on the critical path, whereas activities with slack are not. *(continued)*

Activity	Earliest start (ES)	Earliest finish (EF)	Latest start (LS)	Latest finish (LF)	Slack (LS − ES)	Critical path?
G	16	20	16	20	0	Yes
H	12	15	17	20	5	No
I	12	15	21	24	9	No
J	20	24	20	24	0	Yes
K	24	27	24	27	0	Yes
L	27	29	27	29	0	Yes

This activity analysis reveals two key takeaways, with the first being far more consequential than the second. Our first takeaway is that a substantial number of the project's activities are on the critical path, meaning any delay in these tasks will directly affect the overall timeline. In typical projects, there are usually multiple parallel paths of activities, with only one of these paths being critical. Consequently, the ratio of critical to noncritical activities is generally much smaller than what we observe in the automated reporting tool project. Regardless, project management should be laser-focused on critical path tasks, even at the expense of those activities that have slack; day-to-day monitoring, risk mitigation, and even project crashing strategies should be directed at critical path activities to be impactful. By concentrating on one or more critical path tasks, project managers can effectively expedite the project without unnecessary efforts on noncritical activities.

The second takeaway is that the noncritical activities have considerable, rather than moderate, slack. This slack provides flexibility, allowing these tasks to be delayed without affecting the project's end date. Additionally, the significant slack means there is no immediate risk of these noncritical activities becoming critical. Understanding this distinction helps in planning and resource allocation, ensuring that project management efforts are directed where they are most needed to maintain the project schedule.

Identifying the critical path manually, however, especially from a project plan containing dozens or even hundreds of activities, can be impractical and prone to errors. As project complexity increases, the interdependencies and scheduling nuances become too intricate to handle without automation. Therefore, finding the critical path is best done programmatically. Using Python, we can perform forward and backward passes through a virtual project network, derive the earliest start and finish times for every activity, and subsequently classify tasks as critical or noncritical. Manual methods can't scale with project complexity, so we need to understand how to apply programmatic solutions to project management techniques like the CPM.

13.3.4 Finding the critical path programmatically

Having manually demonstrated the CPM, we will now automate it using a mix of common Python libraries and user-defined functions. By first creating a pandas data frame with the required data—activities, their dependencies, and their expected durations derived from optimistic, pessimistic, and most likely estimates—we can replicate the process of calculating earliest and latest start and finish times, thereby determining the slack for each activity and identifying the critical path. This automation streamlines the process, allowing us to efficiently manage complex project schedules and ensure accurate results, even for large and intricate project networks.

Be aware that finding the critical path programmatically, although significantly more efficient than a manual approach, still requires a fair amount of effort, especially for large and complex projects with numerous dependencies and constraints. The process involves careful data preparation, defining logical sequences, and ensuring accurate calculations for early and late start and finish times. However, the consequences of *not* identifying the critical path far outweigh the effort required to determine it. Without a clear understanding of the project's most time-sensitive activities, delays can easily cascade, increasing costs, extending timelines, and potentially forcing reductions in project scope. By automating critical path analysis, project managers can proactively mitigate these risks, allocate resources more effectively, and ensure that high-priority tasks remain on track to meet project deadlines.

CREATING THE DATA FRAME

Our first snippet of code creates a pandas data frame called `plan` that contains the following four attributes:

- `Activity`—A unique code or identifier assigned to each activity or task
- `Description`—A short description of each activity
- `Dependencies`–The preceding activities, if any, that must be completed before the current activity can begin
- `t`–The expected time, in weeks, for each activity, representing a weighted average of the optimistic, pessimistic, and most likely time estimates

The data frame is then displayed by passing `plan` to the `print()` method:

```
>>> import pandas as pd
>>> plan = pd.DataFrame({
>>>     'Activity': ['A', 'B', 'C', 'D', 'E', 'F', 'G', 'H', 'I', 'J',
>>>                  'K', 'L'],
>>>     'Description': [
>>>         'Define Project Objectives and Scope',
>>>         'Assemble Project Team',
>>>         'Gather Requirements from Stakeholders',
>>>         'Data Collection and Integration',
>>>         'Data Cleaning and Preprocessing',
>>>         'Design Report Templates',
>>>         'Develop Data Processing Pipelines',
>>>         'Implement Report Generation Logic',
>>>         'Develop User Interface for Report Access',
```

13.3 Finding the critical path

```
>>>             'Integrate Data Pipelines with Report Generation',
>>>             'Conduct User Testing and Feedback',
>>>             'Finalize and Deploy Automated Reporting Tool'
>>>        ],
>>>        'Dependencies': [None, ['A'], ['A', 'B'], ['C'], ['D'], ['C'],
                            ['E'], ['F'], ['F'], ['G', 'H'], ['I', 'J'],
                            ['K']],
           't': [3, 2, 3, 5, 3, 4, 4, 3, 3, 4, 3, 2]
})

print(plan)
     Activity                                     Description Dependencies  t
0         A                  Define Project Objectives and Scope     None  3
1         B                              Assemble Project Team      [A]   2
2         C                Gather Requirements from Stakeholders  [A, B]   3
3         D                      Data Collection and Integration      [C]  5
4         E                      Data Cleaning and Preprocessing      [D]  3
5         F                              Design Report Templates      [C]  4
6         G                    Develop Data Processing Pipelines      [E]  4
7         H                    Implement Report Generation Logic      [F]  3
8         I                Develop User Interface for Report Access  [F]  3
9         J      Integrate Data Pipelines with Report Generation  [G, H]  4
10        K                    Conduct User Testing and Feedback  [I, J]  3
11        L          Finalize and Deploy Automated Reporting Tool     [K]  2
```

The `plan` data frame is our foundation. Now that it's established, we can proceed with automating the CPM.

WRITING ERROR-HANDLING FUNCTIONS

Error-handling functions are essential for managing and responding to errors that occur during the execution of a program. These functions ensure that the program can gracefully handle unexpected issues, provide informative feedback to the user, and terminate the program if necessary to prevent further errors or data corruption. In the context of our project, we have defined several error-handling functions to proactively address potential problems with the input data. The following code snippets illustrate how we intend to manage any subsequent errors related to the Activity, Dependencies, and t columns in our `plan` data frame:

```
>>> def errorActivityMsg():
>>>     print('Error in input file : Activity')
>>>     sys.exit(1)

>>> def errorDependenciesMsg():
>>>     print('Error in input file : Dependencies')
>>>     sys.exit(1)

>>> def errortMsg():
>>>     print('Error in input file : t')
>>>     sys.exit(1)
```

For instance, the `errorActivityMsg()` function prints an error message related to the Activity variable and terminates the program using `sys.exit(1)`, ensuring that the error is promptly handled and the program stops execution to prevent further issues.

RETRIEVING ACTIVITY INDICES FOR TASK IDENTIFICATION

The `getTaskCode()` function is designed to retrieve the row index of a specific activity code within a pandas data frame. This function is essential for efficiently locating and referencing tasks based on their unique identifiers, which is crucial for project management tasks such as critical path analysis. By checking whether the activity code exists in the `Activity` column and returning the corresponding row index, the function ensures accurate task identification. If the code does not exist, the function calls `errorActivityMsg()` to handle the error gracefully. This mechanism enhances the robustness and reliability of our project management automation:

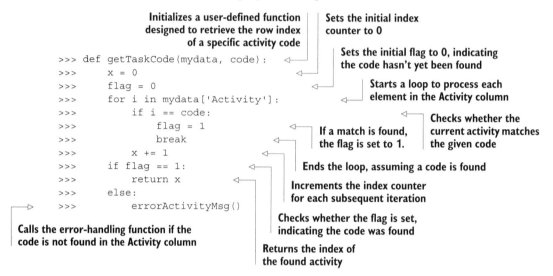

Next, we will demonstrate how to automate the forward and backward passes through the project network to calculate the earliest and latest start and finish times for each activity.

AUTOMATING THE FORWARD PASS IN PROJECT SCHEDULING

The following code implements the forward pass algorithm, a crucial step in project scheduling for calculating the earliest start and earliest finish times for each task. This function iterates through the project's activities, checking their dependencies to determine when each task can begin and end. If a task has no dependencies, it can start at time zero. For tasks with dependencies, the function calculates the earliest possible start time based on the latest finish time of all preceding tasks. This ensures that each task's scheduling considers the completion of its dependent tasks. The resulting earliest start and earliest finish times are then appended to the `plan` data frame, enabling a comprehensive view of the project timeline:

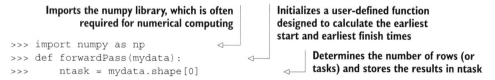

With the forward pass completed, we have successfully automated the calculation of the earliest start and earliest finish times for each activity. Next, we will automate the backward pass algorithm to determine the latest start and latest finish times, further refining our project schedule and identifying potential slack for each activity.

AUTOMATING THE BACKWARD PASS IN PROJECT SCHEDULING

The following code implements the backward pass algorithm, which is essential for calculating the latest start and latest finish times for each task in a project schedule. This function iterates through the project's activities in reverse order, determining the latest times each task can start and finish without delaying the project. By considering the dependencies and successors of each task, the algorithm ensures that all tasks are scheduled efficiently, identifying potential slack and further refining the project timeline. The calculated latest start and latest finish times are then appended to the data frame, thereby providing a complete and automated view of the project's scheduling details:

With the backward pass automated, we now have both the earliest and latest start and finish times for each activity. By taking the difference between the earliest start and latest start times or, alternatively, the difference between the earliest finish and latest finish times, we can calculate the slack for each activity. This allows us to easily determine which tasks are critical, as they have no slack, and which tasks are noncritical, having some degree of flexibility. This comprehensive analysis ensures efficient project scheduling and management, enabling us to identify and focus on key activities that directly affect the project timeline.

AUTOMATING SLACK IN PROJECT SCHEDULING

The following code implements the slack calculation for each activity in the project schedule. Slack represents the amount of time an activity can be delayed without affecting the project's overall timeline. This function iterates through all the tasks, computes the slack by taking the difference between the latest start and earliest start times, and determines whether each task is critical. Tasks with zero slack are marked as critical, indicating they directly affect the project's timeline. The updated data frame includes the calculated slack and critical path information, with just the necessary columns. This comprehensive analysis helps in identifying tasks that need close monitoring to ensure timely project completion:

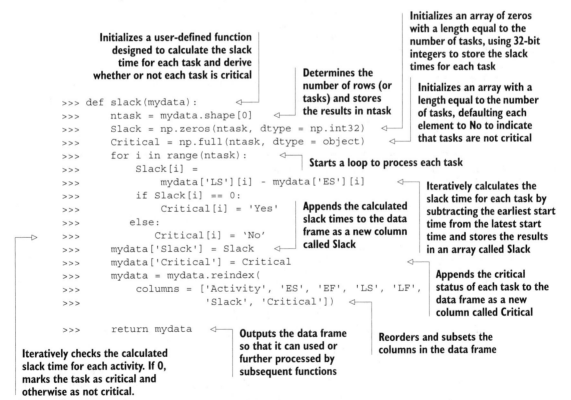

With the columns subsetted and reordered to include only the necessary information, our data frame now provides a clear and comprehensive view of the project schedule, featuring automated calculations for the earliest and latest start and finish times, slack, and critical status for each task. This streamlined format enables efficient project management by highlighting critical tasks that directly affect the project timeline and identifying noncritical tasks with available slack. By automating these detailed analyses, project managers can prioritize resources and focus on key activities to ensure timely project completion, all while minimizing the risk of human error.

FINALIZING AND DISPLAYING THE AUTOMATED PROJECT SCHEDULE

The first snippet of code implements a wrapper function, computeCPM(), that integrates all the necessary steps for automating the CPM calculations. A wrapper function is designed to call multiple other functions, streamlining the process into a single call. Here, compute CPM() sequentially invokes the forwardPass(), backwardPass(), and slack() functions to compute the earliest and latest start and finish times, as well as the slack for each task. This comprehensive approach ensures that all aspects of the project schedule are calculated and updated in the data frame, providing a complete and automated analysis of the project's critical path:

```
>>> def computeCPM(mydata):
>>>     mydata = forwardPass(mydata)
>>>     mydata = backwardPass(mydata)
>>>     mydata = slack(mydata)
>>>     return mydata
```

Another user-defined function, printPlan(), displays the project schedule and slack times in a tabular format. By setting pandas to display all columns, the function ensures that none of the important information is truncated. It prints a header to describe the key metrics and then outputs the data frame containing the calculated values for each task. This visual representation helps project managers quickly understand the project's schedule and identify critical tasks that need close monitoring:

```
>>> def printPlan(mydata):
>>>     pd.set_option('display.max_columns', None)
>>>     print('Automated Reporting Tool: Schedule and Slack Times')
>>>     print('*' * 50)
>>>     print('ES = Earliest Start; EF = Earliest Finish;\nLS = Latest
>>>         Start; LF = Latest Finish;\nSlack = LS - ES')
>>>     print('*' * 50)
>>>     print(mydata)
>>>     print('*' * 50)
```

The next line executes the computeCPM() wrapper function on the plan data frame, which of course encompasses the forwardPass(), backwardPass(), and slack() calculation functions. This single line automates the entire process of computing the earliest and latest start and finish times, as well as the slack for each task, updating the plan data frame with these calculated values. It effectively transforms the initial project data into a comprehensive schedule with critical path analysis, ready for further review or display:

```
>>> plan = computeCPM(plan)
```

And the final line of code calls the printPlan() function to display an automated version of table 13.3. This function outputs the complete project schedule, including the earliest and latest start and finish times, slack, and critical status for each task. It provides a clear and detailed visual representation of the project timeline, helping project managers quickly understand the schedule and identify critical tasks that require close monitoring:

```
>>> printPlan(plan)
Automated Reporting Tool: Schedule and Slack Times
****************************************************
ES = Earliest Start; EF = Earliest Finish;
LS = Latest Start;   LF = Latest Finish;
Slack = LS - ES
****************************************************
    Activity  ES  EF  LS  LF  Slack  Critical
0          A   0   3   0   3      0       Yes
1          B   3   5   3   5      0       Yes
2          C   5   8   5   8      0       Yes
3          D   8  13   8  13      0       Yes
4          E  13  16  13  16      0       Yes
5          F   8  12  13  17      5        No
6          G  16  20  16  20      0       Yes
7          H  12  15  17  20      5        No
8          I  12  15  21  24      9        No
9          J  20  24  20  24      0       Yes
10         K  24  27  24  27      0       Yes
11         L  27  29  27  29      0       Yes
****************************************************
```

With the process now fully automated, project managers can efficiently finalize and display their project schedules. As long as you organize your project plan—specifically, a WBS with the estimated duration for each activity—into a pandas data frame that matches the provided format, you can repurpose this code for your own projects. This method scales seamlessly, allowing you to handle projects of any size and complexity and automatically determine the critical path, ensuring a more effective and streamlined project management process.

13.4 Estimating the probability of project completion

Stakeholders have been apprised that, based on critical path analysis, the automated reporting tool project is expected to take 29 weeks. However, it is crucial for the project to be completed within 30 weeks to ensure that resources can be reassigned to other essential duties. Projects often need to meet specific deadlines for a variety of reasons: to avoid contractual fines, to capitalize on market opportunities by getting a product to market promptly, to align with other project schedules, or to fulfill regulatory requirements.

For example, a delayed product launch could mean missing a critical sales window, resulting in significant revenue loss. In construction projects, delays can lead to penalties or increased costs due to prolonged equipment rentals. In the tech industry, missing a market window can allow competitors to gain a foothold, affecting long-term business viability.

The project manager is concerned because of the variance in many of the critical path activities. If the pessimistic estimates for these activities come to fruition, the likelihood of completing the project in 30 weeks, let alone 29 weeks, could be in jeopardy. This uncertainty necessitates a thorough risk analysis to estimate the probability of project completion within the desired timeframe, taking into account the potential for delays and the effect of these variances on the overall schedule.

The variance for any activity is calculated by inserting the optimistic (a) and pessimistic (b) time estimates into the following formula:

$$\text{Variance} = \left(\frac{b-a}{6}\right)^2$$

So, if Activity A is optimistically estimated to take 2 weeks and pessimistically estimated to take 4 weeks, the variance for that activity is

$$\text{Variance}_{(A)} = \left(\frac{4-2}{6}\right)^2$$

or

$$\text{Variance}_{(A)} = \frac{1}{9}$$

The variance for an activity represents the degree of variability or uncertainty in the activity's time estimates. A higher variance indicates greater unpredictability in the duration, whereas a lower variance suggests more consistency and reliability in the time estimates. Table 13.4 shows the variances for every activity in the automated reporting tool project.

Table 13.4 Variances in time estimates for automated reporting tool activities, with critical path activities highlighted in bold. The project variance is derived, in part, by summing the variances of the critical path activities.

Activity	Optimistic, a	Pessimistic, b	Variance, ((b − a)/6)2
A	2	4	1/9
B	1	3	1/9
C	2	4	1/9
D	3	7	4/9
E	2	4	1/9

13.4 Estimating the probability of project completion

Table 13.4 Variances in time estimates for automated reporting tool activities, with critical path activities highlighted in bold. The project variance is derived, in part, by summing the variances of the critical path activities. *(continued)*

Activity	Optimistic, a	Pessimistic, b	Variance, $((b-a)/6)^2$
F	2	6	4/9
G	**2**	**6**	**4/9**
H	2	4	1/9
I	**2**	**4**	**1/9**
J	2	6	4/9
K	**2**	**4**	**1/9**
L	**1**	**3**	**1/9**

Just as the project duration is derived by summing the expected times for every activity on the critical path, the project variance is derived by summing the variances from only the critical path activities, assuming the activity times are statistically independent. Hence, the project variance is

$$\text{Project Variance} = \frac{1}{9} + \frac{1}{9} + \frac{1}{9} + \frac{4}{9} + \frac{1}{9} + \frac{4}{9} + \frac{4}{9} + \frac{1}{9} + \frac{1}{9} = \frac{18}{9} = 2 \text{ weeks}$$

The standard deviation is equal to the square root of the variance:

$$\text{Project Standard Deviation} = \sigma = \sqrt{2}$$

This is approximately 1.41 weeks.

Assuming project completion times follow a normal probability distribution, we can therefore divide the difference between the due date and the project duration by the standard deviation to get a z-score (see chapter 3):

$$z = \frac{\text{due date} - \text{project duration}}{\sigma}$$

or

$$z = \frac{30 - 29}{1.41}$$

This equals 0.709, where z is the number of standard deviations the due date is above the project duration.

If the project duration represents the mean of a normal probability distribution, there is an equal 50/50 chance of completing the project on time. Therefore, if the due date is beyond the mean, the probability of completing the project within 30 weeks is greater than 50%. The exact probability can be determined by looking up the z-score in a z-score table (see figure 13.4).

z	.00	.01	.02	.03	.04	.05	.06	.07	.08	.09
0.0	.5000	.5040	.5080	.5120	.5160	.5199	.5239	.5279	.5319	.5359
0.1	.5398	.5438	.5478	.5517	.5557	.5596	.5636	.5675	.5714	.5753
0.2	.5793	.5832	.5871	.5910	.5948	.5987	.6026	.6064	.6103	.6141
0.3	.6179	.6217	.6255	.6293	.6331	.6368	.6406	.6443	.6480	.6517
0.4	.6554	.6591	.6628	.6664	.6700	.6736	.6772	.6808	.6844	.6879
0.5	.6915	.6950	.6985	.7019	.7054	.7088	.7123	.7157	.7190	.7224
0.6	.7257	.7291	.7324	.7357	.7389	.7422	.7454	.7486	.7517	.7549
0.7	.7580	.7611	.7642	.7673	.7704	.7734	.7764	.7794	.7823	.7852
0.8	.7881	.7910	.7939	.7967	.7995	.8023	.8051	.8078	.8106	.8133
0.9	.8159	.8186	.8212	.8238	.8264	.8289	.8315	.8340	.8365	.8389
1.0	.8413	.8438	.8461	.8485	.8508	.8531	.8554	.8577	.8599	.8621
1.1	.8643	.8665	.8686	.8708	.8729	.8749	.8770	.8790	.8810	.8830
1.2	.8849	.8869	.8888	.8907	.8925	.8944	.8962	.8980	.8997	.9015
1.3	.9032	.9049	.9066	.9082	.9099	.9115	.9131	.9147	.9162	.9177
1.4	.9192	.9207	.9222	.9236	.9251	.9265	.9279	.9292	.9306	.9319
1.5	.9332	.9345	.9357	.9370	.9382	.9394	.9406	.9418	.9429	.9441
1.6	.9452	.9463	.9474	.9484	.9495	.9505	.9515	.9525	.9535	.9545
1.7	.9554	.9564	.9573	.9582	.9591	.9599	.9608	.9616	.9625	.9633
1.8	.9641	.9649	.9656	.9664	.9671	.9678	.9686	.9693	.9699	.9706
1.9	.9713	.9719	.9726	.9732	.9738	.9744	.9750	.9756	.9761	.9767
2.0	.9772	.9778	.9783	.9788	.9793	.9798	.9803	.9808	.9812	.9817

Figure 13.4 The top of a typical z-score table. The probability is found where the integer and remaining fractional parts of the value intersect.

The probability is found where the first two digits of the z-score, located in the far-left column of the table, intersect with the next two digits of the z-score, located along the top row. For example, a z-score of 0.709 corresponds to a probability of 0.7852, or 78.52%, which is found at the intersection of 0.7 and 0.09. Therefore, there is a better than 78% chance of completing the project within 30 weeks or less.

We can use `scipy.stats` to compute the cumulative probability directly from the z-score without the use of a z-score table:

```
>>> import scipy.stats as stats
>>> due_date = 30
>>> mean = 29
>>> standard_deviation = 1.41
>>> z_score = (due_date - mean) / standard_deviation

>>> probability = stats.norm.cdf(z_score)

>>> print(f'z-score: {z_score:.3f}')
z-score: 0.709
```

```
>>> print(f'Probability of completing the project within '
>>>       f'{due_date} weeks: {probability:.2%}')
    Probability of completing the project within 30 weeks: 76.09%
```

The discrepancy between the probability obtained from the z-table (78.52%) and the probability calculated using Python's `scipy.stats` library (76.09%) can be attributed to differences in precision and rounding methods. Z-tables typically provide rounded values and sometimes use interpolation to offer probabilities between listed points. On the other hand, `scipy.stats.norm.cdf()` computes the probability using precise floating-point arithmetic, which can result in slightly different values. Despite this minor difference, the overall effect on project completion probability is relatively immaterial. Both methods yield a close approximation, and the key takeaway remains that there is a high probability of completing the project within the required timeframe. For most practical purposes, either method provides a sufficiently accurate estimate to inform project management decisions.

To better understand the probability of project completion, it's helpful to visualize a normal probability distribution. Figure 13.5 illustrates this concept, where the due

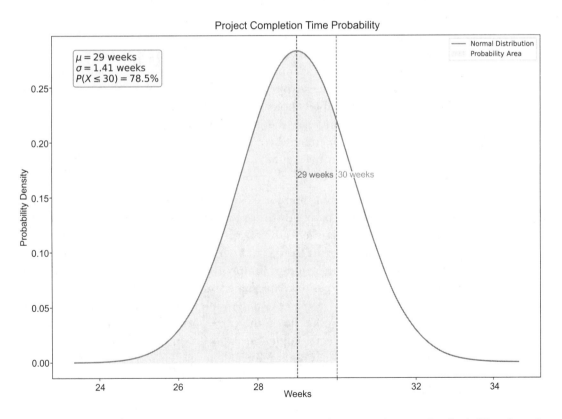

Figure 13.5 Normal probability distribution of project completion time, where the mean duration is 29 weeks and the standard deviation is 1.41 weeks. The due date of 30 weeks is marked, showing a 78.5% probability (using the z-table results) of completing the project within this timeframe.

date is 30 weeks, the expected project duration is 29 weeks, and the project standard deviation is 1.41 weeks. This plot shows the distribution of possible project completion times, and the shaded area represents the probability of completing the project within 30 weeks. The vertical dashed lines indicate the mean and the due date, providing a clear visual representation of how the project timeline aligns with the expected duration and the due date. By examining this plot, we can see that there is a significant probability of completing the project on or before the 30-week deadline, quantified by the shaded area under the curve up to the due date.

Although the automated reporting tool project stands a good chance of being completed within 30 weeks or less, there may still be opportunities to compress the schedule, possibly at an additional cost, without compromising on scope. Implementing schedule compression techniques, such as fast-tracking or crashing, could further increase the probability of meeting the 30-week deadline and provide added assurance to stakeholders.

13.5 Crashing the project

Crashing a project involves accelerating the overall project timeline by reducing the duration of one or more critical path activities. This typically incurs additional project expenses, as accelerating the schedule often requires increased labor costs. It's a fundamental principle of project management that altering one parameter, such as the schedule, inevitably affects other components, like cost or scope. Despite these potential increases in project expenses, exploring options for crashing the project can provide stakeholders with valuable choices. They can decide whether to invest in accelerating the timeline to increase the probability of completing the project within 30 weeks or even less, or to maintain the current schedule, considering that a 76% to 78% chance of finishing on or before the due date is already a favorable likelihood.

To maximize the cost-effectiveness of project crashing, follow these four steps:

1. Change out the expected time for each activity with the most likely time, and recalculate the critical path. For the automated reporting tool project, recalculating the critical path is unnecessary because the expected and most likely times for each activity are similar. However, this is not typically the case. When there is a difference between these times, simply replace the expected times with the most likely times in the pandas data frame and re-run the Python code that automates the critical path processes to determine the new critical path. Otherwise, focus on those activities that lie on the (new or previous) critical path, as these directly affect the project completion date. Crashing noncritical activities will increase the project cost and not reduce the overall project duration.

2. Calculate the weekly crash cost (or other unit of time) for every activity using the following formula:

$$\text{Weekly Crash Cost} = \frac{\text{Crash Cost} - \text{Normal Cost}}{\text{Normal Time} - \text{Crash Time}}$$

This calculation helps to determine the additional cost incurred for each unit of time saved by accelerating an activity, thereby allowing for the prioritization of which tasks to crash based on both cost and time efficiency. It assumes that crash costs are linear.

3. Select one or more critical path activities with the lowest weekly crash costs. Crash these activities to the maximum extent possible or as needed to meet the deadline or significantly improve the probability of finishing before the due date.
4. Ensure that crashing does not alter the existing critical path or create a new critical path. Carefully monitor the project schedule after applying crashing techniques to confirm that the intended activities are shortened without inadvertently shifting the critical path or adding new critical activities, which could negate the benefits of crashing and introduce new scheduling risks. For the automated reporting tool project, this is not a concern due to the significant slack variances between critical and noncritical activities.

The most likely times and crash times per activity, along with their corresponding costs, are then summarized in table 13.5.

Table 13.5 Most likely and crash estimates for the automated reporting tool project in weeks and dollars. The most effective way of accelerating a project timeline is to crash one or more critical path activities with the lowest weekly crash costs.

Activity	Time (weeks) Most likely	Time (weeks) Crash	Cost ($) Most likely	Cost ($) Crash	Weekly crash cost ($)	Critical path?
A	3	2	5,000	6,000	1,000	Yes
B	2	1	4,000	5,000	1,000	Yes
C	3	2	5,000	6,000	1,000	Yes
D	5	4	9,000	11,000	2,000	Yes
E	3	2	5,000	6,000	1,000	Yes
F	4	3	8,000	9,000	1,000	No
G	4	2	8,000	10,000	1,000	Yes
H	3	2	5,000	7,000	2,000	No
I	3	2	5,000	6,000	1,000	No
J	4	2	7,000	10,000	1,500	Yes
K	3	1	5,000	7,000	1,000	Yes
L	2	1	4,000	5,000	1,000	Yes

The most effective way to accelerate the timeline of the automated reporting tool project is to focus on crashing the critical path activities with the lowest weekly crash costs. Based on the data, the best (but not only) candidates for crashing include Activities A, B, C, E, G, K, and L. These activities not only lie on the critical path but also have relatively low additional weekly costs when crashed. These activities each have a crash cost of $1,000 per week, making them cost-effective choices for reducing the project duration. Additionally, Activities D and J, despite having slightly higher weekly crash costs as compared to the other critical activities, still present viable options due to their significant effect on the overall project timeline. By selectively crashing these activities, the project manager can optimize resource allocation, minimize additional costs, and significantly improve the likelihood of completing the project within the desired timeframe.

More complex projects, however, require more advanced crashing methods. To crash the automated reporting tool project (or any project) most effectively, we can set up a constrained optimization problem (see chapter 8). The objective function in this case would be to minimize the total crashing costs, whereas the constraints would include the allowable crash time per activity, the project deadline, and the dependencies between activities.

We have demonstrated how the use of quantitative methods can make a significant difference between unsuccessful and successful project management—and unsuccessful and successful projects. These techniques provide the precision and clarity needed to effectively plan, execute, and control projects. In the next and final chapter, we will focus on establishing quality control measures and visualizing them.

Summary

- Managing projects effectively requires a solid foundation in quantitative skills. These skills enable project managers to analyze data, forecast outcomes, and make informed decisions based on numerical evidence. Proficiency in areas such as scheduling, risk assessment, and resource allocation is critical. These competencies help in structuring plans that are realistic and achievable, ensuring project objectives are met efficiently.
- A work breakdown structure is pivotal in project planning and management. It systematically breaks down a project into manageable sections and tasks, making it easier to organize, schedule, and delegate. The WBS serves as the foundation for the project planning process, helping to identify all necessary activities, allocate resources appropriately, and establish a timeline that supports the project's objectives.
- The program evaluation and review technique is utilized especially in scenarios where there's a lack of analogous estimating data. PERT focuses on calculating time estimates for project activities by considering optimistic, pessimistic, and most likely durations. This approach accommodates uncertainty and variability in project planning, allowing for more robust and resilient scheduling.
- The critical path method identifies the longest sequence of dependent activities and calculates the shortest possible project duration. Automating CPM enhances accuracy in identifying the critical path, reduces manual errors, and

speeds up the reevaluation of the project schedule in response to changes. This automation supports dynamic project management and allows real-time decision-making to keep the project on track.

- Calculating the probability of on-time project completion involves using statistical methods to assess the likelihood of meeting project deadlines. By computing the z-score for the project duration and using it to estimate the cumulative probability, project managers can quantify the chances of completing the project by a specified due date. This method provides a clear, numerical understanding of schedule risks, enabling better planning and decision-making to ensure timely project delivery.

- Project crashing is a technique used to shorten the duration of a project by decreasing the time for one or more critical path activities. This is often achieved at additional costs, typically by assigning overtime to current project team members or by adding resources. The decision to crash a project is usually made when the benefits of completing the project sooner outweigh the additional expenses and other factors.

- Applying quantitative skills to project management requires significant analytical effort and careful planning, even with automation. However, the consequences of inadequate project management—delays, budget overruns, and compromised scope—are often far greater. Poor planning is a leading cause of project failure, and using quantitative methods helps mitigate risks, optimize schedules, and improve overall project outcomes.

Visualizing quality control

This chapter covers
- Quality control measures
- Control charts for attributes (or qualitative data)
- Control charts for variables (or quantitative data)

Quality is a fundamental concept that permeates every aspect of our lives, from the products we use daily to the services we rely on. Defining quality, however, is not always straightforward. In a broad sense, quality can be understood as the degree to which a product or service meets or exceeds customer expectations. This encompasses attributes such as reliability, durability, and performance. But quality is not merely an attribute of a finished product; it is an integral aspect of the entire production and service delivery process. When organizations focus on quality, they aim to ensure that every component of their operations contributes to the creation of a superior final product or service.

To maintain and improve quality, organizations implement controls. Controls are systematic measures put in place to regulate processes, ensuring they function within defined parameters and produce consistent results. Controls can be preventive, aimed at stopping problems before they occur, or detective, identifying issues as they arise. Effective control mechanisms are essential for maintaining standards, reducing variability, and minimizing defects. Without proper controls, processes can deviate, leading to variations that compromise the quality of the final product.

This is where statistical quality control comes into play. Statistical quality control involves the use of statistical methods to monitor and control a process. It is a branch of quality management that employs statistical tools, including control charts for attributes and variables, to identify and rectify sources of variability, ensuring processes remain stable and predictable. The foundation of statistical quality control lies in the collection and analysis of data. By examining data patterns and trends, organizations can make informed decisions that enhance process performance and product quality. Techniques include control charts, process capability analysis, and design of experiments, all of which are geared toward achieving and maintaining high quality.

Visualization plays a crucial role in statistical quality control. The human brain processes visual information far more efficiently than numerical data. This is why charts and graphs are invaluable tools in quality management. They provide a clear and immediate understanding of complex data, making it easier to identify trends, outliers, and patterns. Visual tools like control charts transform abstract numbers into tangible insights, enabling quick and effective decision-making.

Control charts are a quintessential example of how visualization and quality control are inherently linked. These charts, whether for attributes or variables, graphically display process data over time, helping to monitor process stability and control. For instance, a p-chart (proportion chart) tracks the proportion of defective items in a process, whereas an np-chart monitors the number of defective items in a sample. By plotting data points against control limits, control charts highlight any deviations from the norm, signaling when a process is going out of control. This visual representation allows quality managers to quickly pinpoint issues, investigate causes, and implement corrective actions.

The marriage of visualization and quality control is not just a matter of convenience; it is a powerful synergy that enhances the effectiveness of quality management. Visual tools like control charts simplify the interpretation of data, making it accessible to a broader audience, from shop floor operators to senior management. They facilitate a common understanding of process performance and foster a culture of continuous improvement. In the technology industry, similar visualizations are widely used to monitor key performance indicators—such as latency, error rates, and availability—providing guardrails that help teams detect quality issues and maintain service reliability.

In the context of this last chapter, we will explore various quality control charts, including p-charts and np-charts, demonstrating how they can be constructed and interpreted. These tools will serve as practical examples of how visualizing quality control can drive better decision-making and improve overall process quality. By integrating statistical methods with visual tools, organizations can not only maintain but also elevate their quality standards, ensuring that they consistently meet or exceed customer expectations.

To effectively utilize quality control charts, it is crucial to first identify and understand the key measures that are foundational to these tools. These measures provide the necessary insights into process performance and help in making informed decisions to maintain or improve quality.

14.1 Quality control measures

Defining key measures used in common quality control reports is essential for accurately interpreting various types of control charts. Although not all of these measures will appear in every chart demonstrated, they play a crucial role in providing a comprehensive understanding of quality control practices. Gaining familiarity with these metrics ensures a stronger foundation for analyzing and maintaining process quality effectively.

14.1.1 Upper control limit and lower control limit

In quality control charts, the upper control limit (UCL) and lower control limit (LCL) are the most critical measures. These limits are essential for distinguishing between normal process variation and signals that a process may be out of control.

The UCL and LCL are typically defined mathematically as being three standard deviations above and below the mean, respectively. This conventional setting ensures that about 99.73% of all data points should fall within these limits if the process is in control. Imagine a chart where the mean is represented as a central horizontal line, with the UCL and LCL as parallel lines above and below it; data points that fall within these limits indicate a stable process, whereas those outside suggest potential issues that require further investigation. However, it's worth noting that not all industries follow this exact three-sigma convention. In the technology sector, for instance, teams often define custom guardrails for key metrics—such as latency thresholds or error rates—based on operational goals rather than statistical distributions. This ties back to chapter 3, where we noted that approximately 99.73% of a normally distributed data set lies within three standard deviations of the mean—a useful baseline that some industries adapt or reinterpret based on context.

However, the control limits can and should be adjusted based on specific use cases and requirements. For example,

- In highly critical processes, such as pharmaceutical manufacturing or aerospace component production, the control limits might be set at two standard deviations from the mean. This tighter range helps to detect smaller shifts or trends in the process more quickly, ensuring that any potential issues are identified and corrected promptly.
- In processes where some variability is inherent and acceptable, such as agricultural products or construction materials, the control limits might be set at four

standard deviations. This broader range accommodates natural variations without signaling unnecessary alarms.

In quality control charts, the UCL and LCL are typically depicted as horizontal lines above and below the center line (which represents the process mean). Data points are plotted over time to monitor the process performance.

Understanding how to interpret and use control limits is critical for effective quality control. The following points outline the key considerations for evaluating data points in relation to the UCL and LCL:

- When all data points fall within the UCL and LCL, the process is considered to be in control. This indicates that any variations are due to common causes inherent to the process.
- If a data point falls outside these limits, it signals that the process may be out of control. This could be due to special cause variation, which requires investigation and corrective action.
- Even if data points are within control limits, specific patterns, such as runs of seven or more points on one side of the mean or consistent upward or downward trends, can indicate potential issues.

By setting appropriate control limits, organizations can effectively monitor process performance, quickly identify any deviations, and implement corrective actions to maintain high-quality standards. The choice of control limits should be based on the specific context, goals, and requirements of the process, ensuring a balanced approach to quality control.

14.1.2 Mean and center line

The mean is the arithmetic average of a set of values and serves as a central value for the data being analyzed. It is calculated by summing all the individual values and dividing by the number of values. The mean provides a measure of central tendency, representing the expected value in a set of data.

The center line (CL) in a control chart is the horizontal line that represents the mean of the process being monitored. It serves as a reference point for evaluating process performance. Data points are plotted in relation to this line to determine whether the process is stable and in control. The CL helps identify variations from the mean, facilitating the detection of trends and patterns that may indicate issues in the process.

14.1.3 Standard deviation

In the context of quality control charts, the standard deviation is used to measure the variability of a process. For attribute data, such as in p-charts, the formula for standard deviation is different from the general formula used for continuous data. This is because attribute data represents counts or proportions, which have different statistical properties compared to continuous measurements.

The formula for the standard deviation (σ) of a proportion in a p-chart is

$$\sigma = \sqrt{\frac{\bar{p}(1-\bar{p})}{n}}$$

where

- $\bar{p}$ represents the average proportion of defective items over all samples. It is calculated as the total number of defective items divided by the total number of items inspected.
- $1 - \bar{p}$ represents the proportion of nondefective items in the sample. Together with $\bar{p}$ it accounts for the total variability in the sample.
- n is the sample size, indicating the number of items inspected in each sample. The variability of the proportion decreases with larger sample sizes.

Otherwise, the formula uses the square root to transform the variance (the average of the squared differences from the mean) into the standard deviation, thereby providing a measure of spread in the same units as the data.

For continuous data, which involves measurements on a continuous scale, the standard deviation is calculated using a different formula:

$$\sigma = \sqrt{\frac{\sum(x_i - \bar{x})^2}{n}}$$

where

- x_i represents the individual data points or measurements.
- $\bar{x}$ is the mean of all the data points.
- $\sum(x_i - \bar{x})^2$ represents the sum of the squared differences between each data point and the mean. It measures the total variability in the data.
- n is the number of data points in the data set.

The square root of the variance converts it into the standard deviation, which is in the same units as the data points.

Using the correct formula for standard deviation in quality control charts ensures that control limits are appropriately set, allowing for effective monitoring of process performance. By understanding the nature of the data and applying the right statistical measures, quality control charts can accurately detect variations, identify potential issues, and maintain high standards of quality.

14.1.4 Range

Range in the context of quality control charts is a measure of the dispersion or variability within a set of data points. It is calculated as the difference between the highest and lowest values in a sample. The range provides a simple yet effective way to assess the spread of data and is often used in r-charts (range charts) to monitor process variability over time.

The formula for calculating the range (R) is

$$R = X_{max} - X_{min}$$

where

- X_{max} is the maximum value in the sample.
- X_{min} is the minimum value in the sample.

In quality control, the range is particularly useful for detecting changes in the consistency of the process. It helps identify variations that may indicate a loss of control, allowing for timely interventions to maintain process stability and quality.

14.1.5 Sample size

Sample size in the context of quality control charts refers to the number of observations or data points collected from a process during a specific sampling period. It is denoted by n and plays a crucial role in the accuracy and reliability of the control charts.

The sample size affects several aspects of quality control charts, including

- *Control limits*—UCL and LCL calculations are sometimes influenced by the sample size. Larger sample sizes tend to produce narrower control limits, making the control chart more sensitive to small shifts in the process.
- *Statistical power*—A larger sample size increases the ability to detect true variations in the process, enhancing a chart's effectiveness in identifying out-of-control conditions.
- *Variation*—With larger sample sizes, the estimates of process parameters (such as the mean and standard deviation) become more accurate, providing a better representation of the actual process behavior.

In summary, the sample size is a fundamental parameter in quality control charts that affects the precision, sensitivity, and reliability of the monitoring process. It determines the extent to which the control chart can accurately reflect the process's stability and detect deviations from the desired quality standards.

14.1.6 Proportion defective

Proportion defective is a fundamental metric in quality control charts that quantifies the percentage of units within a sample that fail to meet established quality standards. This measure, denoted by p, is particularly critical in attribute control charts like p-charts, where the focus is on tracking the quality of a process over time. By calculating the proportion defective, quality control practitioners gain immediate insight into the overall performance of a process. The proportion defective is determined using a straightforward formula:

$$p = \frac{D}{n}$$

where

- D represents the number of defective units.
- n is the total number of units in the sample.

In the context of p-charts, the proportion defective serves as the primary measure for monitoring the quality of a process over time. By plotting the proportion of defective items in each sample, p-charts help identify variations and trends that may indicate underlying issues in the process. Although the proportion defective itself does not determine the control limits, it is used to calculate the standard deviation, which in turn helps establish the upper and lower control limits. These control limits are essential for distinguishing between common cause variation, which is inherent to the process, and special cause variation, which signals a potential problem that warrants investigation.

Monitoring the proportion defective is crucial for maintaining consistent quality standards and ensuring that the process remains in control. By identifying trends, shifts, or cycles in the proportion of defective items, quality control practitioners can implement timely corrective actions and continuous improvements. This proactive approach helps organizations meet customer expectations, comply with regulatory requirements, and maintain a competitive edge in the market.

14.1.7 Number of defective items

The number of defective items is a crucial measure in quality control, representing the count of units in a sample that fail to meet specified quality standards. This measure, denoted by D, is fundamental in attribute control charts such as np-charts and c-charts. It provides a straightforward way to assess the quality of a process by counting the actual number of defective units.

In the context of np-charts, the number of defective items is the primary measure used to monitor the quality of a process over time. Unlike p-charts, which track the proportion of defective items, np-charts focus on the actual count of defects in a sample. This approach is particularly useful when the sample size remains constant, allowing for a direct and intuitive interpretation of the number of defects. For instance, if a sample of 100 items contains 5 defective units, then $D = 5$, providing a clear picture of the defect level.

For c-charts, the number of defective items is used to count defects per unit in situations where each unit can have multiple defects. This type of chart is helpful for processes where defects can occur in various forms on a single unit, such as scratches, dents, or other imperfections. By tracking the count of defects per unit, c-charts help in identifying patterns and trends in the process, highlighting areas that may require attention.

Calculating the number of defective items involves simply counting the units that do not meet quality criteria in each sample. This measure helps directly assess the level of defects, making it easy for operators and managers to understand and interpret. By plotting the number of defective items on control charts, quality control practitioners can quickly identify when a process is out of control, necessitating investigation and corrective actions.

Monitoring the number of defective items is essential for maintaining high quality standards. It allows organizations to identify variations and trends in the production process, implement timely corrective actions, and ensure customer satisfaction. By using the number of defective items in quality control charts, organizations can effectively track defects, identify areas for improvement, and maintain consistent quality in their processes, thereby meeting regulatory requirements and achieving operational excellence.

14.1.8 Number of defects

The number of defects is a critical measure in quality control that quantifies the total instances of nonconformance or imperfections within a sample. This measure, often denoted by C, plays a pivotal role in attribute control charts such as c-charts and u-charts. Unlike the number of defective items, which counts the units that fail to meet quality standards, the number of defects focuses on the total count of defects within those units, providing a more detailed picture of the quality issues present in the process.

In the context of c-charts, the number of defects is used to monitor the count of defects per unit or per sample over time. This type of chart is particularly useful in processes where each unit can have multiple defects, such as manufacturing, where a single product might have several types of flaws, like scratches, dents, or misalignments. By tracking the total number of defects, c-charts help identify trends and variations that may indicate problems in the production process, enabling timely interventions to maintain quality standards.

Similarly, u-charts utilize the number of defects but normalize this count based on the number of units inspected, providing a defect rate per unit. This normalization is crucial when the sample size varies, allowing for a fair comparison of defect levels across different samples. For example, if 100 units are inspected in one sample and 200 units in another, the u-chart adjusts for this difference, ensuring that the analysis remains consistent and meaningful.

Calculating the number of defects involves counting all instances of nonconformance within a sample. For instance, if a sample of 50 products has a total of 20 scratches and 10 dents, the number of defects C is 30. This measure offers a granular view of quality issues, making it easier to pinpoint specific problems and areas that require improvement.

14.1.9 Defects per unit

Tracking defects per unit is a vital aspect of quality control, particularly in processes where multiple defects can occur in a single unit. Control charts such as c-charts and u-charts are used to monitor the number of defects per unit over time. By capturing and analyzing this data, organizations can quickly identify when the process is deviating from acceptable quality standards. The number of defects per unit can range from zero (indicating no defects) to higher numbers, depending on the complexity of the

14.1.10 Moving range

Moving range is an important concept in quality control, particularly in the analysis of process variability through control charts. It refers to the difference between consecutive data points in a sequence, providing a measure of how much the process varies from one observation to the next. The moving range (MR) is calculated by taking the absolute difference between successive observations:

$$MR = |X_i - X_{i-1}|$$

where

- X_i is the current data point.
- X_{i-1} is the previous data point.

In the context of quality control charts, the moving range is often used in conjunction with individuals-moving range (I-MR) charts. Although the individuals (I) chart monitors the central tendency of a process (i.e., the mean), the MR chart focuses on the variability between consecutive measurements. By tracking these two aspects, I-MR charts provide a comprehensive view of the process, allowing quality control practitioners to monitor both the process average and the consistency of the data.

A stable process typically exhibits a consistent MR, with most values falling within established control limits. When the MR remains stable, it suggests that the process variability is under control and that any observed differences between consecutive data points are within expected limits. However, significant deviations in the MR, such as large spikes, can indicate unusual variability or special cause variation. These deviations may signal potential issues in the process, requiring further investigation to identify and address the root cause.

14.1.11 z-score

The z-score is a statistical measure that quantifies the distance of a specific data point from the mean of a data set, expressed in terms of standard deviations. This measure is crucial in both attribute and variable control charts, as it helps determine whether a process is operating within its expected range or if a particular data point indicates a potential issue. The z-score (z) is calculated using the formula

$$z = \frac{X - \mu}{\sigma}$$

where

- X represents the individual data point.
- μ is the mean of the data set.
- σ is the standard deviation.

Despite the different methods for calculating the standard deviation depending on the type of data, the z-score formula itself remains consistent. This consistency allows quality control practitioners to assess how far any given data point deviates from the mean and whether the data pertains to measurable quantities or defect rates. A z-score of 0 indicates that the data point is exactly at the mean, whereas positive or negative z-scores show how many standard deviations the data point is above or below the mean. This makes the z-score an essential tool in monitoring process stability and identifying when corrective action may be necessary to maintain quality.

14.1.12 Process capability indices

Process capability indices are statistical measures used in quality control to assess the ability of a process to produce output that meets specified quality standards. These indices compare the spread and centering of the process data relative to the specified limits, providing a quantitative measure of how well a process can produce products within the desired specifications.

The process capability index (C_p) measures the potential capability of a process by comparing the width of the process variation (measured by six standard deviations, or the process spread) to the width of the specification limits. The formula for C_p is

$$C_p = \frac{\text{USL} - \text{LSL}}{6\sigma}$$

where

- USL is the upper specification limit.
- LSL is the lower specification limit.
- σ is the standard deviation of the process.

A higher Cp value means the process has a greater potential to produce output within the specification limits. However, Cp assumes that the process is perfectly centered between the specification limits, which is often not the case in real-world scenarios.

The process capability index adjusted for centering (Cpk) accounts for the actual centering of the process relative to the specification limits. It adjusts the Cp index to reflect the position of the process mean relative to the specification limits. The formula for Cpk is

$$Cpk = min\left(\frac{\text{USL} - \mu}{3\sigma}, \frac{\mu - \text{LSL}}{3\sigma}\right)$$

Therefore, it provides a more realistic assessment of process capability by considering both the process variation and how well the process is centered within the specification limits. A higher Cpk value indicates that the process is both capable of meeting the specifications and is properly centered within the specification limits.

With a solid understanding of the key quality control measures, we're now ready to see how these elements come together in practice. Next, we'll explore control charts for attributes, where we'll apply many of these measures to monitor and control processes involving categorical data.

14.2 Control charts for attributes

Control charts for attributes are essential tools in quality management, used to monitor and control processes where the data is categorical in nature, such as the number of defective items or the proportion of defective units in a sample. Unlike control charts for variables, which deal with continuous data, attribute control charts focus on tracking the quality of a process based on the presence or absence of specific characteristics. These charts provide valuable insights into the stability and capability of a process, helping to identify trends, variations, and potential issues that could affect overall quality. In this section, we will explore some of the key attribute control charts, demonstrating how they are constructed and interpreted to ensure that processes remain within acceptable limits and consistently meet quality standards.

The choice of which control chart to use, or whether to use multiple charts, depends on the specific characteristics of the process and the nature of the data being monitored. For example, a p-chart, which tracks the proportion of defective items in a sample, is particularly useful when sample sizes vary from one period to the next. However, if sample sizes are consistent, an np-chart, which tracks the number of defective items rather than the proportion, might be more straightforward and effective. Similarly, although multiple control charts might be necessary to monitor different aspects of a complex process, a single chart could suffice for simpler processes with fewer variables to track. The key is to select the most relevant chart or combination of charts that best suit the specific quality control needs of the process.

14.2.1 p-charts

Proportion charts, typically referred to as p-charts, are a fundamental tool in quality control for monitoring the proportion of defective items in a process over time. They are particularly useful when dealing with attribute data, where each item is classified as either defective or nondefective. The p-chart helps to determine whether the process is stable and operating within acceptable limits by tracking the proportion of defective items in successive samples.

In practice, p-charts are essential for processes where the focus is on the rate of defects rather than the number of defects. For example, in a manufacturing process, a p-chart might be used to monitor the percentage of faulty products in daily production batches. By plotting the proportion of defects and comparing it against established control limits, quality control practitioners can quickly identify trends, shifts, or any unusual patterns that could indicate potential issues with the process.

We have a pandas data frame called `oj` containing synthetic data representing the number of defective units across 64 batches of orange juice cans. Potential defects could include physical damage, improper sealing, incorrect or missing labels, rust or corrosion, or the presence of foreign objects or contaminants inside the can or under the lid. Before accessing and analyzing the data, the `pd.read_csv()` method must be called to import the data set. In this example, we've used a discretionary parameter to load only three specific columns from the .csv file, thereby focusing our analysis on just the relevant variables.

The `info()` method displays a concise summary of a pandas data frame, including important details such as the column names, the number of non-null entries in each column, and the data types of each column. This information is valuable for understanding the structure and contents of a data frame before performing further analysis:

```
>>> import pandas as pd
>>> print(oj.info())
<class 'pandas.core.frame.DataFrame'>
RangeIndex: 64 entries, 0 to 63
Data columns (total 3 columns):
 #   Column  Non-Null Count  Dtype
---  ------  --------------  -----
 0   sample  64 non-null     int64
 1   D       64 non-null     int64
 2   size    64 non-null     int64
dtypes: int64(3)
memory usage: 1.6 KB
None
```

Each batch, or sample, is represented as a single row in the `oj` data frame, which includes the following attributes:

- `sample`—A numeric variable that serves as a unique identifier for each batch of orange juice cans, numbered sequentially from 31 through 94. This column contains no null values. In our p-chart, the `sample` variable will be used as the *x* axis to plot the proportion of defective units across the batches.
- `D`—A numeric variable indicating the number of defective orange juice cans in each sample. This column also contains no null values.
- `size`—A numeric variable representing the total number of cans inspected in each sample; consistently set at 50 across all entries. This column contains no null values.

A subsequent call to the `head()` method returns, by default, the first five rows of the `oj` data frame. This allows us to visually inspect the initial data, providing context and confirming the integrity of the data frame beyond the summary provided by the `info()` method:

```
>>> print(oj.head())
   sample   D  size
0      31   9    50
1      32   6    50
2      33  12    50
3      34   5    50
4      35   6    50
```

The `oj` data frame provides the defect count for each sample, but to better analyze the quality control process, we want to examine the *fraction* of defective units per sample. To do this, we will create a derived variable called `proportion`, which represents the ratio of defective cans (`D`) to the total cans inspected (`size`). This can be achieved with the following line of code:

```
>>> oj['proportion'] = oj['D'] / oj['size']
```

Now we have the *y*-axis variable for our p-chart.

A p-chart must include a center line, which represents the average proportion of defective units across all samples. Additionally, it requires an UCL and LCL, which are calculated to identify the thresholds beyond which the process is considered out of control.

The next line of code creates a variable called `p_bar`, which stores the computed mean of the `proportion` values across all rows in the `oj` data frame. This average serves as the CL in the p-chart, representing the overall defect rate across all samples:

```
>>> p_bar = oj['proportion'].mean()
```

The following snippet of code calculates the upper and lower control limits for the p-chart, which are critical in determining whether the process is within control. The UCL and LCL are derived from the standard deviation of the proportion of defective units, calculated using the `numpy` library and the following formula:

```
>>> import numpy as np
>>> oj['sigma'] = np.sqrt((p_bar * (1 - p_bar)) / oj['size'])
```

This standard deviation accounts for the variability in the proportion of defects. The UCL and LCL are then determined by adding and subtracting three times the standard deviation from the mean proportion (`p_bar`), respectively:

```
>>> oj['UCL'] = p_bar + 3 * oj['sigma']
>>> oj['LCL'] = p_bar - 3 * oj['sigma']
```

With all the necessary attributes and measures calculated, we are now ready to show the p-chart using the `matplotlib` library. This chart will plot the proportion of defective units for each sample, along with the CL (`p_bar`), UCL, and LCL, allowing us to assess the stability and control of the process over time:

```
>>> import matplotlib.pyplot as plt          ⟵ Imports the matplotlib library
>>> plt.figure()                              ⟵ Initializes a matplotlib figure, creating a
>>> plt.plot(oj['sample'], oj['proportion'],     blank canvas for the upcoming plot
>>>          marker = 'o',
>>>          linestyle = '-',                 ⟵ Plots proportion against sample using a solid
>>>          label = 'Proportion Defective')     line and circular markers; adds a label
>>> plt.axhline(y = p_bar,
>>>             color = 'r', linestyle = '--',  ⟵ Draws a horizontal dashed
>>>             label = 'p-bar (Mean)')           red line at the height of p_bar
                                                   on the plot; adds a label
```

14.2 Control charts for attributes

```
>>> plt.plot(oj['sample'], oj['UCL'],
>>>          color = 'g', linestyle = '--',
>>>          label = 'UCL')
>>> plt.plot(oj['sample'], oj['LCL'],
>>>          color = 'g', linestyle = '--',
>>>          label = 'LCL')
>>> plt.fill_between(oj['sample'], oj['LCL'], oj['UCL'],
>>>          color = 'g', alpha = 0.1)
>>> plt.title('p-Chart')
>>> plt.xlabel('Sample')
>>> plt.ylabel('Proportion Defective')
>>> plt.legend(loc = 'upper right',
>>>          bbox_to_anchor = (1, .95))
>>> plt.grid(True)
>>> plt.show()
```

- Draws a green dashed line representing the UCL across all samples; adds a label
- Draws a green dashed line representing the LCL across all samples; adds a label
- Fills the area between the control limits across all samples with a light green color
- Adds a title atop the plot
- Adds a label to the x axis
- Adds a label to the y axis
- Adds a legend in the upper right corner of the plot, nudged downward
- Adds horizontal and vertical lines to the plot
- Displays the plot

Finally, we can now display the p-chart to show the proportion of defective units across the samples: see figure 14.1. It reveals that the process of producing orange juice cans is generally in control, as all the data points fall within the upper and lower control

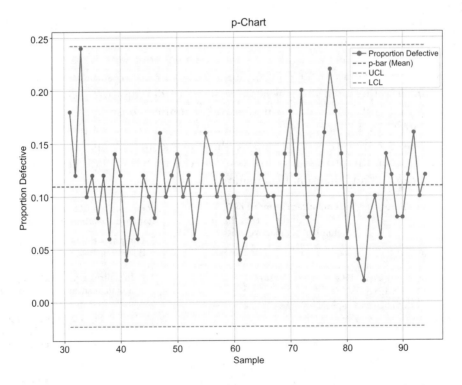

Figure 14.1 This p-chart illustrates the proportion of defective units in each sample of orange juice cans, with the dashed line across the middle representing the mean proportion. The dashed lines at the top and bottom indicate the UCL and LCL, providing boundaries for expected variation in the process. Data points within these limits suggest that the process is in control, and any points outside these limits would signal potential issues requiring investigation.

limits. This indicates that the variations in the proportion of defective units across the samples are due to common causes inherent to the process rather than any special cause variations. However, the proportion defective fluctuates noticeably around the mean, with some samples showing higher defect rates. These fluctuations, although within the control limits, suggest that there could be areas for improvement to reduce variability and enhance overall process stability. Continuous monitoring is essential to ensure that the process remains stable and that any potential issues are identified and addressed promptly before they lead to defects that fall outside the control limits.

14.2.2 np-charts

In the field of quality control, np-charts serve as a valuable tool for monitoring the number of defective items in a sample, particularly when the sample size remains consistent across different observations. Unlike p-charts, which focus on the proportion of defects relative to the sample size, np-charts directly track the count of defective items, making them simpler to interpret when dealing with uniform sample sizes. Given that the `oj` data frame maintains a constant sample size of 50 for each batch of orange juice cans, it is well-suited for demonstrating how to construct and interpret an np-chart. This chart will allow us to easily observe and analyze variations in the number of defects across the various samples, providing insights into the process's stability and quality over time.

To refine our analysis and make the np-chart more sensitive to variations in the process, we've adjusted the control limits to be within two standard deviations from the mean, rather than the typical three standard deviations. This change allows for earlier detection of potential issues, providing a more conservative approach to quality control. Additionally, we've incorporated logic into our Matplotlib code to highlight any data points that fall outside these new control limits, making it easier to identify when the process is out of control. The following code demonstrates these enhancements and their implementation:

```
>>> np_bar = oj['D'].mean()
>>> UCL_np = np_bar + 2 * np.sqrt(np_bar)
>>> LCL_np = np_bar - 2 * np.sqrt(np_bar)
>>> plt.figure()
>>> plt.plot(oj['sample'], oj['D'],
>>>          marker = 'o',
>>>          linestyle = '-',
>>>          label = 'Number of Defective Items')
>>> out_of_control = \
>>>       (oj['D'] > UCL_np) | (oj['D'] < LCL_np)
>>> plt.plot(oj['sample'][out_of_control],
>>>          oj['D'][out_of_control],
>>>          marker = 'o', color = 'r', linestyle = 'None',
>>>          label = 'Out of Control')
>>> plt.axhline(y = np_bar,
```

- Computes the mean of D, which represents the number of defective units
- Computes the UCL to be two standard deviations above the mean
- Computes the LCL to be two standard deviations below the mean
- Initializes a matplotlib figure, creating a blank canvas for the upcoming plot
- Plots D against sample using a solid line and circular markers; adds a label
- Establishes out-of-control conditions
- Plots out-of-control data points in red; adds a label

14.2 Control charts for attributes

```
>>>                    color = 'r', linestyle = '--',
>>>                    label = 'np-bar (Mean)')
>>> plt.axhline(y = UCL_np,
>>>                    color = 'g', linestyle = '--',
>>>                    label = 'UCL')
>>> plt.axhline(y = LCL_np,
>>>                    color = 'g', linestyle = '--',
>>>                    label = 'LCL')
>>> plt.fill_between(oj['sample'],
>>>                  LCL_np, UCL_np,
>>>                  color = 'g', alpha = 0.1)
>>> plt.title('np-Chart')
>>> plt.xlabel('Sample')
>>> plt.ylabel('Number of Defective Items')
>>> plt.legend(loc = 'upper left',
>>>            bbox_to_anchor = (0.1, 0.9))
>>> plt.grid(True)
>>> plt.show()
```

- Draws a horizontal dashed red line at the height of np_bar on the plot; adds a label
- Draws a horizontal dashed green line at the height of UCL_np on the plot; adds a label
- Draws a horizontal dashed green line at the height of LCL_np on the plot; adds a label
- Fills the area between the control limits across all samples with a light green color
- Adds a title atop the plot
- Adds a label to the x axis
- Adds a label to the y axis
- Adds a legend in the upper left corner of the plot, nudged downward and to the right
- Adds horizontal and vertical lines to the plot
- Displays the plot

The np-chart in figure 14.2 visually represents the number of defective items per sample, with control limits set at two standard deviations from the mean. It demonstrates

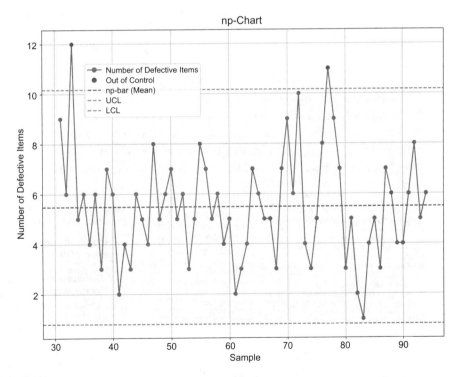

Figure 14.2 This np-chart displays the number of defective units in each sample of orange juice cans, including a pair of data points above the UCL. This type of chart is a better option than a p-chart when the sample sizes are consistent.

that even with the tighter control limits set at two standard deviations from the mean, the process is largely within control. Only a pair of data points fall above the UCL, indicating that the process is generally stable with occasional variations that may require attention. An np-chart, as shown here, is particularly effective when sample sizes are consistent across observations, offering a clear view of the number of defective items per sample. The out-of-control points suggest potential issues that could be due to special cause variation, warranting further investigation to maintain process quality. Overall, this chart is a useful tool for monitoring process stability and identifying areas that may need corrective actions to keep the process within desired quality standards.

14.2.3 c-charts

A c-chart is a type of control chart specifically designed to monitor the number of defects per unit in a process. Unlike p-charts and np-charts, which focus on the proportion or count of defective items within a sample, a c-chart tracks the total number of defects found in individual units over time. This makes c-charts particularly valuable when defects are counted rather than measured as a proportion of the whole. For instance, if you're inspecting units of a product for multiple types of defects—such as scratches, dents, or other flaws—a c-chart helps you determine whether the variation in the number of defects per unit is consistent with an in-control process or if it signals an underlying issue that needs correction. Because c-charts plot the actual count of defects rather than a proportion, they provide a straightforward way to assess the quality of a process where the number of defects is expected to be variable but within a predictable range.

We will generate a synthetic data set to demonstrate how to create and plot a c-chart. To simulate the number of defects per unit, we use a Poisson distribution, which is commonly applied in quality control to model the occurrence of rare events (like defects) over a fixed interval. This approach allows us to create a realistic data set that reflects the expected variability in a process where defects are infrequent but possible. We'll then use this data set to plot a c-chart and analyze the results:

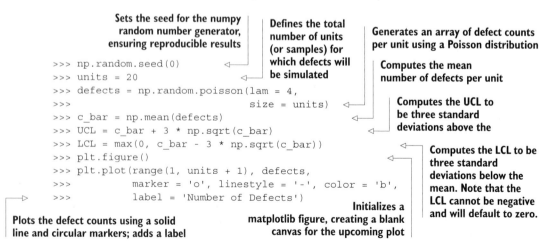

```
>>> plt.axhline(c_bar,
>>>             color = 'r', linestyle = '--',
>>>             label = 'Center Line')
```
◁── Draws a horizontal dashed red line at the height of c_bar on the plot; adds a label

```
>>> plt.axhline(UCL,
>>>             color = 'g', linestyle = '--',
>>>             label = 'UCL')
```
◁── Draws a horizontal dashed green line at the height of UCL on the plot; adds a label

```
>>> plt.axhline(LCL,
>>>             color = 'g', linestyle = '--',
>>>             label = 'LCL')
```
◁── Draws a horizontal dashed green line at the height of LCL on the plot; adds a label

```
>>> plt.title('c-Chart')
>>> plt.xlabel('Unit Number')
>>> plt.ylabel('Number of Defects')
>>> plt.xticks(range(1, units + 1))
>>> plt.legend(loc = 'upper right',
>>>            bbox_to_anchor = (1, .95))
>>> plt.grid(True)
>>> plt.show()
```
◁── Sets the title, labels the axes, adjusts the x-axis ticks, places the legend in the upper right corner, enables the grid, and displays the plot

The c-chart in figure 14.3 shows the number of defects per unit, helping to identify any patterns or trends in the defect counts across the 20 units. It shows the number of defects identified across 20 units, with the CL (center dashed line) representing the average number of defects per unit. The chart also includes a UCL and a LCL (defaulted to zero because it can't be negative), marked by the upper and lower

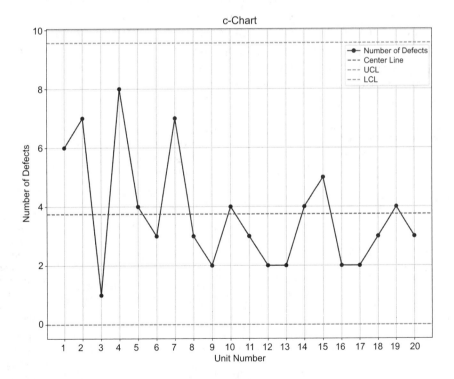

Figure 14.3 This c-chart displays the number of defects per unit for 20 units. All data points fall within the control limits, indicating a stable process.

dashed lines, which are set to monitor process variation. All data points fall within these control limits, indicating that the process is stable and under control. Although there is some variability in the number of defects, with several data points above the CL, no points exceed the control limits, suggesting that the variations observed are within the expected range of process behavior. This consistency reinforces that the process is operating as expected, without any signals of special cause variation.

14.2.4 g-charts

A g-chart is a type of quality control chart specifically designed to monitor the number of units or opportunities between occurrences of a specific event, such as defects or failures. Unlike p-charts, np-charts, and c-charts, which focus on the proportion or count of defects in a sample, the g-chart tracks the gaps or intervals between such events. This approach is particularly valuable when the events of interest are relatively rare and it is more informative to measure the time or number of units between occurrences. G-charts are crucial in identifying patterns that suggest whether a process is improving or deteriorating over time, offering a different perspective on process stability and performance. As the last type of control chart for attributes that we will explore, the g-chart provides a unique and powerful tool for quality control, especially in processes where defects are infrequent but critical to monitor.

To demonstrate how to create and plot a g-chart, we'll generate a synthetic data set that simulates the number of units between defects in a process. This type of data is ideal for a g-chart, which is used to monitor the intervals between occurrences of rare events, such as defects or failures. By applying this data to the g-chart, we can analyze the process's performance and detect any unusual patterns or trends that might indicate process instability. The following code will create the necessary data and plot the g-chart to show these intervals:

Creates a pandas data frame, df, with a defect sequence and the corresponding number of units produced between defects

Computes the average number of units between defects from the units_between_defects column in df and stores it in g_bar

Computes the LCL to be three standard deviations below the mean. Note that the LCL cannot be negative and will default to zero.

```
>>> data = {
>>>     'defect_sequence': np.arange(1, 21),
>>>     'units_between_defects': [50, 30, 45, 60, 55, 35, 40,
>>>                               70, 65, 80, 75, 50, 85, 90,
>>>                               95, 60, 55, 100, 105, 110]
>>> }
>>> df = pd.DataFrame(data)
>>> g_bar = df['units_between_defects'].mean()
>>> UCL = g_bar + 3 * np.sqrt( \
>>>     g_bar * (g_bar + 1))
>>> LCL = max(g_bar - 3 * np.sqrt( \
>>>     g_bar * (g_bar + 1)), 0)
>>> plt.figure()
>>> plt.plot(df['defect_sequence'], df['units_between_defects'],
>>>          marker = 'o', linestyle = '-',
>>>          label = 'Units Between Defects')
```

Computes the UCL to be three standard deviations above the mean

Initializes a matplotlib figure, creating a blank canvas for the upcoming plot

Plots units_between_defects against defect_sequence, using a solid line and circular markers; adds a label

```
>>> plt.axhline(y = g_bar,
>>>             color = 'r', linestyle = '--',
>>>             label = 'g-bar (Mean)')         ◁──┐ Draws a horizontal dashed
>>> plt.axhline(y = UCL,                             red line at the height of g_bar
>>>             color = 'g', linestyle = '--',      on the plot; adds a label
>>>             label = 'UCL')              ◁──┐ Draws a horizontal dashed green line at
>>> plt.axhline(y = LCL,                            the height of UCL on the plot; adds a label
>>>             color = 'g', linestyle = '--',
>>>             label = 'LCL')              ◁──┐ Draws a horizontal dashed
>>> plt.fill_between(df['defect_sequence'], LCL, UCL,   green line at the height of LCL
>>>                  color = 'g', alpha = 0.1)  ◁─ on the plot; adds a label
>>> plt.title('g-Chart')                           Fills the area between the
>>> plt.xlabel('Defect Sequence')                  control limits across all samples
>>> plt.ylabel('Units Between Defects')            with a light green color
>>> plt.legend()
>>> plt.grid(True)      ┌─ Sets the title, labels the axes, adds a legend,
>>> plt.show()       ◁──┘  enables the grid, and displays the plot
```

The g-chart in figure 14.4 shows the number of units between defects over the defect sequence (see figure 14.4), with the defect sequence plotted on the *x* axis and the units between defects on the *y* axis. The center dashed line represents the average (g-bar) of units between defects, and the upper and lower dashed lines denote the UCL and LCL. This chart is significant in monitoring the frequency of defects over time, helping to

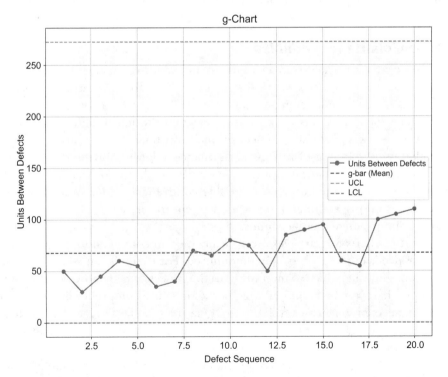

Figure 14.4 This g-chart displays the number of units between defects; it highlights process stability, with all points falling within the control limits. Additionally, it shows an improving process, as the number of manufactured units between defects is trending upward.

identify whether a process is consistently producing a certain number of units between defects or if there are any unusual patterns that indicate the process is out of control. In this case, all the data points fall within the control limits, suggesting that the process is stable and within expected variability. The g-chart's value add lies in its ability to highlight shifts in process reliability, providing a visual tool to detect and address issues before they lead to significant quality problems.

So far, we've explored the most common control charts for attributes, including p-charts, np-charts, c-charts, and g-charts. Using the Matplotlib library, we demonstrated how to create these charts step by step, providing the necessary tools and knowledge to plot and interpret them effectively. By understanding these charts, you're now equipped to monitor and control processes where the quality of products or services is measured in terms of discrete attributes, such as the number of defects or the proportion of defective items.

As we move forward to control charts for variables, it's important to note that although these charts differ in what they measure, the underlying concepts remain consistent. Due to the repetitive nature of the plotting process and because the essential techniques have already been thoroughly covered, we will not be sharing the Matplotlib code for each subsequent chart. Instead, the focus will be on understanding the specific applications and interpretations of these charts, using the skills you have already developed. This approach allows us to avoid redundancy while ensuring that you grasp the critical aspects of quality control for both attributes and variables.

14.3 Control charts for variables

Control charts for variables are crucial tools in quality management, designed to monitor and control processes where the data is continuous and can be measured on a numerical scale. Unlike control charts for attributes, which focus on counting the occurrence of defects, variable control charts track the actual values of a process characteristic to assess its stability and consistency over time. These charts provide a more detailed understanding of process performance, allowing for the detection of small shifts or trends that might indicate underlying issues. In this section, we will delve into some of the most commonly used variable control charts, demonstrating their construction, interpretation, and application to ensure processes remain under control and within specified tolerance limits.

Control charts for variables are typically used in combination, depending on the specific needs of the process being monitored. For example, an x-bar chart might be used alongside an r-chart to monitor both the process mean and variability. Although multiple charts can be employed together to provide a comprehensive view of process performance, in some cases, a single chart may be sufficient to monitor the most critical aspect of the process. The choice of charts depends on the complexity of the process and the specific characteristics that need to be controlled

We'll be using a pandas data frame named `pistons` as our data source throughout, which contains the diameter measurements of 200 piston rings produced in a manufacturing process. These measurements are equally divided across 40 batches, or

14.3 Control charts for variables

samples. Before working with the data, the pd.read_csv() method must be called to import the data set into Python. A subsequent call to the info() method provides a summary of the data frame's essential details:

```
>>> print(pistons.info())
<class 'pandas.core.frame.DataFrame'>
RangeIndex: 200 entries, 0 to 199
Data columns (total 2 columns):
 #   Column    Non-Null Count  Dtype
---  ------    --------------  -----
 0   diameter  200 non-null    float64
 1   sample    200 non-null    int64
dtypes: float64(1), int64(1)
memory usage: 3.3 KB
None
```

Each measurement of piston ring diameter is represented as a single row in the pistons data frame, with five rows corresponding to each batch or sample. Here's a brief overview of its attributes:

- diameter—Represents the measured diameter of each piston ring, recorded as a floating-point number (or real number with fractional parts). The measurements are taken in millimeters. There are no null values.
- sample—A numeric variable that uniquely identifies each batch of measurements, sequentially numbered from 1 through 40. Each sample number corresponds to five individual diameter measurements.

The describe() function in pandas provides a quick statistical summary of numerical data in a data frame. When applied to the diameter variable in the pistons data frame, it will return key metrics such as the mean, standard deviation, and range, giving us a comprehensive overview of the distribution of piston ring diameters:

```
>>> stats = pistons['diameter'].describe()
>>> print(stats)
count    200.000000
mean      74.003605
std        0.011417
min       73.967000
25%       73.995000
50%       74.003000
75%       74.010000
max       74.036000
Name: diameter, dtype: float64
```

The summary statistics for the diameter variable reveal minimal differences between the minimum (73.967 millimeters) and maximum (74.036 millimeters) values, with a very small standard deviation of approximately 0.011 millimeters. This suggests that the piston ring manufacturing process might be highly consistent, producing rings with very little variation in diameter. As we move forward to create control charts for variables, these small variations indicate that the process is (presumably) stable and tightly controlled, which is a positive sign for maintaining quality standards.

Finally, a call to the `head()` method gives us a glimpse at the top 10 observations in the `pistons` data frame:

```
>>> print(pistons.head(10))
    diameter  sample
0     74.030       1
1     74.002       1
2     74.019       1
3     73.992       1
4     74.008       1
5     73.995       2
6     73.992       2
7     74.001       2
8     74.011       2
9     74.004       2
```

These initial rows confirm the consistent measurements within each sample, reinforcing the earlier observation of minimal variation in the manufacturing process. With the foundational data now explored and understood, we are ready to transition to our first control chart: the x-bar chart, which will help us visualize the stability and consistency of the piston ring manufacturing process.

14.3.1 x-bar charts

An x-bar chart is used to monitor the central tendency of a process over time. Specifically, it tracks the mean of a sample, or subgroup, across a series of measurements, allowing quality practitioners to assess whether the process remains stable and predictable. In the context of our piston ring manufacturing process, the x-bar chart will help us determine whether the average diameter of piston rings remains consistent across different batches, ensuring that the process is producing parts within the desired specifications.

The x-bar chart is constructed by first calculating the mean diameter of piston rings within each sample or batch. This is done using the `groupby()` method in Python, which groups the data by sample and then calculates the mean diameter for each group, resulting in a series of sample means. The overall mean, or the central line on the chart, is then determined by taking the average of these sample means. This overall mean represents the expected average diameter if the process is in control.

To assess the variability of the sample means, we calculate the standard deviation of the sample means. This measure of dispersion is then used to establish the control limits, which are typically set at three standard deviations above and below the overall mean. If a sample mean falls outside these limits, it signals that the process may be experiencing an assignable cause of variation, which requires further investigation. The x-bar chart thus provides a clear visual representation of the process's stability, highlighting any shifts or trends that may indicate a need for corrective action (see figure 14.5). By closely monitoring the x-bar chart, manufacturers can ensure that their processes remain consistent, producing high-quality products that meet the desired specifications.

14.3 Control charts for variables

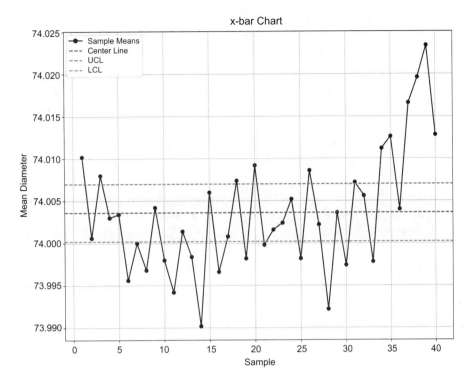

Figure 14.5 This x-bar chart displays the mean diameter of piston rings across 40 samples, with control limits set at three standard deviations from the overall mean. The chart helps monitor the consistency of the manufacturing process, ensuring that the average diameter remains within acceptable limits, signaling that the process is stable and in control.

This x-bar chart shows the mean diameters of piston rings across 40 samples, with the control limits set at three standard deviations above and below the overall mean. Several data points fall above or below the upper and lower control limits, respectively, indicating that the process may be out of control. Specifically, the data points toward the end of the sequence exhibit a rising trend, with several points exceeding the UCL. This suggests that there might be a systematic issue in the manufacturing process that requires investigation and corrective action to bring the process back under control and ensure consistent product quality. The x-bar chart is crucial in identifying these variations and maintaining the stability of the process.

14.3.2 r-charts

An r-chart, also known as a range chart, is used to monitor the variability within a process. Unlike x-bar charts, which track the mean values of a process, r-charts focus on the spread of data within each sample, making them particularly useful for detecting changes in the dispersion of the process over time. The range of a sample is calculated as the difference between the maximum and minimum values within that sample. By plotting these ranges on an r-chart, we can visualize how the variability within the process shifts, helping us to identify any points where the process might be going out of control.

The key measures in an r-chart include the average range, which is calculated as the mean of all the individual sample ranges, and the control limits, which are set at three standard deviations above and below the average range. The UCL and LCL help determine whether the variability of the process is within acceptable bounds. If the range for any sample exceeds the UCL or falls below the LCL, it signals a potential issue with the process that warrants further investigation.

Displaying these measures on an r-chart allows for a straightforward interpretation of the data (see figure 14.6). When all the points fall within the control limits, it suggests that the process variability is stable and consistent. However, if points fall outside these limits or show a pattern, such as increasing or decreasing trends, it indicates that the process variability may be changing, which could affect the overall quality of the product. By using r-charts in conjunction with x-bar charts, quality control practitioners can gain a comprehensive understanding of both the central tendency and variability of the process, enabling them to take timely corrective actions to maintain process control.

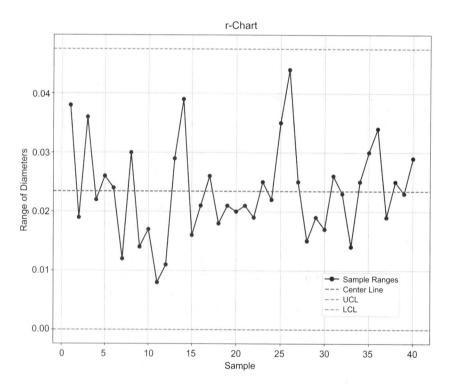

Figure 14.6 This r-chart displays the range of piston ring diameters across 40 samples, with control limits set at three standard deviations from the mean range. The chart helps monitor the variability in the process, indicating that all of the sample ranges fall within the control limits, suggesting the variability in the process is stable.

The r-chart shows that the variability in the diameter measurements of the piston rings appears to be stable, with all data points falling within the control limits. This indicates that the process's range of variability is under control. However, it is important to cross-reference these results with the x-bar chart, where several points were out of control. The discrepancy between the x-bar chart and the r-chart suggests that although the overall process variability is stable, there might be shifts in the process mean that need to be addressed. This could indicate issues such as tool wear or calibration drift that affect the central tendency without significantly affecting the range of measurements. Further investigation is necessary to ensure that the process remains within both range and mean control.

14.3.3 s-charts

An s-chart, or standard deviation chart, is a critical tool in quality control that monitors the variability within a process by tracking the standard deviations of sample measurements over time. Unlike the r-chart, which focuses on the range of data within each sample, the s-chart provides a more accurate representation of variability, especially when sample sizes are large. This chart is particularly valuable when consistent precision is required, as it helps identify shifts or drifts in the process that could lead to defects or non-conformance.

To construct an s-chart, we first need to calculate the standard deviation of the measured characteristic (in this case, the diameter of piston rings) for each sample. This is done by grouping the data by sample and then calculating the standard deviation of the measurements within each group. The average of these standard deviations across all samples serves as the central line of the chart, or the expected average variability if the process is in control.

Control limits are established to help identify when the process variability is outside of acceptable bounds. The control limits are derived from the following formulas:

$$\text{UCL} = \bar{s} + 3\left(\frac{\bar{s}}{c4}\right)$$

$$\text{LCL} = \bar{s} - 3\left(\frac{\bar{s}}{c4}\right)$$

where

- $\bar{s}$ is the average standard deviation.
- $c4$ is a correction factor that accounts for bias in the standard deviation estimates. It is derived by taking the square root of the square root of the ratio of 2 to the sample size minus 1.

If the standard deviations of the samples fall outside these control limits, it indicates that the process variability is out of control and requires investigation.

An s-chart therefore offers a precise method for monitoring the consistency of a process, ensuring that variations remain within predictable limits (see figure 14.7). It is particularly useful in manufacturing processes where maintaining a consistent level of quality is crucial. By understanding the distribution of standard deviations and their control limits, quality managers can detect early signs of process instability and take corrective actions before significant quality issues arise.

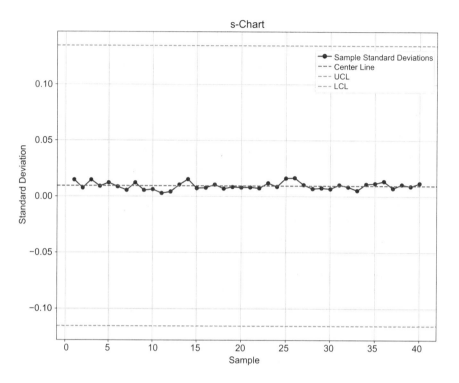

Figure 14.7 This s-chart displays the sample standard deviations for each batch of piston rings, with the CL representing the average standard deviation across all samples. The control limits (UCL and LCL) are set to identify any variations in the process, ensuring the process remains stable within the expected range.

The s-chart shows the standard deviation of piston ring diameters across 40 samples, with the center dashed line representing the average standard deviation (CL). All data points are well within the control limits (UCL and LCL), indicating that the variation in the process is stable and consistent across the samples. This stability suggests that the process is in control, with no signs of significant variability that would indicate a problem. The close clustering of the points near the CL further reinforces that the process is producing consistent results, with minimal variation from sample to sample.

Reconciling the results of the s-chart with the x-bar chart reveals an interesting dynamic in the manufacturing process. Although the s-chart provides another indication that the variability in the piston ring diameters is stable and within control limits, the x-bar chart shows several data points outside the control limits, suggesting that the process mean is not consistently centered. This discrepancy implies that although the process variation is well-controlled, the process may still be drifting from the target mean, leading to potential issues with meeting specific quality standards. Therefore, even though the variability is stable, the process might require adjustments to bring the mean back within control limits, ensuring that the product consistently meets the desired specifications.

14.3.4 I-MR charts

An I-MR chart is a powerful tool in statistical process control, particularly useful when measurements are taken individually rather than in subgroups. This type of control chart is ideal for monitoring processes where data points are not grouped into batches but instead are collected in a time-ordered sequence. The I-MR-chart is composed of two distinct charts: the individual (I) chart and the moving range (MR) chart. The I-chart tracks individual data points over time, allowing for the detection of shifts or trends in the process mean, whereas the MR-chart monitors the variability between consecutive data points, providing insights into the stability of the process variation.

To construct an I-MR chart, we first calculate the mean of the individual measurements, which forms the CL of the I-chart. The control limits for the I-chart are then determined by adding and subtracting three standard deviations of the individual data points from the process mean. This gives us the UCL and LCL, which define the range within which the data points should fall if the process is in control.

Next, we calculate the MR, which is the absolute difference between consecutive data points. The average of these moving ranges forms the CL of the MR-chart. The control limits for the MR-chart are derived using constants $D4$ and $D3$, which are specifically chosen based on the number of data points used to calculate the moving range. The control limits for the MR-chart are calculated from the following formulas:

$$\text{UCL} = (D4)(\bar{R})$$

$$\text{LCL} = (D3)(\bar{R})$$

where

- $D4$ is a constant derived from statistical tables used specifically to calculate the UCL in quality control charts, based on the sample size; it equals 3.267.
- $D3$ is another constant derived similarly to $D4$; equals 0.
- $\bar{R}$ represents the average of the MRs.

These limits provide a visual reference for the variability in the process; if the MR exceeds these limits, it signals potential instability in the process.

The I-MR chart is particularly valuable because it enables the detection of both small shifts in the process mean and changes in process variability that might not be evident with other types of control charts (see figure 14.8). By analyzing the I-chart and the MR-chart together, quality control practitioners can gain a deeper understanding of the process's overall stability. If either chart shows points outside the control limits, it indicates that the process may be out of control, necessitating further investigation and potential corrective actions. This makes the I-MR chart an essential tool for maintaining high quality standards in processes where individual data points are critical to monitoring and controlling production.

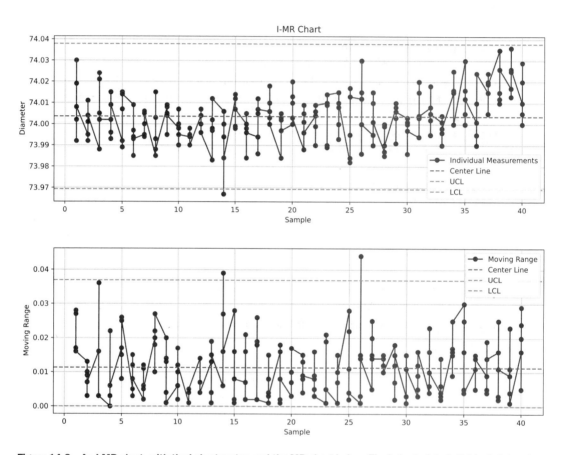

Figure 14.8 An I-MR chart, with the I-chart on top and the MR-chart below. The I-chart plots individual piston ring diameters for each sample, highlighting variation around the process mean. UCL and LCL lines indicate acceptable limits. The MR-chart tracks the moving range, or the difference between successive measurements, reflecting process variability. Lines connect data points from one sample to the next, illustrating changes in measurements and variability across samples.

The I-MR-chart provides a detailed view of both individual measurements and the variability within a process. The top part of the chart, the I-chart, displays individual piston ring diameters across 40 samples. Each point represents a single measurement, and the lines connect these points from one sample to the next. The chart's UCL and

LCL define the control limits, within which most data points should ideally fall. In this case, the measurements are generally within control, but there are some points close to the limits, indicating potential areas to monitor for process drift.

The bottom part of the chart, the MR-chart, shows the moving range, which is the absolute difference between consecutive measurements. This chart helps to detect sudden shifts in process variability that might not be visible in the individual measurements alone. The MR-chart reveals that the variability is mostly stable, with the moving ranges staying within the control limits. Together, the I-chart and MR-chart offer a comprehensive picture of the process, making it easier to identify any unusual patterns that could indicate a problem, such as a shift in the process mean or an increase in variability. This dual-chart approach is valuable in monitoring processes where individual data points and their variations need to be closely controlled.

14.3.5 EWMA charts

An exponentially weighted moving average (EWMA) control chart is a powerful tool used in quality control to monitor the performance of a process over time. Unlike traditional control charts that treat each data point equally, the EWMA chart places more emphasis on recent observations while still considering past data. This approach makes it particularly sensitive to small shifts in the process mean, which can be crucial in detecting trends or gradual changes that might go unnoticed with other types of control charts.

The key measures displayed in an EWMA chart, such as the CL (EWMA mean) and control limits (UCL and LCL), are derived using a smoothing constant, often denoted as λ. The smoothing constant controls how much weight is given to the most recent data point versus the historical data. In the calculation process, the first EWMA value is set to the first measurement in the data set. Each subsequent EWMA value is calculated as a weighted average of the current data point and the previous EWMA value, with λ determining the weighting. This process ensures that the EWMA line is less sensitive to noise and more reflective of genuine shifts in the process.

The control limits on the EWMA chart are calculated similarly to those in traditional control charts but take into account the smoothing constant. The formula for the control limits includes the standard deviation of the original data and adjusts it using λ, making the limits narrower and more responsive to recent changes. The UCL and LCL help determine whether the process is staying within acceptable boundaries or if there are signals that the process is shifting. If the EWMA crosses these control limits, it indicates that the process may be moving out of control, necessitating further investigation and possible corrective actions (see figure 14.9).

The EWMA chart offers a powerful way to monitor subtle shifts in a process over time, particularly when dealing with processes that require early detection of trends or small shifts. In this chart, each point represents the EWMA of the piston ring diameters across 40 samples, giving more weight to recent observations. The CL, or the overall EWMA mean, serves as a benchmark against which individual data points are compared. The UCL and LCL define the range within which the process is expected to operate under normal conditions. In this EWMA chart, most data points fall within these control limits, indicating that the process is generally in control. However, as we approach the latter samples, there's a noticeable upward trend, similar to what our x-bar chart first revealed, suggesting a potential shift in the process. This could be an early warning of a systematic change, warranting further investigation to determine whether corrective actions are necessary to maintain process stability.

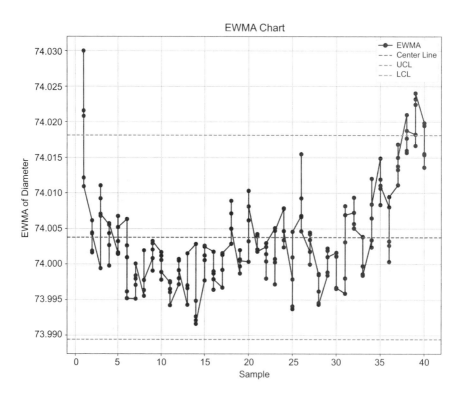

Figure 14.9 This EWMA chart displays the exponentially weighted moving average of piston ring diameters across 40 samples. The chart shows how the process mean evolves over time, with recent data points having more influence on the chart's trajectory than older ones. The CL represents the overall EWMA mean, whereas the UCL and LCL indicate the expected range of variation. Data points within these limits suggest the process is under control, whereas any point outside may signal a shift or trend that requires further investigation.

As we close this book, it's our hope that the statistical and other quantitative techniques explored have equipped you with a solid foundation for tackling real-world challenges. These methods are not just tools but a lens through which you can make informed decisions and drive meaningful outcomes. Thank you for embarking on this journey and continuing to develop your expertise.

Summary

- Understanding key quality control measures, such as control limits, mean, and standard deviation, is crucial for interpreting control charts effectively. These measures provide the foundation for analyzing process stability and identifying areas for improvement.
- Control charts for attributes, including p-charts, np-charts, c-charts, and g-charts, are essential tools for monitoring categorical data. These charts help in tracking defects, proportions, and other attribute-based metrics to ensure processes remain within acceptable limits.
- Control charts for variables, which focus on continuous data such as measurements and process variations, were also covered. These charts, including x-bar charts, r-charts, s-charts, I-MR charts, and EWMA charts, are valuable for assessing the precision and consistency of manufacturing processes.
- It's crucial to use multiple control charts to comprehensively assess whether a process is in or out of control. Relying on just one chart can lead to incomplete or misleading conclusions, as different charts highlight different aspects of process performance. By using a combination of charts, such as x-bar and r-charts, you gain a more accurate and complete understanding of process stability and potential areas for improvement.

index

Symbols

| operator 92

Numerics

68–95–99 rule 44

A

A_ub matrix 234–236
absorbing states 295, 311–317
　obtaining fundamental matrix 313
　predicting 315
　predicting programmatically 316
ACF (autocorrelation function) 197
　plot 199
'add' parameter 218
add_edges() method 290
addition rule 23
agent fees variable 285
agg() method 118, 152
Agile methodology 223–224, 226
AIC (Akaike information criterion) 210
Amount column 336
anytree library 283, 287
append() function 235
Apple 187
apply() method 90, 331, 334
AR (autoregression) 185
　autoregression component 192, 205–207
　moving average component 206
Area variable 125

ARIMA (autoregressive integrated moving average) 185
　class 207–208
　models 192–215
assign() method 321, 326–327, 338
astype() method 332
AUC (area under ROC curve) 137
Augmented Dickey–Fuller (ADF) test 201

B

b_ub vector 234–236
bagging (bootstrap aggregating) 141
basketball games 73
benford library 332
Benford's law 320–324
　distortion factor and z-statistic 343
　mantissa statistics 344
　mean absolute deviation 342
　validating 338
Besni class label 117
beta distribution 355
BIC (Bayesian information criterion) 210
binom module 53
binomial distribution 50
　computing probabilities 54
　properties 51
bln_msk Boolean mask 197
boldface type 285
bounded, defined 37
Breusch–Pagan test 108
budget 350
　constraints 231

C

c-charts 394–396
CDF (cumulative distribution function) 33, 37–39, 245
chance nodes 282
chi-square test 338
   chi-square statistic 339
   degrees of freedom 341
   p-value 341
CL (center line) 381
Class variable 117–118, 121–123, 125, 128
classification metrics 131
   accuracy 136
   area under ROC curve 137
   confusion matrix 132
   false positive/negative rate 135
   misclassification rate 136
   ROC curve 138
   sensitivity 133
   specificity 134
clf object 160–161, 163
close_prices data frame 188, 214, 262, 265
close_prices index 189
coef (coefficients) 95
coeff parameter 211
collectively exhaustive 296
combinations 23–30
   with replacement 24–30
   without replacement 25–27
complement rule for probability 65–66
conditional covariance 198
conditional probabilities 72–77
   examples of 72–73
   formulaic approach to 76–77
      calculating P(A | B) 77
      calculating P(A and B) 76
      calculating P(B) 76
      defining events 76
   independence and 73
   intuitive approach to 74–76
conditional variance 198
confusion matrix 132, 161, 178
conservative approach 277
constraints 231, 233–236
contingency table 74–75
continuous random variables 30–34
   cumulative distribution function 33
   examples 31
   probability density function 32
control charts
   for attributes 388–398
   for variables 398–408

CONVERT class labels 161, 165, 181
CONVERT variable 146, 159
ConvexArea variable 125
copy() method 327
corr() method 123
count variable 326–327
counting rules 22–30
   addition rule 23
   combinations 23–30
   multiplication rule 22
   Pascal's triangle 27
   permutations 23–30
counting, continuous random variables 30–34
   cumulative distribution function 33
   examples 31
   probability density function 32
Counts column 338
covariance (Cov) 198
CPM (critical path method) 349
criterion function 160
cross-tabulation 74
cumulative probability distribution, computing 248–249

D

data
   exploring 115–116, 118–119, 122, 148, 150, 152, 154–155
   importing 186–191
   plotting 190
   understanding 189
data definition 231
data exploration 88
data filtering 144
data transformation 145
data type conversion 146
dataclass decorator 232
decision trees 140–142, 157–173, 271, 282–292
   advantages and disadvantages of 173
   creating schema 283–289
   decision-making without probabilities 273–282
   evaluating model 161
   exploring data 148, 150, 152, 154–155
   fitting 141–142
   fitting model 160
   fitting random forests 174–183
   importing data 142
   interpreting and understanding 164–173
   predicting responses 161
   splitting data 158
   understanding data 143
   wrangling data 144–146

decision variable bounds 231, 236
decision-making without probabilities 273–282
    EV method 279–282
    Maximax method 273–276
    Maximin method 277
    Minimax Regret method 277–279
DecisionTreeClassifier() method 160, 175–176
defects per unit, quality control measures 386
dependencies, defined 351
derived variable 146
DES (double exponential smoothing) 216–217
descriptive statistics 3
DF (distortion factor) 343
diameter variable 399
differencing 195
    purpose 195
    stationarity and 197–205
    types 195
discrete random variables 30, 35–39
    cumulative distribution function 37–39
    examples 35
    probability mass function 36
discrete uniform distribution 56
    computing probabilities 58
    properties of 56
distortion factor 343
distributions, discrete uniform 56
dot product 302
dot() method 305
DOWN variable 144
dropna() method 202, 263
Durbin–Watson test 107

E

Eccentricity variable 125–126, 128
empirical probabilities 19
ensemble techniques 141
epic constraints 231
epics list 235
equilibrium conditions 295, 307–311
    predicting programmatically 308–311
equilibrium distribution 308
EV (Expected Value) method 272, 279–282
EV data frame 281
evaluating model, confusion matrix 161
EWMA charts 407
examples, number sequences
    payment amounts 336
    street addresses 330–333
    world population figures 334–335
excess kurtosis measures 345
Expected column 338

expected value calculation 255
explanatory variable 81
ExponentialSmoothing class 217–218
Extent variable 125–126, 128

F

F-statistic 103
factorial() method 26, 28–29
false positive/negative rate 135
feature importance 179
features list 233
fetch_stock_data() function 187–188
fillna() method 145
financial data, fetching 187–189
financial investments 73
first_digit variable 331, 334–337
first_probability variable 49
first-digit law 320
first-order differencing 202–205
fit() method 160, 176–177, 208, 217
fitting linear regression
    interpreting and evaluating results 95, 99, 103, 105
    simple linear regression 87
    testing model assumptions 105–108
fitting models 93, 160
    decision trees 141–142
    random forests 141–142
    time series 215–220
    time series models 192–215
        AR and MA components 205–207
        autoregression (AR) component 192
        combining ARIMA components 192
        differencing 195
        evaluating model fit 209–213
        fitting models 207–209
        forecasting 214
        integration (I) component 192
        MA (moving average) component 192
        stationarity and differencing applied 197–205
            ACF plot 199
            Augmented Dickey–Fuller (ADF) test 201
            first-order differencing 202–205
            PACF plot 200
            visual inspection 197
        stationarity, statistical properties 193
floats 189
Forecast variable 214
forecasts, distinguishing from predictions 185
fundamental matrix 313

INDEX

G

g-charts 396–398
Gini impurity 165
GM (General Motors) 261
groupby() method 118, 165, 326, 400

H

head() method 89, 116–117, 130–131, 147, 189, 195, 326–327, 331, 334, 336, 345–346, 389, 400
heat maps, correlation 122
histograms, logistic regression 119
historical data 259
history() method 188
Holt's linear trend model 217
Holt–Winters exponential smoothing (H-W) 216
Holt–Winters model 218–220
　forecasting 219
　model evaluation and comparison 219
homoscedasticity of residuals 107
HQIC (Hannan–Quinn information criterion) 210

I

I-MR charts 405–407
IDEs (integrated development environments) 6–7
IDLE (Integrated Development and Learning Environment) 6
iloc attribute 75
importing data 142, 186–191
　fetching financial data 187–189
　logistic regression 115
　　computing basic statistics 118
　　correlation heat maps 122
　　histograms 119
　　understanding data 115
　　viewing data 116
　plotting data 190
　understanding data 189
independence 73
　of residuals 107
inequalities 230
inferential statistics 3
info() method 88–89, 115, 146, 189, 330, 334, 336, 389, 399
integration (I) component 192
intercept 94
internal nodes 164, 169–173

investment_alternatives vector 274
ISO 8601 date formats 188

J

Jarque–Bera test 109
Jupyter Notebook 7

K

Kecimen class label 117
kurtosis() method 346

L

lambda functions 152
law of anomalous numbers 338
LCL (lower control limit) 380
leaf nodes 164, 169–173
len() method 132, 197
line of best fit 85
linear equations 230
linear programming 222
　developing linear optimization framework 229–241
　　constraints 233–236
　　data definition 231–232
　　decision variable bounds 236
　　linear equations and inequalities 230
　　objective function 233
　　result evaluation 239–241
　　solving linear programming problem 236–238
　problem formulation 223–229
　　approach 225–227
　　challenge 224
　　feature summaries 227–229
　　scenario 224
linear regression 81–87
　conditions for best fit 86–87
　fitting 79
　　interpreting and evaluating results 95, 99, 103, 105
　　testing model assumptions 105–108
　　with simple linear regression 87
　fitting model 93
　goodness of fit 85
　importing and exploring data 88–92
　linear equation 81–83
　vs. logistic regression 113
linearity between variables 106
list comprehensions 233

INDEX

list() method 321
LLR (log-likelihood ratio) 126
llr p-value 130
log returns 259, 262
log variable 345
log_model regression 125
logistic function 113
logistic regression
    defined 111
    exploring data 115–116, 118–119, 122
    fitting model 125
    fitting, classification metrics 131–139
    importing data 115–116, 118–119, 122
    interpreting and evaluating results 128–130
    multiple logistic regression 115
    vs. linear regression 113
logit() method 125, 128
lower_threshold 92

M

MA (moving average) component 192–207
    autoregression component 205
    moving average component 206
machine learning, overview 4
MAD (mean absolute deviation) 342
MAE (mean absolute error) 141
MajorAxisLength variable 125
majority vote 141
mantissa statistics 344
map() method 117
Markov analysis 294
    absorbing states 311–317
    equilibrium conditions 307–311
    mechanics of 295
    states 296–307
Markov property 295
MAs (moving averages) 185
math.comb() method 28, 30, 70–71
math.factorial() method 55
math.perm() method 26, 71
matplotlib library 83, 179, 322, 390
matrices, of transition probabilities 300–307
    making future state predictions programmatically 305–307
    predicting period 1 given period 0 302
    predicting period 2 given period 0 303–305
    predicting period 2 given period 1 302
max (maximum) 118
max_depth parameter 160
maximax data frame 276
Maximax method 272–276
    identifying possible states of nature 274

list of payoffs for each alternative and state of nature combination 274
list of possible alternatives 273
selecting decision-making method and making decision 275
maximin data frame 277
Maximin method 272, 277
Maximum column 278–279
mds data frame 94
mean 90, 118, 345
    quality control measures 381
mean() method 150, 152, 343, 346
median 90, 118
medical testing 72
metrics_accuracy_score() method 177
min (minimum) 118
Minimax Regret method 272, 277–279
MinorAxisLength variable 125–128
misclassification rate 136
missing values 145
MLE (maximum likelihood estimation) 208
model class 208
model_fit method 208
model_fit.forecast() method 214
model.fit() method 208
models, fitting time series models 192–215
    AR and MA components 205–207
    autoregression (AR) component 192
    combining ARIMA components 192
    differencing 195
    evaluating model fit 209–213
    fitting models 207–209
    forecasting 214
    integration (I) component 192
    MA (moving average) component 192
    stationarity, statistical properties 193
Monte Carlo simulations 242
    applications and benefits of 243
    automating simulations on continuous data 259–270
        analyzing historical data 261
        analyzing results 268–270
        calculating log returns 262
        computing statistical parameters 264
        generating random daily returns 265
        predicting stock prices with Monte Carlo simulations 259
        simulating multiple trials 267
        simulating prices 266
    automating simulations on discrete data 255–259
        plotting and analyzing results 257–259

416   INDEX

Monte Carlo simulations *(continued)*
   staffing levels example 246–255
      analyzing results 254
      computing cumulative probability distribution 248–249
      establishing interval of random numbers for each variable 250–252
      establishing probability distribution 246
      expected value calculation 255
      generating random numbers 252
      simulating series of trials 253
   step-by-step process 244
moving range, quality control measures 386
MSE (mean squared error) 141
mu parameter 266
multicollinearity 110
multiple logistic regression 115
multiplication rule 22
multistate systems, vector of state probabilities for 297–300
mutually exclusive 296

N

NaN (Not a Number) 145
naturally occurring number sequences 324
Negative class 75
Newcomb–Benford law 321
nfl_pbp data set 158, 165
nondecreasing 37
nonnegativity 36
norm module 47
normal distribution 42
   computing probabilities 48
   probability density function 46
   properties of 42
normality, testing for 91
   of residuals 108
np-charts 392–394
np.arrange() method 51, 327
np.dot() method 306–307
np.log() method 324
np.random_choice() method 327
np.random.normal() method 44
np.random.randint() method 326, 329
np.std() method 344
num_days parameter 266
num_simulations parameter 266
num_trials parameter 256
number of defective items, quality control measures 384–385
number sequences 319
   Benford's law 320–324

   chi-square test 338–339, 341
   distortion factor and z-statistic 343
   examples 330–336
   mantissa statistics 344
   mean absolute deviation 342
   naturally occurring 324
   plotted distributions 328–330
   random distributions 325–330
   uniform distributions 325–330
   validating Benford's law 338

O

objective function 231, 233
OFFENSIVE_TEAM_VENUE variable 145, 154, 171
oj data frame 389–390, 392
OLS() method 93, 127
opg method 209
optimistic approach 273
optimization 4
optimize module 237
order of magnitude 324
order parameter 207–208
outliers 86
   detecting 92

P

p_bar variable 390
p-charts (proportion charts) 379, 388–392
p-value, chi-square test 341
PACF (partial autocorrelation function) 197
   plot 200
pandas library 88, 115–116, 143
Pascal's triangle 27
payments data frame 336
payoff table 275–278, 280–281
pd.concat() method 165
pd.DataFrame() method 75, 321
pd.read_csv() method 88, 115, 143, 330, 334, 336, 389, 399
pd.set_option() method 147
PDF (probability density function) 32, 42
Perimeter variable 125, 128
permutations 23–30
   with replacement 24
   without replacement 25
PERT (program evaluation review technique) 349
pessimistic approach 277
pistons data frame 399–400

planning, overview 350
PLAY_TYPE variable 144, 155, 165, 171
plot_acf() method 199
plot_pacf() method 200
plot_tree() method 163
plot() method 149
plotted distributions 328–330
plotting
   data 190
   decision tree 163
PMF (probability mass function) 35–36, 51
pmf_values variable 58
Poisson distribution 60, 247
   computing probabilities 62
   properties of 60
poisson module 62
poisson_table data frame 247
poisson.cdf() method 249
poisson.pmf() function 62
populations data frame 334, 338, 342, 345, 347
Positive class 75
pow() method 25, 66
predicting responses 161
prediction variable 131
predictions, distinguishing forecasts from 185
predictor variable 81
print() function 338
print() method 89, 161, 177, 233–234, 237
priority scores 225
Prob (f-statistic) 105
probability 3, 16
   complement rule for 65–66
   computing 48
   converting and measuring 19
   counting rules 22–30
   examples and solutions 68–71
   of on-time completion 349
   reference guide for 67
   types of 19
probability density function 46
probability distributions 42
   and conditional probabilities 41
   binomial distribution 50–51, 54
   establishing 246
   normal distribution 42
   Poisson distribution 60, 62
probability_not_4 variable 65
probability_not_4_both variable 66
process capability indices, quality control measures 387
programming, making future state predictions programmatically 305–307

project crashing 349
project management 350
   estimating activity times with PERT 354–357
   WBS (work breakdown structure) 350–354
proportion defective, quality control measures 383
proportion variable 390
pseudo R-squared 129
PyCharm 7
PyDev 7
Python 4–6
   ease of learning 5
   ecosystem 4
   IDEs 6
   industry adoption 6
   online support and community 5
   using for precision and efficiency 13
   versatility 6

Q

Q–Q plot 108
quality control
   control charts for attributes 388–398
      c-charts 394–396
      g-charts 396–398
      np-charts 392–394
      p-charts 388–392
   control charts for variables 398–408
      EWMA charts 407
      I-MR charts 405–407
      r-charts 402
      s-charts 403
      x-bar charts 400
   visualizing 378
quality control measures 380–388
   defects per unit 386
   mean and center line 381
   moving range 386
   number of defective items 384
   number of defects 385
   process capability indices 387
   proportion defective 383
   range 382
   sample size 383
   standard deviation 381
   UCL and LCL 380
   upper control limit and lower control limit 380
   z-score 386
quantitative methods 2–4
QUARTER variable 148

R

r-charts 402
R-squared 8, 82, 85, 99
random daily returns 260
random distributions 325–330
random forest classifier object 175–177
random forests 140–142
    fitting 141–142, 174–183
    importing data 142
    understanding data 143
    wrangling data 144
random numbers
    establishing interval of 250–252
    generating 252
random variables 30, 59
    continuous 30–34
    discrete 35–39
random_distribution variable 327
random_state parameter 160
RandomForestClassifier() method 175
range, quality control measures 382
rank variable 346
recall_score() method 134
rectangular distribution 56
regression
    analysis 4
    line 81, 85
    table 94
regret data frame 278
reset_index() method 326
residual error 83
residuals 211
    homoscedasticity of 107
    independence of 107
    normality of 108
response variable 81
result evaluation 231
right-continuous 38
ROC (receiver operating characteristic) curve 138
roc_auc_score() method 137
root node 164–167
round() method 321
row_number variable 325, 327

S

s-charts 403
sample size, quality control measures 383
sample variable 389, 399
samples array 45
schedule 350
scipy library 47, 59, 339
scipy.stats 59, 62
scope 350
SCORE_DIFFERENTIAL variable 145, 152, 171–172
seaborn library 123
second_probability variable 49
sensitivity 133
SES (simple exponential smoothing) 216–217
set_option() method 116
set() method 331
shape attribute 159
shapiro() method 92
shift(1) method 263
sigma parameter 266
sigma2 parameter 211
sigmoid function 113
SimpleExpSmoothing class 217
simulating multiple trials 260
simulating prices 260
simulation 4
simulation_df data frame 266
size variable 389
size() method 165, 326
skew() method 346
skewness measures 345
sklearn (scikit-learn) library 134
sklearn.tree module 163
sort_values() method 346
specificity, defined 134
splitting data 158
sprints, defined 352
Spyder 7
SSE (sum of squares error) 103
SSR (sum of squares regression) 99–100, 103
SST (sum of squares total) 99–100
stage1 predictor variable 94
standard deviation 90
    quality control measures 381
states 296–307
    matrix of transition probabilities 300–307
    vector of state probabilities for multistate systems 297–300
stationarity 193
    differencing applied 197–205
        ACF plot 199
        Augmented Dickey–Fuller (ADF) test 201
        first-order differencing 202–205
        PACF plot 200
        visual inspection 197
    statistical properties 193
statistical parameters 260

statistics
    benefits of learning 8–11
    book structure 12–14
    overview 1
    probability distributions and conditional
        probabilities 41
    quantitative methods 2–4
    what this book does not cover 14
stats module 92, 339
stats.chisquare() method 339–341
stats.randint() method 59
statsmodels library 93, 125, 127, 199–200, 207
statsmodels.stats package 107
statsmodels.stats.diagnostic module 108
statsmodels.tsa.arima.model module 207
statstools module 107
Stays Healthy node 292
std (standard deviation) 118
std err parameter 211
steady-state probabilities 308
stock_data data frame 188
street addresses 330–333
Strong column 278
strong_econ estimate 281
strong_economy vector 275
subjective probability 19
subtasks 351
subtrees 288
sum() method 97, 322
summary statistics 90
summation, defined 36
symptoms variable 75

T

tail() method 89, 116–117, 130–131, 189,
    326–327, 346
target variable 81
tasks 224, 351
terminal nodes 164
test data frame 197, 214
test_results variable 75
theoretical probabilities 19
three-sigma rule 44
Ticker object 188
ticker symbols 187
time series models 184
    distinguishing forecasts from predictions 185
    importing and plotting data 186–191
time series, fitting models 192, 207–220
    applicability 216
    AR and MA components 205–207
    autoregression (AR) component 192

choosing between ARIMA and exponential
    smoothing 217
combining ARIMA components 192
differencing 195
evaluating model fit 209–213
forecasting 214
Holt–Winters model 218–220
integration (I) component 192
MA (moving average) component 192
mathematical properties 216
model structure 216
SES and DES models 217
stationarity 193
stationarity and differencing applied 197–205
types of 216
total_cost variable 234
total_outcomes variable 58
traffic 72
train data frame 197, 202, 208
train_diff data frame 204
train_test_split() method 159
transition probabilities, matrix of 300–307
    making future state predictions
        programmatically 305–307
    predicting period 1 given period 0 302
    predicting period 2 given period 0 303–305
    predicting period 2 given period 1 302
trees, decision trees 157–173
    advantages and disadvantages of 173
    evaluating model, confusion matrix 161
    fitting model 160
    interpreting and understanding 164–173
    plotting 163
    predicting responses 161
    splitting data 158
trials, simulating series of 253
two-way table 74

U

UCL (upper control limit) 380
uniform distribution of mantissas 324
uniform distributions 325–330
    discrete 56, 58
uniform module 59
uniform_distribution vector 326
unique_values variable 331
upper_threshold 92
usecols parameter 143, 330
user stories 224

V

value_counts() method 148
var (variance) 118
variance measures 345
vector of state probabilities 296
VIF (variance inflation factor) 126
visual inspection 197
VS Code (Visual Studio Code) 7
vstack() function 235

W

WBS (work breakdown structure) 349–354
weak_econ estimate 281
weak_economy vector 275
weather forecasting 72
world population figures 334–335
wrangling data 142, 144
    data filtering 144
    data transformation 145
    data type conversion 146
    derived variable 146
    missing values 145

X

X_test test data 177
x-bar charts 400

Y

y_pred object 161, 177
y_train test data 177
YARDS_GAINED variable 145–146, 159
yf alias 187
yfinance library 187

Z

z parameter 211
z-score, quality control measures 386
z-statistic 343